In 1848 a torrent of revolutions ripped through Europe. The storm all but swept away the conservative order that had held sway since the fall of Napoleon in 1815, suppressing dreams of national freedom and of constitutional government. Over the course of the spring and summer, crowds of working-class radicals and middle-class liberals in Paris, Milan, Venice, Naples, Palermo, Vienna, Prague, Budapest, Krakow, Munich, and Berlin toppled the old regimes and began the task of forging a new order. Political events so dramatic had not been seen in Europe since the French Revolution of 1789 and would not be witnessed again until the revolutions of Eastern and Central Europe in 1989.

1848 is a comprehensive account of this extraordinary year. Historian Mike Rapport traces the roots of the revolutionary fervor and then, with breathtaking pace, chronicles the explosive spread of violence across Europe. A vivid narrative of a continent in revolt, *1848* tells the thrilling story of a violent and tumultuous age—and explains the many ways in which 1848 continues to shape the modern world.

1848

1848

YEAR OF REVOLUTION

MIKE RAPPORT

BASIC BOOKS

A Member of the Perseus Books Group
New York

For Helen, of course,
and for Michael H. Rapport (1917–2007)
and John Bell (1964–2008):
de mémoire glorieuse et éternelle

CONTENTS

PREFACE

In 1848 a violent storm of revolutions tore through Europe. With an astounding rapidity, crowds of working-class radicals and middle-class liberals in Paris, Milan, Venice, Naples, Palermo, Vienna, Prague, Budapest, Kraków and Berlin toppled the old regimes and began the task of forging a new, liberal order. Political events so dramatic had not been seen in Europe since the French Revolution of 1789 – and would not be witnessed again until the revolutions of Eastern and Central Europe in 1989, or perhaps the less far-reaching Bolshevik Revolution of 1917. The torrent severely battered the conservative order that had kept peace on the continent since the end of the Napoleonic Wars in 1815, but which in many countries also suppressed dreams of national freedom and constitutional government. The brick-built authoritarian edifice that had imposed itself on Europeans for almost two generations folded under the weight of the insurrections.

The story of 1848 has been retold many times.[1] It is a complicated one and telling it poses some interesting challenges. One historian has described it as a problem of 'historical synchronisation',[2] but Italians have a much more colourful phrase: '*un vero quarantotto*' – 'a real 48' – which means 'a right royal mess'.[3] While the main purpose is therefore to tell the story and to do so in a way that will hopefully be enjoyed, the book is also driven by the belief that the revolutions of 1848–9 are worth revisiting because they have such contemporary resonance. In general I let the reader draw her or his own conclusions and connections from the evidence and

narrative presented here, but every so often I give what I hope will
be a helpful nudge. In 1848 the revolutionaries were faced with the
problem of constructing liberal, constitutional regimes, while facing
issues that are strikingly modern. For the Germans, Italians,
Hungarians, Romanians, Poles, Czechs, Croats and Serbs, the year
was to be the 'Springtime of Peoples', a chance to assert their own
sense of national identity and to gain political recognition. In the
cases of the Germans and the Italians, it was an opportunity for
national unification under a liberal or even democratic order.
Nationalism, therefore, was one issue that came frothing to the
surface of European politics in 1848. While rooted in constitutionalism and civil rights, it was a nationalism that, ominously, made
little allowance for the legitimacy of claims of other national groups.
In many places such narrowness of vision led to bitter ethnic conflict, which in the end helped to destroy the revolutionary regimes
of Central and Eastern Europe.

A second problem was the question of constitutions and democracy. The revolutions were scarred almost everywhere by a bitter,
often violent, political polarisation. Moderates wanted parliamentary government – but not necessarily to enfranchise everyone – and
they were challenged by radicals who wanted democracy – frequently combined with dramatic social reform – without delay.
This split between liberals and democrats divided the revolutionary
alliance that had so easily toppled the conservative order; and the
resulting political polarisation had tragic consequences, not just in
1848, but for the future of liberal government and democracy in
many parts of Europe deep into the twentieth century.

A third issue that came boiling to the surface in 1848 and never
left the European political agenda was the 'social question'. The
abject misery of both urban and rural people had loomed menacingly in the thirty or so years since the Napoleonic Wars. The
poverty was caused by a burgeoning population, which was not yet
offset by a corresponding growth in the economy. Governments,
however, did little to address the social distress, which was taken up
as a cause by a relatively new political current – socialism – in 1848.
The revolutions therefore thrust the 'social question' firmly and

irrevocably into politics. Any subsequent regime, no matter how conservative or authoritarian, ignored it at its peril. In 1848, however, the question of what to do about poverty would prove to be one of the great nemeses of the liberal, revolutionary regimes.

The revolutions were also genuinely European, in the sense that they arose across the continent. Even countries such as Britain and Russia that were not directly affected by insurrections were touched by the impact. This European dimension raises the interesting issue of how far Europe, in its historical development, is merely the sum of its different national parts, or how far those parts are linked by common experience, shared problems and similarities in ideals and aspirations. This question, too, has an important contemporary significance.

This book will explore these issues through a narrative of the events of 1848–9, which will draw on eyewitness accounts, memoirs and a wide range of secondary sources. This is a period of European history that is little explored outside academic texts, yet it is replete with its own drama: many of the images of European revolution – workers and students on barricades, red flags, tricolours – were present in 1848. The insurrections and their repression brought to centre-stage an impressive cast of characters, including: Metternich, the architect of the old conservative order; Louis-Napoleon Bonaparte (later Napoleon III), who became the French Second Republic's nemesis by trading on his famous uncle's name; Garibaldi, the red-shirted hero of the struggle for Italian unification; Mazzini, the near-religious inspiration behind Italian democratic republicanism; Bismarck, the Machiavellian dark horse of German history; and Radetzky, the wily, octogenarian Austrian field marshal who might legitimately have claimed to have been the main saviour of the Habsburg Empire. There are others who are perhaps not household names in the English-speaking world, but are no less the stuff of drama: the Croatian commander Jelačić; the fiery Hungarian revolutionary Kossuth; the bespectacled, inspiring Venetian republican Manin; the French historian and poet Lamartine, who had a flair for the dramatic. The 1848 revolutions present a complex and fascinating story, which combines the high politics of diplomacy, state-building and constitution-making with the human tragedy of revolution, war and social misery. Yet, at the same time, they had their truly uplifting and inspiring moments: 1848 was a revolution of hope as well as despair.

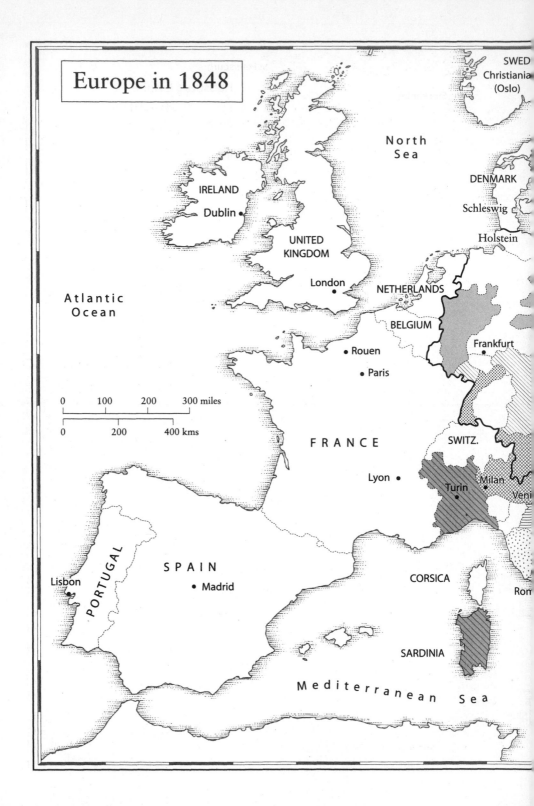

Europe in 1848

SWED
Christiania
(Oslo)

North
Sea

DENMARK

Schleswig

Holstein

IRELAND

Dublin

UNITED
KINGDOM

NETHERLANDS

BELGIUM

Frankfurt

London

Atlantic
Ocean

Rouen

Paris

0   100   200   300 miles

0   200   400 kms

FRANCE

SWITZ.

Lyon

Milan

Turin

Veni

PORTUGAL

SPAIN

Madrid

CORSICA

Rom

Lisbon

SARDINIA

Mediterranean   Sea

I

THE FOREST OF BAYONETS

Underneath a darkening January sky, a convoy of horse-drawn sledges cut trails across a glowing, snow-covered plain. The procession halted at a barrier, the passengers' passports were inspected by a sergeant and a grizzled old soldier huddling under an oilskin, his rifle slung heavily over his shoulder, raised the barrier: it was the Russian frontier with Prussia. The sledges crunched once again through the snow. Turning his head, the lead passenger, a man named Alexander Herzen, heard a Cossack wish him a happy journey, the soldier holding the bridle of his own hardy mount, its shaggy coat hanging with icicles.[1] Herzen did not know it then, but he would not see Russia again. It was January 1847 and he was embarking on a European journey, accompanied by his wife Natalie, their three children, his mother, and two nannies. He was a member of the Russian gentry but also a socialist, escaping the stifling environment of life under Tsar Nicholas I and eager to learn more about 'the West', to make comparisons with Russia and, he hoped in vain, to return with the fruits of his learning.[2]

I

The Europe through which the Herzens were about to journey was a continent on the edge of an uncertain future. Politically, it was dominated by a conservative order. Of the five great powers – Austria, Prussia, Russia, France and Britain – only the last two had parliaments to temper royal power, but they were far from democratic. A parliamentary system had been evolving in Britain – albeit with bloodshed and political opposition – for generations. In 1832 had come the first great modern reform of the system, whereby urban property-owners were given the right to vote, while the cities – many of them hitherto absent or poorly represented at Westminster – were allowed to elect Members of Parliament. This was not democracy, for only one in five adult males (women were excluded as a matter of course) was enfranchised in England and Wales (and only one in eight in Scotland) and the composition of Parliament, which consisted of gentry and aristocratic landowners, remained virtually unchanged.

France had become a constitutional monarchy in 1814, when Napoleon was packed off to his genteel exile on Elba, and then again in 1815, after which the incorrigible Emperor was held under stricter conditions on the remote island of Saint Helena until his death in 1821. The Bourbon monarchy was restored, represented first by the portly Louis XVIII, younger brother of the guillotined King Louis XVI, and then, on his death in 1824, by their younger brother, the slender and ultra-conservative Charles X. The French constitution, the Charter of 1814, provided a parliament whose lower house, the Chamber of Deputies, was elected by the wealthiest 110,000 taxpayers. In 1830 Charles's royal intransigence in the face of repeated liberal electoral victories provoked the final overthrow of the Bourbon dynasty. It is said that Charles had once declared that he would rather be a hewer of wood than rule like a British monarch. It was therefore a sublime irony that, as he made his way towards exile (he would live in Holyrood Palace in Edinburgh), at one staging-post Charles's courtiers had to cut a table down to size so that everyone in the royal retinue could be accommodated in the small dining room. Back in Paris the Charter was retained by the new regime. This was the 'July Monarchy', named for the month when the Revolution occurred, under King Louis-Philippe, the scion of the rival Orléans dynasty. The Charter was slightly modified, so that the electorate swelled to include only 170,000 of France's richest men: this was a mere 0.5 per cent of the French population, a sixth of those who enjoyed the vote in Britain after 1832.[3]

The other three great European powers were absolute monarchies and, of these, Austria was in many ways central to the conservative European system. 'Austria' was the Habsburg Empire, a polyglot assembly of territories enveloping no fewer than eleven different nationalities: Germans, Magyars, Romanians, Italians, and the Slav peoples – Czechs, Slovaks, Poles, Ukrainians (then known as Ruthenians), Slovenians, Serbs and Croats. This veritable Tower of Babel was held together by the Habsburg dynasty, ruling from its imperial capital, Vienna. From the end of the Napoleonic Wars in 1815 right up to 1848, the dominant figure in Austrian politics was one of the giants of the nineteenth century, Klemens von Metternich. A long-serving Austrian diplomat, Metternich had been the Habsburg monarchy's foreign minister since 1809 and Chancellor since 1821. He was intelligent, arrogant, aloof and, as a British diplomat once put it, 'intolerably loose and giddy with women'.[4] He was not Austrian, but was born in 1773 in Koblenz, a town then ruled by one of the many states of the Rhineland, the Archbishopric of Trier. Like the other small German principalities, Trier reposed within the protective shell of the Holy Roman Empire, at the pinnacle of which was the Emperor, who was chosen by the prince-electors and who was invariably a Habsburg, since this dynasty had for centuries been the most powerful and therefore the best placed to defend Germany. In the autumn of 1794 the French revolutionary armies overran the Rhineland and with the triumph of the blue-coated hordes came the republican retribution against the local nobility. The Metternich estates were confiscated and Klemens fled to Vienna, where he subsisted on an imperial pension and the income from his last remaining land in Bohemia. His inexorable climb up the ladder of Austrian diplomatic service began in 1801, when he took the post of Austrian minister to Saxony. With Napoleon rampaging across Central Europe – abolishing the thousand-year-old Holy Roman Empire in 1806 – Metternich began to develop the idea that the multi-national Habsburg monarchy, held together by a strong imperial government in Vienna, could become the new 'foundations of a European political system'.[5]

By 1815 Metternich's background and direct experience gave him a strong sense that the Habsburg monarchy was not only a German, but also a European, necessity. In a positive way, Metternich believed that a powerful state in Central Europe had a chance of protecting the smaller German states and of playing a leading role in preserving the social and political stability of the entire continental order. In a more negative sense, if the Habsburg monarchy failed, then the multi-national empire at the heart of Europe would fragment and, where once there was order, there would be civil strife, revolutionary conflict and terror, the effects of which no European state could hope to escape. Metternich was the main architect of the entire conservative order. Perhaps his greatest achievement was the diplomatic role that he played at the Congress of Vienna in 1815. After the protracted agony and slaughter of the Napoleonic Wars, this great international conference tried to reconstruct a European political system that aimed not only to maintain international peace, but to keep under the hammer the twin threats of liberalism and nationalism. This attitude was shared by Metternich's fellow diplomats. The legacy of Napoleon Bonaparte and the carnage of the wars that now bear his name (and killed proportionately as many Europeans as the First World War) weighed heavily on the minds of policy-makers. So, too, did the grim, angular shadow of the guillotine. For conservatives across Europe, liberalism and nationalism meant revolution – and that could only be the bleak herald of destruction and death, whether it came in the shape of revolutionary armies streaming across the continent, respecting neither life, nor religion, nor property, or in the form of a bloodthirsty social war waged by scythe-wielding peasants, or by the desperate, dispossessed urban masses, against all those who had a stake in the established order. The post-Napoleonic political system therefore tried to be muscular in the face of subversive threats to its existence; this was precisely because it was all too aware of what failure might mean.

For the chief organiser of this order, the only monarchy worth the title was an absolute monarchy. In 1820, fearful that Alexander I of Russia was flirting with the hair-raising idea of introducing a constitution, Metternich addressed to the Tsar his 'profession of political faith'. Monarchs, he argued, had to be 'placed above the sphere of passions which agitate society':

> it is in times of crisis that they are principally called upon . . . to show themselves for what they are: fathers invested with all the authority which belongs to heads of families; to prove that, in dark times, they know how to be just, wise and, by that alone, strong, and that they do not abandon the peoples, whom they have the duty to govern, to the play of factions, to error and its consequences, which will fatally lead to the destruction of society.[6]

Among the 'factions' that threatened 'society' were liberals and nationalists who called for constitutions, national independence and political unity. Sovereigns should not yield to these demands, not even in an effort to make timely concessions to avoid revolution: 'Respect for everything that exists; liberty for all Governments to watch over the well-being of their own peoples; a league between all Governments against the factions in all States; mistrust for words devoid of sense ["the cry for Constitutions"], which have become the rallying cry of the factions.' For Metternich, however, absolute rule did not mean despotism, which was government at the capricious whim of a single man. Rather, monarchs had to rule through a framework of law and regular administration: 'The first and greatest of matters . . . is the fixity of laws, their uninterrupted working, and never changing them. So may Governments govern, may they maintain the fundamental bases of their institutions, old as well as new; for if it is always dangerous to interfere with them, it could not be useful to do so now, in today's general turbulence.'[7]

The Habsburg regime, in fact, was not especially oppressive – at least not by the standards of modern dictatorships. Its bureaucracy was generally honest and efficient. Moreover (and despite his advice to the Tsar), Metternich used his considerable diplomatic influence to press mild reforms on the more benighted absolute rulers whose intransigence threatened to provoke violent opposition: in 1821 he promised military aid to King Ferdinand I of Naples against the monarch's rebellious subjects, on the condition that Ferdinand made some minor concessions. Despite all the talk of the rule of law and of the benevolence of the monarchy, Metternich and other conservatives feared that, should constitutional or revolutionary movements have arisen among the diverse peoples of the Habsburg monarchy, then the very integrity of the empire would be endangered. In theory, it was held together by the subjects' loyalty to the dynasty, the common institutions of the monarchy (including the administration and the imperial army) and, although there were religious minorities such as Jews and Protestants, the Catholicism of most Austrian subjects. In 1815 perhaps only the Germans, the Magyars, the Poles and the Italians had a deep sense of their own national identity. The first three, in particular, also dominated the other subject-nationalities of the empire, politically and socially. In Hungary the Magyar gentry lorded over the peasants who in the north were Slovaks, in the east were Transylvanian Romanians and in the south were Serbs or Croats. In Galicia the Poles tended to be the landlords holding the Ukrainian peasantry in such a state of servitude that they were practically beasts of burden. The Czechs, at least, with their high standards of education and (by 1848) the most advanced manufacturing base in the Habsburg monarchy, were beginning to challenge German hegemony in Bohemia, but one of the seething resentments among the non-Germans was that since the machinery of the state was centred in Vienna, it was dominated by German officials, whose language was usually the official medium in the law, education and administration. Even so, a developed sense of national identity was primarily shared by the aristocratic elites and the urban, middle classes, who were of course precisely the people most frustrated that opportunities in the bureaucracy, the law and in higher education were closed off unless one spoke German. This had not yet trickled down to the mass of peasants, many of whom saw the Emperor as their guardian against the depredations of their landlords, but the very fact that social difference coincided with ethnic divisions would aggravate the frequently bloody conflicts among the nationalities of Central Europe.

The resentment of the Magyars against what they saw as German dominance and overbearing Habsburg authority was potentially very dangerous to the empire. Unlike most of the other nationalities, the Magyars had a constitutional voice: the Hungarians had a diet, or parliament, which was dominated by the Magyar nobility, the clergy and the burghers of the free royal towns. Thus the 'Hungarian nation' – meaning in contemporary parlance those who were represented in the diet – made up a small proportion of the total population. The rest were legally defined, with graphic aptness, as the *misera plebs contribuens* – the poor tax-paying plebians (Latin was still, to the chagrin of patriotic Magyars, the official language of Hungarian politics and administration). The Magyar nobility none the less consisted of a fairly sizeable proportion of the Hungarian population – some 5 per cent compared to an estimated 1 per cent in pre-revolutionary France – and some of them were poor enough to be dubbed the 'sandalled nobles', since, it was said, they were so penniless that they could not afford boots. Yet, since these men only had their privileges and titles to distinguish them from the rest of the toiling masses, they were often the most resistant to any reform that endangered their status. Although the Habsburg Emperor, who also held the title of King of Hungary, could summon and dismiss the diet at will (and Emperor Francis sulkily refused to call the troublesome parliament between 1812 and 1825), it was difficult to raise taxation without consulting it, so it met in 1825, 1832–6, 1839–40, 1843–4 and, most dramatically, in 1847–8. Moreover, even when the parliament was not in session, the Hungarian gentry entrenched their opposition to the Habsburg

monarchy in the fifty-five counties, where they elected and salaried
the local officials, and where their assemblies (or 'congregations'),
which often met annually, were sometimes so bold as to claim the
right to reject royal legislation.[8]

In 1815 the Italians of Lombardy and Venetia fell under Habsburg
rule. They, too, had an institutional outlet because they both had
congregations, chosen from among local landowners and the towns,
as well as the united 'Congregations General', which drew together
delegates from the two provinces. These assemblies had the right to
decide how to implement laws handed down by the government,
represented by a viceroy living in Milan, but not to make legislation
of their own. The Habsburgs had to tread carefully, for northern
Italy was one of the jewels in their crown: Lombardy's fertile, irrigated
plains were a bright patchwork of wheat, of well-kept vines and of
mulberry bushes, upon which silk worms produced their precious
fibres. The duchy's capital and, to the irritation of the proud
Venetians, of the two provinces together, was Milan, which was
culturally one of the most vibrant cities in Europe, thanks in part
to the lighter touch of the censor, as compared with elsewhere in the
Habsburg Empire. Lombardy-Venetia accounted for a sixth of the
monarchy's population, but contributed close to a third of its tax
revenue – a fact that was not lost on Italian patriots. The Austrians
worked hard to ensure that northern Italy was well and fairly governed, but the inevitable tensions arose. Educated Lombards and
Venetians grumbled that Austrians occupied some 36,000 government posts, preventing Italians from enjoying their fair share of
state patronage.[9]

Outside Hungary and Lombardy-Venetia, there were no representative institutions worthy of the name in the Habsburg Empire.
Since 1835 the Emperor had been the mentally disabled Ferdinand
(in one famous outburst, he yelled at his courtiers, 'I am the
Emperor and I want dumplings!'). He was loved by his subjects,
who affectionately referred to him as 'Ferdy the Loony', but of
necessity the task of government was left to a council (or
Staatskonferenz), dominated by Metternich. The rejection of constitutional government made repression almost unavoidable, since

Metternich's political vision would not admit the legitimacy of any opposition. There was a secret police, which operated out of offices on the Herrengasse in Vienna, but the number of officers was small – some twenty-five, including thirteen censors – so in the imperial capital they relied upon the regular police (which also handled a plethora of other tasks), while in the provinces local bureaux had to deal with both regular and secret policing. This was not a particularly intense system of surveillance, but it is also true that the activities of printers, publishers and writers were hemmed in with a range of petty, irritating regulations.[10] Since only one of four categories of books was fully permitted, this fostered a climate that assumed a publication would be forbidden unless it was explicitly allowed.[11]

The repression was particularly tough in Russia, the second of Europe's pre-eminent absolutist regimes. If Metternich cast Austria in the role of Central Europe's policeman, then Tsar Nicholas I saw himself as gendarme for the entire continent. The Russian empire had been in his iron, autocratic grip since the death of Alexander I in 1825. He had founded the notorious Third Section, the secret police, an organisation which had a tiny number of officials, but which worked through the gendarmerie and a larger number of informants, who made as many as five thousand denunciations a year. The very existence of police spies created an atmosphere in which it took a brave soul to express dissent openly. One widely believed myth held that in one office of the Third Section headquarters in Saint Petersburg there was a trap door: during a seemingly innocuous conversation, a perfectly innocent individual summoned before the police officials could be lured into saying a minor indiscretion, whereupon a lever would be pulled and the victim would fall into a dungeon below to be subjected to all sorts of unspeakable horrors.

The real oppression was bad enough for those who dared to voice their thoughts too loudly. In 1836, when the liberal intellectual Petr Chaadaev lambasted Russia for its backwardness, he met the fate that would be shared by some twentieth-century Soviet dissidents: the government declared him insane and confined him to an asylum.[12] Even (or perhaps, given his quick temper, especially) the great poet Pushkin had to tread carefully: he was tolerated because the Tsar liked his work, but even he was subjected to the occasional rap on the knuckles. Intellectuals and writers cautiously circulated their writings in manuscript among friends first, and only later approached publishers – if they approached them at all. The Tsarist regime did not only fear dissent from among Russia's intellectuals, it was anxious – perhaps more justifiably – of the possibility of a mass uprising by the peasantry, twenty million of whom were serfs and who had risen up with startling vengeance in the past, most recently under the renegade Cossack Emilian Pugachev in the early 1770s. It also worried about opposition from the downtrodden subject nationalities of the Empire, especially the Poles, who bore their subjugation only between fits of rebelliousness.

The third great absolute monarchy in Europe, Prussia, had been governed since 1840 by King Frederick William IV, who moved rapidly after his accession to dash liberal hopes that he would introduce a constitution. His father, Frederick William III, had promised his eager subjects to abandon absolute rule several times, but that had been during the Napoleonic Wars, when he wanted to arouse the patriotism of his loyal Prussians against the hated French. A generation later, Frederick William IV explained to a disappointed liberal official that 'I feel I am king solely by the grace of God.' A constitution would, he said, make the whole idea of monarchy 'an abstract concept, by dint of a piece of paper. A paternal governance is the way of true German princes.'[13] Prussia did have provincial estates, but these representative bodies were stacked heavily in favour of the nobles and great landowners and they were not permitted to correspond with one another, to avoid any notion that they could merge into a national parliament. This was especially galling to liberals, many of whom were Prussians of recent vintage. The Rhineland, with its advanced economy and relatively positive experience of Napoleonic rule, had been given to Prussia in 1815, to strengthen Germany against France. This made Prussia a kingdom of two halves – the east dominated by the landed nobility, with their great estates and their peasants, who until 1807 had been enserfed, and the west, with its strong manufacturing base and burgeoning middle class. One of the latter, on learning of the imminent Prussian annexation of the Rhineland in 1815, sniffed that they had married into poor relations – meaning the agrarian, noble-dominated east. It was perhaps no surprise that much of the liberal leadership of the Prussian revolution in 1848 sprang from the Rhineland. As well as its formidable army, it was however the combined wealth of its manu-facturing and agricultural bases that made Prussia one of the greatest powers not just of Germany but of Europe.

Thanks, then, to the peace settlement at Vienna in 1815, Central and Eastern Europe had been thrust under the domination of these three absolute monarchies. Since 1795 the old Polish kingdom (except for the Napoleonic interlude of the Grand Duchy of Warsaw, established in 1807), had been wiped off the map, parti-tioned between Russia, Prussia and Austria – and this was confirmed at the peace congress. The three 'eastern monarchies' therefore tried (in vain) to asphyxiate Polish nationalism under their combined weight.

They were equally determined to keep German nationalism locked inside its Pandora's box. Austria shared with Prussia a dom-inant position in Germany, which, after the destruction of the Holy Roman Empire and a dramatic reordering of territory under Napoleon, was now divided into thirty-nine states (including Austria and Prussia), bound together in a confederation (Bund), with a diet that met at Frankfurt. This assembly was not a parlia-ment of elected representatives, but rather a meeting of diplomats sent by the governments of the separate states, a sort of German 'United Nations'. Its purpose was not to encourage Germany into closer union – quite the opposite. The Bund was intended to pre-serve the conservative order and to ensure that disputes between the states were resolved peacefully, which of course reassured the smaller 'middle states' that they would be protected against the domineer-ing tendencies of Prussia and Austria. It could call on the various German governments to provide soldiers to defend Germany from foreign invasion, but also against domestic revolutionary threats. In 1819 it issued the repressive Karlsbad Decrees against the German radical and liberal movements, and especially against the student nationalist organisations, the *Burschenschaften*. These edicts were reiterated in 1832 in response to a wave of revolution and protest that swept across Europe. Behind the decrees stood Metternich, who had also looked askance at the constitutionalism beginning to take root in Germany in the years immediately following the Napoleonic Wars. The southern German states of Baden, Württemberg, Bavaria, Nassau and Hesse-Darmstadt had all emerged with constitutions. This process was actually in keeping with the act that created the German Confederation, and which declared that all German states should have 'constitutions of the territorial estates'. This, however, was a deliberately ambiguous phrase, since it could mean either (as the southern German states interpreted it) a modern, parliamentary monarchy or a more conservative style of traditional 'estates' in which the nobles, the clergy and the good burghers of the towns were separately represented, ensuring that the estates were always weighted towards conservative interests. Metternich had exerted his influence on King Frederick William III of Prussia and then on the German Confederation to ensure, first, that Prussia did not join the constitutional dance and, second, that the Bund's 'Final Act' of 1820 interpreted the term 'constitution' in Metternich's sense, to mean estates rather than parliaments. Even then, they were to be stacked in favour of the 'monarchic principle', meaning that the prince would always enjoy most of the power.[14]

It was in Italy, however, that Metternich pursued the most active counter-revolutionary and anti-liberal policies. He famously derided the claims of Italian nationalists for unification by calling Italy 'a geographical expression',[15] split as it was among ten kingdoms, duchies and statelets. He saw Austria's role to keep it that way. Besides ensuring that Austria had a strong direct Italian presence, by virtue of its annexation of Lombardy and Venetia in the north, the Congress of Vienna had arranged Italian affairs so that Austria would be the predominant power in the entire peninsula. After the long experience of Napoleonic occupation, the purpose was initially to ward off French influence, but the role soon developed into one of repressing Italian liberalism and nationalism.

Tuscany was ruled by a Habsburg grand duke, while the Duchies of Parma and Modena were also governed by relatives of the Emperor. Beyond these dynastic ties, the Austrians were given the right to garrison the fortress of Ferrara in the Papal States. The Bourbon King of the Two Sicilies (meaning southern Italy and the eponymous island, since 1816 deprived of its separate parliament and ruled directly from Naples) signed an alliance and a military convention with Austria, which bound the kingdom tightly to Habsburg policy. Only the north-western Kingdom of Sardinia (which included the island of the same name and, on the mainland, Piedmont and Genoa) remained completely independent: it was militarily the most powerful of all Italian states and provided a strong buffer between France and the Austrians in Lombardy. Yet Austrian power in Italy was such that it was able to intervene militarily against liberal revolutions in both Naples and even in Piedmont itself in 1820–1. In the aftermath the Austrians tried over ninety leading Lombard liberals (although they had little to do with the uprisings) and condemned forty of them to rot in the dark Spielberg fortress in Bohemia. Among them was Silvio Pellico, who on his release in 1830 wrote *My Prisons*, a testimony to both Austrian oppression and to the power of religious faith in the face of adversity. The book became a bestseller and contributed to a 'black legend' of Austrian misrule in Italy. Metternich merely reinforced the grim image of Germanic oppression when he again sent troops southwards in 1831–2 to crush insurrections in Modena, Parma and the Papal States (where the Austrians had the brass neck to hold on to Bologna until 1838).

Austrian power and influence therefore spread from Germany down to the toe of Italy and into Eastern Europe. It was, Count Anton Kolowrat-Liebsteinsky disparagingly said, a 'forest of bayonets'. Kolowrat was no liberal, but he was Metternich's great rival in the Staatskonferenz. He agreed with the Chancellor 'that people must strive for conservatism and do everything to achieve it. Yet we differ about means. Your means consist of a forest of bayonets and fixed adherence to things as they are. To my mind, by following these lines we are playing into the hands of the revolutionaries.'[16] Metternich's more rigid form of conservatism, he fretted, would merely create such pressure that 'your ways will lead us . . . to our ruin'. The outspoken British statesman Lord Palmerston bluntly criticised Austria's 'repressive and suffocating policy' because it 'will lead to an explosion just as certainly as would a boiler that was hermetically sealed and deprived of an outlet for steam'.[17] Kolowrat was also deeply concerned about the financial cost of maintaining Austrian power in Europe at such intensity: between 1815 and 1848, the army swallowed some 40 per cent of the government budget, and paying interest alone on the state debt digested a further 30 per cent. One of the great weaknesses of Metternich's 'system' that was exposed in 1848 was that it had scant money left in its coffers to cope with the worst economic downturn of the nineteenth century and so could do little to soothe the people's distress.

II

The political restrictions imposed on Europe could not help but provoke opposition. Just as Metternich and his ilk felt the heavy weight of recent history in their political calculations, so that same history proved to be an inspiration to their opponents. The French Revolution of 1789 and its Napoleonic progeny had provoked dread among conservatives, but – in the true Romantic fashion of the age – their memory could stir the blood of liberals, radicals and patriots who felt constricted in the stifling atmosphere of Metternich's Europe. The first post-war generation of European liberals had personally engaged in the struggles of the revolutionary era. With the final allied victory in 1815, they had lost either because they had supported Napoleonic rule – and its often empty promises of freedom – or because, having opposed the French, they had hoped in vain that from the ruins of the old European order would rise a new, constitutional system.

There were unsuccessful revolutionary outbreaks in Italy in 1820–1, led in Naples by liberal army officers (including Guglielmo Pepe, a former Napoleonic officer with a central role to play in 1848), who were members of a secret revolutionary society called the

Carbonari, dedicated to the overthrow of Austrian domination and to the establishment of a liberal order in Italy. The French equivalent, the Charbonnerie, drew much of its strength from the seething resentment felt by former servants of the Napoleonic state who had been purged in the royalist reaction, the violent 'White Terror' of 1815 – so-called to distinguish it from the 'Red' Jacobin Terror of 1793–4. Among those who joined the underground opposition was a teenage Louis-Auguste Blanqui. His family had fallen on hard times after his father, the Napoleonic prefect of the Alpes-Maritimes, lost his post when the territory (better known as Nice) was returned to Piedmont in the peace settlement of 1815. Blanqui thus began a lifetime of revolutionary activism that would last until his death in 1881. In Spain the liberals yearned for the Constitution of 1812, which had been forged in Cadiz by a parliament that had met not far from the hostile muzzles of cannon belonging to the besieging French army. Yet when King Ferdinand VII returned triumphantly in 1814, he brushed aside the constitution and sent many of the liberals scurrying into exile. They had their revenge in 1820, when they seized power and compelled Ferdinand to rule as a constitutional monarch for three years – until they in turn were overwhelmed by French troops (the '100,000 sons of Saint Louis') sent over the Pyrenees by Louis XVIII, who was intent on restoring the royal absolutism of his fellow Bourbon.

Even autocratic Russia could not remain untouched by the explosive legacy of the Napoleonic epoch. Russian army officers who had marched across Europe during the war, ultimately occupying Paris, had met their French, German and British counterparts and, over the course of the genteel, intellectual conversations with these fellow officers, began to wonder at the backwardness of their own country, while absorbing western ideas of constitutional government and civil liberties. This germinating seed finally bore its bitter fruit in Russia's first revolution, the Decembrist uprising of 1825. In the month which gave the insurrection its name, liberal army officers, taking advantage of the confusion following the sudden death of Tsar Alexander I, raised the standard of revolt against his successor, Nicholas I. The insurrection was easily crushed by loyal troops, first in Saint Petersburg and then in the Ukraine, but it was this experience at the very moment of his accession that set the new Tsar on a reactionary course for his entire reign – although there were some occasional, hopeful glimmers that serfdom would be reformed.

The most dramatic wave of revolutions occurred several years later. In 1830 the Bourbon Charles X was toppled by a three-day uprising in the streets of Paris, to be replaced by the more liberal-minded Louis-Philippe. This was rapidly followed by a revolution in Belgium, where liberals overthrew Dutch rule (imposed in 1815), eventually to secure an independent state with a constitutional monarchy. In Germany the French example inspired liberal opponents of the conservative order to demand – or force – constitutions from their rulers, so that Hanover, Saxony and a few others joined the still small group of German states that had representative institutions. The opposition pressed for more, unleashing a protest movement that culminated in the Hambach Festival of 1832, a mass meeting – the largest in Germany before 1848 – demanding political reform and a united Germany. This display of opposition muscle spurred Metternich into repeating the Karlsbad Decrees.

The most dramatic surge of resistance to the conservative order came in Poland, where in November 1830 the patience of the patriotic Polish nobility within the Russian partition snapped when the Tsar mobilised the Polish army in response to the revolutions in Western Europe. The insurrection lasted ten months and was crushed – after some bloody and intense fighting – by a 120,000-strong Russian army under General Ivan Paskevich (who would help repress another revolution in 1849). In the retribution that followed, a staggering eighty-thousand Poles were dragged off in chains to Siberia. There were also revolutions in Italy, but these were flattened, mostly by Austrian troops. The revolutions of the 1830s were nowhere near as widespread as those of 1848, but on a European scale they loosened Metternich's grip on the conservative, international order. When the Austrian Chancellor heard the first news of the revolution in France, he collapsed at his desk, moaning, 'My entire life's work is destroyed.'[18] His despair was exaggerated, however, for the cautious behaviour of the July Monarchy, which rapidly swung on to a conservative tack, would do much to bury his worst fears. He was not troubled, either, by another crack in the conservative edifice, in the shape of Greek independence. After a brutal, atrocity-ridden war which lasted eight and a half years between 1821 and 1829, the Greeks won their freedom from Turkish rule. Yet Metternich's international system did not descend into crisis because the final Greek victory had been secured, first, with military intervention by Russia, Britain and France and then by the diplomatic recognition of the great powers at the Treaty of London in 1830. The new kingdom of Greece was therefore rapidly enveloped within the folds of the post-Napoleonic order.

Metternich saw revolution as an essentially French disease: in late 1822 he had written to the Tsar that 'nationality, political boundaries, all have disappeared for the [revolutionary] sect. Without doubt, it is in Paris that the directing committee of the radicals of all Europe is today established.'[19] Metternich was once again overstating the case, but he illustrates the truth of the cliché that just because someone is paranoid, it does not mean that some people are *not* out to get him. The 1830s witnessed the emergence of a new wave of very real and resilient underground, revolutionary networks. These were energised by a new generation of intellectuals, romantics and patriots who were not old enough to have any clear recollection of the French Revolution, but who lived and breathed the glorious memories of its liberating promise. For the French republican historian Jules Michelet, born in 1798, and writing in 1847 the preface to his epic history of the French Revolution, that great historical moment was driven by the entire people – an unstoppable, providential force whose destiny was to spread the benevolent gospel of liberty, equality and fraternity across the globe.[20] Following the exhilarating example of 1789, some visionaries believed that revolution would be the means by which a freer, more equitable world would be born and they now dedicated their entire lives to bringing about that glorious day.

Unsurprisingly, perhaps, this epoch therefore witnessed the birth of the 'professional' revolutionary, who plotted tirelessly for the violent overthrow of the conservative order. Those of the French Revolution of 1789 had been unexpectedly hurled – often from obscure, drab provincial lives – into the maelstrom that eventually convulsed Europe for more than two decades: they became revolutionaries by accident and often quite reluctantly. Those of this new generation were self-consciously and actively trying to provoke a revolution. Foremost among them was the inspirational, if rather quixotic, figure of Giuseppe Mazzini. Born in Genoa in 1805 and a member of the *carbonari* from 1829, Mazzini was devoted not only to expelling the Austrians from Italy, but also to unifying the country in a democratic republic. Although this Italian patriot was far from giving his unqualified admiration to the revolution of 1789, he held that the French had proclaimed the rights of the individual, while demonstrating that great revolutions were possible even against the odds and in the most unexpected of places. Even failed uprisings, Mazzini argued, had their purpose, because 'ideas ripen quickly when nourished by the blood of martyrs' – and the ideas would ferment even as the insurgents were mown down by cannon and musketry.[21] The modern-day revolutionaries, he wrote in 1839, 'labour less for the generation that lives around them than for the generation to come; the triumph of the ideas that they cast on the world is slow, but assured and decisive'.[22] Mazzini was convinced that the next great revolution would bring genuine liberty to all the oppressed peoples of Europe. In this vision, he cast the Italians in the leading role – this was a people who, once they had rid themselves of their Austrian and princely masters, were predestined to unleash their immense but as yet untapped energies and resources for the good of the entire continent: 'It is in Italy that the European knot must be untied. To Italy belongs the high office of emancipation; Italy will fulfill its civilizing mission'.[23] Mazzini's dream was of a Europe of nationalities, equally free and each with their own character: indeed, from the mid-1830s, he used the term 'nationalism' as a term of abuse, declaring that while struggles for national freedom against foreign oppressors were absolutely necessary, patriotism should never stand in the way of 'the brotherhood of peoples which is our one overriding aim'.[24]

Mazzini's ideas were very influential on his countrymen. His underground organisation, 'Young Italy', founded when he was in exile in Marseille in 1831 after the failure of the *carbonari* movement, probably (by Metternich's own estimate in 1846) had no more than a thousand active members in Italy itself, but many thousands more offered moral support and read its banned literature. Mazzini also enjoyed overt backing among Italian expatriates, including some five thousand subscribers to its journal in Montevideo and Buenos Aires. One of them was another professional revolutionary named Giuseppe Garibaldi who had been exiled from Piedmont since 1833 and was now fighting for revolutionary causes in Brazil and Uruguay. His exploits made him famous throughout Italy.

Mazzini proved to be a truly inspiring figure for revolutionaries of all nationalities. Alexander Herzen met him on a number of occasions (in this instance, in 1849):

> Mazzini got up and, looking me straight in the face with his piercing eyes, held out both hands in a friendly way. Even in Italy a head so severely classical, so elegant in its gravity, is rarely to be met with. At moments the expression of his face was harshly austere, but it quickly grew soft and serene. An active, concentrated intelligence sparkled in his melancholy eyes; there was an infinity of persistence and strength of will in them and in the lines of his brow. All his features showed traces of long years of anxiety, of sleepless nights, of storms endured, of powerful passions, or rather of powerful passion, and also some element of fanaticism – perhaps of asceticism.[25]

Such was his attraction as a theorist and an apostle of revolution that Mazzini felt able to draw revolutionaries of all nationalities into a pan-European movement. While in exile in Berne in 1834, he gathered around him a small number of political refugees from Poland and Germany, as well as Italy, to create an organisation called 'Young Europe', aimed at liberating the oppressed nations and at coaxing the peoples of Europe – eventually – to settle their differences peacefully. This glorious vision proved tragically too elusive, but 'Young Italy' and 'Young Europe' inspired a wealth of imitators in other countries: there was a 'Young' Ireland, Switzerland, Poland and Germany and later the world would boast a Young Argentina and a Young Ukraine. Metternich was not, therefore, being entirely unreasonable when he lost sleep over the existence of a revolutionary network: it was just that it did not take its orders from Paris. He was perhaps nearer the mark when he castigated the Italian as the most dangerous man in Europe – certainly some anxious European rulers wholeheartedly agreed. In 1834 Mazzini, Garibaldi and other members of Young Italy were condemned to death *in absentia* by a Piedmontese military tribunal, while the Pope ordered his police to be watchful over the 'immense designs of this extraordinary man'.[26] There were even some sweaty palms in the Belgian and Dutch governments when they learned that Mazzinian propaganda was circulating in the Low Countries, yet as parliamentary regimes they almost certainly had much less to fear from its influence. By the crisis year in 1847, Mazzini had become such a bogeyman for the authorities that there were simultaneous sightings of him in Malta, Switzerland, Germany and Italy.[27] For all this, when faced with the golden opportunities that 1848 offered, the great visionary proved capable of seizing them with some political pragmatism.

The revolutionaries were not merely romantic dreamers, but were willing to take grave personal risks in the single-minded pursuit of their brave new world. Many of them also sacrificed comfort and financial security: Mazzini relied heavily on his parents for money (they kept paying up in the hope that – someday – he would get a 'proper' job). While living in exile in London in the ten years or so before 1848, he lived austerely, bemusing his British friends and patrons by eschewing the expense of taking cabs, so appearing at social events spattered with the mud of the filthy city streets. Herzen was better off, since he was living off his inheritance from his father, but his friend, the anarchist Mikhail Bakunin, another scion of the Russian gentry, had burned his bridges with his well-heeled family and had an irritating habit of asking his new acquaintances for loans. When not being paid for his military services in South America, Garibaldi, who came from a seafaring family in Nice (which then belonged to Piedmont), earned a living, variously, as a sailor, as a cattle drover in the Argentinian pampas and as a ship's broker.[28]

The revolutionaries did not create the conditions for revolution in 1848, nor were they responsible for the initial outbreaks of the violence that year, which arose from a confluence of much broader circumstances. Yet they were poised for action when the moment arrived and, more importantly, they had the support of organisations that could mobilise significant numbers of activists when the time came for insurrection. More importantly, this organised, revolutionary opposition to the conservative order could not have flourished if it had been the work of only a few thousand isolated fanatics. It was, rather, rooted in the frustrations of a wider, civil society. While the vast majority of Europeans had no intention of becoming active revolutionaries – and indeed they dreaded the violence and social dislocation that an insurrection would bring – the grievances and aims of the activists found sympathetic echoes among the more passive majority of the population. In this sense, the lurid picture of a bloodthirsty, all-embracing revolutionary movement, painted by conservatives to justify their repressive policies, became something of a self-fulfilling prophecy. Legislation which targeted genuine revolutionaries may have been acceptable to most people, but much of it – like the Karlsbad Decrees in Germany – also struck more broadly at the press, at education, at public associations, at workers' unions and at cultural societies. In many countries, censorship, government or church interference in education and restrictions on the freedom to assemble, to form associations and to discuss politics freely, frustrated many educated, articulate and ambitious people who genuinely felt that they had something positive to contribute to both state and society. There was also a sense that the existing political systems – constitutional or absolutist – did not represent the interests of those social groups such as the manufacturers, artisans and educated middle class like lawyers, professors and low-ranking officials, who felt, first, that they performed roles useful to the state and, second, that the political system was not arranged to protect or further their own interests. Consequently, there were broad segments of society which, while they may have abhorred the prospect of revolution and social upheaval, at least understood the revolutionaries' grievances and shared some of their aims.

Underlying this wider dissatisfaction with the conservative order was the growth of public opinion. Since the eighteenth century, new concepts of 'civil society' had been emerging, fostering the idea that there was – or should be – a cultural and social space independent of the state, where individual citizens could engage in discussion, debate and criticism of everything from art to politics. Civil society was to be the independent arbiter of artistic taste and the legitimate source of political opinion and judgement. This, of course, assumed the existence of an educated, cultured and politically conscious section of society that could sustain such interests. By the nineteenth century, that did indeed exist everywhere, although it varied in scope and size from one part of Europe to the next. Among the great powers, it was perhaps broadest in Britain and France, where censorship was lighter (or where there were ways to avoid it) and literacy was higher. In France by 1848, some 60 per cent of the population could read (a figure closely matched by the Habsburg Empire, which boasted 55 per cent), whereas in Russia the figure was a lowly 5 per cent. In Prussia, where there was a well-established tradition of state schooling, an impressive 80 per cent of people were literate.[29]

Public opinion was expressed not only in print, but in societies and clubs, with their membership drawn from among the progressive middle classes and nobility. These often covered their political purposes with more innocuous activities, including scientific discovery (a favourite in Italy), gymnastics (popular with the perennially healthy Germans), music and shooting (although this last, of course, had its revolutionary uses). 'Public life', wrote one German observer, 'stormed and raged in the theatre and the concert hall because there was nowhere else it was allowed to storm and rage.'[30] Alexander Herzen – for so long used to the oppressive atmosphere in Russia – found even this limited freedom refreshing. Soon after his arrival in Prussia, he visited a grubby theatre and left exhilarated not by the play, 'but by the audience, which consisted mostly of workmen and young people; in the intervals people talked freely and loudly'. He was also so delighted by the caricatures of the Tsar on sale in a bookshop that he bought 'a whole stock of them'.[31] From 1839 the annual Italian scientific conference gathered together hundreds of the most learned minds from up and down the country to discuss the latest developments in technology, medicine and science. In the particularly tense year of 1847, it was held in the Doge's Palace in Venice. The name of the national hero of the day, Pope Pius IX, was invoked as often as possible and even discussions of agriculture provided opportunities to fulminate against the Austrians, since the northern Italians traditionally nicknamed the Habsburg soldiers 'potatoes'.[32] That there were ways around government restrictions none the less did nothing to soothe resentment when governments tried to determine what people could and could not read or discuss and how, when and with whom they could meet. German liberals liked to joke that a typical conservative sign would read 'It is permitted to walk in this field', the assumption being that people were not allowed to do anything unless it was explicitly allowed. In other words, there was a parting of ways between the conservative state and civil society.

This was perhaps to be expected in the absolute monarchies, but it was also true in liberal France. This was because the July Monarchy did not meet the expectations of a wide section of French society. King Louis-Philippe had solid liberal credentials: as 'Général Égalité' (as he was briefly known), he had distinguished himself in the opening campaigns of the French Revolutionary Wars in 1792, before fleeing to Belgium at the end of the year, as Louis XVI was put on trial for his life. After being persuaded (above all by his strong and devoted sister, Adélaïde) to take the throne in 1830,[33] Louis-Philippe initially held fast to his liberal convictions. When he arrived in Paris, he symbolically embraced the aged Lafayette, hero of both the American and French Revolutions, on a balcony at the Hôtel de Ville, the seat of the capital's municipal government. The July Monarchy also reconnected with France's revolutionary heritage by restoring the tricolour: never again would the Bourbon white banner flutter as the national flag. There was no lavish coronation, but a simple ceremony in which the new 'Citizen King', dressed in National Guard uniform, promised to uphold the Charter of 1814, albeit with some changes, including a mild extension of the suffrage, the expunging of the crown's emergency powers and the deletion of phrases in the preamble making reference to divine right monarchy.

Yet these moderately liberal reforms did little to please those Parisian artisans who had done most of the fighting on the barricades in 1830. For them, Louis-Philippe's Orléans dynasty was no better than the Bourbons who had just been deposed. During the insurrection, cries of both 'Long live Napoleon!' – meaning the Emperor's ailing son, Napoleon II, living in gilded captivity in Vienna – and 'Long live the Republic' were heard above the rattle of musketry. With Louis-Philippe's enthronement, the artisans now received very little in return for shedding their blood, for the new order wanted to avoid what it saw as the extremes of democracy (which evoked memories of the braying Parisian mob of the 1789 Revolution) and Bourbon absolutism. Among the people, however, there was a strong sense that 'their' revolution had been 'filched' (*escamotée*) by the complacent rich landowners, industrialists and financiers. There were, moreover, other powerful undercurrents in French society resentful at their exclusion from political life, including middle-class professionals, officials, lesser landowners and entrepreneurs whose fathers or grandfathers had been the backbone of the 1789 Revolution. This opposition found expression either in republicanism, which looked back nostalgically to the democratic days of the First Republic of the 1790s, or in Bonapartism, which wanted to restore the dynasty that, while preserving some of the heritage of the Revolution, also recalled the glorious days when Napoleon took Europe by storm. This nationalist vision of a France exporting the libertarian principles of 1789 to the wider world had widespread appeal. The opposition to the July Monarchy bore with impatience the humiliation of the peace treaties of 1815, which had reduced France (after more than twenty years of warfare) back to its frontiers of 1792.

Yet the July Monarchy by and large sought to avoid foreign

adventures; in fact, it tried very hard to be unheroic and rather boring. This was because, quite reasonably, it wanted peace abroad and stability at home so that France could prosper. The regime would therefore do little to try to reverse the 1815 peace settlement, but it succeeded in prodding France into some of the fastest economic growth in its history. In the late 1830s it expanded and improved the road system. In 1842 the government embarked on the construction of a railway network, laying some nine hundred miles of track, which made new demands on heavy industries like coal, iron, steel and engineering, so that they expanded in turn. For this reason, some economic historians identify the 1840s as the period of 'take-off' in French industrialisation.[34] Karl Marx would describe the July Monarchy scathingly as a joint stock company for the exploitation of French national wealth. Indeed, the stolidly 'bourgeois' nature of the regime was represented by Louis-Philippe himself, who usually appeared in public not in royal regalia, but in a plain suit, a black frock coat and carrying that ultimate symbol of middle-class respectability, an umbrella. This was precisely the safe image that the monarchy wanted to display to the world, but it did not impress the republicans, who seethed at both the regime's unadventurous foreign policy and its resistance to wider political participation. Republican uprisings in 1832 in Paris and two years later in both the capital and Lyon were crushed. The Parisian insurrection of April 1834 – the inspiration for the uprising in Victor Hugo's *Les Misérables* – ended with a massacre on the rue Transnonain, when enraged soldiers clearing revolutionary snipers from a tenement room by room indiscriminately slaughtered twelve civilians whom they found sheltering there.

The killing of innocents left an indelible stain on the July Monarchy, but at least the regime had the support of the well-heeled electorate, which was petrified by the prospect of another revolution. The government therefore felt strong enough to prosecute republican newspapers and imposed restrictions on political associations and workers' unions. Among the organisations proscribed was the paramilitary Society of the Rights of Man, which was founded in 1832 and recruited from workers. It was divided into small revolutionary cells called 'sections' – a term recalling the old Parisian districts that had been the hotbeds of popular militancy during the 1789 Revolution. This was not an organisation devoted to peaceful persuasion: rather, it sought to drill and discipline its artisanal membership in preparation for an insurrection to establish a democratic republic. It planned the Parisian uprising of 1834, and so it suffered accordingly in the repression: no fewer than 1,156 arrests were made in the initial swoop by the police, although 736 were released within five months.[35] The republicans reacted with more violence, including, in 1835, a truly horrific assassination attempt on the King by a twenty-five-barrelled gun, dubbed an 'infernal machine', in which some fourteen people were killed – but not Louis-Philippe, who escaped with a single bruise. This was one of eight efforts on his life, a frequency that prompted the satirical magazine *Charivari* to quip on one occasion that the King and his family had returned from an outing 'without being in any way assassinated'.[36]

The years 1834–5 represented the start of a cycle of violence and repression, in which the republicans became increasingly embittered by the regime, while the monarchy had abandoned its original liberal principles and became ever more repressive. The September Laws of 1835 imposed press restrictions: newspapers could be prosecuted for proposing another system of government or for insulting the King – although that did not stop the bold caricaturist Honoré Daumier (who was prosecuted for his cartoons) from transforming Louis-Philippe's jowly features into a pear shape, an image which stuck. Legal procedure was also changed to make it easier to pursue political prosecutions.[37] The liberal monarchy had, despite the King's own misgivings, abandoned some of the very principles that had differentiated it from the Bourbons. This transformation seems to have been encapsulated in the slogan used in support of the September Laws: 'Legality will kill us'.[38]

At the same time, the violence and repression split the republican opposition into the moderates, who wanted to use legal methods to persuade the regime to grant political reforms (this tendency took its name from its newspaper, *le National*), and the radicals, who wanted to destroy the monarchy by revolution. On the extreme fringe of this militant tendency Louis-Auguste Blanqui and his friend Armand Barbès forged the insurrectionary Society of Seasons, so-called for the way in which it was structured. To keep the identities of its members secret from the prying eyes of the police, its cells consisted of seven revolutionaries, each named after a day of the week. Four weeks were bound into a month and three months were grouped into the largest unit of all – a season. The catechism to which its members had to subscribe condemned all society as 'gangrened', which justified 'heroic remedies . . . to achieve a healthy state', by which was meant not only a revolution, but also a period of 'revolutionary power' – that is to say, a form of authoritarian rule until the 'people' were ready for democracy and the old ruling elites were exterminated. This was an early, grisly herald of Karl Marx and Friedrich Engels's 'dictatorship of the proletariat'. Indeed, Blanqui started to insist that ensuring all citizens the 'right to existence' would involve some redistribution of wealth.[39] The Seasons was on the extreme left of the republican movement and was responsible for an abortive uprising in May 1839, in which Barbès fell wounded, bleeding from a head wound. Despite the failure – and the captivity that followed – Blanqui remained convinced that revolutions could be made by acts of will: insurrection alone was enough to begin the process of extirpating the old order and of building the world anew. The rest of the republican left was not so sure: in 1843 the left-wing newspaper *La Réforme* was founded, backed with the money of Alexandre Ledru-Rollin, who was rich enough to have been elected to the Chamber of Deputies, but whose sympathies were with the left. The journal's editors and contributors saw themselves as 'the General Staff' of the coming revolution, but their main thrust was persuasion through propaganda. *Réforme* advocated not only political democracy (as did the *National*), but social reform. In 1845 it denounced what it called 'communism' (whereupon Blanqui and his followers castigated the paper as 'aristocratic'), but it certainly entertained socialist ideas.

In Italy, Germany and the Habsburg Empire, liberalism coincided with nationalism. The idea of Italian unification had developed under the ideological impact of the French Revolution of 1789 and the practical experience of Napoleonic rule, under which previously separate states had been lumped and administered together. Yet there were divisions between the moderates, who wanted to ensure the survival of the existing princes within an Italian confederation, and the republicans, like Giuseppe Mazzini, who sought a unitary, democratic state. Others still, devoted to their native city or region, envisaged a republican revolution in their own state, which they hoped would then co-exist with all the others – whether monarchist or republican – in a loose federation. Among the proponents of this solution was the Milanese teacher and intellectual Carlo Cattaneo. Perhaps the leading intellect behind the moderate, monarchist vision was Vincenzo Gioberti, who in 1843 published an influential book, entitled *Of the Moral and Civil Primacy of the Italians*, which by 1848 had sold no less than eighty-thousand copies, making it a bestseller by nineteenth-century standards. The title alone could not fail to appeal to a people who in various ways were squirming under foreign domination. For Gioberti, the model for the Risorgimento – Italy's 'resurgence' – was not the French Revolution. Indeed, French influence in the shape of Napoleon Bonaparte had disrupted, not nurtured, Italy's national development. The French, in fact, were not the great people many took them to be, for (Gioberti argues crushingly) 'France is not inventive, not even in the ranks of error'. Italy's primacy stemmed not from imported ideas of nationhood, but from the Pope, for religion by its very nature dominated all that was human. Gioberti therefore proposed a federation of the existing Italian states led by the political and moral authority of Rome: this would give Italy, 'the most cosmopolitan of nations', its rightful place in the world.[40] The unitary, republican vision was of course expressed by Mazzini, who in explaining Young Italy's goals declared:

> Young Italy is republican and unitarian – republican because theoretically every nation is destined, by the law of God and humanity, to form a free and equal community of brothers; and the republican government is the only form of government that ensures this future:

because all true sovereignty resides essentially in the nation, the sole progressive and continuous interpreter of the supreme moral law . . . Young Italy is unitarian, because, without unity there is no true nation; because, without unity there is no real strength; and Italy, surrounded as she is by powerful, united, and jealous nations, has need of strength above all things.[41]

German nationalism was also divided between liberal and radical wings, as became eminently clear at the Hambach Festival in 1832. There, republican orators proclaimed, under streaming black, red and gold banners, the goal of a unitary, democratic German republic. This horrified liberals, who, like their moderate Italian counterparts, wanted to persuade the existing German states to grant constitutions and join a German federation, which would guarantee individual and political liberties. This vision was driven in part by a sincere belief that this was the best way of reconciling freedom with unity. As one Baden liberal put it in a tongue-tied turn of phrase, 'I desire unity only with liberty, and I would prefer liberty without unity to unity without liberty.'[42] For the liberals, the radical vision of a unitary republic would lead to such an uncertain future that constitutional and individual freedoms would be put at risk. Many of them sought simply to develop the Prussian-sponsored customs union, the Zollverein (in existence since 1833 and which excluded Austria), into something more than just a common German market. The divisions between radicals and liberals would prove to be among the gravest weaknesses of both the Italian and the German nationalist movements in 1848.

In the multi-ethnic Habsburg Empire, Metternich had initially encouraged the local elites to engage in literary activities, to explore the language of their people and to research their national past, because it seemed like a harmless diversion from political activity.[43] It transpired that he was playing with fire, for it was precisely such cultural life among the Magyars, Czechs, Croats, Serbs, Romanians and others that fed into a developing sense of national identity. Sooner or later, these identities would be given political expression, and in 1848 they would endanger the very fabric of the

Habsburg Empire. Metternich started to understand this sometime before the cataclysm. He fell particularly hard on the Hungarian liberals. The lawyer and nobleman Lajos Kossuth, elected to the Diet of 1832–6, had circulated in manuscript form his 'parliamentary reports' which argued for a root-and-branch reform of both Hungarian society and the Habsburg monarchy in general. He was arrested in 1837 and was imprisoned for three years. Undeterred, he went on to publish his own newspaper, the *Pest News*, from 1841 and emerged as one of the fiery leaders of the Hungarian revolution. To counterbalance the Magyar opposition, in 1835 Metternich gave government support to the Croatian intellectual Ljudevit Gaj in publishing the journal *Danica* (*Morning Star*), which argued in favour of the 'Illyrian ideal', or a united kingdom of southern Slavs (Serbs, Croats and Slovenians). Yet, by 1842, southern Slav nationalism itself became sufficiently worrying for Metternich to change his mind and withdraw his support for Gaj.

Liberalism and radicalism may well have been confined in each country to a few thousand intellectuals and the alienated gentry and middle classes, but opposition to the conservative regime was popularised by one of the most pressing issues of the age: the 'social question'. This meant the problem of poverty and the dislocation caused by the painful economic transformation that was under way. Pauperism stemmed mostly from the sustained rise in population, which had begun in the mid-eighteenth century and continued relentlessly ever since. Ultimately, economic growth, stimulated by industrial capitalism, would ease the pressure by creating a wide range of different types of jobs and by raising standards of living, but in most parts of Europe these benefits became apparent only after 1850, primarily in the last quarter of the nineteenth century. The decades prior to 1848 certainly saw the onset of industrialisation (defined as the application of large-scale technology to manufacturing processes concentrated in factories, bringing sustained economic growth). Indeed, the European landscape across which Alexander Herzen and his family travelled in 1847 was in the first stages of a transformation that would only accelerate in later decades: factories on the outskirts of cities belched fumes into the air, mingling with the more familiar smoke rising from the chimneys of the increasingly crammed working-class tenements. Telegraph wires were just beginning to thread their way across the landscape and railway tracks, with their engines travelling at speeds hitherto unthinkable to most people, were spreading across Europe like an incipient spider's web.

The boom in the heavy industries that supported the railways and the mechanisation of textile manufacturing (which experienced the first phase of industrialisation in the west) were particularly intense in isolated pockets, namely in Britain, Belgium, parts of northern and south-eastern France, some regions of Germany (particularly the Rhineland and Silesia), and in the enclaves in the Czech lands of the Habsburg Empire and around Vienna. Even so, artisans and craft workers, who had formerly enjoyed existences as small-scale producers, found that their skills and independence were being threatened not only by the introduction of machinery, but by new ways of organising production, in which unskilled or semi-skilled workers – including women – could produce the same goods in greater numbers and at lower cost, although (the beleaguered artisans argued) of poorer quality. Desperation pushed some craft workers into revolt. In June 1844 the Silesian hand-weavers, sinking underneath the tide of competition from both the British textile industry and recently established Polish mills, rose up against the merchants who were profiting from the situation by driving down the prices of their homespun wares. Roughly three-quarters of the forty thousand weavers simply did not have enough money on which to feed their families. Factories were sacked, but no one was hurt until the Prussian army stepped in to crush the weavers, killing ten of them.[44] Moreover, artisans and craft workers faced with the prospect of succumbing to the factory system found little to recommend life in service to the machine. The working day, which previously had followed gentler rhythms, was now relentlessly timed by the clock. The introduction of gas lighting may have been a boon in a domestic setting, but for European workers it meant that they regularly spent fourteen to fifteen hours a day at the machine, since there was no longer any reason to knock off when daylight faded.[45]

Industrialisation was not sufficiently widespread to create a middle class or bourgeoisie that owed its wealth primarily to large-scale capitalism. Such bourgeois did exist, of course, but the European middle classes were a much more variegated and a far from socially united group of people. Many of them were landowners, often pretentiously imitating aristocratic lifestyles. In France the wealthiest landed bourgeois fused with the older nobility to form a fifteen-thousand-strong class of super-rich *notables* who dominated political life under the July Monarchy. In Prussia over 40 per cent of landed estates were held by non-nobles. Beneath this stratum of bourgeois landowners, there was a plethora of smaller proprietors, professionals, officials and businessmen, as well as a lower middle class of retailers and master-craftsmen. The main problem facing the middle class was that while many of them had enjoyed a good standard of education, there were not enough positions in the professions and the government to provide them all with employment. So the middle classes experienced the population pressure in the shape of 'an excess of educated men'. As one French satirist put it, there must have been a population explosion because 'there were twenty times more lawyers than suits to be lost, more painters than portraits to be taken, more soldiers than victories to gain, and more doctors than patients to kill'.[46]

In social terms, therefore, the collapse of the conservative order in 1848 was a crisis of 'modernisation' in the sense that the European economy and society were changing, but they had not yet been adequately transformed to absorb the intense pressures of population growth and, above all, to address the desperation of artisans, craft workers and peasants. In the countryside overpopulation threatened to create a crisis of Malthusian proportions in some parts of Europe, leaving much of the population living on the margins of existence and especially vulnerable to famine when poor harvests struck. Landless labourers saw their wages driven down by proprietors who could draw from an ever-increasing pool of rural workers desperate for jobs: the growth of the rural population was such that between the Napoleonic Wars and 1848, the number of landless agricultural workers in Prussia grew at almost double the rate of the overall population. Even peasants who had some land struggled to scratch out a living: dividing what fields they owned among their children meant that their holdings were ever more subdivided and unproductive, until there was nothing left to do but to sell to a landowner rich enough to buy up these parcels of land. It has been estimated that a hundred thousand Prussian landowning peasants disappeared in this way, joining the struggling masses of the landless rural labourers.[47] Such pressure on the land was also acute in France, where from around the 1820s the population outstripped the countryside's capacity to feed all French families, making imports of food essential and workers and peasants particularly vulnerable to price rises.

There was also the problem of the downtrodden peasantry of Central and Eastern Europe. They were either serfs (as in the Russian Empire and Austrian-ruled Galicia) or were obliged to pay heavy dues to their landlords while also being forced to perform compulsory labour services (the *robot*) on their lord's land, as in Bohemia and Hungary. Besides the *robot*, Czech peasants were also weighed down by payments in money and kind to their landlords – and this was in addition to taxes owed to the state and the tithe paid to the Church. Moreover, peasants were meant to be subservient in their behaviour: right up to 1848 they had to address state officials as 'gracious lord' and landlords could strike a peasant with a fist at will, although beating with a cane required the formal approval of the district government official.[48] Outside the Russian Empire, the Ukrainians of Galicia almost certainly bore the worst conditions of all European peasants. On average, more than a third of all the days of the year were spent performing the *robot* on their (usually Polish) landlords' estates, but they also had to work for the government repairing roads and using their draught animals for transportation. Serfdom (for such it was) was enforced through violence: since 1793 landlords were not permitted to use cudgels with which to batter their serfs, but the prohibition was almost universally ignored; so much so that the government had to reiterate the ban repeatedly, the last time in 1841. A Polish democrat despaired on seeing the way in which his aristocratic compatriots treated their Ukrainian subjects: 'The peasant in the eyes of the magnate was not a man, but an ox, destined to work for his comfort, whom it was necessary to harness and thrash with a whip like an animal.'[49]

Compared with some of the peasantry, workers were much better off, but they, too, had reasons to be fearful. The growth of industry was fitful, rather than sustained, so there were 'boom and bust' trade cycles, in which production overtook demand, causing a collapse in prices and commerce, leading to unemployment and despair. One such crisis arose prior to the 1830 revolutions. The worst of them struck in the years before 1848. Even outside these periods of crisis, the conditions in which the poorest people lived shocked observers. Rural poverty meant that many peasants either had to face hunger – and perhaps starvation – in the countryside, or take their chances in emigration to North America (some 75,000 left Germany in the crisis year of 1847)[50] or to the cities. Neither course was an easy option. While manufacturing offered wages higher than those gleaned by rural labourers, the costs of living were also greater. One estimate suggests that food and drink for a working-class family swallowed up between 60 and 70 per cent of its income, which left little for rent and clothing.[51] Indeed, studies conducted by worried middle-class philanthropists in the 1840s suggested that German workers did not have half the income required to live decently: some noted that they survived essentially on potatoes and on hard spirits, providing a standard of living below that of convicts in prisons – an observation that was echoed by similar studies in Prague. German workers also wore the same clothes in the summer as they did in the winter, with no additional layers against the bitter cold.

The towns and cities were teeming with poverty-stricken masses crammed into hideously overcrowded tenements. The building of affordable housing, the provision of sanitation and the delivery of a clean water supply did not keep pace with the migration of the rural poor from the countryside. People were stunned at the sight of half-naked children playing in filthy, narrow streets: close to half did not live to see their fifth birthday, while those who survived could expect, on average, to live until their fortieth.[52] In 1832 a report on the northern French industrial town of Lille described the squalor in which the poorest workers lived: 'In their obscure cellars, in their rooms . . . the air is never renewed, it is infected; the walls are plastered with garbage . . . If a bed exists, it is a few dirty, greasy planks; it is damp, putrescent straw . . . The furniture is dislocated, worm-eaten, covered with filth.'[53] A resident of the slums in one crowded Parisian district could expect to have on average some seven square metres of living space in the dark, dirty and damp housing of the city centre. 'No where else', declared one newspaper, 'is the space more confined, the population more crowded, the air more unhealthy, dwelling more perilous and the inhabitants more wretched.'[54] These were the days before the reconstruction of the city by the Baron Haussmann, Emperor Napoleon III's Prefect of the Seine, who from the 1850s was responsible for slum clearance and the construction of the airy, elegant boulevards for which the French capital is still famous. Miserable lodgings, a contaminated water supply and open sewers running down the middle of narrow streets provided the unsanitary conditions in which a ghastly new disease, cholera, made its first appearance in western Europe in 1832. The urban squalor also persuaded moralists and reformers that cities were breeding grounds for vice and criminality. In Berlin, a city of 400,000 people by 1848, there were no less than 6,000 paupers being helped by the state, 4,000 beggars, 10,000 prostitutes, 10,000 'vagabonds' (meaning people of no fixed occupation) and, it was thought, a further 10,000 engaged in criminal activity. Collectively, these people living on the margins outnumbered the established burghers of the Prussian capital by two to one.[55] Since poverty was seen by liberals and conservatives alike as a sign not of economic circumstance but of idleness, vice and even stupidity, there was no welfare state or safety net of social security. There was some relief provided by public works in times of dire emergency, but otherwise paupers had to rely on assistance in the harsh conditions of the workhouse or on handouts, both of which were organised at parish rather than state level, so were dependent on the willingness of local communities to pay for them. Otherwise, paupers could beg for help from private charities.

Some intellectuals therefore pondered the question of poverty and emerged with a wide range of ideas which collectively came to be known as 'socialism'. This term, first used by the French radical Pierre Leroux in 1832, arose because its adherents gave priority to resolving the 'social question' rather than to political reform. Some 'utopian' socialists, such as Etienne Cabet and Charles Fourier, envisaged ideal communities that would erase inequalities of wealth, but there were other, 'scientific' socialists, such as Karl Marx and Henri de Saint-Simon, who tried to analyse society as it was and to offer a practical vision for the future. Poverty – and the fact that there were people willing to exploit it for political purposes – deeply alarmed anyone who had something to lose from a social revolution. In the 1840s a British observer issued the stark warning of the masses in Hamburg that their 'lack of well-being encourages the pathological lust for destruction which . . . turns against the possessions of the better-off'.[56] Such psychological fears among the well-to-do were given material evidence by some serious outbursts of working-class violence. In 1844 – the same year as the Silesian uprising – the cotton printers of Prague rose up and the authorities lost control of the city for four days until they were crushed by troops under General Alfred Windischgrätz, an act that shrouded him in notoriety and was still remembered by the Czechs four years later.

These workers were driven to such extremes because the mid-1840s was a period of dire economic distress. A cyclical trade slump combined with harvest failures ensured that the bleak era would be remembered as the 'hungry forties'. The crisis began in earnest in 1845, but then continued unabated until almost the end of the decade. The great tragedy was that, while the grain harvests failed, so too did the potato, which was the main back-up crop. It was afflicted by a fungus, popularly called the 'blight', which turned the tubers into a rotten mush. The disease affected almost all of Europe, from Ireland to Poland. It was in the former that the results were the most tragic, for the blight unleashed the Potato Famine, during which up to 1.5 million people died. In Germany there was a wave of food riots and hunger marches,[57] while in France the price of bread, the main staple of the bulk of the population, rocketed by close to 50 per cent, provoking angry scenes at the bakeries, and food riots. Furthermore, since people had to spend an even greater proportion of their earnings on food, unemployment in the industrial and artisanal sectors spiralled dangerously upwards, as demand for manufactured goods slumped. In the northern French textile manufacturing towns the numbers of jobless reached catastrophic proportions: in Roubaix some eight thousand out of thirteen thousand workers were thrown on to the street; in Rouen, people endured wage cuts of 30 per cent to stave off the calamity of unemployment.[58] In Austria ten thousand workers were laid off in 1847 in Vienna alone, which, at a time when food prices were reaching all-time highs and there was no government help for the poor, was disastrous. To compound the misery, there were outbreaks of typhoid in many of the cities of the empire.[59]

In January 1847, surveying the deep and widespread distress, a Prussian minister wrote, 'the old year ended in scarcity, the new one opens with starvation. Misery, spiritual and physical, traverses Europe in ghastly shapes – the one without God, the other without bread. Woe if they join hands!'[60] The possibility of the opposition to the conservative order harnessing the economic despair was not just a phantom conjured up by conservative imaginations. Popular anger focused, not unnaturally, on the conservative order – and the liberals were quick to capitalise on this. Economic despair, which had always simmered threateningly beneath the delicate surface of the social order, now reached an intensity which the political structures of the old regime were scarcely equipped to contain. The first months of 1848 would be a fleeting but crucial moment in which the distress of the masses fused with the long-nourished frustrations, anxieties and aspirations of the liberal opposition to the conservative system. Metternich's Europe, which had seemed so triumphant in 1815 and which had weathered so many storms since, suddenly seemed extraordinarily vulnerable and the liberals smelled blood. The confluence of the acute social crisis with the sense that political change was now possible led even the more cautious opponents of the old order to press for reform, if not for revolution.

In France the hostility to the July Monarchy was channelled by the republican movement into a campaign for parliamentary reform, demanding universal male suffrage. Since 1840 the French political landscape had been dominated by the figure of François Guizot, whose ministerial portfolios had at various times included education, the interior and foreign affairs but who in 1848 was effectively prime minister. A historian, he was Protestant, bourgeois, eloquent, bright and rather arrogant: when pressed with demands to extend the right to vote, he famously replied, '*Enrichissez-vous*' – 'Get rich' – in order to qualify for the suffrage. Yet an indication of the extent to which civil society was excluded from formal political life was the fact that in Paris for every man who had the right to vote, there were ten who subscribed to a newspaper. In other words, a great many people had political opinions, but could not participate directly in the parliamentary system. Guizot's intransigence therefore did much to alienate the July Monarchy from the mass of public opinion. In 1847 the government's opponents – both republicans and members of the 'dynastic opposition' (the latter meaning those who did not want to topple the monarchy, but rather wished to take the existing ministry's place) – pressed their demands. They avoided an official ban on political meetings by arranging a series of banquets across the country. At these frequently massive gatherings, speakers would harangue the revellers with calls for reform. In Britain such an activity might have seemed harmless, but in France, where there was such a chasm between government and public opinion, it was explosive.[61] Among the more sought-after speakers was the historian and poet Alphonse de Lamartine, whose *History of the Girondins*, a narrative of the 1789 Revolution published in 1847, had tapped into the zeitgeist and become a bestseller. At a packed, rain-drenched banquet at Mâcon in July that year, Lamartine addressed the people who also happened to be his constituents (for he was their representative in the Chamber of Deputies). With a reference to the great revolution of 1789, he declared, 'It will fall, this royalty, be sure of that . . . And after having had the revolution of freedom and the counter-revolution of glory, you will have the revolution of public conscience and the revolution of contempt.'[62] Thus, Lamartine expressed what many people felt about the July Monarchy and the fate it deserved.

Elsewhere in Europe the liberal opposition tested the strength of the conservative order, sometimes with tragic consequences. In the Habsburg province of Galicia in 1846, Polish nobles tried to raise the standard of patriotic revolt against Austrian rule. Although they promised in their proclamation to free their serfs, the mostly Ukrainian peasantry did not listen. Instead, they killed and mutilated some 1,200 Polish nobles – men, women and children alike – and set ablaze or plundered some 400 manor houses. The serfs' loyalties remained fixed on the Habsburg Emperor who, it was said, had used his divinely ordained authority to suspend the Ten Commandments, allowing the peasants to kill their hated landlords with impunity.[63] The upshot of this abortive Polish insurrection was the annexation by Austria of the last candle that burned for Polish independence, the free city of Kraków, which was the epicentre of the revolt.

More positively for European liberals, in 1847 a civil war in Switzerland between the liberal and conservative cantons ended. The conservatives had formed themselves into a league, the Sonderbund, which Metternich had supported with Austrian money and weapons, but the liberals emerged victorious in the struggle. In Italy patriotic enthusiasm was aroused with the election of a 'liberal' Pope, Pius IX, in 1846. 'Pio Nono' was known to have read Gioberti's popular book, and when he took power in Rome he immediately relaxed censorship, freed all political prisoners and promised to look into political reform. For Italian nationalists, here was a figurehead who could unite all strands of Italian opinion, provide moral leadership for the campaign to free Italy from Austrian domination and give the country some sort of political unity. Metternich responded in 1847 by reinforcing the Austrian garrison at Ferrara, but this merely gave Pius the chance to show off his liberal and patriotic credentials by protesting vehemently; his star among Italian liberals soared even higher. In northern Italy the opposition engaged at first in a 'lawful struggle', the *lotta legale*, seeking to work within the limits of the Congregations to secure political reforms from the Habsburgs. Metternich's intransigence, however, would ensure that the Italian patriots would be forced to choose between abandoning the struggle or plotting a revolutionary course. In Lombardy this opposition was led by the nobility frustrated by the lack of opportunity for status and position in the viceregal court and bureaucracy in Milan, but which was also the backbone of the liberal movement in the various societies that had been formed in the city. Foremost of these was the 'Jockey Club', an imitation of a British club, which also had a serious political and cultural purpose.

Elsewhere in the Habsburg Empire, the elections to the Hungarian Diet in 1847 returned a parliament which included radical liberals like Kossuth and was willing to debate peasant emancipation and the abolition of the nobles' tax privileges. In Austria the cash-strapped monarchy summoned the Estates of Lower Austria for March 1848. This became the focus of the hopes of liberals who pored over one of the few permitted foreign newspapers, the *Augsburger Allgemeine Zeitung*, for news of the outside world, and who met in Vienna's Juridical-Political Reading Club, among others. In Germany, where nationalism had reached boiling point with an anti-French war scare in 1840 (provoked by one of the July Monarchy's rare bouts of sabre-rattling), membership of liberal organisations had swollen dramatically: the 'gymnastic societies' by 1847 could claim 85,000 members in 250 branches, while choral clubs boasted 100,000 adherents, who met annually in national festivals between 1845 and 1847. In constitutional states such as Baden, Württemberg and Bavaria, the liberals began to flex their parliamentary muscles, but it was in Prussia that their resurgence would have the most dramatic effect. King Frederick William IV needed money to pay for one of his pet schemes, the development of the railways, but a law of 1820 stated that, if the monarchy wanted to raise new loans, the estates of the whole kingdom would have to be consulted. In 1847, therefore, the United Diet met, chosen from among members of the provincial estates. This assembly became a platform from which Prussian liberals could press for permanent constitutional reform, and the irritated King dismissed it in June. Yet public interest had been aroused and the question of the Prussian estates and of constitutional reform became the subjects of excited and expectant conversations in cafés and social clubs across the country. In September the radical wing of the opposition, pressed by the expansive and eloquent figure of Friedrich Hecker and the renegade aristocrat (and vegetarian) Gustav von Struve, gathered other democrats together at a meeting in Offenburg in the grand duchy of Baden. They stopped short of calling for a unitary German republic, but called for (among other things) the repeal of all repressive laws passed by the diet of the German Confederation, the abolition of censorship and an elected assembly for a federal Germany. The moderate liberals – including the stalwart Heinrich von Gagern – responded the following month with a gathering at Heppenheim in the grand duchy of Hesse. They proposed that the already extant Zollverein, the customs union, be converted into a political body, with the people having a say through elected representatives, so that over the course of time it would bring greater German unity.

With the pressure on the conservative order – and with actual breaches being knocked through its ramparts – almost everyone expected a great revolutionary crisis to sweep across Europe. As a priest in Rome declared when giving his oration at the funeral of the great Irish reformer Daniel O'Connell in mid-1847, there was arising a 'revolution which threatens to encompass the globe'.[64] This was a source of great hope for some, including Alexander Herzen, who later wrote of a 'dream' which he had about his arrival in Paris in 1847, but which would prove to be an illusion shattered like broken glass:

> I . . . was carried away again by the events that seethed around me . . . the whirlwind which set everything in movement carried me, too, off my feet; all Europe took up its bed and walked – in a fit of somnambulism which we took for awakening . . . And was all that . . . intoxication, delirium? Perhaps – but I do not envy those who were not carried away by that exquisite dream.[65]

2

THE COLLAPSE

Many of those who would participate in the events of 1848 awoke to the New Year with a nagging sense of foreboding, suspecting that the various crises which had punctuated the previous two years were yet to reach their climax. On 29 January, Alexis de Tocqueville rose in the Chamber of Deputies and warned his colleagues that sooner or later the grumbling discontent of the French masses would explode in the most fearful of revolutions: 'I believe that right now we are sleeping on a volcano . . . can you not sense, by a sort of instinctive intuition . . . that the earth is trembling again in Europe? Can you not feel . . . the wind of revolution in the air?' He urged the government to concede parliamentary reform and to shake off the odour of corruption and intransigence that was losing it public confidence. Tocqueville was no alarmist, but his speech was derided by the government majority, who mocked the drama of his intervention, while the liberal opposition politely applauded an attack on the ministry by an unlikely, conservative ally. Even Tocqueville's friends thought that he had overdone the histrionics.[1] Yet the great historian and social thinker would be proven right: almost the entire continent was teetering on the very edge of a revolutionary abyss.

I

The first violent confrontation of 1848 arose in Milan in the form of perhaps the first concerted anti-smoking campaign in modern history. The young nobles of Milan, gathering in the Jockey Club, long chafing at the scant opportunities for advancement in the German-speaking regime and encouraged by the liberal-sounding noises coming from the Vatican, wanted to hit the Austrians where it would hurt most: the treasury purse. Since Austria's Italian provinces were among its most lucrative sources of taxation, the Italian notables, inspired by the example of the Boston Tea Party of 1773, organised a boycott of tobacco, the tax on which gave the Viennese treasury a significant portion of its revenue. The nobles also knew that taxation was a source of resentment among Lombardy's humbler citizens, so they had little difficulty in winning popular support. On New Year's Day, the Milanese gave up smoking. In response, the Austrian garrison, encouraged by their officers, took up smoking with gusto, ostentatiously waving their cigars in the faces of the citizens. Relations between the Italians and the Austrians had been tense since at least the previous autumn, so tempers – no doubt frayed by nicotine withdrawal – almost inevitably snapped. On 3 January, a Milanese, offended by an Austrian soldier puffing exaggeratedly at a cigar, knocked it out of his mouth. A scuffle ensued and some citizens were beaten up by soldiers. A larger crowd of civilians then gathered and retaliated by attacking the troops. The garrison came out in strength, putting down the 'tobacco riot' by killing six and wounding fifty civilians.[2] The commander of the Austrian forces in Italy, Marshal Joseph Radetzky, warned Metternich that he needed reinforcements to contain any further outbreaks, but he was ignored. In fact, the Milanese nobles did not want to provoke revolution. Rather, the tobacco boycott was intended to be a means of continuing the *lotta legale* and of securing peaceful reform. More prosaically, one Milanese nobleman explained to Metternich that what the Lombard elites really desired was more access to the higher state positions usually reserved for Austrians. In neighbouring Venetia, Daniele Manin and Nicolò Tommaseo pursued the *lotta legale* by petitioning the Central Congregation of the Austrian provinces for political reform, but the Austrian authorities threw both men in prison on 18 January.

The tobacco riots and the arrests of two popular Venetian leaders created *causes célèbres* that helped to broaden the basis of support for the liberal campaign. Meanwhile, the Austrian government was convinced of its strength against the hot air spouted by Venetian and Milanese liberals. On 16 January, the steely octagenarian Radetzky assured his men that Italian liberalism ('fanaticism and the insane mania for innovations') would be smashed on their courage, 'like fragile surf against hard rock'.[3] The entrenched positions of both sides ensured that northern Italy was in 'a state of undeclared war'.[4] The explosion, when it came, would yield considerably more than the limited reforms originally demanded by the liberal leadership.

The battle lines had hardened in the north partly in response to developments in the south, where the year's first full-blown revolution took place, in Sicily. The fiercely independent islanders had long been convinced that their 'tyrannical' government, the autocratic Bourbon monarchy in Naples, was wilfully ignoring their interests. This impression was reinforced by the state's feeble response to the desperate poverty that became entrenched in a dreadful winter. On 12 January, a crowd in Palermo 'celebrated' the Neapolitan King Ferdinand II's birthday by building barricades high across the streets and unfurling the Italian tricolour, crying, 'Long live Italy, the Sicilian Constitution and Pius IX!' They were soon joined by shady people with less lofty motives. Peasant bandits from the impoverished countryside and the *squadre*, an early form of mafia who lived by running protection rackets against hapless villagers, slipped into the city. They bristled with a grisly array of home-made weapons, hooks and blades of all kinds, and proceeded to terrorise the Neapolitan garrison in the street fighting. The government forces bombarded Palermo from the grim Bourbon fortress of Castellamare, while gunners scattered their lethal charges of grapeshot into the crowd in front of the royal palace and cathedral before they were overwhelmed by the insurgents. The police head-quarters was invaded and its records incinerated. Some thirty-six people were killed before the army withdrew from the city. Within days, the Sicilian countryside was literally in flames as peasants joined the revolution, torching the tax records and land registers in village halls. Eventually, the only royal troops left on the island were those besieged in the citadel of Messina. A General Committee assumed the powers of a provisional government in Palermo under the liberal nobleman Ruggero Settimo, Prince of Fitalìa, who was a veteran of the British-inspired parliament of 1812 and the revolution of 1820. The General Committee included both moderate liberals and more radical democrats, but for now both were willing to work together to protect lives and property from the rampaging peasantry and the urban poor. They also faced the hardest task of all: that of imposing legal rule over those areas controlled by the *squadre*. The revolutionary leadership called for elections to the Sicilian parliament, which had not been allowed to meet since the union of Sicily with Naples in 1816.[5]

When news of the Sicilian revolution reached Naples by steamship, the populace took to the streets. Meanwhile, King Ferdinand had embarked some five thousand troops on steamers bound for Sicily to crush the uprising. He thus denuded the mainland of forces just as the revolution took hold there. Swelling the crowd in Naples were the notorious *lazzaroni* – the poverty-stricken slum masses whom Herzen, who would arrive in the city in February, described as having 'wild features . . . the servile manners of the Neapolitan mob . . . a hybrid of all the slaves, the lower stratum of everything defeated, the remnant of ten nationalities, intermingled and degenerate'.[6] Normally, government-sponsored charity kept them in a state of uneasy quiescence, but the disastrous economic crisis had bit exceptionally hard and, in a pattern that would be repeated elsewhere in the coming months, the government proved unable to help the people out of the depths of their distress. The *lazzaroni* therefore turned against the authorities and, meanwhile, the peasants of the Cilento rose up against their landlords.

This, and the rumour that some ten thousand of them were marching on the city, provoked the uncomprehending fear of townspeople
for the scythe-bearing rural mob. It was enough to push the
Neapolitan nobility and bourgeoisie into demanding some political
changes in order to meet the crisis. The panic infected the court
itself and, learning that his own troops were at best reluctant to
fight, Ferdinand sprang the liberal leader Carlo Poerio from prison.
This at last gave the liberals a figure around whom they could rally.
On 27 January they organised a 25,000-strong demonstration on the
great piazza in front of the royal palace. When cavalry trotted out to
disperse them, the crowd surged around the horsemen and persuaded them to stand down; their commander even offered to take
a petition to King Ferdinand.[7] Afraid of losing his entire kingdom,
Ferdinand promised a constitution, which was published on 10
February. It was based heavily on the French Charter of 1814, so it
was a long way from enfranchising the masses. The Sicilians, who
demanded the restoration of the constitution of 1812 and political
autonomy with merely a dynastic link to Naples, remained implaca-
ble. Some Neapolitan liberals, however, hoped that Naples was at
last joining an inexorable current rolling towards Italian unification. The onetime republican but now moderate liberal Luigi
Settembrini returned to the city from exile in Malta on 7 February
to find the port efflorescent with the Italian tricolour.[8]

The collapse of the absolute monarchy in the south reverberated
up the mountainous spine of Italy. In the Papal States, public pressure on Pius IX, who now wanted to slow the pace of reform,
became more intense. When he tried to placate the Roman masses
by declaring a day of prayer for peace in the Kingdom of the Two
Sicilies, he merely provoked a night-time demonstration that filled
the Corso on 3 February. The avenue blazed with torches as the
people of Rome cheered, '*Viva Pio Nono*', but now added, '*e la cos-
tituzione e la libertà*'. The civic guard – formed in the summer of
1847 as a concession to liberal demands – defiantly tore off the
white-and-yellow papal cockades and pinned tricolours to their hats
instead. A few days later, rumours that the Austrians were preparing
to restore order in Italy by sending their army southwards brought

out another massive protest, which filled the Piazza del Popolo. The demonstrators called on the Pope to raise an army to defend the frontiers. According to the alarmed Belgian ambassador, there were also cries of 'Death to the cardinals! Death to the priests!' With little means of coercion at his disposal, the chastened Pope promised to summon a new government in which laymen as well as ecclesiastics would serve as ministers. Yet, the Belgian diplomat concluded on 12 February, 'the party of movement, now master of the field, will not check itself in the middle of such favourable progress, and its last word . . . is a *constitution*'.[9]

It would be a month (14 March) before the Romans received that from the Pope, but further north Leopold of Tuscany saved his grand-ducal throne by granting a constitution on 11 February, while King Charles Albert of Piedmont had promised one three days before and produced the definitive document on 4 March. This was a seismic shift in Italian politics, for the country's most powerful monarchy, the Savoyard dynasty, had abandoned its age-old absolutist tradition. This would carry heavy weight in the future development of Italy. The proclamation prompted a flamboyant reaction from the people of Turin: patriotic women took to wearing black riding habits, with the skirts lifted up to reveal red-white-and-green petticoats. Church bells pealed so exuberantly that the peasants in the surrounding countryside took up arms in the belief that the ringing was a warning of an Austrian invasion.[10] The Dukes of Modena and Parma stood firm for now, but only because they were under the immediate protection of Austrian troops, while Lombardy and Venetia simmered resentfully. It would take wider European events to make those two provinces boil over and, when they did, Italian nationalists were gifted the long-awaited opportunity to fight for Italian unity.

II

The first of these ground-breaking European events was the revolution in Paris, where the republicans and the dynastic opposition

were campaigning for political reform. Their way was blocked
inside parliament by an intransigent government, but they kept up
the pressure outside by pursuing the banquet campaign. One such
gathering provided the unexpected flashpoint for the revolution in
France, and thereby sparked the explosions that would erupt across
Europe. The banquet was to be held in the 12th Arrondissement in
Paris – which then covered the area around the Panthéon and
included one of the heartlands of Parisian republicanism, with radical traditions reaching back to the days of the 1789 revolution.
The choice of location left the moderates fretting that the banquet
might provide an occasion for a more strident, popular demonstration. The leader of the dynastic opposition, Odilon Barrot, who did
not lack physical courage, but who was politically cautious, therefore had the banquet moved to the well-heeled Champs-Elysées,
scheduling it for 22 February, which prompted the republicans to
call for a protest march that day. The moderates reacted by can-
celling the event altogether. They achieved this at a hastily arranged
meeting of all opposition deputies and journalists in Barrot's home
in the evening of 21 February. Even Armand Marrast, editor of the
republican *National*, agreed. They were all scrambling back from a
collision with the authorities and from the radical forces that such
violence might unleash. But it was too late: Marrast's own paper had
advertised the order of march for the demonstration and the radical republicans insisted that it must go ahead. At a crisis meeting of
republicans of the left-wing *Réforme* tendency, held that same night,
the radicals agreed that the protest would take place as planned, but
it would disperse at the first show of strength by the authorities:
even they were eager to avoid an uncontrollable, unpredictable
clash with the government. No one envisaged a revolution.[11]

Paris arose the next morning to a grey sky heavy with rain. Gusts
of wind drove a miserable drizzle down its streets, but by nine
o'clock plenty of demonstrators – unemployed workers, women
and children – had gathered on the Place de la Madeleine, the start-
ing point for the march. The authorities had called out the National
Guard, but the crowd was steeled by the arrival of some seven hundred students who crossed the River Seine singing 'The Marseillaise'.

According to the left-wing writer and activist Marie d'Agoult, this electrified the atmosphere.[12] Emboldened and reinforced, the crowd now surged across the Place de la Concorde towards the Chamber of Deputies to demand reform, only to be pushed back without bloodshed by National Guards and dragoons. In the battle that then heaved back and forth on the Place de la Concorde that afternoon, it was, however, the Municipal Guard which bore the brunt of the people's frustration:

> This elite corps [Marie d'Agoult explained], composed of experienced men who remained attached to the government thanks to high pay, aroused the jealousy of the troops of the line because of its privileges and was detested by the people because of its policing duties. Its discipline was severe, it fulfilled its missions with rigour. From its frequent conflicts with the Parisian population arose a reciprocal animosity which, in circumstances such as these, could only precipitate hostilities.[13]

The violence erupted when stones were hurled by the crowd at the Municipals, who reacted by forcing their way through the tumult, sabres drawn, and knocking people over. One of the victims was an old woman, who died when her head hit the paving stones; elsewhere a worker was hacked down by a sabre. The first blood had been spilled and now fighting broke out across the city: outside Guizot's home in the Foreign Ministry on the rue des Capucines, on the Champs-Elysées, on the Place de la Bastille and at the stock exchange. The insurgents had armed themselves first with iron railings torn down from fences, then with arms pillaged from gun shops.[14] The forces of order managed to protect the public buildings, but the crowds simply retreated into the labyrinthine streets of the artisanal districts.

While Paris rioted, Guizot faced Barrot's demand for impeachment for corruption and for betraying the constitution. Yet, with the spectre of revolution now hovering over them, even most opposition deputies were in no mood to weaken authority and the motion attracted only fifty-three signatures. Guizot allowed himself to listen to the charges with a contemptuous smile.[15] Moreover, since the rioting was spontaneous and unexpected, the republicans themselves were uncertain what to do. That night the journalists of *La Réforme* discreetly met among the shadowy colonnades of the Palais-Royal, but they could not agree on the best course of action. Some republicans chose to wait on events, but others returned to their districts to mobilise the rank and file of the revolutionary secret societies and to harness the insurrection.

Overnight, barricades arose in the narrow streets of central and eastern Paris. With their sheer weight of numbers, the forces of order ought to have remained masters of the city: there were some 31,000 regular troops, 3,900 Municipals and 85,000 National Guards from Paris and the suburbs. Yet the regulars could act only on the express order of the Prefect of Police – and the Royal Council that night, fearful of provoking a popular backlash, wisely advised prudence.[16] As for the National Guard, it was a citizens' militia composed of taxpayers – a bourgeois force upon which Louis-Philippe thought he could rely. But even those who came from the more conservative western districts baulked at defending an unpopular ministry and helping in the unsavoury task of putting down the insurgents. Some of those who responded to the call-out were badgered and then talked around by crowds of workers. Others, particularly those of the radical Twelfth Legion, which had meant to attend the original banquet at the Panthéon, reacted to the call to arms with defiant cries of '*Vive la réforme!*' The National Guards therefore mustered only in tiny numbers, leaving the hated Municipals almost alone in the struggle to keep control of the streets. The insurgents cut off, attacked and disarmed their more isolated guard posts, while their comrades joined the regulars in spending a miserable night huddled around camp fires and bivouacking in the rain.[17]

Through the following day the National Guard played a pivotal role in mediating between the insurgents and the Municipals. For example, a detachment of the latter was defending the Lepage Brothers' firearms shop, at a crossroads on the rue Bourg l'Abbé, which became a hornets' nest of musketry: by the afternoon of 23

February one of the street corners had been so riddled with bullets that it collapsed in a heap of rubble. The fighting ended only when a detachment of National Guards marched in and divided the two sides, allowing Étienne Arago, one of the founders of *La Réforme*, to negotiate the Municipals' surrender.[18]

His military position weaker than he had expected it to be, Louis-Philippe, who up to now had been stubbornly resistant to concessions, reluctantly decided that the time had come to sacrifice his hated first minister. In the early afternoon of the 23rd Guizot was summoned to the Tuileries Palace, where the King expressed his bitter regret at having to end their long-standing collaboration. Guizot returned to parliament, where, according to d'Agoult, his breathing seemed to be 'stifled by an internal weight',[19] but he threw his head back as if, Tocqueville thought, he was afraid of bowing. The opposition received his announcement of his dismissal with thunderous applause, drowning out his voice, while he was mobbed – like a pack of dogs tearing at their quarry, Tocqueville acerbically remarked – by pro-government deputies, for whom Guizot's fall meant the loss of patronage, position and power.[20] The leaders of the dynastic opposition, Barrot and Adolphe Thiers, congratulated themselves on forcing a change of ministry without – as they thought – toppling the monarchy.

For a few hours this illusion did not appear to be unfounded. When National Guards and breathless deputies ran from barricade to barricade spreading the news of Guizot's dismissal, the firing gradually died down and the menacing crowds began to celebrate. Yet the fate of the regime was still finely balanced. The King had sacrificed his minister to the crowd, but the underlying political and social pressures remained. Moreover, the republicans began to sense that they might secure more than just the fall of a ministry. They continued to harangue the artisans and National Guards, who were uncertain as to whether the time had come to dismantle the barricades. As so often happens in these precarious moments in history, an accident tipped the scales against the regime. On the evening of 23 February coloured lights garlanded the boulevards, where *tricolore*-waving Parisians gathered to celebrate Guizot's demise. At 9.30 p.m., into this festive crowd marched an orderly phalanx of six or seven hundred workers from the radical eastern districts. The revellers joined this march, singing patriotic songs. According to Jean-François Pannier-Lafontaine, a former army paymaster who was marching in the front rank, the people were yelling '*Vive la Réforme! A bas Guizot!*' but raising no hue and cry against the King. Outside the offices of *Le National*, they stopped to listen to Marrast, who urged the people to demand reform and the impeachment of other government ministers, but there was still no talk of deposing the monarchy. Yet the collision was not far away, for further down the boulevard some two hundred men of the 14th Line, the regiment protecting Guizot's lodgings in the Foreign Ministry, heard the singing and, through a light haze of smoke, could see the glow of torches as the swollen crowd approached the rue des Capucines. As a precaution their commander ordered his men to block the boulevard. When the marchers came to a halt, they pressed against the soldiers, and the officer, apparently hoping to nudge them back a little, ordered his men to 'Present bayonets!' As the troops performed the manoeuvre, a mysterious shot burst into the night air. In a knee-jerk response the nervous soldiers let off a volley, the bullets killing or wounding fifty people. Pannier-Lafontaine was knocked over and trapped beneath one of the falling bodies, while one of his companions was wounded. There was panic, as people fled in all directions, trying to find cover from a second volley which never came.[21]

News of the slaughter pulsated around the city: for Parisians, the massacre seemed to signal the onset of a government effort to reassert its authority by crushing force. After midnight people huddling fearfully behind closed shutters were drawn out by a spectacle worthy, d'Agoult wrote, of Dante's Inferno: a horse and wagon, drawn by a muscular, bare-armed worker, bore five lifeless bodies, including 'the corpse of a young woman whose neck and chest were stained with a long stream of blood'. The tableau was lit by the flickering, reddish reflections of a torch held aloft by 'a child of the people, with a pallid complexion, eyes burning and staring . . . as one would depict the spirit of vengeance'. Behind the cart another worker shook his sparkling torch, 'passing his fierce gaze over the crowd: "Vengeance! Vengeance! They are slaughtering the people!"' The insurgents, fired up again, prepared to fight once more and they raced back to the barricades. 'At that moment,' noted d'Agoult, 'the corpse of a woman had more power than the bravest army in the world.'[22]

When Louis-Philippe heard of the massacre, he yielded more of his crumbling ground by appointing Thiers and Barrot to form a government, all too aware that it would be a mere cooling drop in a boiling ocean. He also put on his mailed fist, by appointing Marshal Thomas Bugeaud to command all forces in Paris. Bugeaud was a veteran of the recent colonial wars in Algeria, and he had a hardline reputation as the 'butcher' of the rue Transnonain. Thiers and Barrot proclaimed their new ministry, hoping that the change of government would be enough to persuade the Parisians to cease fire. Barrot courageously rode from one fortification to the next, calling on the insurgents to stand down, but he was stunned by mocking cries of 'We don't want cowards! No more Thiers! No more Barrot! The people are the masters!' The Parisians had paid too dearly for there to be a repeat of 1830, and now the journalists of *La Réforme* stole from barricade to barricade, uttering the electrifying word '*République*'.

In the early hours of 24 February, Bugeaud unleashed his forces, sending four strong columns of troops through the city in an attempt to clear away the barricades. Yet the King, understanding that more bloodshed would make the situation utterly irretrievable, had ordered that the officers in charge should negotiate before firing on the insurgents. Consequently, there were stand-offs across the city, which led nowhere. The lack of determination at the very top showed that the regime's self-confidence had faltered. By midmorning, even Bugeaud was beginning to doubt the wisdom of his strategy. His officers understood that there was little chance of prevailing over the barricades without immense carnage; the National Guards had either joined the insurgents or were reluctant to fight against them; many barracks in the city were under siege; and the revolutionaries had managed to capture a convoy of munitions from the arsenal at Vincennes. The marshal ordered all his troops to fall back on the Tuileries, to consolidate the defence of the royal palace. Tocqueville witnessed the humiliating retreat of the column commanded by General Alphonse Bedeau: it 'looked like a rout. The ranks were broken, the soldiers marched in disorder, heads down, exuding both shame and fear; as soon as one of them briefly fell out with the mass, he was quickly surrounded, seized, embraced, disarmed and sent on his way; all that was done within the blink of an eye.'[23] To the east the Hôtel de Ville, the seat of the city government, was taken by National Guards who had joined the revolutionaries. To the west Tocqueville, caught on the Place de la Concorde by a crowd of insurgents, escaped being beaten up or worse by a timely shout of '*Vive la Réforme!* You know that Guizot has fallen?' 'Yes, monsieur', came a mocking reply from a short, stocky worker, who pointed at the Tuileries, 'but we want more than that.'[24] Both the massacre on the rue des Capucines and the retreat of Bedeau's column symbolised successively the July Monarchy's loss of legitimacy and of power.[25]

With the revolutionaries closing in on the palace, Thiers urged the King to withdraw from the city, bring up regular troops and smash the revolution with overwhelming force from outside. It was a strategy Thiers would adopt much later against the Paris Commune in 1871. In 1848, however, he was rebuffed by his horrified colleagues, including Barrot, and Thiers, in power for less than a day, resigned and stole out of the palace. He was later spotted by a threatening crowd and he escaped by jumping into a cabriolet, which drove him to safety; throughout the journey, he was 'gesticulating, sobbing and pronouncing incoherent words'.[26] Outside the palace, the royalist scholar and diplomat Adolphe de Circourt was on the Place du Carrousel, drawn up with his National Guard battalion – one of the few units (all from the wealthier, conservative western districts) still defending the regime. Louis-Philippe rode out in front of these loyal troops, but to Circourt he seemed 'pale and virtually set in stone'. The street-fighting raged just a few hundred yards away, producing 'a storm of noise which combined a roaring with a tempest . . . One felt vaguely that, behind the first detachments which gave combat, rolled an immeasurable crowd which no moral or intellectual power could any longer stop or turn back.'[27]

The last stand took place at the Château d'Eau, which guarded one of the main access routes to the Tuileries. The Château d'Eau was a two-storey guard post with barred windows, centred on the fountain from which it drew its name. It was defended by some hundred men of the now despised 14th Line and ten Municipal Guards. In bitter fighting vividly described by Gustave Flaubert, the air buzzed with bullets, was torn by the cries of the wounded and rattled to the beating of drums.[28] In the carnage the masonry of the fountain itself was torn apart by the musketry, and the water spilled out over the square, mingling with the blood of the slain and wounded. The insurgents took the awful decision to end the murderous fighting by crashing carriages, laden with burning straw and spirits, into the guard post. As the fire caught, an officer, choking on the smoke, opened the door to escape, only to be shot down. His men piled out behind, throwing their weapons on the ground in a frantic gesture of surrender. The victorious assailants surged forward and then struggled to put out the fire, tripping over blackened corpses and charred debris.[29] Among the wounded on the revolutionary side was the tailor Buacher, who was hit by several musket balls. His shattered arm was later amputated and his signature at the bottom of his testimony in the archives has all the unsteadiness of someone writing with the wrong hand.[30]

While the Château d'Eau burned, the King collapsed in a chair in his study, watched by his hapless courtiers. Politicians offered him conflicting advice, but it was the slippery newspaperman Émile Girardin, editor of *La Presse*, who at midday strode forward and brusquely urged Louis-Philippe: 'Abdicate, Sire!' On being told that no further defence was possible, the exhausted King sat down at Napoleon's old maple desk and formally vacated his throne, leaving it to his grandson, the ten-year-old Count of Paris, with the boy's mother, Hélène, Duchess of Orléans, acting as regent. Louis-Philippe, dressed (as he liked to do) in plain, bourgeois clothes, walked briskly with his wife Marie-Amélie through the

Tuileries Gardens and boarded a carriage waiting on the Place de la
Concorde, from where, escorted by loyal cavalrymen, they drove off,
reaching Honfleur on 26 February. There, the British vice-consul
(showing either a profound lack of imagination or a wry sense of
humour) gave the royal couple the alias of 'Mr and Mrs Smith'. On
3 March they landed in Britain, where Louis-Philippe would die
in August 1850.[31]

The revolutionaries burst triumphantly into the now almost
deserted palace. In another scene described by Flaubert, the crowd
'surged up the stairs, a dizzying flood of bare heads, helmets, red
bonnets, bayonets and shoulders'. Workers took turns to sit on the
throne (the first, Flaubert writes, 'beaming like an ape'). On the
royal seat was written: 'The People of Paris to All Europe: Liberty,
Equality, Fraternity. 24 February 1848'. Then the proceedings took
a more sinister turn, as the crowd smashed up furniture, china and
mirrors.[32] The following day the throne was taken to the Place de
la Bastille, where it was ceremonially burned.

The Duchess of Orléans and her son had taken refuge in the
Chamber of Deputies, where she witnessed the demise of France's
last monarchy, 'dressed in mourning, pallid and calm', noted
Tocqueville, who admired her courage. National Guards, their banners flying, jostled with enthusiastic Parisians brandishing sabres,
muskets and bayonets. When they spilled over from the public galleries on to the floor, Barrot, seeking to secure the regency, was
drowned out. (He was later seen wandering aimlessly in the streets,
stunned and dishevelled.) Lamartine, 'his tall frame thin and
upright', rose to the tribune.[33] He was no republican, but, scholar
of history that he was, he also knew that regencies had generally
been disastrous in France's past.[34] To the acclamation of the crowd,
he now read out a list of members of a provisional government –
arranged by prior agreement with the republicans of the *National*
tendency. Yet he was also pressed to acknowledge the Parisian role
in the revolution, so, responding to the cry of 'To the Hôtel de
Ville!', the poet stepped down and fell in step with the likeable, left-
leaning, eloquent republican Alexandre Ledru-Rollin. As they
marched together towards the traditional seat of Parisian radicalism,

the portly Ledru-Rollin struggled to keep up with Lamartine's long strides. To his breathless complaints, Lamartine replied, 'We are climbing Calvary, my friend.'[35] The provisional government was announced, minister by minister, from the windows of the city chambers; it revealed a compromise between the *National* and *Réforme* tendencies in the republican movement. The moderate majority included Lamartine as foreign minister, the astronomer and member of the French Institut François Arago at the army and navy, and Louis-Antoine Garnier-Pagès at finance. The strong minority appointed from the *Réforme* tendency included Ledru-Rollin as minister of the interior and two ministers without portfolio – the socialist Louis Blanc and a worker named Alexandre Martin, known as 'Albert', who had won his republican and social-ist spurs in the revolutionary underground. A living link back to the First Republic was found in the symbolic appointment of the aged veteran republican Jacques-Charles Dupont de l'Eure as another minister without portfolio. In the early hours of 25 February, Lamartine dramatically strode out on to a balcony, declaring: 'The Republic has been proclaimed!' His words unleashed a roar of ecstatic cheering.

III

Word of the February days in Paris spread like a dynamic pulse and electrified Europe, hastened by the wonders of the modern world: railway, steamboat and telegraph. In the words of William H. Stiles, the American chargé d'affaires in Vienna, it 'fell like a bomb amid the states and kingdoms of the Continent; and, like reluctant debtors threatened with legal terrors, the various monarchs hastened to pay their subjects the constitutions which they owed them'.[36] The news spilled rapidly into Germany. At the University of Bonn, the eighteen-year-old radical student Carl Schurz was interrupted while at work in his garret by a friend bearing the tidings. He threw down his pen and joined the throng of other excited students in the market place: 'We were dominated by a vague feeling as if a great outbreak of elemental forces had begun, as if an earthquake was impending of which we had felt the first shock, and we instinctively crowded together.' The black–red–gold of German unity, formerly banned as revolutionary, now fluttered openly, and even the good, cautious burghers of the city wore the colours in their hats.[37]

The enthusiasm among German liberals and radicals was infectious. In Mannheim in the Grand Duchy of Baden on 27 February, the republican lawyer Gustav Struve organised a political rally, drafting a petition demanding freedom of the press, trial by jury, a popular militia with elected officers, constitutions for every German state and the election of an all-German parliament. The Grand Duke, faced with a massive demonstration in his capital Karlsruhe, yielded two days later, appointed a liberal ministry and permitted work on a new constitution. Struve's petition was printed and circulated all over Germany and thrust before German rulers during the dizzying days of March. This is why the Mannheim programme became known as the 'March demands'. The rulers of Württemberg and Nassau gave in. In Hesse-Darmstadt the Grand Duke abdicated in favour of his son on 5 March rather than yield himself. The only other German ruler to lose his throne in 1848 was the unfortunate King Ludwig of Bavaria, whose colourful and controversial mistress, the dancer and femme fatale Lola Montez, had been targeted by the opposition. While Lola had escaped the odium of the Munich crowd by fleeing the country on 12 February, the liberals struck the following month, while the iron of revolution was still hot. On the 4th, the royal armoury was stormed, and two days later Ludwig acceded to the March demands. Yet his relationship with Lola had shocked Catholic sensibilities at court and even the conservatives abandoned him. The situation was salvaged by the sage, moderate Prince Karl von Leiningen, who persuaded Ludwig to stand aside and allow his son, Maxmilian, to take the helm of the liberalised state. Leiningen was calmly performing this service to the Bavarian monarchy as his own estates in Amorbach were being invaded and ransacked by peasants. Further east, demonstrations organised in Dresden by the radical Robert Blum and the moderate liberal journalist Karl Biedermann on 6 March forced King Frederick Augustus II of Saxony to summon the Estates to enact reform and to dismiss Falkenstein, his unpopular conservative minister.

While individual states were being reformed, liberals and radicals sensed the opportunity to recast all of Germany into a new, more unified shape. In Heidelberg on 5 March an assembly of fifty-one delegates from the freshly liberalised states brushed aside the weakly protesting Diet of the old German Confederation and cut its own path towards the future. Working with a feverish sense of urgency, the meeting convoked 'a more complete assembly of trusted men from all German peoples',[38] a 'pre-parliament', which would gather in Frankfurt to arrange elections for a German national assembly, which in turn would draft an all-German constitution.

So far the German revolution had swept up only the 'Third Germany' – the smaller states lying between the two great power blocs of Prussia and Austria, which at first refused to buckle before the storm. In the west the Prussian Rhineland was swept along by the torrent – and it sent delegates to the Heidelberg Assembly. There was a demonstration of workers in Cologne on 3 March, led by the radical socialist Andreas Gottschalk, demanding, among other things, the right to work, free education and welfare measures to protect the poor. The army moved in and dispersed the three-thousand-strong protest, arresting its ringleaders. Prussia, therefore, had not as yet lost its footing. Nor had the other great German power, Austria, where the absolute monarchy, though its grip was weakening, still had a hold on its European empire. The uprising in the great Habsburg capital of Vienna of 13 March therefore gave fresh impetus to the revolution not only in Germany but through-out Europe. If the February revolution in Paris was the first great shock to the European conservative order in 1848, the second, equally fundamental blow for the old regime was the fall of Metternich.

The ageing Chancellor had been told of the revolution in France in a telegram from his friend, the banker Salamon Rothschild, whose tidings arrived at 5 p.m. on 29 February, just before the rest of the Viennese population learned the news from one of the few permitted foreign newspapers, the *Augsburger Zeitung*. The diplomat William Stiles observed that 'the people, collected in groups throughout the streets, in the cafés, and reading-rooms, expressed themselves with a freedom and an earnestness altogether foreign to the habits of the calm and phlegmatic Germans'.[39] The Chancellor himself remained sanguine: during the first ten days of March the chief of police, Count Josef von Sedlnitzky, never one to play down the risk of subversion, assured Metternich that there was nothing to fear in Vienna. Events in perennially troublesome Hungary, however, would dash this prediction. On 1 March word of the Parisian revolution reached the Hungarian Diet, which had been meeting at Pressburg since November. The parliament had been holding agonising debates about serfdom, but now even wider, root-and-branch reform seemed possible. On 3 March the fiery Lajos Kossuth rose in the lower house and gave the speech that would prove to be 'the inaugural address of the revolution'.[40] Habsburg absolutism, he declared, was 'the pestilential air which . . . dulls our nerves and paralyses our spirit'. Hungary should be 'independent, national and free from foreign interference', tied to Austria only through the dynastic link of having the Emperor continue as King of Hungary. Kossuth went further and remarked that a political overhaul which benefited Hungary would not be safe for as long as the rest of the empire remained unreformed, so fundamental change was needed for all the subjects of the Emperor. 'The dynasty', he thundered, 'must choose between its own welfare and the preservation of a rotten system.'[41]

This lion's roar of a speech would have a profound impact, and it reached Vienna via a manuscript version translated into German and sent to the Legal-Political Reading Club. Very soon copies were clandestinely printed and circulating around the imperial capital. Initially, the meeting of the Lower Austrian Estates, due on 13 March, was the focus for liberal hopes and expectations. In excited anticipation a radical 'party of progress', led by Alexander Bach, gathered several thousand signatures on a petition (carried by Bach through the streets on horseback). This demanded parliamentary government and Austrian participation in the reform of the German Confederation.[42] Yet the Staatskonferenz – the inner circle of family and ministers that acted as a regency council on behalf of Emperor Ferdinand – was divided between those who advocated some concessions and those, including Metternich, who urged no weakness. Initially, the latter held sway.

The liberal opposition received an injection of youthful energy from the students of the University of Vienna. Many of these young people were the archetypical, impoverished, garret-dwelling scholars who relished banned political literature, joined secret societies and were taught by stuffily conservative professors. Now, intoxicated by the political excitement, the students circulated a petition that demanded freedom of the press, speech, religion and teaching, improvements in education, popular representation in government and the participation of all German-speaking parts of the empire in the new Germany. They were galvanised further at early morning mass on Sunday 12 March by the passionate oratory of the liberal and popular theologian Anton Füster, who declared that Lent was a time of hope and that truth would triumph if the students acted courageously.[43] They occupied the Aula, the university's great hall, where, with tumultuous enthusiasm, the petition was soon covered with signatures. 'The stormy air permeated everybody,' recalled one student. 'The students gave orders to the professors for the first time. A topsy-turvy world was beginning. Pedants tore their hair and thought that the world was going to pieces or that the whole youth must receive a "2" in the next examination . . . Had the light or reflection of dawn finally broken through the dismal sky?'[44] The students agreed that the following day they would march *en masse* to the opening of the Landhaus to present their petition to the Lower Austrian Estates. That night, to garner muscle for their cause, posses of students stole through the city gates into the poorer suburbs, where they roused the Viennese workers. To counter this the authorities put the gates under close guard, while it began to dawn on the court that some concessions might be necessary. These would prove to be too little, too late.

Early in the morning of 13 March some four thousand students streamed out of their lectures, deaf to the warnings of their professors, and marched on the Landhaus, which happened to be just around the corner from Metternich's Chancellery on the Ballhausplatz. A large, respectable gathering of mostly middle-class professionals – well-to-do lawyers, doctors, entrepreneurs and the odd bohemian writer and flamboyant artist – joined the throng in expectation as the Estates opened. Watching from the windows of the Chancellery, Metternich's third wife Melanie scornfully remarked, 'All they need is a stand selling sausages to make themselves happy.'[45] Yet, as the protest was running out of steam, a pale, bearded young doctor named Adolf Fischhof silenced the directionless hubbub when, standing on the shoulders of four companions, his booming voice declared, 'It is a great, significant day on which we find ourselves assembled here,' and he urged the people to present the Estates with the demands of the liberal opposition.[46] Now speaker after speaker – 'pale with terror at their own daring,'[47] noted Stiles perceptively – climbed on to railings and balconies to harangue their audience, which cheered the orators and turned its anger towards Metternich.

No sooner had the president of the Estates, Count Albert Montecuccoli, tried to pacify the crowd by allowing a delegation to present the petition in the Landhaus than a Tyrolean journalist named Franz Putz arrived on the square. Holding aloft copies of Kossuth's speech, he clambered on to the central fountain. Everyone knew of the great Magyar's oration, but few had read or heard the precise content. Putz's powerful lungs now bellowed the explosive words – including 'liberty', 'rights' and 'constitution' – across the sea of enthralled faces. When a window of the Landhaus squeaked open and copies of the Estates' own petition fluttered down to the crowd, it was disappointingly meek by comparison and 'each paragraph . . . was saluted with ringing laughter'.[48] The constitutional cat was now out of the bag: students angrily tore up the Estates' supplication. Cries of 'No half measures!', 'No delay!' and 'Constitution! Constitution!' rippled through the crowd. The mood was beginning to turn ugly, but a minor blunder now tipped it into violence. With commendable but, in the circumstances, tactless efficiency, the porter performed his noonday duty of locking the side door of the Landhaus. For the people unaware of the routine, this was a sign that their twelve delegates were being arrested. A crowd of students and, as Baron Carl von Hügel put it curiously, 'intruders of the better class'[49] battered down the doors and invaded the meeting chamber. To calm tempers, Montecuccoli agreed to adopt the liberal programme and to proceed to the royal residence in the Hofburg to present the demands to the Emperor.

By now the imperial court had finally ordered its soldiers out of barracks under the command of Archduke Albert. His orders were to compel the crowds to disperse, but to avoid any loss of life if at all possible. The flood of humanity now stretched from the Landhaus, poured into the Ballhausplatz and spilled towards the Hofburg, where it confronted the gaping mouths of cannon and a line of fixed bayonets. The crowd showered the stone-faced soldiers with a barrage of insults and missiles. Vienna drew breath for a violent confrontation: retailers boarded up their shops and clusters of workers, who had marched in from the suburbs armed with tools, iron bars, pitchforks and wooden shafts, tramped through the streets. The authorities stemmed the proletarian flow by closing all the gates to traffic, but the workers tried to smash their way through. In the fighting the lamp-posts that lit the glacis – the open ground in front of the city walls – were torn up for use as battering rams. The hissing, escaping gas ignited and cast an eerie halo around the city. The troops won the first battle for the city gates and wheeled cannon on to the bastions. Barred from joining the political revolution taking place within, the frustrated workers now gave full vent to their economic grievances. They broke into factories and smashed up machinery, plundered bakeries and groceries and attacked landlords' property.[50]

Outside the Hofburg, Archduke Albert was struck by a rock when he called on the citizens to return to their homes. The troops at last moved forward, but they were bombarded with stones and even furniture hurled from upper windows. His nerves at breaking point, a regimental commander barked out the fateful order: 'Move forward with fixed bayonets and fire!' The first shots of the Austrian revolution killed four people and a woman was trampled to death as the crowd stampeded away from the smoking muskets.[51] Street-fighting now exploded across the city and only the timely intervention of his soldiers prevented Archduke Albert from being hauled off his horse.[52] The suburban workers finally crashed through one of the city gates – the Schottentor – and tried unsuc-cessfully to storm the arsenal. The troops could control the main thoroughfares and squares, but the crowds of students, bourgeois and workers defended the side-streets with barricades. At 5 p.m. an uneasy truce was negotiated, in which the bourgeois militia, the Bürgergarde, promised to maintain order provided that the troops were withdrawn from Vienna, that the students were allowed to form their own militia (an 'Academic Legion') and that Metternich was dismissed by 9 p.m. The government conceded all but Metternich's head. The Viennese willingly submitted to the Bürgergarde and the Academic Legion, for they had already been alarmed by the destructive power of the factory workers. It was for this reason, as much as enthusiasm for the revolution, that the ranks of the civic guard were suddenly swelled by new, middle-class recruits, who cleared some forty thousand arms from the arsenal.

The minutes ticked away as the Staatskonferenz argued about Metternich's fate. The Chancellor, who had reached the Hofburg from the Ballhausplatz under guard, resplendent in his green coat and silk cravat and bearing his gold-handled cane, was agonisingly pressed into resigning. Metternich slipped out the Hofburg minutes before the deadline expired. He and Melanie left Vienna that night in a discreet fiacre, boarded another carriage outside the city and drove to a train, which spirited them across Europe. They spent almost a fortnight in The Hague, waiting until the apparently rev-olutionary threat from the Chartists had dissipated in London. *The Times* announced their arrival off a steamer from Rotterdam on 21 April.[53]

As daylight broke on 14 March the Viennese celebrated the fall of Metternich, but they suspected – rightly – that the government would yield not another inch and hoped to restore order by impos-ing martial law. Metternich's last act as Chancellor had been to persuade the Staatskonferenz to give the fire-breathing Prince Alfred Windischgrätz full civil and military powers to restore imperial authority in Vienna. The army was still a brooding presence outside the city walls and, except for press freedom and the creation of a new National Guard, there were no further promises of civil liberties or a constitution. The balance was finally tipped when, on 15 March, Windischgrätz declared Vienna under a state of siege in all but name. The embers of revolution were fanned once more – although in the suburbs they had never died down, since working-class attacks on factories and shops had continued almost unchecked. At midday Ferdinand was persuaded to ride through the city to soothe passions, and he was cheered sincerely by the crowds. Yet this parade was merely a panacea, for people still hovered expectantly around the Hofburg that afternoon. It had at last dawned on the Staatskonferenz, including a thunder-faced Windischgrätz, that it was better to grant a constitution and then resist any further demands than risk the possibility of a mass insurrection. At 5 p.m. on 15 March a herald rode up to the palace gate and read the imperial proclamation. All Austria would be asked to send delegates to an assembly that would discuss 'the Constitution which We have decided to grant'.[54] The imperial capital, at last, rejoiced:

> In Vienna, the whole aspect of things seemed changed, as it were, by a magician's wand . . . The secret police had entirely disappeared from the streets; the windows of book-stores were now crowded with forbidden works, which, like condemned criminals, had long been withdrawn from the light of day; boys hawked throughout the city addresses, poems, and engravings, illustrative of the Revolution – the first issues of an unshackled press; while the newly-armed citizens formed into a National Guard, marched shoulder to shoulder with the regular military, and maintained in unison with them, the public tranquillity.[55]

One Viennese wrote excitedly that 'The word "constitution" is giving a new movement to the waves of the time – a movement that will be

felt over the whole globe and which will strike many a pillar of absolutism with thunder and lightning.'[56] Those parts of Central
Europe that so far had merely effervesced at the news from Paris
now boiled over on the word from Vienna.

IV

In the small hours of 14 March Archduke Stephen, the Palatine
(Viceroy) of Hungary, was woken by a messenger from Vienna who
had come thundering down the road on horseback, bearing the
news of Metternich's fall. Stephen had Hungarian sympathies and
he summoned an emergency meeting of the upper house of the
Hungarian Diet in Pressburg. There, everyone agreed that the Diet
would demand a separate Hungarian government, with reform of
the counties, wider representation of the people and (here the
theme of nationalism rose to the surface) the full union of
Transylvania with Hungary. It was also decreed that delegates from
both houses would travel to Vienna and present this petition to the
Emperor in person. That night Kossuth was hailed as a hero by students in a torchlit procession. In return, Kossuth was emboldened
to present the liberal Count Lajos Batthyány as the next Hungarian
prime minister. The following day, underneath a blustery, cloudy
sky, a 150-strong Hungarian deputation – including the firebrand
Kossuth and the moderate Count Istvan Széchenyi – boarded two
steamers on the Danube for Vienna. Their arrival in the imperial
capital at 2 p.m., just hours before the Emperor promised his
Austrian subjects a constitution, was triumphant. Dubbed the
'Argonauts' because they had arrived by boat, the Magyars were
resplendent in plumed fur caps, gold-braided frock-coats, red
trousers, richly ornamented scabbards and knee boots clinking with
spurs.

On the morning of 16 March Kossuth was carried to the
Hofburg on the shoulders of cheering Austrians. At the palace the
Hungarians found that the Emperor – drained, pale, and his head
lolling – had already been persuaded by the Staatskonferenz to con-

cede all that the Magyars asked. Overnight, in fact, Széchenyi and Batthyány had quietly persuaded Archduke Stephen to stand up to the arch-conservatives at court by arguing that it was better to yield than to provoke a rebellion for full Hungarian independence. Now the Hungarians pushed even further, also demanding that Batthyány be called to form a government and that all legislation passed by the Hungarian Diet be automatically ratified. This was going too far for the Emperor's inner circle, which rejected these new demands outright. What now followed would later ensure that Batthyány would end his life facing a firing squad and Stephen would finish his political career in exile. Stephen rushed straight to the Emperor himself – bypassing the Staatskonferenz altogether – and extracted the feeble-minded Ferdinand's personal agreement that Batthyány be made Hungarian Prime Minister. The Imperial Rescript that emerged on 17 March therefore gave Hungary its own government, responsible to the Diet, and appointed Stephen as the Emperor's plenipotentiary, with full powers to implement the reforms. Stephen immediately officially appointed Batthyány as his premier. The new cabinet included a kaleidoscope of views from the gradual reformist Széchenyi to the radical Kossuth. The former bristled at the thought of serving alongside the latter: 'I have just signed my death sentence!' he wrote, adding later that 'I shall be hanged with Kossuth.'[57]

The Staatskonferenz had been so pliable because Habsburg authority appeared to be collapsing in every corner of the empire – in Budapest, Prague, Milan and Venice. Concessions were made out of the grim necessity for survival. While Hungary's political leaders were wringing far-reaching constitutional concessions from Vienna, there was a full-blooded revolution occurring in Budapest. After he had delivered his famous speech of 3 March, Kossuth, anticipating stiff conservative opposition, opened a second front by urging the radicals of the capital – including fired-up students and journalists – to back his parliamentary speech with the weight of a popular petition. The radicals scheduled an enormous French-style banquet for 19 March, the date of a huge trade fair at which the petition could be signed by thousands of people. The task of drafting the document fell to the Society of Ten, drawn from a circle of Hungarian democratic writers who called themselves 'Young Hungary'. Its leader was the poet Sándor Petőfi, but the petition was penned by the young journalist József Irinyi, whose 'Twelve Points' became Hungary's revolutionary programme. They included the standard demands of 1848 – free speech, 'responsible government' (meaning a ministry answerable to parliament), regular parliaments, civil equality and religious freedom, a national guard, equality of taxation and trial by jury. They called for the release of all political prisoners and an end to all 'feudal burdens' for peasants. There was also some radically nationalist content. Besides a separate government in Budapest, all non-Hungarian troops should be evacuated from Hungarian soil. Transylvania, the Magyars argued, should become part of Hungary, regardless of Romanian feelings. The multi-ethnic character of Hungary made the apparently standard demand for a national guard especially acute. The regular Hungarian army was regarded by the radicals as a reactionary force: it was drafted mostly from the non-Magyar peasants of the kingdom, while many of its officers were German-speaking nobles.[58]

As these Twelve Points were being discussed, news of Metternich's departure arrived by steamer in Budapest on 14 March. At a pre-dawn meeting in Petőfi's apartment on 15 March, a small group of radicals decided to act immediately. 'Till tomorrow, then,' Petőfi said as his comrades turned in for a few hours' sleep, 'when the time will come to trample a few double-headed eagles underfoot!'[59] In the morning they walked through the pouring rain to the Society of Ten's watering hole, the Café Pilvax, where a cheering, expectant crowd had assembled. 'Inside the café', wrote one eyewitness, there was 'great turbulence, excited talk and violent outbursts'. The Twelve Points were read out to explosions of cheering and applause. Petőfi then recited a poem, written only two days previously, the 'National Song', the refrain of which brought a roar of approval: 'We swear by the God of Hungarians, we swear, we shall not be slaves any more!'[60] At 3 p.m. Petőfi addressed a ten-thousand-strong crowd in front of the National Museum before leading them to the city chambers. The masses filled the square outside 'like a roaring sea before the storm'.[61] The startled president signed the Twelve Points and a new municipal government – the Committee of Public Safety – was appointed, including radicals like Petőfi, pro-Kossuth nobles and liberals from the old Council. The National Guard was established, but since this was to be a citizens' militia, there was no uniform except for armbands and cockades in the Hungarian colours of red, white and green.[62] The revolutionaries then marched across the river via a pontoon bridge (since Széchenyi's famous chain bridge was still under construction) and then tramped up the hill to Buda Castle, where the Vice-Regal Council met. 'We marched', wrote the radical Alajos Degré, 'with unbound enthusiasm up to the fortress where we saw artillery men standing next to their cannons holding burning fuses, the multitude in front of them shouting "Long live liberty! Long live equality!"'[63] Confronted by a crowd now twenty thousand strong and with no clear direction coming from Vienna, the Palatine's councillors could do little else other than yield. Both sides, in fact, seemed thunderstruck by the situation. The Committee of Public Safety's spokesman presented the Twelve Points, 'stammering in all humility and trembling like a pupil before his teacher', Petőfi later recalled scornfully, adding that 'their Magnificences, the Vice-Regal Council, turned pale and were graciously pleased to tremble also. Within five minutes, they consented to everything.'[64]

With Habsburg rule now in full retreat, the Czechs were also able to assert themselves. Late in the night of 29 February the cream of the city's intelligentsia was holding a masqued ball, during which the first letters arrived from Paris, bearing the news of the republic. To avoid the ubiquitous ears of the police, the word was whispered among the revellers. Quietly, friends clustered together and toasted the revolution.[65] The hopes and expectations grew when word of Kossuth's speech reached Prague. On 8 March the liberal organisation Repeal posted up placards calling a public meeting at the Saint Václav's Baths on 11 March. The venue was perilously close to the working-class quarter of Podskalí, and the time of 6 p.m. on a Saturday gave the district's workers ample opportunity to draw their wages and down some alcohol before attending. The destructive power of the workers had been brutally demonstrated (and then equally brutally repressed) only four years previously, and the social fear among the propertied classes was now reignited. Even the leading liberal lights of Bohemia, the historian František Palacký and journalist Karel Havlíček, stood aloof from the political activities, because they were reluctant to stray from the path of 'legality'. The mayor (or Burgermeister) Josef Müller called out the respectably bourgeois civic guard, but he turned down the request of Prague's wealthiest citizens, who were mostly German-speaking industrialists, to allow all burghers to bear arms. The manufacturers also demanded that the authorities ban the meeting altogether. This the governor of Bohemia, Rudolf Stadion, would not do, for fear of sparking a confrontation; but he put the garrison on alert.

Several thousand people turned out on the appointed day. Eight hundred of the more 'respectable' demonstrators – young intellectuals, officials, burghers, artisans, almost all of them Czech – were allowed into the baths by Repeal's ushers. The excluded workers huddled together in the street, battered by a heavy rain. The almost complete absence of Germans at the meeting suggested that it attracted those who had been aroused by the Czech national movement and felt frozen out of Bohemian political structures.[66] A petition was read out, demanding a constitution, press freedom and trial by jury, and, more radically, the 'organisation of work and wages' for the workers and the abolition of both labour obligations (the *robot*) and manorial courts for the peasants. Nationalism was expressed in the demand for a union of all the lands of the ancient Czech crown: Bohemia, Moravia and Silesia, collectively represented by a single assembly of the Estates, the official equality of Czech with the German language, the reduction of the standing army and a bar on 'foreigners' – the meaning was ambiguous – from holding office. The meeting ended with the election of a committee of twenty to prepare the petition for signature. It was only now that Palacký lent his considerable intellectual weight to the demands.

On 15 March thousands of people signed the petition under clear blue skies. In the festive atmosphere that evening a train from Vienna arrived bearing the news of the imperial promise of a constitution. 'Champagne', one newspaper reported, 'flowed in torrents' and total strangers embraced one another on the streets. The word 'constitution' suddenly became fashionable, as artisans started to produce 'constitutional' hats and parasols, while 'constitutional pastries' rose in bakers' ovens. The newspaper *Bohemia* suggested that it was no longer polite to doff one's hat in greeting, as this seemed counter to the equality promised by a constitution and, in any case, it was inconvenient in inclement weather.[67] As in Vienna, a national guard and academic legion were set up in Bohemia and Moravia to keep order. These organisations recruited from both Germans and Czechs, but the Saint Václav committee also established Svornost, an exclusively Czech militia. Meanwhile, the students formed a political society, the Slavie, or Slavic Linden.

Emperor Ferdinand received a Bohemian delegation that presented the Saint Václav Petition on 22 March, but the Viennese court sensed the reluctance among both Moravians and Bohemian Germans to subscribe to Czech nationalism and got away with giving only vague promises of concessions. The celebrations planned in Prague were cancelled and popular anger at seeing their hopes dashed turned on the Czech delegates themselves, some of whom had their windows smashed.[68] On 28 March there was a stormy meeting, at which members of the Saint Václav Committee struggled to make themselves heard over fierce cries of 'Republic!' and chants against the Bohemian nobility. The committee drafted a more strident petition, demanding the unity of all the Czech lands, represented in a single, modern parliament elected on a wide franchise: the Estates were now jettisoned as archaic. Like the Hungarians, the Czechs now wanted a separate, unified kingdom, retaining only a dynastic link with the Habsburg monarchy. This new list of demands was gathered up and carried by the armed militia to Stadion's offices. The seething, humiliated governor was forced to fix his seal to the petition and, shortly afterwards, he resigned after warning Baron Pillersdorf, the minister of the interior in Austria's new cabinet, that he 'could answer for nothing if all was not granted'.[69]

This time Vienna conceded, though not completely. The imperial reply of 8 April did not promise a single Czech parliament, but separate Bohemian and Moravian estates, elected on a franchise limited to property-owners, salaried employees and taxpayers, thus excluding the urban workers, domestic servants and rural labourers. The Czech language would be taught in all schools and used at every level of administration in the Czech lands, alongside German.[70] These concessions – along with the later abolition of the obligations that weighed on the peasantry – were the high-water mark of the Czech revolutionary achievement in 1848.

V

As absolutism collapsed in the Austrian Empire, the other great pillar of the conservative order in Germany – Prussia – could not resist for long. Adolphe de Circourt, fresh from the street-fighting in Paris, had been appointed French ambassador to Berlin, where he had arrived on 9 March. Watching the capitulation of one German government after another, he commented that Prussia was surrounded by 'a circle of fire'.[71] When the explosion came, the Prussian capital would be the scene of the most grisly of all the revolutionary outbursts of March 1848. Students had excitedly filled cafés to read the European news, but of some fifteen hundred at the university, perhaps only a hundred were seriously engaged in politics. The obvious focal point for popular hopes and expectations, the permanent committee of the United Landtag, which had been meeting since January, was dismissed by the King on 6 March, on the grounds that at a time of crisis he needed unity rather than 'party quarrels': 'Rally around your King, around your best friend, like a bronze wall.'[72] This, and Frederick William's promise that the Landtag would meet every four years, became the principal talking point. On Sundays, Berliners – artisans, workers, students, office workers, journalists – habitually wandered among the cafés, beer-halls and sausage-sellers of the Zelten (literally, the 'tents', which had stood in the park before the permanent buildings were constructed). On 7 March a crowd gathered as journalists and academics stepped on to the bandstand to harangue them with speeches about the King's promise.[73] A petition was drafted and signed by thousands of people on the spot, asking for the immediate recall of the Landtag and press freedom. When the King refused to receive the demands, the petitioners sent them to him in the post. Berliners also took to wearing the black–red–gold of German unity.

The following day the crowds grew bigger on the Zelten and the chief of police warned the King that he did not feel confident in his ability to control the situation. He suggested that the twelve-thousand-strong garrison be used in support. Frederick William, fatefully, agreed.[74] Up to this point the crowds had been good-natured, even carnivalesque, but the appearance of army patrols clattering though the streets created a more menacing atmosphere and, to compound matters, the King reinforced the garrison with fresh troops from other provinces, eventually swelling the military presence to twenty thousand. Berliners always resented being given orders by soldiers, but this surged into anger when one violent incident after another flared up between the citizenry and the troops between 13 and 18 March. The initial engagements, noted General Leopold von Gerlach, the King's adjutant-general, were easily dealt with by the army. However, he later remarked, this was what caused such complacency among the authorities when the insurrection broke out in earnest on 18 March.[75] The sight of troops breaking up public meetings by striking out with the flats of sabres, or clearing city squares at the point of the bayonet, turned the popular mood from one of cheerful excitement to dark anticipation. Circourt noted the change of atmosphere: 'Everywhere there were gatherings, confused cries, whistling and vagabonds taking sinister shape on their nocturnal prowls.'[76] Berliners hooted and threw stones at the soldiers, many of whom were drawn from the rural provinces of eastern Prussia and were unused to city life and suspicious of urban ways.

The pressure intensified when the news of Metternich's dismissal reached the Prussian capital on 16 March. To defuse the situation, Frederick William was persuaded to make concessions, but only after a ferocious debate among his ministers, with diehard conservatives like Gerlach and the Prince of Prussia (the heir to the throne, who in 1871 would become the first emperor of the newly united Germany) roaring that the shooting of rebellious subjects would make an impression. Instead, on 18 March, Frederick William let it be known that a proclamation was imminent. At 2 p.m. a herald in fact read out two proclamations to an expectant crowd gathered outside the royal castle. The first abolished censorship. The second promised to call the Prussian Estates on 2 April and to consider the reform of the German Confederation, including a German law code, flag and the creation of a German navy (this last was an important aspiration for nationalists). Inside the palace, Gerlach fumed, 'I had rather have had a hand chopped off than have signed these edicts',[77] but when Frederick William himself appeared on the balcony, he was cheered by the joyful crowds.

Yet one promise had not been made: to pull the troops out of the city. A well-dressed cohort of some twenty civilians began to shout in chorus, 'Away with the military!' – a chant that was taken up by everyone else. This was a revolutionary stake thrust at the very heart of the Prussian monarchy. The King's foremost role was to lead the Prussian army, which was itself virtually a state within a state. Liberals may have wanted the King to rest his authority instead on the trust and goodwill of all citizens, but this was to ask Frederick William to kick away the central pillar of the Prussian monarchy. The revolutionary challenge stiffened the King's resolve and strengthened the ultra-conservatives, who replaced the dithering General Ernst von Pfuel with the reactionary martinet General von Prittwitz as Governor of Berlin. This conservative pill was sugared by the appointment of a new ministry that included the Rhenish liberal businessman Ludolf Camphausen. Prittwitz then made the fateful decision to clear the square in front of the Schloss. The dragoons rode forward at a slow trot, led by Prittwitz himself, who drew his sabre to make his orders clear over the tumult. The horsemen followed suit, making their advance look like a charge. Some civilians surged forward to seize the bridles of the horses, crying, 'Soldiers back!' When two infantry companies also marched out, two mysterious shots were fired. No one was hurt, but the crack of musketry was enough to scatter the crowd in all directions. There were yells of 'Betrayal!' and 'They're killing people on the Schlossplatz!' The newly appointed prime minister, Count von Arnim-Boitzenburg, tried haplessly to calm the situation by appearing on the square waving a white flag, but he was ignored.[78]

Within hours, hundreds of barricades had been thrown up in the streets and topped with black–red–gold banners. One flag was rather defiantly hoisted above the luxurious d'Heureuse confectioner's shop, in full view of the royal palace. Men, women and children put their backs into the construction of the barricades, 'which was achieved with astonishing virtuosity, as if the population never had any other business', and they used the material that modern urban life offered: 'cabs, omnibuses, a post wagon which had been stopped, wool sacks, beams, overturned well-enclosures'.[79] They were fashioned from the heavy paving stones prised out of the streets, planks of wood torn from buildings, guttering, barrels, overturned carriages and stalls. The square in front of the Rosenthal Gate was turned into a fortress, with barricades blocking every entrance. The ensuing battle was one of civilian against soldier, in which all the fury stoked up on both sides was unleashed. Prittwitz himself later wrote of the soldiers' sense 'of having a definite enemy in front of them and of having reached the end of the hitherto existing trial of their patience'.[80] Artisans clambered into the church towers and pealed the bells, sounding the tocsin of revolt. Middle-class property owners, respectably dressed in top hats and long black coats, journalists and professionals, the 'petty bourgeoisie' of shopkeepers, low-ranking officials, teachers and skilled artisans, about a hundred students and, of course, the workers all mounted the barricades. Summoned by the bell-ringing, the Borsig locomotive workers picked up their iron bars and hammers and determinedly marched some nine hundred strong towards the fighting, still wearing their oily smocks. Women and children brought food and drink to the insurgents.

The battle for Berlin was one of the most ferocious anywhere in Europe in 1848. When the troops attacked the barricades, they used artillery and then marched head-on against the fortifications. Gerlach, who commanded troops during the fighting, said that the cannonballs ricocheted along the street. Everywhere the soldiers were confronted by one barricade after another. 'One could discern three, maybe four barricades, one behind the other, on which construction had taken place continually in our presence,' wrote Gerlach. 'At the artillery fire everybody ran from the first . . . and also from the second barricade, but when the troops advanced towards the following barricade, they were met with violent rifle fire and with many stones from the houses, particularly from those at the corner.' On the other side a witness wrote:

> The thunder of cannons resounded in increasingly quick succession. Individual barricades already began to collapse into the street, and the more and more embittered and enraged advancing soldiers began a frightful hand-to-hand fighting . . . The whole street swam with blood. The houses were overcrowded with dead and wounded. At the corner of the Spandauerstrasse cannons were driven up whose shots were intended to clear the streets completely. The houses themselves were hit again and again and damaged by rifle shots. Throughout the city there began this time a frightful sounding of the alarm bells which was kept up through the whole night by armed artisans who had climbed the church towers.[81]

Even the most experienced of the officers were unaccustomed to the kind of battle being waged in the narrow confines of Berlin's old streets. Faced with the ferocity of the insurgents, the frustrated, furious and often frightened soldiers fired indiscriminately into houses, through doors and windows. Gerlach's men were equipped with tools that allowed them to break into the buildings; but once inside, the attackers were stabbed and shot at point-blank range.[82] Houses burst into flames and burned through the night. In all some nine hundred people were killed in an afternoon and night of fighting – eight hundred of them on the insurgents' side.

By the end of the day the army had control of the main thoroughfares and, unlike in Paris, there was little danger that the troops, with their rural origins and iron discipline, would be converted by the revolutionaries. None the less, Prittwitz was aware that the horrifying and exhausting experience of street-fighting had taken its toll on his men's morale. That night he told the King that, unless the rising was put down within the first few days, there would be nothing else to do other than pull out his troops, besiege the city and bombard it into submission. The King was torn apart by conflicting emotions. The Berliners were rebels, but Frederick William's own sense of Christian kingship found the idea of spilling his subjects' blood utterly abhorrent. When Prittwitz had first asked for the order to advance, the King had cried, 'Yes, all right! Only no shooting!'[83] At the first crash of artillery, he had wept. So it was that Georg von Vincke, a moderate Westphalian aristocrat who had led the liberal opposition in the United Landtag and had ridden hard to reach Berlin, found a willing audience in Frederick William when he appeared at the palace still dressed in his travelling clothes. Vincke argued that the fighting would continue for as long as the people had no confidence in their King. A withdrawal of the troops and entrusting the King's own safety to the citizens would reawaken their natural sense of loyalty. Gerlach, listening to this, joined in the mocking laughter at what he called the politician's 'miserable controversialist dialectic', to which a furious Vincke snapped that they might well laugh now, but the following day they would not.[84]

At midnight, therefore, Frederick William told Prittwitz to cease operations, after which he sat down at his desk and drafted a further proclamation 'To my dear Berliners', which was hastily printed and distributed across the city in the early hours. The King promised that, once his subjects had returned 'to their peaceful ways' and dismantled the barricades, he would pull his troops back to defend only the Schloss, the armoury and several other government buildings: 'Hear the paternal voice of your King, inhabitants of my loyal and beautiful Berlin.'[85] The mauled and bloodied Berliners greeted the rather syrupy language with some scepticism. Yet an uneasy truce did hold across the city that Sunday morning. When Prittwitz went out himself to investigate, the first person he met was not an insurgent, but a servant girl who had been sent out to buy pastries.[86] The revolutionaries also allowed churchgoers to pass freely across the barricades on their way to worship. Encouraged, the King, meeting with Prittwitz and the Prince of Prussia in the palace's red corner room, ordered all forces to pull back to barracks.[87] The Prince hurled his sword on the table in disgust.

With the Schloss all but denuded of troops, the insurgents picked their way across the debris-strewn streets and gathered outside the palace. This time they were in no mood for cheering the King. They were drawing biers upon which the broken bodies of those killed lay covered with flowers. They howled at the windows above: 'Bring him out, or we will throw these dead right in front of his door!'[88] The King emerged on to a balcony with the alarmed Queen clutching his arm. The carriages were drawn closer and, in a symbolic gesture of humility, the King removed his hat in respect. The Queen fainted. At this point the crowd serenaded the royal couple with a Lutheran hymn, 'Jesus, my Refuge', and the procession moved away. Meanwhile, the army was marching out of the city, drums beating. A Bürgerwehr, or civic guard, was hastily organised to ensure order, and the King, self-consciously wearing a German black–red–gold cockade in his hat, met its commanders on 21 March, whereupon he thanked them for restoring peace to his capital. He was saluted with cries of 'Long live the German Emperor!' That day, swept along by the popular tide, he issued a further proclamation, in which he declared: 'I have today taken the old German colours and have put Myself and My people under the venerable banner of the German Reich. Prussia henceforth merges into Germany.'[89] This was deliberately vague, but for now it seemed to satisfy the clamour for Prussian leadership of a united Germany.

On 22 March the dead from the street-fighting were buried. On that emotional day of mourning Frederick William finally announced that he would grant a constitution. Yet, playing the role of revolutionary monarch did not suit a king who had been forced to yield most of the concessions. Three days later he and his family abandoned the city for Potsdam and the royal palace of Sans-Souci, protected by elite guard regiments. Safe in his palace, the King began bitterly to feel the humiliation of the March revolution: 'We crawled on our stomachs.'[90] He was now surrounded by plenty of hardliners, among them the Prince of Prussia and Gerlach, all of whom were itching for a counter-revolution.[91] Among them was Otto von Bismarck, who had travelled to Potsdam from his estate at Schönhausen to offer the services of his deferential, armed peasants to the King. When Prittwitz asked what could be done to restore royal authority, the tough nobleman, who was sitting by a piano, began to play the Prussian infantry charging-march.[92]

VI

Of all the constitutions wrung from Italian rulers in the first months of 1848, the Piedmontese constitution, or *Statuto*, of 4 March would prove to be, historically, the most significant for the future of Italy, since it became the constitution of the united Italy in 1860 and remained the fundamental law of the country until 1946. Power was to be shared between the King and the parliament, which comprised a senate and a chamber of deputies. The monarch retained control of the armed forces and foreign policy, and could call and dissolve parliament, but any financial act, including taxation, had to be approved by both chambers. Moreover, if the King prorogued parliament, it had to be summoned again within four months, so there could be no long-term rule without it. Civil rights were also guaranteed.[93] The *Statuto* resonated across the frontier into Austrian-ruled Lombardy, where Milanese liberals now dared to dream of the possibility of a military invasion by the Piedmontese army, which would chase out the Austrians at the point of '100,000 bayonets'. Lombards took to wearing grey capes, in imitation of the uniforms of Charles Albert's army. To turn the dream into reality, Count Carlo d'Adda, a Lombard émigré taking refuge in Turin, and Count Enrico Martini acted as emissaries of Milan's liberal nobility, pressing the King to strike the decisive blow against Austrian rule.[94]

Milan and Venice, the great cities of Austria's two Italian provinces, had been simmering since the Tobacco Riots in early January. During his last weeks in power, Metternich became ever more preoccupied with Italy and was determined to resist the march of the revolution there. To do so he wanted to ensure that all the Austrian authorities – military and civil – coordinated their efforts not only with one another but with those Italian states yet to succumb to the torrent. For that he needed a trustworthy diplomat, who could keep in constant contact with the different Italian governments, to encourage them to resist revolution, to assure them of Austrian military support and to present the Austrian view through the press. The man he chose for the job was Count Joseph von Hübner, who received his brief in Vienna on 21 February. Remarking that Metternich's confidence in his abilities 'frightens more than it flatters me', Hübner boarded the train from Vienna on 2 March, changed to post-horses and arrived in Milan seventy-two hours later. He did not know that the news of the Paris revolution had encouraged the liberals to organise a peaceful protest aimed at persuading the Austrians to grant Lombardy greater autonomy within the Habsburg monarchy, including press freedom and a civic guard. Martial law had been declared across Lombardy and Venetia on 25 February. Hübner found the city tense and the Austrian authorities in a state of defeatism, if not utter paralysis. At dinner on 5 March Count Ficquelmont, whom Metternich had sent to Milan the previous August to advise the local government, told Hübner, 'I have been asked to do the impossible. All that I have done and all that you will do here are like sword blows on water.'[95] Ficquelmont and his wife left Milan a few days later for Vienna, where he would become the foreign minister of the first post-Metternich government.

Matters only became worse for the Austrians when word of Metternich's fall and the imperial promise of a constitution reached Milan on 17 March. That night the leaders of the liberal opposition

met to discuss their response. They could wait and see what benefits the promised constitution would bring, or they could fully
exploit the regime's weakness and try to expel the Austrians altogether. The latter option carried great risks: the commander of the
Austrian forces in Italy – the wily, redoubtable Marshal Joseph
Radetzky – controlled a thirteen-thousand-strong garrison of imperial troops who were subject to iron-hard discipline but also had
genuine respect and even devotion for their leader. The republican
teacher and intellectual Carlo Cattaneo argued that there could be
no insurrection against such forces: the people had neither the military leadership nor the weapons for such an undertaking. Later he
frankly avowed that he suspected the moderates of seeking to provoke a premature uprising that would be powerful enough to tempt
Charles Albert of Piedmont to intervene against the Austrians,
thereby giving the revolution a monarchical stamp, and making it
too weak to gather a republican momentum of its own. After much
debate the Milanese agreed that the demonstration would be peaceful
and led by Count Gabriel Casati, the podestà (mayor) of Milan. As
the most highly placed Italian in the local municipal administration,
Casati had worked closely with the Austrians, but he had some patriotic sympathies. This was an awkward division of loyalties that led
him to allow one son to serve with the Piedmontese artillery and
another to study at the University of Innsbruck. Cattaneo commented
wryly that 'Casati would have divided himself in two to serve both
courts at the same time; unable to split himself, he wanted to split his
family instead.'[96] Yet, early the next morning, Casati did sterling work
in persuading the vice-governor, Heinrich O'Donnell, not to call out
the garrison, since that would merely inflame the situation. As a precaution, Radetzky primed his men for combat, fortifying the city
gates with artillery and reinforcing the guards on the walls. On the
night of 17 March Hübner was struck by the eerie silence in the streets:
'There were here and there small groups of people, but they were
whispering into each other's ears and they dispersed at our approach.'[97]
The Austrian viceroy, Archduke Rainer, prudently left for the safety of
Verona.

On 18 March the call was raised 'Men to the street, women to the windows!' Some fifteen thousand people marched, while countless others cheered and waved them on with red, white and green handkerchiefs. Casati himself, though dressed soberly in a black suit, wore a tricolour rosette while an Italian flag fluttered above his head. Women tossed tricolour ribbons from the windows. At the Palazzo del Governo a handful of sentries were swept aside by the popular torrent. Hundreds of people surged up the stairs and found O'Donnell in the council chamber. He had already made the last-minute concession of lifting censorship, but now, confronted by a respectable but potentially aggressive crowd, he had little choice but to sign the order for the establishment of a civic guard, to be made up of Milanese of independent means. As surety, the crowd took the unfortunate vice-governor hostage.

With this act, the frustrated Radetzky, who had been watching events furiously from the sidelines, struck back. His troops double-quicked through the streets to protect such buildings as the police headquarters, the law courts and the army engineering depot. Tyrolean marksmen were posted high among the marble needles of Milan's great cathedral, from where they would snipe at all and sundry – be they insurgents or hapless citizens caught in the cross-fire. The Milanese quickly threw up barricades in the narrow streets of the old city. Bells rang from the church towers to summon people to the defences. At first these fortifications were makeshift, comprised of overturned carriages, barrels and hastily chopped-down trees. Soon they were bolstered by paving stones, sofas, beds, pianos and church furniture. Among the first to stand on them were young democratic republicans like the twenty-seven-year-old Enrico Cernuschi, nicknamed 'the little Robespierre', who had studied law before giving it up to work in a sugar refinery.[98] They were joined rapidly by artisans and workers, who formed the backbone of this spontaneous uprising. The republican Carlo Osio sped home from the demonstration and gathered a pistol, a stiletto and an iron bar – making him look more like a street thug than the doctor he was – before running back to help his brother Enrico and others build the barricades. Carlo careered headlong into a police patrol, narrowly escaped their gunshots, then beat a hasty retreat home again, this time to gather the rifle, bayonet and ammunition that he had stowed there. He was a veritable human arsenal.[99]

The more conservative patricians implored the insurgents to stand down and avoid the 'inevitable massacre'.[100] Yet few listened – not the comfortable merchants who opened their warehouses to allow the revolutionaries to search for weapons and matériel, not the chemists who helped to make gunpowder, nor the students, workers, women and children who helped to build the barricades and then took part in the fighting. Crossing the piazza in front of the cathedral, Hübner was caught up in a crowd armed with batons, 'among them sinister faces recalling Paris during a day of rioting'. The sky, echoing to a confusion of noise, 'was the colour of lead, and a fine rain, turning later into a downpour, never stopped falling'.[101]

While the Milanese held the narrow streets of the historic heart, the Habsburg forces – largely Croats and Hungarians – were firmly installed in some of the major buildings and enveloped the city by holding the walls. In the first few days the fate of the insurrection – which had no plan and no overall leadership – was desperately uncertain:

> The parts of the city where the insurrection made most progress were not all in communication with each other . . . beyond there were very broad streets, thinly populated and very difficult to barricade and to defend, down which the enemy's fire could fall . . . It was calculated that all the city that first night had only three to four hundred rifles of all kinds available.[102]

From the Casa Vidiserti – which served as the first, impromptu headquarters of the uprising because that was where Casati, its reluctant figurehead, had taken refuge – a civic guard was hastily organised. Osio – who, like many of the insurgents, appeared at the house to receive instructions – was made a corporal in the new force. He would eventually be put under the command of the young, democratic nobleman Luciano Manara, whose platoon fought for the next four days almost without respite. For now, one of Osio's first duties was to guard the captive vice-governor O'Donnell, who had been transferred to the safer Casa Taverna in the Contrada de' Bigli.[103] It was there that the republicans under Cattaneo tried to seize the political initiative on 19 March, creating a four-man council of war, including Cattaneo himself and Cernuschi. For now, its main purpose was to impose some firm leadership and military direction: Cattaneo had to deploy his great powers of persuasion to dissuade the younger, hotter heads from declaring a Milanese republic then and there. How, he asked, would Lombardy then gain the support of the other Italian states, which were still ranged under monarchist regimes and whose constitutions had barely begun to see the light of day? Instead of enjoying freedom, Italy would be engulfed in civil war. This analysis was perceptive, but the establishment of the Council of War still created a rival – and republican – seat of power against Casati's liberal, monarchist municipality.[104]

By dawn on 20 March it was clear that the imperial troops were struggling under the horrifying effects of street combat. Hübner, trapped by the fighting since 18 March in a tenement near the cathedral, occasionally peered over the balcony and witnessed the carnage. He saw two Hungarian horsemen cut down by rifle fire and Croatian infantry marching stoically into a hail of musketry. Among the insurgents, 'no one could be seen: they were men armed with rifles, women armed with stones and jugs of boiling water, hidden behind closed blinds, seeing without being seen themselves. It was this invisible enemy, which seemed to murder rather than fight, which worked on a soldier's imagination, which upset his nerves and demoralised him.' The noise was deafening: 'the infernal racket of shouting voices, the cries of *evviva* mixed with the irritating chiming of the bells and the *maestoso* of the great guns of Father Radetzky'. By the third day the shutters of the apartment had been shattered by bullets, while gunsmoke wafted in from the street. Insurgents were on the roof and upper floors, firing down on the Austrians below, while the troops returned fire upwards and stray bullets occasionally tore the air around the terrified residents, all women. For their safety, Hübner gathered them all in an internal room, where they huddled behind a shelter of mattresses (the young Austrian was especially impressed by the sang-froid of a Swiss woman 'into whose profession I did not pry', who seemed to be used to the rough side of street life).[105]

On the Milanese side, witnesses were no less struck by the horrors of the battle. When the insurrection spread to the eastern districts, Cattaneo had himself rowed across a canal to investigate the situation in the district by the Porta Ticinese, which presented a desolate sight. Apart from the barricades, 'the broad streets were empty and deserted, all the houses were shut up; the explosions from a battery . . . and the ceaseless rumbling of fusillades kept falling into this silence of the dead; a thick smoke cast a dismal pall over everything'. The Austrians had smashed holes through the adjoining walls of apartments, gardens and stables, so that they could advance without exposing themselves to gunfire in the streets. Women and children caught between the two forces huddled together fearfully in the houses, blocking the doors and windows to protect themselves from ricocheting bullets.[106]

Both sides would later claim that atrocities had been committed. The Milanese were said to have found an Austrian soldier carrying a severed woman's hand, cut off for the rings on her fingers. Whole families were said to have been trapped and then burned alive by the Habsburg forces. The Austrians, meanwhile, claimed that one of their soldiers had been crucified to a sentry box, while others, captured by the Milanese, had been blinded. The very nature of the fighting means that claims of brutality (if not the grisly details) cannot be dismissed lightly, while the stories themselves – and the readiness with which they were believed – show how inflamed both sides were.[107]

Ever more insurgents picked up weapons from fallen Austrian soldiers, or by swamping and disarming isolated detachments by sheer force of numbers. The want of munitions grew less acute as, one by one, the Austrian barracks fell.[108] Radetzky was forced to abandon his home and take up residence in the castle. He concluded that he could no longer reduce the barricades, since the army would destroy one only to be confronted with another. He withdrew his troops to the walls, from where he would besiege the city. With the fighting now moving towards the periphery, Hübner and the company of women now picked their way through the streets to the safety of the home of a Tyrolean banker. Yet the only way out of Milan for Hübner, as an Austrian diplomat, was to negotiate with the municipality. In doing so, however, he effectively became a prisoner of the insurgents. He was arrested on 21 March and marched through streets fluttering with tricolours and echoing to cries of 'Long live Italy! Long live Pius IX!'[109] Yet the divisions between Milanese monarchists and republicans were already widening. When, that same day, Radetzky sent one of his officers to open negotiations for a truce, Casati hesitated, perhaps seeing in the proposal a chance to buy time for Charles Albert to make his long-awaited commitment to send in his army against the Austrians. Cattaneo, for precisely this reason, refused to entertain any talk of a pause in the fighting.[110] The power struggle between liberal monarchists and republicans – a fault-line that would run right through the Italian revolutions of 1848–9 – was already taking shape.

The Milanese, meanwhile, deployed all their ingenuity to break the siege:

> To reconnoitre enemy movements on the bastions and outside the city, astronomers and opticians climbed into the observatories and the bell-towers; they sent down bulletins every hour. Instead of wasting time descending staircases . . . they attached their reports to a small ring which they lowered at the end of an iron wire. Cernuschi organised straight away a message system served by the pupils of the orphans' schools . . . Recognisable by their uniform, they would slip rapidly through the crowds which gathered around the barricades, performing this service with as much intelligence as precision. Soon afterwards, someone thought of releasing small balloons carrying proclamations which would be spread across the countryside. The Croats, encamped on the bastions . . . fired their rifles at the balloons in vain . . . An attempt was made to make wooden cannon, held together by iron rings, which were capable of firing a small number of shots.[111]

Milan's novel air-mail service carried appeals to the Lombards to support the insurrection. Some of them drifted into Piedmont while others were blown as far as Switzerland. The call had already been heeded, for the independent-minded peasantry of upper Lombardy had risen and marched into provincial towns like Como and Monza, forcing the small Austrian garrisons there to beat a hasty retreat. Meanwhile, Casati and the moderates received a fillip with the surprise appearance of Count Martini, who had crept into the besieged city. He and d'Adda had spoken with King Charles Albert on 19 March and asked for military aid against Austria. The Piedmontese monarch replied that his army would march provided that Milan's municipality formally asked him for assistance, since he would need to justify his invasion to the other European powers. Charles Albert also faced a domestic challenge from Piedmontese radicals, who threatened a revolution of their own, unless the King served the cause of Italian unity and sent his army against the Austrians. His primary motive, however, was to satisfy his own dynastic ambition of annexing Lombardy and Venetia, thereby forging a northern Italian kingdom under the Savoyard dynasty. It was therefore also necessary to nip the republican movement in the bud since it would fight for a broader form of Italian unity on a democratic basis. So it was that Martini made his way back to Milan, bearing the King's message. He stole into the city disguised as a worker delivering salt in the night of 21–2 March.[112]

After trying in vain to persuade the Milanese leadership to rebut Charles Albert's offer, Cattaneo yielded to the municipality and agreed to a compromise, whereby the call for assistance was issued in the name of Milan to '*all* the peoples and *all* the princes of Italy and specifically those of Piedmont, its warlike neighbour'.[113] Armed with this appeal, Martini made his way back to Turin. In the early hours of 22 March Casati at last formed a provisional government which unambiguously assumed leadership of the insurrection. Cattaneo immediately recognised it. He also subscribed to the provisional government's proclamation declaring that political arguments were to be postponed until the fighting was over: 'After the victory [*A causa vinta*], it will be for the nation to discuss and pronounce on its own destinies.' 'A causa vinta' was Cattaneo's great concession: it was, he said, 'the only order which could delay the explosion of political passions'.[114]

Yet time was on the side of the monarchists, for it would not be long before the Piedmontese army would arrive and tip the political balance decisively in their favour. Not for the last time, an Italian republican had surrendered a chance of taking power. Why Cattaneo should have done so is an intriguing question. He himself later said that it was because the republicans were ready to shelve their sectional interests and their dogma for the sake of the wider struggle for independence.[115] It is almost certainly true that Cattaneo wanted to avoid civil war at all costs, and it seems he realised that the republican movement was in a minority against the monarchists. However, he may well have underestimated the amount of support and prestige that the radicals now enjoyed: the insurrection had popularised the republican movement, while there was even some evidence of republican sentiment in the small towns and villages of the surrounding countryside. Yet it was not easy to forge these inchoate sympathies into the hard steel of a single revolutionary movement. In the rural areas the handful of radical leaders could not prevail against the dominant, conservative influence of landlords and priests who supported the monarchists. In Milan itself, 'a causa vinta' allowed the provisional government to establish itself and reap the political fruits of the victory over the Austrians.[116]

That victory was assured when the Milanese made a determined effort against the Porta Tosa in a day-long battle on 22 March. It was at the Tosa that the Austrian-held bastions came closest to the heart of the city, and Milanese army officers advised strongly that it was here that the enemy should be driven back. The idea was not only to secure the city centre but to open the gate to the Lombard insurgents who had been spotted in their hundreds in the distance pouring down from the hills. The fight began – after reconnaissance from the rooftops by Carlo Osio – at 7 a.m., when the Italians started blasting cannon and fired from windows, rooftops and behind garden walls at the Austrian positions on the gate, in the customs post and at the nearby Casa Tragella. The imperial troops replied with Congreve rockets and one house burst into flames. The final assault took place under the ingenious protection of moving barricades. There was a bitter and murderous exchange of fire – Osio later said that he alone fired 150 cartridges.[117] Manara and another aristocrat with democratic principles, Enrico Dandolo, were the first to make the final dash to the customs house, with the former waving a tricolour as the rest of the attackers surged on behind. They were cheered on by women watching from nearby balconies. The gate was beaten down and the triumphant Milanese, crossing the moat on the other side of the bastions, at last embraced the Lombard peasants and small-town artisans, led by local professionals and priests, who poured into the city. Radetzky's siege had been broken.

He now had to contend with the imminent Piedmontese invasion and peasant insurrections in the mountains to the north. His exhausted troops, though still in good order, could not attempt to retake Milan and at the same time contend with the rural uprising and the crushing weight of Charles Albert's army. To avoid being pinned against the walls of the city by this combination of hostile forces, he ordered his troops to withdraw, but only once his artillery had rained down a vengeful barrage on the city. Hübner, sheltering with his captors in a cellar, spent an uncomfortable night listening to the muffled roar of the guns, followed by 'a fitful noise like someone running up or down a spiral staircase in clogs' – the sound of tumbling masonry. The bombardment continued until one o'clock in the morning and the worst of the damage was done closest to the castle, where most of the Austrian guns were emplaced. The cathedral, churches and public buildings were not scarred, because Radetzky had told the gunners to spare them: he had little doubt that the Austrians would be occupying them again soon.[118] Nevertheless, the city centre was now strewn with debris, walls riddled with bullets, tiles scattered across the streets and charred houses still smoking. On 23 March Radetzky's troops pulled northwards to the so-called Quadrilateral of fortresses at Verona, Peschiera, Mantua and Legnano that barred the way into Austria itself. That same day Charles Albert declared war on Austria and sent his army across the River Ticino, his personal Rubicon, which separated him from his dynastic ambitions. Milan's 'Five Glorious Days' were over. Among those who celebrated was the composer Giuseppe Verdi, who was in Paris when he heard the news. He dashed off to the city, but did not arrive until early April. Once there, he wrote to a friend: 'Yes, yes, a few more years, perhaps only a few more months, and Italy will be free, united and a republic. What else should she be?'[119] He was not alone, for another great Italian had also arrived in Milan: the republican revolutionary Giuseppe Mazzini. The uprising was over, but the tough politics of the Italian revolution had only just begun.

Meanwhile, the Venetians had rallied around the *causes célèbres* of Daniele Manin and Nicolò Tommaseo after their arrest in January. Little could hold back the gathering tide once the news of Metternich's fall reached Venice, brought by the Lloyd Line steamer from Trieste on 17 March. A crowd swept across Saint Mark's Square, calling for the release of the two political prisoners. They stormed the governor's residence on the piazza, where they confronted its trembling occupants, Aloys Palffy and his shaken wife, on the main staircase. A posse of Manin's friends rushed to the nearby prison to release the two men. The jailers prudently calculated that surrender was safer than resistance and yielded the two captives. Manin was convinced that times were now sufficiently propitious to free Venice of Austrian rule. The stakes were raised on 18 March, when Croatian and Hungarian troops tried to haul down the Italian tricolours that had been fluttering over Saint Mark's Square since the day before. The crowd jeered at the soldiers, whereupon an enraged officer gave the order to fire. After the smoke cleared from two volleys, nine Venetians lay dead or wounded. With the mood of the crowd boiling over into blind fury, Manin approached Palffy with the proposal to create a civic guard that would keep order and defend property. A moderate republican, Manin genuinely wanted to avoid social revolution, but of course he also hoped that the new civic guard could be used against the Austrians when the time came. Palffy, trusting that Radetzky would soon be able to send troops to his aid, tried to stall Manin with a promise that he would consult the viceroy, Archduke Rainer, who was now in Verona. Seeing through this ruse, Manin defiantly organised a two-thousand-strong militia regardless. That night the streets of the city were being patrolled by men wearing white sashes.[120]

The Austrian authorities could have been forgiven for believing that they had weathered the storm by 19 March, when word arrived from Trieste of the promised imperial constitution. To cries of 'Long live Italy! Long live the Emperor!', Palffy read out the Emperor's proclamation to the ecstatic crowd. That night he and his wife were cheered by the audience at a concert at La Fenice. Yet all was not well. No one could quite believe that a Habsburg emperor would grant a constitution freely. The garrison was still strong and there were rumours that the army would try to bombard the city into submission from the arsenal. This fear mingled with hope: stories about the insurrection in Milan were now circulating and keeping Venetian enthusiasm aflame. Manin decided that now was the time to act, especially when he received word that the Croatian troops in the arsenal were soon to be reinforced. He held a meeting with other Venetian revolutionaries that night and they explored their subversive contacts in the imperial navy, including an officer named Antonio Paolucci, who would try to mobilise the Italian sailors in support of an assault on the arsenal. Key, however, were the fifteen hundred workers – the *arsenalotti* – who bore plenty of grievances against their Austrian employers, particularly the military commander, Captain Marinovich, who had refused pay increases and banned the workers from supplementing their income by their traditional practices of repairing gondolas and helping themselves to 'spare' naval supplies. The date for the insurrection was set for 22 March, when the civic guard would converge on the arsenal gates at midday and, with the help of the workers, force it to surrender.

That day the *arsenalotti* made the first move spontaneously, when they angrily confronted Marinovich with their own demands. The captain was left virtually defenceless when the naval commander in Venice, Admiral Martini, ordered the Croatian guard to stand down for fear of provoking the crowd. Paolucci tried to help Marinovich escape the *arsenalotti* in a covered gondola, but the luckless captain was spotted and chased on to the roof. He was dragged downstairs, beaten to a pulp and left to die in a boatshed. Manin was horrified by this brutality and sent forward an advance company of militia to prevent any more violence. When he himself arrived with the rest of the civic guard, he summoned the workers by ringing the arsenal's great bell and took over formal control of the works from a chastened Martini. An Austrian attempt to retake the arsenal failed when their mostly Italian troops refused to follow orders. Instead, they trained their rifles on their Hungarian officer, and he was saved from certain death only by the intercession of one of Manin's associates. With this mutiny, the rest of the Italians in the garrison succumbed. They joined the revolution, tearing the Austrian eagle from their caps and replacing it with the Italian tricolour: the black and gold Habsburg emblems were later seen floating in their hundreds in the city's canals.

A detachment of civic guards then easily took the cannon which were lined up in front of Saint Mark's Cathedral. The guns were wheeled about to face the governor's palace, where Palffy desperately summoned Venice's municipal government, mostly noblemen anxious to prevent the city falling into grubbily bourgeois and republican hands like Manin's. Yet, as the councillors and the governor debated the best course of action, a mounting clamour intruded from outside. Manin's followers had unfurled a huge tricolour topped with a red Jacobin cap, while Manin stood on a table outside the Café Florian and hailed: 'Long live the republic! Long live Saint Mark!' The only republican among the city councillors, the outspoken lawyer Gian Francisco Avesani, demanded that all non-Italian troops be withdrawn from Venice and that all forts be surrendered, along with the ordnance, weaponry and pay chests. The infuriated Palffy resigned as governor, handing over control to the Austrian garrison commander, Count Ferdinand Zichy. The latter, fortunately, did not share Radetzky's unbending nature: he recoiled from the idea of bombarding Venice into rubble, since he loved the city, and at 6.30 p.m. surrendered control to the municipality, leadership of which fell to Avesani. It was clear, however, that a government without Manin, the hero of the day, would have little legitimacy for the Venetians, so in the early hours of 23 March Avesani resigned and Daniele Manin was proclaimed president of the new provisional government of the Venetian Republic. The imperial army abandoned the city. The official report to Vienna opened with the words, 'Venice has really fallen'.

VII

Not all European countries experienced violent revolution in 1848. There was some impact from the shockwaves of the revolution in France across the Pyrenees: there were some stirrings in Catalonia, a blundered uprising in Madrid and a military mutiny in Seville, but (except in Madrid) the extent to which the republican movement was involved is unclear. And in Catalonia, the main threat to the government came from a 'Carlist', or ultra-royalist, revolt. The government of the day, led by General Ramón María Narváez, reacted to the European revolutions in March by pushing through the Cortes the suspension of civil rights, extra funds to meet any insurrection and the temporary dissolution of parliament (which in the event lasted for nine months).[121] Narváez sometimes appeared to be the epitome of Spanish militarist reaction: on his deathbed, when asked to forgive his enemies, he replied, 'I don't have to, because I've shot them all.' Yet, while certainly not above authoritarian methods, he had some liberal credentials: he tried to steer a middle, constitutional way between Catholic royalism and republican revolution, but it was a constitutionalism that, he was determined, would give power to the propertied elites. Backed, for now, by Queen Isabella and seemingly the guarantor of political and social stability, Narváez managed to navigate Spain through the revolutionary storms of 1848. Neighbouring Portugal since 1846 had been (with British, French and Spanish backing) under General Saldhanha, who, like Narváez, defended a conservative constitutional order against both reactionaries and radicals with a rod of iron.[122]

Britain – while facing down a small insurrection in Ireland – relied primarily on the robust nature of its constitutional structures and the broad acquiescence of civil society to weather the radical challenge of the Chartists, who demanded the six points of their 'People's Charter' of 1838: universal male suffrage, annual elections, equal electoral constituencies, the payment of Members of Parliament, the abolition of property qualifications for MPs and the secret ballot. They drew strength from the political radicalism of British artisans and skilled workers, and the movement included various, sometimes conflicting tendencies. A radical wing, personified by the likes of Bronterre O'Brien and Feargus O'Connor, considered strikes and violence – or the threat of violence – as necessary tactics, while a more moderate face, exemplified by the London cabinet-maker William Lovett (one of the authors of the People's Charter), sought to exert pressure through education, self-improvement and rational persuasion. On the left the movement certainly had a pink, socialistic tinge, and it was associated with the nationalist opposition in Ireland. In the economic distress of the 1840s O'Connor, with his strident rhetoric and the thirty-thousand-strong circulation of his newspaper, the *Northern Star*, gained ground.[123]

Although much of his rhetoric of revolution was just that, the news of the February revolution in Paris caused some anxiety in official circles that the Chartist agitation might turn into something more aggressive than propaganda and patient petitioning for parliamentary reform. The alarm grew shriller when, on 6 March, there was rioting in Glasgow and London, initially in response to a government proposal (which was in fact withdrawn) to increase income tax. In Glasgow the violence was more serious: most of the demonstrators were unemployed workers, and they looted bakeries and tore up railings as weapons before the authorities called out the troops and read the Riot Act. In the ensuing shooting, one demonstrator was killed and two mortally wounded. 'The alarm', reported *The Times*, 'flew over the city like wildfire, and coupled with the late events in Paris, gave rise to a general dread of some political disturbance.'[124] The London disturbances took place on Trafalgar Square, where a meeting, although banned by the police, attracted up to ten thousand people, who listened to Chartist orators speaking about the glories of the French Republic and finishing with cheers for the People's Charter and the new regime in France. There were some scuffles with the police and a small group of about two hundred protesters smashed shop windows and street lamps. A lady's carriage was stopped by the crowd, who berated her for being an 'aristocrat', but since her husband had only recently been ennobled, she took this as praise. All in all, the day showed that the 'London mob, though neither heroic, nor poetical, nor patriotic, nor enlightened, nor clean, is a comparatively good-natured body,' reported *The Times* with patronising aloofness.[125]

Yet the danger did not appear to be over, since three days later the Chartists called for two hundred thousand people to rally on 10 April on south London's Kennington Common, from where the demonstrators would march on Parliament in support of a petition for parliamentary reform. If, the socialist Chartist Ernest Jones declared, this was imitated in other cities, then Parliament would give way under the intense pressure and the People's Charter would become law. With this announcement, genuine public alarm about the threat of revolution now began to stir, the more so when, on 4 April, a Chartist convention met in London. For a population that had been consuming press stories about the Parisian revolution and its socialist clubs, this appeared to be a malign attempt at a British imitation. Chartist rhetoric merely intensified the anxieties: on the eve of the massive demonstration, Jones told the cheering convention, 'So help me God I will march in the first rank tomorrow, and if they attempt any violence, they shall not be 24 hours longer in the House of Commons.'[126] The government's alarm was sufficiently great for it to persuade Queen Victoria and her family to travel to Osborne House on the Isle of Wight. The authorities – with some involvement from the aged Duke of Wellington – prepared for trouble by putting professional police on the Thames bridges, while tactfully keeping regular troops out of sight, but close to strategic points. The Bank of England was fortified with sandbags and mounted with cannon. Some 85,000 citizens were sworn in as special constables, prompting Charles Dickens to turn down the opportunity on the grounds that 'special constable-ing' was becoming an epidemic.[127] Indeed, the overwhelming support for the government of the middle classes, from the wealthiest to the 'petty bourgeoisie' of shopkeepers, clerks and the like, was an essential difference between the situation in London in April and that which had prevailed in Paris in February.[128]

Yet, so too was the restraint showed by the Chartists themselves. Despite the strong words, the aim of the protest was primarily to exert pressure, not to purge Parliament and topple the government. Now, faced with an impressive show of coercive might, even the fiery Feargus O'Connor, learning from the police that the mass meeting but not the march on Parliament would be permitted, showed some relief when he mounted a carriage and told the dense ranks of Chartists 'not to injure their cause by intemperance or folly'. Jones, more reluctantly, agreed, since he felt the movement was not yet ready for an 'attempt at collision with the authorities'.[129] In the end the Chartists' demands were presented by a small delegation led by O'Connor. The petition was ridiculed in Parliament – MPs were especially amused by the false signatures it contained (one joker had apparently signed as 'Queen Victoria') – but the suspicion must be that the laughter was borne as much of relief as it was of derision. A relieved Palmerston, the British foreign secretary at the time, declared 10 April 'the Waterloo of peace and order'.[130] Although it was not immediately obvious, the wind had been taken out of the Chartists' sails, and while a radical wing chose to turn to violence in the summer, most of its leaders, including Jones, were arrested.

The defeat of the Chartists almost guaranteed the failure of the opposition in Ireland in 1848, since the Whig government in London had no need to make concessions to the Irish nationalists in order to muster all their strength against a revolutionary threat in Britain. Almost immediately, the lord lieutenant in Dublin Castle turned the screws: in March three leaders of the nationalist 'Young Ireland' movement – William Smith O'Brien, Thomas Francis Meagher and John Mitchel – were arrested and charged with sedition. The government wanted to silence troublemakers before they could whip up a revolutionary storm among a population devastated by the famine (O'Brien had already accused the British government of deliberately allowing hundreds of thousands of Irish to die).[131] Yet the pre-emptive strike was counter-productive as the three men became nationalist heroes. The case against the first two collapsed when the jury could not reach a verdict, and when Mitchel was sentenced to fourteen years' transportation the previously fractious nationalist movement was pushed into unity, with the moderates of the Repeal Association (so called because it wanted to repeal the 1800 union of Ireland with Britain) under John O'Connell joining with the more militant Young Ireland to form the Irish League. Young Ireland's seventy-odd 'confederate clubs', with a total membership of some twenty thousand, mostly in the cities (half of them were in Dublin), were allowed to arm and were regarded as an Irish 'national guard'. In the event, however, weapons were in short supply and the confederates did not have the time to train properly. Nevertheless, all the bluster about revolution provoked another round of government repression: in July it banned possession of arms in Dublin, suspended habeas corpus and arrested a number of confederates. Facing suppression, it was hard for the moderates to hold the middle ground, but the League's executive voted – albeit by a very narrow margin – to wait for more propitious times before pressing for an insurrection. It authorised the confederate clubs to use force in defending themselves, but not to rise up. Only Smith O'Brien and a few other Young Irelanders, including Meagher, soldiered on. At the end of July they tried to rouse the countryside around Kilkenny in revolt, but they gathered only a few hundred recruits. Smith O'Brien and his closest colleagues ended up taking a stand in a farmhouse and its cabbage patch. There was some heavy shooting, with the flashes from the police musketry lighting up the dark. Meagher, who would later serve with distinction on the Union side in the American Civil War, claimed that the Irish revolutionaries took as much fire that day as he did at Gettysburg.[132] The insurgents scattered, but Smith O'Brien was later caught at a railway station and was eventually transported to Tasmania.[133]

The established order in the British Isles therefore emerged from the trauma of 1848 unaltered. Some other European governments – such as those of the Netherlands and Belgium – made timely concessions before anything like a groundswell of opposition could pose a serious challenge. Russia, meanwhile, took the opposite tack and brutally repressed the stirrings of revolutionary opposition, and the Swedish government also used force to rebuff demands for reform.

In the Netherlands King William II, who governed under parliamentary restraints that were far from robust under the 1815 constitution, had declared – prior to the outbreak of the European revolutions – that he was willing to listen to the Estates-General debate proposals for mild constitutional reform. When the time came for the debate on 9 March, however, the revolutionary torrent was now cascading across the continent. Still, ignoring the advice of a minority of his cabinet, William set his face firmly against any reform beyond the original bill. The widespread disappointment was articulated by the liberal leader Johan Thorbecke, who called the bill 'a small, poor spoonful out of our kettle'.[134] Yet, four days later, influenced by (unreliable) reports that the people of Amsterdam were becoming restive, the King – without consulting his cabinet – yielded, summoning the leader of the lower house of parliament to discuss a more radical reform programme. His conservative ministers resigned *en masse*, prompting popular celebrations that, in The Hague on 14–16 March, developed into peaceful demonstrations of support for Thorbecke's demands for an independent commission to decide on the scope of the reforms. The King, after much agonising (and with his will shaken by the sudden death of his son), appointed the commission, which in turn appointed a new cabinet and drafted far-reaching reforms, including freedom of the press, assembly, association and religion. (This last point was essential for the large Catholic minority who had hitherto felt like second-class citizens.) Ministers would be responsible to parliament, which would be elected by direct election, albeit on a limited suffrage, and at legally defined intervals. When these proposals, having been accepted by the King, were finally brought before parliament on 19 June, the conservatives rejected many of them. The Dutch were therefore in the rather peculiar position (for 1848) of having a government that was trying to implement a political reform programme being frustrated by an elected assembly. In the end a compromise was hammered out and the various amended proposals were all accepted after fresh elections to a new, reformed parliament were held in September. This meant that, when the reaction took hold elsewhere in Europe, the Netherlands had a liberal government, under Thorbecke, between 1849 and 1853. According to the American ambassador, this gave 'a consoling Spectacle to the friends of freedom throughout Europe'.[135] The events of 1848 also strengthened the belief that, because the Netherlands was a small, weaker European state with no great international mission (although it was still a colonial power), it could *afford* to give greater liberties to its subjects since it had no need for a strong, coercive government. In this sense, 1848 enabled the Dutch to comfort themselves over the obvious decline of the Netherlands (since the later eighteenth century) as a world power by suggesting that this very fact made Dutch liberties at home possible.[136]

In neighbouring Belgium there was no revolution partly because the constitution was of recent vintage (1831), arising as it did from the struggle for independence from the Netherlands: prior to 1848 it was widely admired as a model for liberals in other countries. Armed with a parliamentary order that would have satisfied the opposition elsewhere in Europe, the Belgian constitutional monarchy was therefore barely shaken by the republican movement that flashed briefly in the pan in February and March. There was widespread distress in this most industrialised of European countries, and there was certainly socialist agitation and a rash of riots in March, but the government, under the astute liberal Charles Rogier, had already acted promptly, on the 2nd of that month, by broadening the suffrage, which placated the potential middle-class leadership of the opposition. The economic suffering was then addressed by investment in public works, by giving poor relief to the indigent and by reforming the system of workhouses and municipal pawnshops. These timely measures helped to soothe popular distress and took the sting out of the radical opposition. By the time the government faced a small invasion by expatriate republicans sallying across the frontier from France at the end of March, the threat could be met and repressed easily. The government felt strong enough not to carry out the seventeen death sentences that were passed on the insurgents, and it triumphed in the elections of June. There was, moreover, as yet no vigorous Flemish nationalist movement that might otherwise have threatened Belgium with ethnic strife.[137] The King of Denmark, Frederick VII, implemented the constitutional reforms of his father Christian VIII, who had yielded to liberal pressure at the very end of his life, creating the Joint Estates of the Realm, which held legislative and fiscal powers. When the new king signed the edict abolishing royal absolutism, there was a 'silence so profound that the stroke of the pen could be plainly heard'. It was 29 January 1848. The timing could not have been more fortuitous.[138]

While concessions were made in the Low Countries and Denmark, the situation in Russia and Sweden was very different. In Sweden a banquet was held in Stockholm on 18 March at which banners demanded reform and a republic. The authorities were sufficiently anxious to call out the army, and thirty people were killed, leaving the capital restless for several days before calm was restored. King Oscar I, who had enjoyed a liberal reputation before 1848, now set himself against political reform and there would be no extension of the franchise in Sweden for more than a decade. In Norway, which had been in a political union with Sweden since 1815, an assembly of delegates representing local branches of a Chartist-style movement for universal male suffrage and social reform, led by the socialist Marcus Thrane, met in Oslo (then called Christiania). It was broken up and 117 people were imprisoned, including Thrane, who served four years before he left for the United States.[139]

Uncompromising as the authorities were in Sweden and Norway, though, the initial repression was even harsher in Russia. On hearing word of the February revolution in Paris, Tsar Nicholas I is alleged to have burst into a palace ballroom, proclaiming, 'Saddle your horses gentlemen! A Republic has been declared in France.'[140]

In fact, the Tsar refused to act impetuously – at least, not in foreign policy. He partially mobilised his forces along the western frontiers of the empire, declaring that he was ready to meet his enemies 'wherever they may appear', but this was a defensive posture, for he also declared that Russia would not intervene in Europe 'unless anarchy crossed her frontiers'.[141] Nicholas's pronouncements suggest that he would be circumspect in foreign policy, but it is equally apparent that he was anxious about the spread of the 'political illness' into his empire, which, the Prussian ambassador wrote, he believed was 'very far from being immune from infection'.[142] The partial Russian mobilisation was not, therefore, a precursor to a counter-revolutionary assault on Europe, but was intended to meet the warlike noises coming from Germany, where overzealous liberals were calling for a revolutionary war against Russia to liberate Poland and cement German unity. It was also aimed at persuading the oppressed Poles that an insurrection of the kind attempted in 1831 was not worth repeating. Although many Europeans (perhaps understandably) feared Russia's designs, Nicholas had no intention of provoking a major European war. He was well aware that Britain was becoming concerned about the expansion of Russian influence, particularly in the Middle East and Asia, and he saw Britain, as the only other great power unaffected by revolution, as a potential diplomatic partner in restoring stability to the continent. He also feared that the revolutionary virus would contaminate Russia: consequently, his instincts were not to strike outwards, but to isolate his empire from the rest of Europe and to turn inwards, repressing all domestic dissent.

In late March he banned the publication of news relating to the European revolutions, ordered all Russian subjects abroad to return home (this proved a counter-productive measure, since on their return home these eighty-thousand-odd excited or frightened people simply babbled the stories of the revolutions that they had just witnessed), banned all Russians from leaving the empire and forbade entry to all foreigners (except for merchants and those with the Tsar's express permission). Having tried to seal Russia off with a cordon sanitaire, Nicholas also tried to choke all expressions of internal dissent, however mild. On 2 April (in the then Russian calendar, which ran twelve days behind the Gregorian version used elsewhere in Europe) he created a committee that would supervise the state's censors, who were now deemed to be too lax. Some of the first to feel the sting of the tsarist lash, therefore, were not revolutionaries at all, but loyal servants of the regime. Among the reasons for the establishment of the 'Committee of 2 April' was that the minister of education, Sergei Uvarov, was felt to be too 'liberal' – yet he was the author of the regime's ideology of 'official nationality', whereby a loyal subject was defined as Orthodox, obedient to the Tsar's autocracy, and fervently Russian. Uvarov may well have been among the least benighted of Nicholas's ministers, but he was scarcely a wild-eyed radical.[143] Intellectuals had always needed to be circumspect in the way they expressed their ideas, but the likes of Pushkin, Gogol, Lermontov and others had always been indulged somewhat. Now, though, the atmosphere was positively stifling. Perhaps most damaging of all in the long run was that Nicholas, who appears to have been earnest in trying to find ways of tackling the problems of serfdom and had passed a series of edicts at least to improve the lives of peasants, now retreated from all reform.

The repressive screws turned even tighter in 1849, when the authorities struck ruthlessly at a circle of Saint Petersburg intellectuals who had been meeting under the leadership of Mikhail Petrashevskii. During the 1840s this group, which included the budding writer Fedor Dostoevskii, had met to discuss the state of Russian society, new ideas and the future, including socialist solutions to the problems of poverty, serfdom and oppression. They had even managed to get some of their ideas in print in 1845 by publishing a *Dictionary of Foreign Words*, which gave the authors scope to discuss the concepts as well as to define their meaning. This was, however, no revolutionary organisation. There were some hotheads, led by Nikolai Speshnev, who on news of the February revolution in Paris wanted to press immediately for a *coup d'état* and the assassination of the Tsar. Most of the Petrashevtsy (as the group became known) were enthusiastic about the revolution, but recalled the fate of the Decembrists, the liberal army officers who failed to topple the Tsar in a military coup in 1825. This more cautious majority, including Petrashevskii himself, took a Fabian approach, wanting to prepare the ground by a long campaign of propaganda among the peasantry, winning hearts and converting minds, so that when, in the distant future, the revolution finally came, it could be sure of mass support. In the acrimonious split, Speshnev and the extremists started preparing for an immediate peasant revolution.

Yet the essential moderation of the majority availed the Petrashevtsy nothing. They had been under close surveillance since February 1848, and only the slow collection of evidence delayed the almost inevitable government crackdown. In 1849 an undercover agent of the Third Section, the Tsar's secret police, revealed Speshnev's plans to his bosses and in the night of 23 April the authorities swooped, arresting some 252 people, all of whom were interrogated. Fifty-one were exiled and twenty-one sentenced to death.[144] 'A handful of nonentities, the majority of them young and immoral, has tried to ride rough-shod over the sacred rights of religion, law and property,' read the damning indictment.[145] The death penalties were commuted, but only at the very moment when the sentences were about to be carried out, on 16 November. A traumatised Dostoevskii was one of the victims of this mock-execution. His sentence was reduced to four years' exile in Siberia. Among the collateral damage in the crushing of the Petrashevtsy was Uvarov, who was forced to resign as minister of education after Nicholas, a week after the arrests, severely curtailed student admissions to the universities, which he regarded (with some reason) as seedbeds of dissent.

There was, therefore, no revolution in Russia, but in the long run the tsarist regime arguably paid a high price: it was a 'Pyrrhic victory'.[146] Prior to 1848 the regime and the intelligentsia (writers, poets, historians and the like, mostly of noble background, who substituted for civil society in Russia) had lived in an often stuffy atmosphere, but there was at least some give and take in the relationship. After the thoroughgoing repression, the 'parting of ways'[147] between the state and the intellectuals became virtually an unbridgeable chasm. The failure to press home the reform of serfdom (Nicholas had already made it clear that he did not feel able to abolish it outright) ensured that Russia would lag behind the rest of Europe, where the institution was finally abolished (in those places where it still existed) in 1848. Moreover, by keeping the non-Russian peoples of his empire under his heel, Nicholas simply stoked up the resentment of the Poles, the Ukrainians and other subject nationalities. The Tsar simply left these potentially poisonous issues to his successors. The shortcomings of the tsarist state and of Russian society were exposed in the disastrous Crimean War of 1854–6, and it was left to Tsar Alexander II to pick up the pieces. He made admirable strides, abolishing serfdom in 1861 and introducing other reforms, but Nicholas's hardline position against dissent had ensured a hardening of positions on both sides, between the state and the hard kernel of opposition. The uncompromising nature of the repression convinced the radical intelligentsia, once and for all, that there could be no constructive accommodation with the regime and that meaningful progress would be attainable only by violent means.[148] The harshness of Nicholas's reaction to 1848 ensured that, when the critics of the regime resurfaced from the 1860s onwards, this time they would give genuinely revolutionary expression to their frustration.

Although these countries on Europe's periphery did not experience the great upheavals that swept across the continent's geographical centre, they do show that they did not remain entirely untouched or even emerge unchanged by the shockwaves of the revolutions. Even with these exceptions, too, what happened in the few weeks between late January and the end of March was breathtaking in its rapidity and geographical scope. Underlying the broad range of the revolutions was the economic crisis of the later 1840s: although the European economy was strikingly diverse from one region to the next, and although the social structure and political institutions of each country varied, the intense economic pressure placed on almost every section of society across the continent ensured that there was a widespread sense of distress and frustration with the inability of the existing governments to do much to meet the crisis. Yet this does not explain why the responses should have been spontaneously *revolutionary* in so many places, in such a short space of time, nor why the revolutions should have achieved such startling success.

The first reason is that the insurrections of 1848 were preceded by a widespread – indeed, near universal – demand for political reform across Europe, even in those countries like Britain, Sweden and Norway, Spain and the Netherlands that managed to navigate this tumultuous year without serious revolutionary disturbances. The political ferment of 1846–7, which included the Galician uprising, the Sonderbund War in Switzerland, the liberal resurgence in Germany, mounting tensions in Italy and the banquet campaign in France, was symptomatic of a growing and widespread frustration within civil society with the limitations of the conservative order. These outbursts of violence and protests had already seemed like portents of something more serious.

That a truly dramatic upheaval of tectonic proportions appeared to be stirring came with the eruption in Paris. The French capital sent shockwaves across Europe because France's now well-established revolutionary tradition made it the single most important source of inspiration or fear (depending upon one's point of view). The great French revolution of 1789 had been studied carefully by reactionaries, reformers and revolutionaries alike for lessons and warnings. In the initial revolutionary sweep of Europe in the first three months of 1848, the historic French example led governments to make gloomy prognoses as to their prospects of facing down the rising tide of opposition. Moreover, the memory of revolutionary France bursting its banks and flooding into neighbouring countries, as it did in the 1790s, encouraged some governments to make concessions at home the better to meet the anticipated challenge from the French.

So it was that the February revolution in Paris – rather than the opening shots heard in Palermo and Naples in January – set the European heather alight. The demands, ideals and even some of the institutions immediately established by the European revolutionaries of 1848 drew in some measure from the models of 1789: the Committee of Public Safety and the National Guard established in the Budapest revolution of March are cases in point. Moderate liberals were also conditioned by memories of the 1789 revolution, admiring the freedoms achieved then but anxious not to repeat the events of 1792–4, which showed that terror and social conflict were potentially the consequences of revolution – and perhaps even of democracy.[149]

Yet in 1848 the Parisian events were not the only impulse. It is significant that, in Germany, the February revolution in France sparked revolutionary movements in the smaller 'middle states', but it did not immediately provoke political change in Berlin, the capital of one of the two hegemonic powers in the confederation. Instead, it was the news that Metternich had fallen in the other great German metropolis, Vienna, which intensified the political pressures in the Prussian capital before exploding into the insurrection of 18 March. The March revolution in Vienna – not the February revolution in Paris – also brought about the unravelling of the conservative order in the Habsburg Empire. It is true that the citizens of Budapest, Prague, Milan and Venice stirred in excitement with the news from France, but it took the ousting of Metternich and the imperial promise of a constitution to spur the liberals to make the decisive revolutionary push.

Moreover, while events in Paris and Vienna were undoubtedly triggers, opposition had been simmering everywhere, albeit with various degrees of intensity, before the revolutions of February and March 1848. Social and economic distress, combined with the gathering momentum of constitutional demands in almost every European state from the mid-1840s – and the weakness and lack of confidence evident in government responses in 1848 itself – gave the revolutions their explosive power and ensured their initial victory. The speed with which the wave of revolutions swept across Europe was due to the wonders of modern technology. In 1789 it took weeks for news – carried, at its fastest, on horseback or under sail – for the fall of the Bastille to be relayed across Central and Eastern Europe. In 1848, thanks to steamships and a nascent telegraph system, reports were being heard within days or even minutes.

The liberal opposition was also momentarily able to seize the advantage over the conservative order because of the temporary weakness of the old regime. Its shortcomings – particularly its reluctance to countenance anything other than the most sedate of reforms and the most limited of social intervention – were exposed harshly by the economic despair. Moreover, the sharp decline in tax revenue that was a consequence of high unemployment, the agrarian disaster and the manufacturing slump made governments seriously doubt their ability to deploy the armed might at their disposal for very long. Yet governments appeared to have suffered from a crisis of confidence that went beyond a mere question of finance and force. Rather, the wider atmosphere and expectations of the later 1840s seem to have made ministers and even some military commanders doubt their own ability to weather the crisis. The failure of the old regime was therefore one of leadership as well as of structural problems such as the economic crisis and the schism that had opened up between government and civil society. Confronted with determined protests backed by the actual or implicit threat of insurrection, the authorities lost their nerve and either gave way without a fight or offered only muddled, contradictory responses to the challenge of the opposition. Referring to Frederick William's dithering while the street-fighting raged in Berlin, General Leopold von Gerlach commented 'we were at that time all so inexperienced in this kind of warfare that we did not consider how every postponement only made matters worse'.[150] Watching the Prussian army pull out of Berlin after the March revolution, the French ambassador, Adolphe de Circourt, remarked that the troops were 'gloomy, irritated, but obedient . . . never before had good troops been so undeservedly abandoned and even disavowed by their leaders'.[151] Even the most determined and disciplined of troops were often left to go into battle unsure about the overall purpose or strategy for which they were fighting. This was certainly the case in Paris, where Louis-Philippe (for quite admirable reasons) commanded that no blood should be shed and that negotiations must take place prior to any assault on the barricades. Such orders merely left his commanders uncertain as to their next step once talks had failed: were they ultimately to clear the streets with force or to wait in a stand-off until the government decided what to do next? The Orléanist Charles de Rémusat, who was with Louis-Philippe when he abdicated on 24 February, noted that the King's confidence had evaporated in a matter of hours: 'it is our attitude', he reflected later, 'the powerlessness of our will, that humiliates me when I think it over'.[152] In Milan the Count von Hübner had no doubt about Radetzky's inspirational abilities. Rather he blamed the paucity of the logistical and moral support that the latter received from Vienna for his failure to hold on to the city. Metternich, Hübner wrote prior to the Five Glorious Days,

> speaks of intervention, but I do not see how military preparations are being made. I believe, on the contrary, that Marshal Radetzky has been refused the help which he has said is necessary for poorly conceived reasons of economy . . . The prince is isolated, paralysed – in a word, powerless. He is only granted half-measures, timid attempts which can only finish with miscalculations if not catastrophe.[153]

It was not, however, only the weakness of the old order that ensured the success of the uprisings. The revolutionaries themselves also showed a unity of purpose, across social and political divisions, which enabled them to prevail. In Milan Cattaneo, who normally saw the middle class as the mainspring of the national movement (unfairly, in fact, since much of the political and cultural leadership of the liberal opposition prior to 1848 came from the nobility), emphasised the social unity of the Five Glorious Days. He described the moment when incredulous peasants burst into Milan to meet 'such elegant women who had built barricades and loaded weapons with their own hands'.[154] As a republican, it was in Cattaneo's interests to stress the social unity of the Milanese revolution, with the cause of liberty transcending divisions of wealth, poverty and gender. However, his view is corroborated by that from the other side of the barricades. Hübner, who was marched as a prisoner through the streets of Milan, noted armed peasants guarding barricades, young women helping to build fortifications, a large number of priests wearing 'broad-rimmed hats decorated with tricolour cockades and carrying swords or sabres in their hands', noblemen and bourgeois 'who seemed a little awkward with their rifles, which they often shifted from one shoulder to the other, a little astonished at the part which they had been made to play'.[155] The Church played an important role in Italy, in particular. As a figurehead, Pius IX managed to transcend social and political divisions and offer a striking unifying focus to the Italian insurrections, but the local clergy played an important, galvanising role as well. As violence erupted in Milan on 18 March, the archbishop 'excited an indescribable enthusiasm' when he appeared wearing the Italian tricolour and, Carlo Osio claimed, those who accompanied the clergyman were among the first to give the orders to raise the barricades.[156] In Hungary nobles provided almost all the leadership of the revolution, backed by the urban population of Budapest and by the threat of a peasant insurrection.

The peasantry gave the revolutions – temporarily, as it turned out – mass support and ensured that the old order could not depend on the countryside: in France, western Germany, Lombardy, Venetia and the south of Italy, rural unrest lent the revolution a particularly wide social basis and contributed to the evaporation of confidence among the conservatives. In the urban insurrections, the workers and artisans provided the strong backbone to the risings. A sympathetic, though anonymous, account of the March revolution in Berlin claims of the nine-hundred-strong Borsig workers that 'it was above all due to their heroic courage and endurance behind the barricades on the night of 18 March that a battle was fought which allowed the cause of the people to appear with an importance which could no longer be denied'.[157] Women engaged in the initial, peaceful demonstrations everywhere; and, when the fighting erupted, they helped to build and repair barricades, loaded weapons, kept the insurgents fed, tended the wounded or gave encouragement by cheering on the revolutionaries waving flags and shouting slogans, often at the very scene of the battle.

The defection to the revolution of the usually quiescent property-owners – middle class or otherwise – was often decisive. On 24 February Tocqueville came across a battalion of National Guards from his own, well-heeled neighbourhood who were abandoning the July Monarchy: 'the fault lies with the government, so the danger is theirs; we do not want to get ourselves killed for people who have managed affairs so badly'.[158] The July Monarchy fell because its bedrock – property-owners, entrepreneurs and small business-owners whose conservatism was tinged with a mild liberalism – had, at a moment of acute crisis, deserted it. These same people would then spend the next two years trying to reassert stability and order, which they saw as their safeguard, against the more radical elements that had been unleashed in February 1848. Yet, no matter how half-hearted the defection of the bulk of the middle class may have been, in many places it proved to be essential to the success of the revolutions because they provided the rank and file of the various citizens' militias, which either pre-existed (as in Paris, Prague and Vienna) or were created (as in Budapest, Venice and Berlin). Since these citizens' militias recruited primarily from among property-owners and burghers who had stakes in law and order, their lack of confidence in the old regime severely weakened its ability to keep control of the streets except by the terrible and (as it turned out) counter-productive use of regular troops. Liberal nobles, clerics, bourgeois, artisans, workers, students, peasants, women, men and even children all played, in different ways from one insurrection to the next, parts in supporting the revolutions.

This social unity, however, could not last. The revolutions of 1848 were to some extent built on what Georges Duveau has called a 'lyrical illusion'.[159] This 'illusion' rested, first, on the idea that the people had indeed triumphed over the old regime and even defeated its armed forces. There was some truth in this, but in most European states affected by the revolutions the structures of the old order were battered and severely damaged but not entirely levelled – except in France, the only country where the revolution destroyed the monarchy. Everywhere else, the monarchy remained – and with it ministers and advisers who were determined to resist further change or to undo the revolution altogether. They also kept control, vitally, of the armed forces, a factor that would prove to be decisive before the year was out. Second, the 'lyrical illusion' was also founded on the idea that the revolutions marked a new beginning, one in which the unity of all classes and people could nurture the delicate growth of a new freedom and a new, liberal order. That this hope was problematic, to say the least, became obvious almost immediately, for the nascent liberal regimes were beset, to varying degrees and in different ways, by two fundamental problems that would ultimately tear them apart. The first was the 'national question' – the problem of political unity and the place of ethnic minorities within the new liberal order. The second was the 'social question' – how to deal with the desperate poverty that afflicted so much of the population, both as part of the wider structural changes in the economy and in the acute distress of the 1840s. These two questions provide the themes for the next two chapters.

3

THE SPRINGTIME OF PEOPLES

'A new era begins,' mused Fanny Lewald in her diary on 28 February. 'What will it bring the French? New battles? Murder and the guillotine? A short epoch of peace and then new tyranny? I cannot believe that . . . War between civilized peoples is the last vestige of brute animal behaviour and must vanish from the earth. I believe in mankind, in the future, in the survival of the Republic.'[1] German liberals would dub 1848 the *Völkerfrühling* – the 'Springtime of Peoples' – a name pregnant with the liberating hopes of the early weeks of the revolutions, when national aspirations suddenly seemed possible. On 5 March the Heidelberg Assembly proclaimed that Germany must not intervene in the affairs of other states and that 'Germany must not be caused to diminish or rob from other nations the freedom and independence which they themselves ask as their right.'[2]

Yet there was a dark side to the liberal nationalism of 1848. The revolutions provided European liberals with the unprecedented opportunity to realise ideals of national independence or unity, but their fulfilment often conflicted with those of neighbouring peoples, or there were national minorities within the presumptive boundaries of the emerging liberal states. Most patriots of 1848, in

The architect of the conservative order: Prince Klemens Wenzel von Metternich shortly before his death in 1859. (akg-images)

The Legislative Stomach. The Revolution of 1830 had altered the French constitutional Charter of 1814 minimally. Here, Honoré Daumier's satirical comment on parliamentary life in 1834 reflects republican disappointment. (akg-images)

King Frederick William IV of
Prussia, by Franz Krueger, c. 1845.
(akg-images)

The distress of the Silesian workers, 1844: a factory owner turns down the goods of the
weavers. Painting by Carl Wilhelm Hübner, 1844. (akg-images)

THE COLLAPSE OF THE OLD ORDER

The final hours of the July Monarchy: the fighting around the burning Château d'Eau, Paris, 24 February 1848, by Eugène Hagnauer. (Bridgeman Art Library)

Some of the bloodiest fighting took place in Berlin: here the formidable barricade on the Alexanderplatz holds out against the Prussian troops. (akg-images)

The climax of Milan's Five Days: the storming of the Porta Tosa on 22 March. This painting by Carlo Canella illustrates the social unity among the insurgents: a priest waves an Italian tricolour, a bourgeois in top hat joins the fight alongside artisans and women lend their support. (akg-images)

Daniele Manin, shortly to become the inspirational leader of the Venetian Republic, is freed from prison and carried shoulder-high on 17 March, by Napoleone Nani, 1874–6. (akg-images)

France Proclaiming Liberty, 1848. The spirit of Lamartine's 'Manifesto to Europe' in the hopeful early days of the 1848 Revolution: France declares freedom for all peoples. (Bridgeman Art Library)

Guiseppe Mazzini: the prophet of democratic revolution, loved and feared in equal measure. (Bridgeman Art Library)

The thundering tribune of the Hungarian Revolution: Lajos Kossuth as legislator in 1848, by August Prinzhofer. (akg-images)

Revolution in Transylvania: *The Rally of the Romanian Peasants at Blaj on 15 May 1848.*
(Bridgeman Art Library)

The focus of liberal German aspirations: the opening of the German Parliament in Saint Paul's Church, Frankfurt, on 18 May, with Philipp Veit's image of *Germania* reminding deputies why they were there. Heinrich von Gagern is presiding. (akg-images)

THE REVOLUTION AS EMANCIPATION

Two views of women's role in the revolution:

Heroic: *An Episode of Milan's Five Days in the Piazza Sant'Alessandro*, by Carlo Stragliati, Museo del Risorgimento, Milan. Milanese women risk their lives to support the insurrection. (www.immaginidistoria.it)

Satirical: *The Socialist Women* – an ironic view by Honoré Daumier on the *démoc-soc* refusal to support Jeanne Déroin in the elections of May 1849. The caption reads: 'The delegates of the central socialist club have unanimously rejected the candidature of Jeanne Déroin!' 'Oh! The aristocrats! . . .' (Bridgeman Art Library)

Proclamation of the Abolition of Slavery in the French Colonies, 23rd April 1848, by François Auguste Biard, 1849. (Bridgeman Art Library)

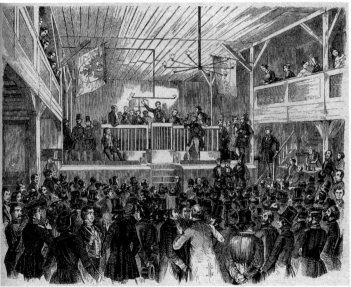

A Berlin political club. Women are clearly not allowed to participate: they must watch from the gallery above. (akg-images)

The explosion of the press after the abolition of censorship: people (and a dog) from all walks of life and all parts of the Habsburg Empire, including the Magyar twirling his whiskers and a Tyrolean complete with rifle, flock to enjoy the fruits of the free press in Vienna. (akg-images)

claiming national rights and freedoms for their own people, were in the process willing to trample on the liberties of others. All too soon the hard iron of national self-interest invariably won out over the more fragrant universal principles of 1848. Consequently, in many places where the 'national question' arose, Europeans would experience the brutalities of ethnic conflict, setting the revolutionaries against each other and providing the conservatives with the opening into which they could pour the hot lead of counter-revolution.

Initially, it was to France that European eyes anxiously looked. While European liberals were inspired by the February revolution, they were also uncomfortably aware that the First French Republic had been aggressively expansionist. The intensity of European anxieties was such that Piedmont initially deployed its forces not against Austria, but along the French frontier. The Belgian and Dutch governments put aside their mutual dislike to discuss measures for common defence against France. Prussian troops in the Rhineland were put on high alert, and other German states, great and small, followed suit.[3] The frontier state of Baden was tormented by panic – the 'French alarm' – in which peasants took the distant beating of German military drums to be the sound of a marauding French army.[4]

French radicals certainly expected the provisional government to pursue an energetic foreign policy, to erase the humiliation of the defeat of 1815. For the republican left, this meant reconnecting with the revolutionary heritage of the 1790s, sending patriotic armies bursting forth, liberating Italy and Poland and spreading the gospel of democracy.[5] The new socialist prefect of police, Marc Caussidière, wrote that the February revolution was like 'a sacred promise of emancipation for all the peoples of Europe', which explained why the Hôtel de Ville was being inundated with addresses from radicals from 'all parts of the globe'.[6] These foreign political refugees kept French revolutionary proselytism on the boil. In better times, cities like Paris and Lyon were hives of economic activity, attracting foreign workers (there were some 184,000 in the capital in 1848),[7] many of whom now languished in unemployment. Their poverty made them fertile ground for the revolutionary seeds sown by their more politically minded compatriots. The largest of these expatriate groups were the Germans, of whom there were 55,000; the Poles, although numbering just 4,000, were probably the most energetic. In Paris the German expatriate poet Georg Herwegh organised a paramilitary force of some eight hundred German exiles and workers to spearhead a republican revolution in Germany. 'In three magnificent days', he told his French hosts, 'you have broken with the past and raised the banner for all the people of the earth.'[8] Over the course of the spring, making patriotic appeals for an aggressive foreign policy was a way for French radicals to recapture the political initiative that they had lost to the moderates on the creation of the provisional government. On 26 March, up to seven hundred Polish democrats led a march of Parisian radical club members – some twenty thousand strong – on the Hôtel de Ville, ignoring Lamartine's urgent pleas the night before to cancel the demonstration. In the event, the protest, which demanded arms and weapons from the French government, finished peacefully after the foreign minister assured the Poles of France's sympathies, but offered nothing beyond financial aid to help them return home.[9]

Lamartine was in an invidious situation, since it was his task to reassure France's neighbours of the new Republic's pacific intentions. The tricky balancing act that he had to perform was illustrated on 25 February, when he persuaded radical demonstrators to abandon their demand that the red flag be adopted as the banner of the Second Republic, but in order to do so he had to appeal to their nationalist impulses: 'The red flag . . . has been dragged in blood around the Champ de Mars[10] . . . The tricolour flag has gone around the world carrying freedom in its folds.'[11] Yet the British ambassador, Lord Constantine Normanby, saw Lamartine's symbolic victory in a positive light and felt able to report to London that most French people appeared to support the new government and 'trust to the efforts to moderate the popular feeling and re-establish order and confidence'.[12] Lamartine's colleagues also helped the next day when, seeking to break all associations with the Terror of the First Republic, they abolished the death penalty for political offences. More importantly, Lamartine's 'Manifesto to Europe' (a declaration issued on 4 March) deftly balanced his sincere desire to ensure peace with the urgent domestic political need to absorb the radical pressure. The soothing words claimed that monarchies and republics could live together. While he denied the justice of the peace treaties of 1815, he declared that France accepted them as 'facts to be modified by general agreement'. Nevertheless, there was some iron beneath the velvet glove. In an attempt to satisfy nationalist pressure, Lamartine declared that, if attacked, France would be a formidable enemy: 'her martial genius, her impatience of action, and her force . . . would render her invincible at home, dreaded, perhaps, beyond her frontiers'. France would also not hesitate to protect her neighbours – specifically Switzerland and Italy – in their own attempts to democratise or to unite, if they were attacked by conservative powers. The Republic, however, hoped to lead by example, not by force:

> It will make no secret propagation or incendiarism among its neighbours. It knows that no liberty is durable, save that which is born upon its own grounds. But it will exercise, by the light of its ideas, and by the spectacle of the order and peace which it hopes to display to the world, the sole and honest proselytism – the proselytism of esteem and sympathy.[13]

Yet the firebrands were not listening. Instead, they actively supported foreign revolutionaries in their efforts to topple their own governments – and the provisional government was still wary of taking rigorous measures to prevent them from exporting the republican revolution. A massive demonstration on 17 March, in which some hundred thousand members of the left-wing Parisian clubs participated, was an impressive show of force that put the ministers on the defensive. Consequently, the government reacted belatedly to the efforts of Lyon radicals who helped the attempt of expatriates from Savoy, then under Piedmontese rule, to prepare the duchy for its annexation by France. A fifteen-hundred-strong legion crossed into Savoy, taking Chambéry on 3 April, but the local peasantry did not take kindly to the ragged, poorly armed invaders. The next day they swept from the mountains and expelled the legion, killing five men and capturing eight hundred.[14] Even more serious was an armed clash on the Belgian frontier, when some two thousand unemployed Belgian workers in Paris, organised into legions by republican exiles, travelled northwards to topple the monarchy in Brussels. Cautiously, the French authorities offered no more support than providing rail transport for the unarmed Belgians as far as the border. The first train, though, was accidentally allowed to roll over the frontier, delivering its consignment of would-be revolutionaries into the waiting arms of the Belgian authorities. A second, twelve-hundred-strong Belgian legion, however, was allowed to acquire weapons in Lille and, in the night of 28 March, it stole into Belgium. There it marched straight towards the gun-muzzles of the primed Belgian forces. In an hour-long skirmish at the aptly named village of Risquons-tout, the legion was torn apart by musket fire and grapeshot.[15]

Lamartine had to work hard to defuse these diplomatic bombshells. The exasperated foreign minister smoothed over one fiasco by (rather redundantly) offering French military assistance to Charles Albert in expelling the legion from Savoy.[16] The assault on Belgium was potentially more damaging, since Britain was a guarantor of Belgian neutrality and took any French intrusion there as a serious threat to its own vital interests. Lamartine calmed tempers by frankly avowing that the provisional government was not yet secure enough to use force against radical troublemakers within France, but he accepted that other governments were perfectly entitled to receive them 'with gunshot'.[17]

Adroitly managing these profound embarrassments, Lamartine made diplomatic headway. While only the American ambassador to Paris, Richard Rush, gave immediate and full recognition to the Second Republic, the Manifesto to Europe did soothe the inevitable fears about French intentions. Lamartine privately explained the finer points to various European ambassadors, and, one by one, each European state – even Russia – declared its intention not to intervene against the new republic.

I

Initially, the potential threat from France – and the grim possibility of being directly in the path of any Russian army intent on crushing revolution in Europe – had concentrated German minds on building up national strength through unity. The Mannheim Petition of 27 February neatly encapsulated the German sense of being trapped between the French hammer of revolution and the Russian anvil of reaction: 'In a few days French armies might well be standing on our borders, while Russia assembles its own armies to the north . . . Germany can no longer stand by patiently and allow itself to be kicked.'[18] Yet the drive for German unity was powered not only by fear: in the immediate aftermath of the March days it was also energised by hope and expectation. The German republican Carl Schurz would later recall the 'People's Springtime' for its 'enthusiastic spirit of self-sacrifice for a great cause which for a while pervaded almost every class of society with rare unanimity . . . I knew hosts of men who were ready at any moment to abandon and risk all for the liberty of the people and the greatness of the Fatherland.'[19] The first problem was precisely what form that 'liberty' would take. Should the new, free Germany be a democratic republic or a parliamentary monarchy? The other question was: where should the boundaries of the 'Fatherland' lie? The latter problem revolved, first, around the national minorities who lived within the boundaries of the existing German states – particularly the Danes and the Poles – and second, around to what extent Austria – with its polyglot empire – should be included. The liberals and radicals clashed over the former question politically at the meeting of the 'pre-parliament' in Frankfurt, and then violently in the Grand Duchy of Baden.

The 574-strong pre-parliament consisted of members invited from existing German state assemblies, others summoned individually for their progressive reputations, and a handful who had been spontaneously elected by popular meetings. The radicals managed to send a respectable number of delegates because their networks were already primed to seize any opportunities offered by the political crisis. Most notable among the radical leadership was the Prussian Johann Jacoby, the Saxon Robert Blum and the Badensians Gustav Struve and Friedrich Hecker.[20] The rupture between liberals and radicals occurred at the very first meeting on 31 March. Struve rose and pressed his republican programme for a single, unitary and democratic German state, watched in awe by the two thousand spectators crammed into the public galleries. The following day, Heinrich von Gagern, a moderate, liberal-minded nobleman from Hesse (who had fought at Waterloo at the age of sixteen), stemmed the radical assault. Fanny Lewald – no great political admirer – described him as 'tall and strongly built . . . his posture, his voice, his manner of expression all bear the imprint of his masculinity'.[21] Gagern believed in law, order and monarchy, but he accepted that it was necessary to wrest the initiative from the radicals – 'to become revolutionary in order to avoid a revolution', as one observer put it.[22] He and other moderates respected the individual German states, but believed that some overarching political unity was required if Germany were to be strong and succeed in realising its mission as a great, civilising influence. For the liberals, Germany would be a federation of constitutional monarchies, with an emperor chosen by its parliament. On 1 April Gagern rose to the tribune and silenced the noisy assembly with a sweep of his steely gaze, but his victory was almost a foregone conclusion, for some 425 deputies were liberal monarchists by conviction. The moderates pressed their advantage when the pre-parliament separated on 3 April, electing a 'Committee of Fifty', which would act as a caretaker until the actual German parliament was due to meet in May. Neither Hecker nor Struve was elected on to this committee. Hecker stormed out, taking a rump of deputies with him, while the more compromising Blum and the other democrats stayed, hoping to work for a federal Germany that would allow for the coexistence of both monarchies and republics. Blum stood apart from many of his fellow democrats not only because of his eloquence (which spoke directly to the impoverished masses since he drew on his childhood experience of privation) or because of his shaggy beard and the worker's blouse that he sometimes wore, but because he saw the wisdom of political compromise.[23] Yet the radical left was not only defeated but irretrievably fractured.

These early defeats convinced some radicals that 'the reaction' was already gathering pace and that, as Carl Schurz recalled, 'there was no safety for popular liberty except in a republic'.[24] But there was no chance of a republic being established by legal means. Hecker fumed: 'Nothing can be done in Frankfurt. We have to strike in Baden' – where grassroots republicanism had found rich soil. The grand duchy had been politically one of the most liberal since 1815, but its territory included large landed estates that belonged to princes or knights of the former Holy Roman Empire who had lost their political power during the territorial reshuffles of the Napoleonic era but still burdened their peasantry with the relics of seigneurialism. During the March revolution, peasants in the Black Forest seized their landlords' property and demanded weapons to defend their claims. Such rebels offered a willing ear to republican propaganda,[25] but the Baden republicans had more than just peasant anger to sustain them. Over the Swiss border, a German 'national committee' recruited a paramilitary force from among the twenty thousand expatriates, while the former soldier Franz Sigel organised his own republican legion at Mannheim and, in Paris, Georg Herwegh, leader of the eight-hundred-member German Democratic Society, was boasting that he could raise a force of some five thousand Germans. The Prussian ambassador to Baden warned that 'with a word – that may already have been spoken – an army of more than twenty thousand desperate and fanatic proletarians could unite under [Hecker's] command'.[26]

A new revolution in Baden itself was certainly feasible, but Hecker and his comrades seem to have vastly overestimated the appeal of their democratic ideas across Germany as a whole. They thought that, with one decisive push in the grand duchy, they could bring about the collapse of the entire monarchist edifice in Germany. But the March revolutions had not swept away much of the old conservative order, and it was already beginning to show signs of renewed vigour. The thoroughly alarmed Baden liberal

government appealed to the still-existing German Confederation
for military assistance on 4 April, and the Diet granted it.
Meanwhile, the radical-turned-moderate Karl Mathy and the cool-
headed democrat Adam von Itzstein – both Badensian members of
the Committee of Fifty – travelled to Baden to try to dissuade
Hecker from fomenting civil war. The uprising was sparked, however, when the capable republican propagandist Joseph Fickler was
arrested at Karlsruhe railway station – Mathy himself spotted the
journalist and ordered the stationmaster to prevent his train from
leaving. With this news, Hecker made his way to Konstanz, where
he met up with Struve. Donning a blue worker's shirt, a slouch hat
with a cock's feather and pistols in his belt, he proclaimed a republic on 12 April and called on all able-bodied men to join him
in marching on the grand duchy's capital, Karlsruhe. Hecker's
small group of sixty followers grew as it moved north-west until
it numbered some eight hundred men – mostly representing a
cross-section of urban or small-town life: professionals, tradesmen,
master-craftsmen, journeymen, students and workers.[27]

Many were armed with scythes rather than firearms, and
Hecker's band could not combine with the other republican forces.
The German legion in Switzerland was blocked by the Swiss army,
determined that their neutrality should not be violated. In France
the government was desperate to wash its hands of Herwegh's trou-
blemaking legion, which endangered Lamartine's finely balanced
foreign policy. Warning the Baden and Bavarian governments of
Herwegh's intentions, Lamartine promised not to arm the legion,
but he added that the provisional government was not yet strong
enough to force it to disband.[28] Meanwhile, Herwegh sent his
indefatigable wife Emma into Germany in an effort to make contact with Hecker's men. Dressed in trousers, a dark blouse,
feathered slouch hat and with a brace of pistols in her belt, she
found Hecker on his march and told him that her husband's
twelve-hundred-strong force was poised uncertainly on the French
frontier. She asked Hecker for a time and place for the two legions
to link up. Hecker was surprisingly vague – possibly because he
believed that Herwegh's legion was full of foreigners, which would

make its incursion look like a foreign invasion. Meanwhile, the more professionally minded Franz Sigel was marching his well-disciplined force – all three thousand of them – across southern Baden in an attempt to find Hecker. One evening, after a gruelling march through snow, mud and driving rain, Hecker, his wet clothes steaming as he luxuriated in the warmth of an inn, scornfully rejected an appeal from the Committee of Fifty to abandon his enterprise.[29]

Meanwhile, the liberal Baden government had mustered a crushing superiority in professional soldiers. While Grand Duke Leopold's own army was of questionable loyalty, the German Confederation had sent forces from Hesse and Nassau, joined by troops from Württemberg and Bavaria. This combined army of thirty thousand men was put under the command of Friedrich von Gagern, Heinrich's brother, who insisted on dressing in civilian clothes, the better to convey the image of a 'citizen general'. This, after all, was no struggle between revolution and counter-revolution, but a fight between moderates and radicals.

The two forces clashed at the village of Kandern on 20 April. Leading from the front, Gagern was the first to fall, but the professionalism and sheer numbers of the government forces soon told. Hecker's legion scattered in all directions, while its leader scampered across the Swiss frontier which lay fewer than ten miles away. Some of his men ran into Sigel's force, which was finally and belatedly following their tracks. The cool-headed soldier managed to rally the fugitives, but his force was then crushed at Freiburg when, attacked on three sides, they ran out of ammunition. Sigel himself managed to escape. In the night of 24 April, Herwegh's legion crossed secretly from France into Baden, where they heard of the disasters at Kandern and Freiburg. Emma and Georg Herwegh agreed that it was best to abandon the insurrection and march their legion into Switzerland, gather the shattered republican remnants, and try again in more propitious times. But on their way through the Black Forest, their force was ambushed and routed. Some of the fugitives found in the darkness were summarily shot or hanged, their limp corpses dangling from branches of the sombre trees. Emma and

Georg eventually slipped across the border dressed as peasants, carrying pitchforks.[30]

The republican revolution in Baden had irrevocably divided the German revolutionaries. Blum's reaction to the uprising was damning: 'Hecker and Struve have betrayed the country in the eyes of the law – that's trivial – but they betrayed the people by their insane insurrection and checked us on the way to victory. That is a hideous crime.'[31] This analysis of radical political chances was almost certainly flawed, but Blum's indictment illustrated the decisive split in the radical movement. For the liberals, the insurrection was an offence against the emerging constitutional order and they had shown that against the radicals they were willing to use force to consolidate what had been gained in March. Ominously for them, however, the troops had been provided by the German princes involved at the behest of the Confederation, showing that, after the initial shock of the revolution, the old order still had some considerable power.

For the time being, however, the spilling of blood on the snow of the Black Forest did nothing to dampen the revolutionary ardour of the more extreme republicans: they had lost a battle, but the war for the revolution was still to be won. The support gathered by Hecker had suggested that there was still much economic distress and political dissatisfaction among the wider population to be harnessed.[32] Karl Marx's associate Arnold Ruge tried to keep up the revolutionary momentum by appealing to the workers and the poor on the streets of cities like Frankfurt, Berlin and Cologne. His newspaper, *Die Reform*, called openly for a second revolution to establish a Jacobin-style dictatorship that would lay the foundations of a republic and an egalitarian democracy.

While the liberal monarchists and republicans locked horns, the problem of the non-German nationalities also exploded on the political landscape. Trouble arose with the Danes over the duchies of Schleswig and Holstein. Lord Palmerston once remarked with characteristic gruffness that he knew only three men who had ever understood the issue: one was dead, another had been driven insane by it and Palmerston himself, the third, had forgotten what it was all about.[33] In 1460 the King of Denmark had taken over the duchies on condition that they would be forever inseparable. In fact, Holstein (which had a German majority) joined the Holy Roman Empire and then, from 1815, was part of the German Confederation. The Danish sovereign remained its duke, but even the most exuberant Danish patriots agreed with the German nationalists on one thing: that Holstein would always remain part of Germany. The true controversy was over Schleswig, which had a Danish majority. The 'Eider Dane' nationalists argued that Denmark extended to the River Eider, the southern boundary of Schleswig. The thorny issue was therefore whether Schleswig could be separated from Holstein and fully absorbed into Denmark. The nationalists' German opponents, by contrast, declared that Schleswig should be detached from Denmark and, along with Holstein, join Germany. For both sides, this was an emotive issue. Danish feeling had been excited by the news of the February revolution in France. Liberals wanted to press for a 'modern' parliamentary system, in which, by contrast to the Joint Estates promised by King Frederick VII, Schleswig would have no special status, but be incorporated into Denmark as a single province, like any other, with representation proportionate to its population, while Holstein would join the new Germany. Danish nationalism and Danish liberalism were inextricable.[34] Yet the former seemed to have more emotive impact: in March a crowd of fired-up Danish nationalists marching through Copenhagen chanted 'Denmark to the Eider!' The situation was particularly tense in the duchies, because Frederick VII had no heirs, so the succession was open to debate. For German nationalists, the obvious choice was the Duke of Augustenburg, a German of the cadet branch of the ruling Danish Oldenburg dynasty, who would bring *both* duchies into the German Confederation.

The friction between the two sides increased: on 18 March, a meeting of German nationalists in Rendsburg defiantly reiterated the German demands for both duchies. The gauntlet was taken up by the Danes and a massive popular demonstration in Copenhagen on 21 March forced the King to dismiss his conservative government and appoint a more liberal ministry, including the strong-willed figure of Orla Lehmann. Besides freeing the press and improving the lot of the peasantry by abolishing compulsory labour services and corporal punishment, this new government declared the 'reunion' of Schleswig with Denmark 'under a common, liberal constitution', which was given royal assent on 5 June (still celebrated as Denmark's 'Constitution Day'). There was to be a broad male suffrage: all men over the age of thirty of a certain independence – 'with their own cloth and table', as the law picturesquely put it – had the right to vote, although events would prevent the inhabitants of Schleswig from participating in the first elections, which were set for October. Ominously for what was to follow, conscription was also made universal.[35] On 24 March the German nobles in the duchies declared their independence and established a provisional government in Kiel: 'We will not tolerate the sacrifice of German territory as a prey to the Danes!'[36] The issue set German nationalism aflame: the Committee of Fifty in Frankfurt declared Schleswig part of the German Confederation, while German patriots across the country flocked to the black–red–gold colours to support the military preparations being made in the duchies. Carl Schurz recalled fervent students enrolling in hastily mustered volunteer corps, although he himself was dissuaded by his professor and friend Gottfried Kinkel, who sagely argued that professional soldiers would do the job much better than a bunch of enthusiastic amateurs. One of Schurz's friends who did march was so shortsighted that he fired his musket at his own side before being felled by a Danish bullet and taken captive.[37]

On 4 April, responding to an appeal by the provisional government in Kiel, the Diet of the German Confederation asked Prussia to intervene against Denmark and provided contingents from other German states. The Prussian army crossed the Eider ten days later, and the forces mustered by the Bund, who were under the command of the Prussian general Friedrich von Wrangel, followed. On 3 May the German forces entered Denmark itself, provoking an international crisis. King Frederick William, who in any case had serious misgivings about aiding rebels, was soon put under intense diplomatic pressure from Britain, Russia and Sweden, all of whom were alarmed at a surge of Prussian power on the isthmus between the North Sea and the Baltic. The Germans were also in danger of overextending themselves, since the Danish navy was now mounting a blockade of northern Germany to which the Germans could offer no serious reply. In the deadlock, the European powers tried to broker a peace deal. When they succeeded, it would provoke a crisis within the German revolution of 1848.

The conflict revealed, once again, that the old order still had vitality, since it was the old Confederation and the Prussian army, not the Committee of Fifty, which provided the military muscle to prosecute the war. It also demonstrated that the revolutionaries all too easily confused 'Germany' with 'liberty': an essentially aristocratic uprising in the duchies, which offered no liberal reforms to its own people, was conflated with the wider German national cause.[38] The German (and, to be fair, the Danish) reaction to the crisis demonstrated that, when the cosmopolitan flowering of the 'Springtime of Peoples' clashed with brute national interest, the latter would be carried with much more conviction.

This was violently illustrated even more amply by the intractable problem of German–Polish relations. The Poles would prove to be one of the European nationalities that emerged with little to show from 1848.[39] At first glance, this is surprising, because the Poles had been among the most dogged of all the European revolutionaries and, along with the Italians, attracted the most widespread sympathy. The flame of the Polish revolution had been kept alight by the 'great emigration' of Polish exiles, whose activities were concentrated mostly in France, but they were divided among themselves. The more conservative nobles around Prince Adam Czartoryski, 'the uncrowned King of Poland' who conducted his business from his Paris home, the Hôtel Lambert, believed that their country could regain its freedom only if it had broad European diplomatic support and military assistance.[40] The more radical tendency was represented by the Polish Democratic Society, founded in Paris in 1832 by republicans who feared Czartoryski's monarchical ambitions and believed that Poland should rely primarily on its own revolutionary muscle. To this end, the society declared openly in favour of abolishing serfdom and all aristocratic privileges, in the hope of securing peasant support for the next insurrection. On the eve of the 1848 revolutions, it boasted a membership of some fifteen hundred exiles, mostly in France, but with branches in Brussels, London and New York.[41]

The March revolutions in Berlin and Vienna at last opened Prussian-ruled Poznania and Austrian Galicia to the activities of Polish patriots. Czartoryski – seventy-eight years old but energised by new hope – boarded a train for Berlin on 24 March in order to press the liberalised Prussian government into war against Russia. Meanwhile, members of the Democratic Society were behind the great demonstration in Paris on 26 March that demanded money and arms for the coming insurrection in Poland. Over the following week, patriotic Poles left Paris by foot or on trains, and (thanks to free rail transport provided by the German Confederation, which was keen to ensure that no Polish revolutionary lingered) crossed Germany, making their way towards Poznania and Galicia. The conflict of Polish and German interests would be fought out in the former.

Revolutionary relations between the Germans and the Poles began promisingly enough. Some one hundred Polish political prisoners, jailed in Prussia for their part in the abortive 1846 insurrection, were freed on 20 March. As befitted the Springtime of Peoples, most Germans expressed solidarity with the Poles. On 23 March King Frederick William received a deputation from the Grand Duchy of Posen (or, as the Polish majority would have called it, Poznania). The region was part of Prussia's share of partitioned Poland, with a sizeable German minority (figures vary depending on national bias, but there were roughly two Poles for every German). Led by the Archbishop of Poznań, the deputation told the King that, since Germany was about to be united 'on the principle of nationality', it was also 'the hour of Poland's resurrection'.[42] They asked for a 'national reorganisation' to be carried out. The following day the King's liberalised cabinet granted the request, establishing a committee of Germans and Poles to discuss some form of autonomy for the grand duchy. On 4 April, having listened sympathetically to a further declaration from a Polish 'national committee' in Poznań – 'we as Poles cannot and will not join the German Reich' – the pre-parliament declared 'the partition of Poland a shameful injustice' and recognised 'the sacred duty of the German people to collaborate in the restoration of Poland'.[43]

If such aspirations were to be fulfilled, however, it meant war with by far the most powerful of the three partitioning powers: Russia. That was a prospect which was relished by many German revolutionaries: the resurrection of Poland would create a bulwark between the new Germany and reactionary Russia and it would help forge national unity against the common eastern enemy. War between Prussia and Russia was also precisely what Czartoryski, who arrived in Berlin on 28 March, was trying to ignite. Yet he found that the Prussian King was now drawing back in horror from the prospect. Once the implications of his earlier warmth sank in, Frederick William exclaimed, 'By God, never, never, shall I draw the sword against Russia.'[44] Adolphe de Circourt, now French ambassador to Berlin, who met with the Prince daily, found that, by early April, Czartoryski was 'perpetually waiting . . . neither the King of Prussia nor his ministers wanted to meet with him personally'. Moreover, Circourt, mindful of his friend Lamartine's pacific foreign policy, frankly apologised to the Polish aristocrat for being unable to offer any concrete French help to his national cause.[45] Meanwhile, the Russians shrewdly made no hostile gestures against Prussia: if the Polish volunteers crossed into the Russian Empire, it would be they, not the Russians, who would appear to be the aggressors.

The determination of all the great powers to avoid a general, Napoleonic-scale European conflict was therefore the first reason for the failure of the Polish national movement in 1848. With Czartoryski's diplomatic offensive hitting the buffers, the focus shifted to revolutionary efforts on the ground.

In Silesia Polish peasants had risen against their German landlords, while Polish coalminers rioted. The first Polish newspapers appeared and demands were heard for the creation of Polish schools and for the official use of the language. Yet there was no direct challenge to the nascent German state.[46] The situation was different in Poznania, where patriotic Polish nobles had established their National Committee, but they demanded little more than autonomy for the grand duchy, not the reconstruction of the entire Polish state. It was the arrival of agents from the Polish Democratic Society that radicalised the movement and tried to channel energies towards truly national aspirations. Foremost of these delegates was Ludwik Mierosławski, who saw the liberation of Poland as his destiny. Mierosławski (whose mother was French and whose Polish father had fought for Napoleon) subscribed to the all-too-common view among European nationalists of the day that warfare was invigorating and prevented decadence. No sooner was he freed, along with the other Polish political prisoners, from Berlin's Moabit Prison on 20 March than he sent agents into both Poznania and Galicia to arm and train the Poles for war with Russia. Yet, in the former, the fragile solidarity between German and Polish liberals was already falling apart. With the encouragement of the National Committee, the Poles seized local power in the grand duchy, removing unpopular officials and organising militias. On his arrival, Mierosławski was given command of these forces, which numbered ten thousand by the beginning of April. As the realities of separation from Prussia began to bite, the German minority began to protest to Frankfurt: 'We are Germans, and want to remain Germans . . . you cannot, must not, abandon us.' In Poznania itself the Germans started forming their own militias and citizens' committees: 'the German cause', wrote one local schoolteacher, 'was at stake'.[47]

Poles and Germans were clearly on a collision course. At first the now thoroughly alarmed Frederick William sought to negotiate with the Poles, sending General Wilhelm von Willisen to Poznań early in April in an attempt to defuse the tension. Yet conservatives close to the King had persuaded him to reinforce General von Colomb, the Prussian military commander in the region, whose men soon outnumbered Mierosławski's by two to one, although ten thousand of the Prussians were civilians armed only with hunting rifles and scythes. Willisen concluded an agreement with the Poles on 11 April, but by then it was too late. On 14 April the King made it clear that autonomy would be granted only to the 'purely Polish' eastern districts of Poznania. Some cool Polish heads accepted that abandoning their claim to some predominantly German, western areas, albeit with large Polish minorities, was a compromise worth making, but the National Committee itself was adamantly opposed to any such partition. On 19 April Colomb unleashed his army. Mierosławski's volunteers fought a skilful defensive action, holding off Colomb's troops in one action on 29 April before two greater battles, the first the following day, in which the Poles managed to rout the Prussians, and the next on 2 May, when each side mauled the other to a standstill. Mierosławski was defeated only when his troops were caught in the open by Prussian artillery and pulverised. The last detachments surrendered on 9 May and the National Committee disbanded. Mierosławski himself was captured and, having tasting freedom for a mere fifty-one days, was locked up in Poznań's fortress.

In Frankfurt the early German cosmopolitan idealism had evaporated: in a new resolution, the Committee of Fifty still spoke piously of restoring Poland, but only if this did not harm German interests in any way.[48] When the German National Assembly discussed Poznania on 24–7 July 1848, it voted to offer the Poles the 'Duchy of Gnesen', a mere third of the original grand duchy, with only a quarter of its population. In a speech described by Lewis Namier as the 'reveille of German nationalism', Wilhelm Jordan asked whether 'half a million Germans' were to live under the rule of 'a nation of lesser cultural content than themselves'? Darker still, he added that 'the preponderance of the German race over most Slav races . . . is a fact'. The mere existence of a people was not enough to guarantee its independence: it had to have 'the force to assert itself as a State among the others'. One of the few voices to object belonged to a Silesian Pole, Jan Janiszewski, who spat back that 'culture which withholds freedom . . . is more hateful and despicable than barbarism'.[49] Robert Blum, one of the wisest and most eloquent of the German radicals, shook his shaggy mane and remarked sadly on 'the inordinate taste for conquest shown by our young and uncertain freedom'.[50]

II

The other spiky thistle that German nationalists had to grasp was how far Austria should be included in the new Reich. The issue was hotly debated throughout 1848–9 and was not finally resolved until Otto von Bismarck drove Austria out of Germany with Prussian blood and iron in 1866. In 1848, however, the Viennese revolutionaries fully expected to be part of the united Germany. In the night of 1–2 April, a group of students clambered up the tower of Saint Stephen's Cathedral and unfurled a huge red–black–gold German banner. The American diplomat in Vienna, William Stiles, saw that

> A united Germany now became the watch-word of the day, and . . . every house in Vienna . . . was surmounted by a German national flag. The students not only marched under German banners, but paraded the streets decorated with German cockades and ribbons. It was remarkable how all, with one consent, gave up at once their own national standard. To be Austrian had already become a reproach, and the venerable 'Schwartz-Gelb', black and yellow, the only acknowledged colors of the imperial monarchy . . . was by these new lights totally proscribed.[51]

Even the beloved Emperor Ferdinand was spotted gleefully waving a German tricolour on a balcony of the Hofburg. Still, the Hungarian nobleman (of German origin) Count Charles Leiningen-Westerburg noticed that some Viennese hedged their bets, flying the German, Austrian and imperial banners at the same time, so that, 'as required, they can then easily remove the superfluous ones and join in the triumph of the victorious idea'.[52] In fact, the inclusion of Austria in the united Germany would present several intractable problems. Not all – Protestant, economically liberal – northern Germans wanted a Germany to include conservative, Catholic, protectionist Austria. Those who sought to exclude Austria, like Heinrich von Gagern, therefore proposed a 'smaller German' (*Kleindeutsch*) solution. Meanwhile, there were plenty of loyal

Austrian monarchists and southern German Catholics who had no desire to see Austria reduced to the status of a mere southern province of a united Germany, or to see the new state dominated by Protestant Prussia. While they still wanted Austria to be included, they often envisaged a much looser confederation, in which the political structures of the existing states as well as the religious beliefs and economic interests of their subjects would be protected. In proposing to include Austria – the 'greater German' (*Grossdeutsch*) solution – the conservatives were joined by radicals, although they envisaged a democratic, unitary republic of all Germans. Yet the *Grossdeutsch* idea had a major problem of its own: would it involve tearing the German-speaking parts of Austria out of the Habsburg Empire, which would lead to its break-up; or should it bring Austria into Germany along with the entire multi-ethnic empire, creating some sort of federal super-state in Central Europe? What, in other words, would become of the other nationalities of the polyglot monarchy?

This issue was thrust firmly into the limelight in the political conflict between the Germans and the Czechs in the Austrian Empire. In Bohemia, the two ethnic groups initially basked in the glow of revolutionary fraternity. The first resistance to the Czech national movement came not from the Germans, but from the reformed Moravian Diet, which, though it contained both Czechs and Germans, voted against union with Bohemia out of provincial patriotism. This was a heavy blow to one of the cardinal aspirations of Czech nationalists: the unification of the ancient Czech crown lands of Bohemia, Moravia and Silesia. In Prague, meanwhile, Czechs and Germans initially joined together in supporting the Saint Václav Committee, which became Bohemia's informal government and the moral centre of the Czech revolution, since Austrian officialdom had been discredited. Rudolf Stadion tried to create an alternative, conservative seat of power by appointing his own commission early in April from among the worthies of Prague, both Czech and German, including the moderate liberal historian František Palacký and some members of the Saint Václav Committee, but on 10 April it was subsumed by the latter. Three days later Stadion, conservative servant of the Habsburg monarchy that he was, was rather stunned to be chairing a body that now bore the title of 'National Committee'. The new effective government – in which both Czechs and Germans served – prepared for the elections of the Bohemian Diet, called by virtue of the imperial concessions of 8 April. On the streets, the liberal Karel Havlíček's newspaper had put a fly in the soothing ointment of Czech–German cooperation by calling on all Czechs to remove German signs from their workplaces, but protests forced him to backtrack with a cringing apology.[53]

The Czech–German conflict stirred because of a surge of opposite currents: German nationalism and Austro-Slavism. The clash was elegantly summarised by a famous exchange between Frankfurt's Committee of Fifty and Palacký. On 6 April the former invited the great Czech historian to join them: German nationalists assumed that the Czech lands, since they had been under both the Holy Roman Empire and the Confederation, would also be part of the united Germany. The social and cultural elites spoke the language: even Palacký's great works were written in German. Yet, on 11 April, the historian stunned the committee by rejecting its invitation in a published letter.[54] He began with a statement of Czech national identity: 'I am a Czech of Slavonic blood . . . That nation is a small one, it is true, but from time immemorial it has been a nation of itself and based upon its own strength.' Palacký's statement did not come out of the blue – it was rather a feisty product of the accelerating Czech cultural renaissance of the nineteenth century[55] – but it thrust the idea of Czech nationality on to the wider European table for the first time. Yet, while Palacký countered German nationalism with the Czech version, neither he nor any other Czech patriots sought full independence from Austria. The historian explained that the unity of the entire German people (which would include the Germans of Austria) would tear apart the Habsburg Empire. This would leave the smaller nations of Central and Eastern Europe vulnerable to the leviathan to the east – Russia – which 'has become, and has for a long time been, a menace to its neighbours'. The Czechs and other peoples of Central

Europe were sheltered from Russian expansionism by the protective shell of the Austrian Empire: 'Assuredly, if the Austrian State had not existed for ages, it would have been . . . in the interests of Europe and indeed of humanity to endeavour to create it as soon as possible.' Palacký was therefore not only offering a rebuff to German nationalism in general but to the *Grossdeutsch* idea in particular.

His Austro-Slavism – the notion that the Slavonic peoples of Central Europe could find freedom and security within the Austrian Empire – so pleased the imperial government in Vienna that it offered him the position of education minister (which he declined). Yet Austro-Slavism assumed that the Habsburg monarchy would be reformed along lines that would give equal rights and status to all the peoples of the empire – turning it into a multinational federation. It remained to be seen whether this faith was well placed. Meanwhile, the Austro-Germans were downright hostile towards such an idea. They had long seen themselves as the *Staatsvolk* – the people who by virtue of their social position and their language, which they regarded as the *Staatssprache*, would always dominate the Austrian state.[56] This dominance would be challenged by the demands of other nationalities for official recognition of their own languages, equal access to government posts and some degree of political autonomy.

In the Czech lands in early April, some of the Germans, who felt especially threatened because there they were a minority, had already reacted by founding a German League 'for the Preservation of Their Nationality', which opposed many of the demands of the Czech revolution and called for the absorption of the Czech lands into 'Greater Germany'. Palacký's letter now decisively broke open a chasm between the two nationalities and by the end of the month the League boasted a membership of eight hundred, which distributed propaganda in support of the Frankfurt parliament. Germans began to desert the National Committee, leaving it to become a voice of Czech nationalism. Mutual animosity became ever shriller: 'Forward against the German, forward against the murderer, against Frankfurt,' screamed the chorus of one popular Czech song, while newspapers derided the Germans as stupid and murderous and their language as babbling.[57]

The Germans responded in kind. In Frankfurt the Committee of Fifty listened to Arnold Schilling declare on 3 May, 'I believe that since Bohemia cannot be held in the German Confederation by conviction, she must be bound to Germany by the sword's edge'.[58] When the Habsburgs were finally able to restore their authority in Prague in June, they would be applauded by German nationalists of almost every political persuasion.

Palacký's protests of Slav loyalty and his rebuff to German nationalism would ultimately illuminate the path by which the Habsburg monarchy would crush the revolution and reassert its authority. For every German, Italian and Magyar nationalist threatening the integrity of the empire there was a Slav or Romanian who felt their ethnic identity was endangered by the triumphant nationalism among the Germans or Hungarians. This allowed the Habsburgs to play off the national minorities against one another. Yet this was much more than a cynical policy of 'divide and rule': it rested on the genuine loyalty of Habsburg subjects who felt that their security and interests were best defended by the empire.[59] If this was true of the Czechs, it was equally true of other national groups who felt the sting of Magyar or German nationalism. In the process, however, the Springtime of Peoples in the Habsburg Empire rapidly fell into the abyss of civil war.

The recovery of imperial power in 1848 was all the more striking because in the spring the Emperor's new ministers had been powerless against the surging revolutionary tumult in Vienna. The backbone of the radical movement was provided by the students of the Academic Legion, middle-class intellectuals, the urban lower middle classes (such as master-craftsmen, retailers and clerks) and suburban workers who tended to follow the students' political lead. Its leadership was assumed by the Central Committee, originally established to liaise between the Academic Legion and the more moderate National Guard. The radicals split definitively with the liberals when the Emperor issued his promised constitution on 25 April. Liberals were keen to crystallise what they had gained, so were happy with the constitution as it empowered them through a system of indirect elections for a parliament due to meet on 26 June. The Emperor kept important powers, offsetting what were regarded as the pitfalls of democracy. The constitution was greeted joyfully by most Viennese, but it was a bitter disappointment for the radicals. It had been 'granted' by the Emperor, who retained an absolute veto, control over war and peace and the right to make all official appointments. Moreover, there was no promise of universal male suffrage, for the manner of elections to the new parliament was yet to be decided by the government. The students' response was to take to the streets in a traditional form of protest. Over two successive nights on 2–3 May, the Emperor's new first minister, Count Ficquelmont, was 'serenaded' by a powerful crowd of Academic Legionnaires, National Guards and workers, who made an unholy racket outside his home, singing songs at the top of their lungs, hurling abuse up at his windows and demanding his resignation before invading the Foreign Ministry, where a deputation threatened, cajoled and browbeat the startled Ficquelmont into promising to resign within twenty-four hours. On 4 May the minister-president was as good as his forcibly extracted word and he handed over the poisoned chalice to Baron Franz Pillersdorf. It was a resounding victory for the students, and illustrated 'the remarkable fact that a government, which a few weeks before had been . . . one of the most power-ful in Europe . . . had become so weak as to be unable to protect the highest officer of state from the insults and indignities of the rabble'.[60]

The radicals now turned their attention to the constitution, par-ticularly when the suffrage law decreed on 11 May that servants and those who earned daily or weekly wages were to be denied the vote – effectively excluding all workers. The Central Committee quickly organised a 'Storm Petition', presenting a list of demands (including a single-chamber legislature elected by universal male suffrage) backed by the threat of force. The government responded clumsily on 13 May, banning the National Guard from participating in the Central Committee. Tensions in the city mounted as both sides prepared for a new collision: the government closed the city gates 'and a strong guard of regular military [was] stationed in every direction around the palace, with cannons loaded with grape-shot, and torches ready lighted'. Yet the radicals once again triumphed: through the night of 14–15 May,

> the students and National Guard were pressing, on all sides, upon the palace, while workmen by thousands, armed with scythes and axes, thundered for admission at the city gates . . . The government, intimidated by the formidable display made against it – though a single discharge of grape or charge of cavalry into the densely-thronged masses would have mowed down all opposition – yielded.[61]

There was to be universal male suffrage and a unicameral parliament. Only the pitiful pleading of Ferdinand prevented the humiliated ministry from resigning *en masse*. Yet, at the very moment of the radical victory, the mood in Vienna turned. After a day of uneasy peace, the city awoke on the morning of 17 May to read a proclamation that the imperial family had left in the night and set up court at Innsbruck. The echoes of Louis XVI's flight to Varennes during the 1789 revolution in France were lost on no one: it seemed to be the prelude to a republic, which few Viennese wanted. Fear, anxiety and near panic filled the political vacuum. 'In bewildering excitement', wrote Stiles of the Viennese, 'they had wandered upon an unexplored path, and suddenly found themselves, as it were, on the very brink of a precipice . . . whence they retreated in horror.'[62]

The conservatism of the majority of the Emperor's subjects was rekindled. On 20 May a proclamation was issued from Innsbruck in Ferdinand's name, complaining of the behaviour of the Academic Legion and the National Guard and promising to listen to the 'just complaints of my people', provided they were 'genuine popular desires', legally expressed and discussed in the coming parliament.[63] The shamed Viennese responded with a backlash against the radicals. Stiles witnessed a man narrowly escaping being lynched because he had been overheard discussing a republic. The Central Committee disbanded itself, and the more moderate Viennese Citizens' Committee (established on 20 April to address problems of law and order) created a Security Committee to 'maintain the existing laws, to safeguard public security, peace, and order, and to guard the personal and property rights of all inhabitants', against those who wanted 'the overthrow of the whole legal order and . . . the dissolution of all civil society'.[64] Both the chastened Academic Legion and the National Guard submitted to the command of Count Auersperg, the military commandant.

However, the first triumph of the reaction within the empire would come not in Vienna but in Galicia. While Polish nationalism failed in Poznania because it collided with German nationalism backed by Prussian military might, in Galicia it ran into the opposition of the peasantry, who, in the eastern part in particular, were Ukrainian (then called Ruthenians) and had very good reasons to support the Emperor. The gentry who led the Polish patriotic movement were impaled on the dangerously sharp horns of a menacing dilemma: should they sacrifice their social interests to their national cause by abolishing serfdom, thereby securing peasant support, or should they repress the urges of romantic nationalism and protect their masterly sway? When news of the Viennese revolution reached Lwów, the provincial capital, a petition was signed on 19 March by twelve thousand people, mostly Poles, but also Jews and some Ukrainian intellectuals, demanding provincial autonomy within the Habsburg Empire. The Austrian governor, Franz Stadion, who had already tried to stem the tide of protest by abolishing censorship and permitting a National Guard, allowed the Poles to present the petition to the Emperor. The delegation travelled via Kraków, where a Citizens' Committee was formed, and offered to speak for the city when they met Ferdinand. Bearing the red-and-white Polish flag, the deputation finally reached Vienna, where it received a rapturous welcome from the population, still drunk with the heady spirit of revolutionary fraternity. Austrian newspapers saluted the prospect of the Habsburg monarchy taking the lead in restoring Polish freedom and, like Prussian liberals, excitedly anticipated war with Russia. The audience with Ferdinand took place on 6 April, when the delegates expressed their hope that with Galician autonomy Austria would spearhead the reconstruction of an independent Poland.

Meanwhile, Democratic Society agents had been arriving in Kraków: by 23 April the city teemed with twelve hundred fresh revolutionaries, who established newspapers, led patriotic marches and pressured the more staid Citizens' Committee, which was cajoled into accepting radical members and changing its name to 'National'. The surge of radical energy into the province thoroughly alarmed most of the local Polish gentry, who were still shaken by the experience of being put to the scythe at the hands of the Ukrainian peasantry in 1846. The raw memories of that year ensured that the landlords were deeply reluctant to follow the Polish democrats in their call for revolution. It was the question of serfdom – and the innate loyalty of the peasantry to the Emperor – which hamstrung the Polish revolution in Galicia from the start. While all the exiles, moderate and democratic alike, urged the gentry to emancipate their serfs, the Galician landlords feared that such appeals would merely prod the peasants into revolt. The National Committee in Kraków declared Easter Sunday, 23 April, to be 'Emancipation Day'. Yet the inability of the democrats to impose their programme on the Galician elites allowed the Austrian authorities to split the Poles, to gather their own strength and to undercut the revolutionaries. It was probably with some relief that the more conservative Poles had received the orders of the Austrian authorities disarming the National Guard in Lwów and reinforcing the military presence in Galicia. Then Stadion played Austria's ace: pre-emptive emancipation. On 17 April the Viennese court, seeking to shore up its crumbling authority, gave the governor permission to free the serfs in Galicia. On 22 April – the day before the Poles' own deadline – Stadion, in the name of good Emperor Ferdinand, announced emancipation as of 15 May, with compensation for the landlords. With a few neatly penned words, Stadion had ensured that the Galician peasants would remain loyal to the Emperor and immune to the blandishments of Polish democrats, whose appeals to the consciences of the landlords had so signally failed.

After the reform came the reaction: tensions in Kraków and Lwów now reached breaking point. In the former, the Austrian government's commissioner narrowly escaped being lynched on Easter Sunday, and three days later the garrison clashed with Polish democrats when it seized caches of pikes and lances. Barricades were thrown up in the streets and the four thousand troops withdrew into the castle. From there the Austrian cannon roared for two hours, bombarding the city into submission: twenty-eight Poles and eight Austrians had been killed. On 27 April, the National Committee was disbanded and the exiles were expelled. The Austrians had successfully carried out the first counter-attack against the 1848 revolutions.[65]

In eastern Galicia, Stadion ruthlessly exploited the tensions between the Ukrainians and the Poles, whose ethnic division coincided with a social chasm, since the former tended to be peasants, the latter their landlords. While always suspicious of Austrian petty officialdom, the Ukrainians had traditionally regarded the distant Emperor as their benign protector against the depredations of their masters. This was why Stadion's imperial decree emancipating the peasantry was such a masterstroke. He not only harnessed the social grievances of the serfs but was able to play the incipient Ukrainian national movement off against the Polish patriots. Within a week of the suppression of Kraków, Stadion allowed the first meeting of a Supreme Ruthenian Council to take place in Saint George's Cathedral in Lwów (Lviv in Ukrainian). One of its demands was for a separate Ukrainian administration, which would undermine Polish authority in Galicia. The council rapidly established local branches across the province (there were forty-three by October) and on 15 May the first Ukrainian periodical appeared, with Stadion's blessing, selling four thousand copies a week throughout the year; it was soon joined by six others. These were significant developments for the future, since they gave Ukrainian national consciousness a formal voice. It was also through the councils that the peasantry got their first taste of politics and learned a sense of national identity: peasants accounted for a third of the membership in some places. Prior to 1848, Ukrainian peasants expressed their grievances against their landlords primarily in social terms, appealing to the good Emperor in Vienna for his protection. Now, they began to express their aspirations in national terms: as a peasant who attended one of the local councils explained, he had learned that 'the Ruthenian people is eminent, great and powerful, that it is the original inhabitant and numerous in Galicia, that, although until now we have been scorned and humiliated, this is a Ruthenian land and more of us Ruthenians live here than Poles'.[66] The fraught tensions between Polish landlords and Ukrainian peasants posed the severest limitations on the Polish national movement in Galicia. The fearful memories of 1846 explain why even Polish democrats were so reluctant to arm the peasants in their national cause.[67]

III

Appeals to the loyalties of the subject peoples of the empire would prove to be particularly effective in what would turn out to be the monarchy's fiercest battleground: Hungary. There, the constitutional concessions wrested from Vienna in the March revolution were given concrete, legislative form in the 'April Laws'. Late in March the Austrian government had tried to claw back some of its power over Hungary by watering down its earlier promises, but it was powerless to resist Kossuth's thundering oratory in the Diet, backed by a determined show of force by a crowd of twenty thousand in Pest on 27–30 March, led by the city's Committee of Public Safety. Sandor Petőfi kept the agitation on the boil with his own fiery speeches and radical poetry: the day of judgement, he wrote, was approaching for all kings, and the Habsburg monarchy was a tree whose fruit rotted on the branch. The streets resounded with calls of 'We don't want a German government!' and even 'Long live the republic!'[68] Unable to impose its authority by force, Vienna once again yielded. It was a victory for both the Hungarian Diet and the Budapest radicals – an irresistible alliance of parliament and street.

The thirty-one April Laws gave Hungary independence within the Empire. A Habsburg would remain as King of Hungary, with the right to approve and veto laws, but his Hungarian cabinet would sit in Budapest. Ministers would be responsible to the new Hungarian parliament, which was to be elected on a much wider franchise than the old aristocratic Diet, but women, Jews and people who did not meet the property, residence and occupational qualifications – mostly wage-earners and landless peasants – were excluded. In all, a quarter of all adult males received the right to vote. The fiscal privileges of the nobility were abolished and all citizens were guaranteed civil liberties. The laws also incorporated the abolition of both serfdom and the tithe. There were, however, some issues that were ominous for the future of Austro-Hungarian relations: the King alone commissioned army officers and could choose to send Hungarian army units abroad (meaning outside Hungary). There was also the fraught question of transferring the Military Frontier region, which hitherto had been under the direct control of the Austrian council of war, to the authority of Hungary's civilian government. This was a sensitive issue, because the border region was a vital source of some of the monarchy's finest soldiers – the Croats and the Serbs. After much cajoling, the court conceded, but only on condition that the Austrian government retained control of the military there and appointed the ban (viceroy). This, at last, was the most the Hungarians could force from the Habsburgs.[69] The old Magyar Diet was dissolved on 11 April in advance of elections to the new National Assembly.

In celebration, the Hungarian colours were draped from windows of houses everywhere and, while all citizens wore the national cockade, radicals were distinguishable by the addition of huge red feathers. As a mark of equality, everyone now carried swords, once a symbol of noble status: Petőfi's was so enormous that his friends – perhaps only half-jokingly – called it 'the guillotine'.[70] Yet, although the April Laws fell short of their March programme, the radical leaders were willing to submit to the new, legally constituted authorities; the Committee of Public Safety disbanded voluntarily on 15 April. This support was conditional, however.

When on 14 April Batthyány's ministers arrived in Budapest and stepped off the already *de rigueur* steamer, they were greeted by the radical spokesman Pál Vasvári, who in front of a huge crowd reminded the new government that the people of Budapest 'now place the power of the revolution in your hands . . . You will have to account for your actions to a powerful reborn nation.'[71]

It seemed that the Hungarian revolution was over and that the way was open to a peaceful, constitutional era of reform. But it was not to be. Among the problems that the liberal regime faced were the demands of the national minorities within Hungary: Slovaks, Romanians, Serbs and Croats. The relationships between Magyars and the rest would become festering wounds, weaknesses that would be cannily exploited by Vienna. On 25 April the Emperor had made a promise that gave the non-Magyar minorities cause to be loyal to the dynasty: 'All peoples of the Monarchy are guaranteed the inviolability of their nationality and language.' While vague, it certainly was more than anything promulgated by the April Laws, which offered no such commitment. Liberal Hungarian nationalism was rooted in a powerful sense that the nation grew from rich Magyar soil. It assumed that Hungary would include all the historic lands of the Crown of Saint Stephen, encompassing such territories as Slovakia, Transylvania and the Military Frontier. It also expected that the various ethnic groups thus enveloped would be content to live within a state that offered all citizens equal rights and that they would simply assimilate into the liberal order, in which, of course, the Magyars would dominate. On 8 April Kossuth admonished a Serb delegation by saying that 'the true meaning of freedom is that it recognises the inhabitants of the fatherland only as a whole, and not as castes or privileged groups, and that it extends the blessings of collective liberty to all; without distinction of language or religion'.[72] Yet he added that the 'unity' of the kingdom made it necessary for the official language to be Magyar. For Hungarian liberals, the unity of the historic lands meant denying the separate national identities of the non-Magyars, while offering to them their rights as individual citizens. 'I shall never recognize more than one nation and nationality, the Magyar, under the Holy Crown of

Hungary,' Kossuth had declared in December 1847.[73] From this perspective, national demands by the other ethnic groups of Hungary were 'reactionary', but they, in turn, could look to Palacký's vision of a confederation of equal nations within the protective shell of the Habsburg monarchy.

Among the first to stake their claims were the Slovaks, who lived entirely within the Kingdom of Hungary and were backed by Czech nationalists, who saw them as fellow countrymen. This relationship was itself problematic. Some older Slovak patriots, such as the poet Jan Kollár, believed that the two peoples should draw closer together, with the Slovaks adopting Czech as their own language. A younger generation disagreed. They were led by the writer Ľudovít Štúr, who had worked hard to promote Slovak as a literary language in its own right. The small Slovak national movement held its first meeting on 28 March and presented its demands to the Hungarian government, asking only that Slovak be taught in schools and used as an official language in Slovakia, and that the Slovak colours be displayed alongside the Hungarian. The government rejected these modest demands out of hand as a 'manifestation of pan-Slavic activity'. Understanding that the Slovak peasants still cared little for questions of nationality, Štúr and his associates organised a larger meeting at Liptovský Svätý Mikuláš in May, drafting a more comprehensive programme, including the right for peasants to own land and greater political autonomy within the Kingdom of Hungary. Budapest reacted by ordering the arrest of three Slovak leaders, including Štúr, who fled to Prague. Slovak volunteers would later join the Habsburg campaigns against Hungary, supporting the Austrians with a guerrilla war, but they failed to raise the peasantry, who listened quizzically to the patriotic appeals of Slovak nationalists.

The Romanians posed a far greater challenge to the Magyars. The 2.5 million Romanians who lived in Transylvania, in Bukovina to the north and in the Banat to the south, had strong commercial and cultural ties with those who lived beyond the frontier, in the Romanian Danubian principalities of Moldavia and Wallachia, which were theoretically under Turkish sovereignty but were

actually governed by the restrictive 'Organic Statutes' imposed by
Tsar Nicholas I in 1832. The Grand Principality of Transylvania had
long enjoyed a separate status within the Habsburg Empire: it had
its own governor in Kolozsvár (or Kluj-Napoca in Romanian), its
own chancellery in Vienna and a diet – albeit one dominated by the
Magyar landlords. The nucleus of an army existed in the form of
the Romanian border regiments, but these were drawn customarily
from ethnic Magyars known as Székelys. Romanians were divided
religiously between Uniate Catholics, who fell under the authority
of the Hungarian bishops, and Orthodox Christians, who were
subject to the Serb Orthodox hierarchy. As conditions for the union
of Transylvania with Hungary, Romanian nationalists demanded, at
the very least, a separate status for their two churches and legal
recognition of their language and culture. Yet a more radical form
of Romanian nationalism had been fostered by contacts and the
cross-border smuggling of books and pamphlets among Romanian
intellectuals,   schoolteachers,   students   and   journalists   in
Transylvania, Wallachia and Moldavia. In May 1848 a Banat priest
named Daniel Roth published a tract that envisaged a new
Romanian kingdom based on 'Dacia', an old province of the
Roman Empire.[74] In Transylvania the idea of Romanian national
unity naturally meant rejection of the union with Hungary altogether, while in the principalities it meant shaking off Russian
dominance and Turkish suzerainty.

At first, Magyars and Romanians alike in Transylvania enthusiastically celebrated the March revolution. The only people who felt
threatened were the Hungarian and Saxon (ethnic German) magnates
who feared for their privileges. The Magyar gentry of Transylvania
embraced the idea of full union with the Hungarian kingdom, but
they bitterly resented the Hungarian Diet's abolition of serfdom.
As most Romanians in Transylvania were peasants, the nobles fretted
that Romanian nationalists might stoke up their hatred against the
Magyars. Otherwise, in the revolutionary fraternity of the March
days, Transylvanian Romanians went so far as to agree that union
with Hungary would be a step in the right direction, because it
would bind them more closely to their co-nationals in the Banat.

The editor of the influential *Gazeta de Transilvania*, George Bariţiu, argued that union with Hungary could be fruitful if the Romanians were allowed to use their own language in local government, church and education, while establishing cultural organisations that would lay firm foundations for their own sense of national identity.[75]

Yet therein lay the rub, for it ran counter to the vision of Magyar liberals, who denied the legitimacy of such national aspirations within Hungary. An article in the organ of the Budapest radical movement, *March Fifteenth*, praised the Romanians for being different from the Russians and remarked that their language was beautiful, though it needed work to become as pleasant as Italian. It went on to argue implausibly that the Romanians 'would consider it an honour to be allowed to become Magyars'.[76] It was not long before Romanian nationalists woke up to the fact that it would be tough to fulfil their own dreams of nationhood in union with the Hungarians. As early as 24 March, the radical lawyer Simion Bărnuţiu told his countrymen that, instead of trusting to Magyar goodwill, the Romanian patriots should hold a congress that would draw up a national programme – and it must include representatives of the peasantry.

There then followed weeks of feverish activity, in which Romanian journalists, students, teachers and priests criss-crossed Transylvania, the Banat and Bukovina to prepare for the great assembly that was to be held in Blaj, with its schools and seminaries one of Transylvania's intellectual centres. The authorities watched these movements anxiously, particularly when delegates from Moldavia and Wallachia were spotted. Yet no one, at this stage, wanted conflict with Hungary, nor to provoke an uprising of the peasantry. At a preliminary assembly of six thousand peasants held in Blaj on 30 April, Bărnuţiu urged his audience not to upset the inevitable process of reform by taking matters into their own hands: emancipation would come as surely as national freedom, but only if both were sought through legal, constitutional means. He none the less continued to reject union with Hungary, warning a committee drafting the Romanian 'National Petition' not to trust Hungarian promises of individual rights, since this would simply turn Romanians into citizens of a 'Greater Hungary'.[77] The great congress was finally held on the Field of Liberty outside Blaj on 15–17 May and was attended by forty thousand people, mostly peasants:

> An entire people, wearing the same national dress and speaking the same language as our people at home, stood there, magnificent, bathed in sunshine; and among the peasant frocks one could notice, here and there, people clad in town clothes. These town clothes were worn by young intellectuals . . . a young generation of great courage and deep love for the Romanian people.[78]

The National Petition was intended for both the Transylvanian Diet and Emperor Ferdinand – but pointedly not for the Hungarian government. It demanded the abolition of serfdom, civil rights, Romanian representation in the Diet, as well as a separate parliament, militia and educational system for Romanians. A permanent committee was established as a provisional government, with Bărnuţiu among its membership, as well as a National Guard. There was no demand for full independence from Hungary, but it certainly looked that way to the Magyars. The Magyar governor, József Teleki, openly charged the committee with subversion and disbanded it.[79] He had little trouble gaining the support of the Transylvanian Diet at Kluj, dominated as it was by the Magyar and Saxon elites, who dismissed the Blaj demands on 30 May and voted for union with Hungary regardless of Romanian sensibilities. The pill was at least sweetened by the abolition of peasant dues and labour services, but the political absorption of Transylvania into Hungary continued apace. On 10 June Emperor Ferdinand, under Hungarian pressure, ratified the act of 30 May. Batthyány could then legally insist that the National Petition had to be presented to the Hungarian parliament, not to the Emperor. Predictably, when a Romanian delegation duly presented it in Budapest, they were dismissed with the now familiar argument that, as free and equal citizens in a free country, they had no need of special national rights. This rejection left the Romanians with two options: union with the Danubian principalities or becoming a separate state within the Austrian Empire, with a direct link to the Habsburg crown. By June 1848 the first option suddenly looked possible, for, at that very moment, a revolution erupted across the Carpathians and the Transylvanian Alps.

Elsewhere, the southern border of the Kingdom of Hungary was the Military Frontier, where, in order to defend the Habsburg Empire against the Turks, since the sixteenth century the Serbs and Croats had been offered land free of seigneurial obligations between the Adriatic and the River Drava in return for military service. This system was gradually expanded until it encompassed Hungary's entire border region as far as Transylvania. The largest military contribution was made by the Croats, who supplied eight border regiments, with their headquarters at Zagreb, compared to the nine raised on the remainder of the frontier. The Croats, however, had their own grievances: when not at war, they farmed in large communes called *zadruga*, which worked well for army recruitment but struggled to provide enough food to cope with the expanding population. Western Croatia, in particular, had become desperately poor by 1848, but the people remained loyal to the Austrian crown because their freedom from manorial obligations gave them a status above that of other peasants in those parts of 'civil Croatia' ruled by the Hungarian civilian government, who were serfs. Croatian nobles had been happy in the past to let the Hungarian Diet defend elite interests against imperial demands, but Magyar encroachments into Croatian affairs and Magyar nationalism had begun to alarm Serbian and Croatian intellectuals alike. Some Croats had begun to formulate the notion of unity of all Croatian provinces into one 'Triune kingdom', which had been ruled in the past as one state, or, like Ljudevit Gaj, they promoted the 'Illyrian' (later called the 'Yugoslav') ideal, which entailed the unity of all southern Slavs.

Initially, both Serbs and Croats reacted positively to the Hungarian revolution in March 1848: those who were still serfs awaited their freedom, while those on the frontier hoped that compulsory military service might be abolished. Clinging desperately on to their privileges, the Croatian gentry declared that only the Croatian Diet, the *Sabor* – not the Hungarian National Assembly –

could abolish serfdom in Croatia, so the peasants rebelled, refusing to pay their dues or to carry out their labour obligations. On 25 March a Croatian national congress met in Zagreb, abolishing serfdom and demanding the same rights that the Hungarians were extracting from Vienna – essentially, full autonomy within the Habsburg monarchy. These liberal demands were dangerous to Austria, Hungary and conservative Croats alike. These last were also 'patriotic' in so far as they wanted to defend the conservative structures of Croatian society against the revolutionary impulses emanating from the Magyars. The way to do this was to remain loyal to the Habsburg monarchy.

The beleaguered Habsburgs would find one of their champions from among these patriotic, conservative nobles: Baron Josip Jelačić. As a proud Croat who made the right 'Illyrian' noises, he received support from the anti-Magyar liberals in the Zagreb congress, but, as a loyal monarchist, he was the preferred leader of the conservatives. He was also seen as a strongman who could control the peasant uprising that was sweeping the region. In other words, he was the Croatian nobility's best hope of both greater autonomy from Vienna and of retaining their authority over the peasantry. Jelačić was also respected as a commander among the border regiments. The Habsburg court, meanwhile, understood that if it wanted to restore its authority in Hungary, the loyalty and help of the Military Frontier would be invaluable. Jelačić, then a colonel in the 1st Banat Regiment, had been spotted as a shrewd and determined operator by an Austrian military commissioner in Zagreb, who recommended him to Vienna. To the imperial government, he seemed to be the man to harness Croatian patriotism against the Magyars, and he was duly appointed ban of Dalmatia, Croatia and Slavonia on 23 March. He set a tone of gritty and determined defiance against Hungary with a blunt order that, until the Croatian parliament met, all districts should accept orders from no one except himself, as the Emperor's representative.[80] Two weeks later he was given command of the Military Frontier. Early in May – spuriously claiming a Turkish threat – he placed some units on a war footing and refused to recognise the legality of the government in

Budapest. He also asked the War Ministry in Vienna to transfer military supplies from Austria to Croatia; the new, conservative war minister, Count Theodor von Latour, willingly obliged. When the Hungarians protested against Jelačić's aggressive defiance, however, the Austrian government as a whole – which, aware as it was of its continued weakness, was still trying to keep on good relations with the Magyars – felt that Jelačić was moving too far, too fast. The Emperor yielded to the Magyar government on 7 May and placed all troops in Hungary and the Military Frontier under the command of the new War Ministry in Budapest. This allowed the Hungarian government to appoint Baron János Hrabovszky to lead the imperial forces to restore order along the southern border.[81] His first targets were not the Croats but the Serbs.

The Serbs supported Jelačić's appointment as ban. On 13 May, with the backing of the independent Serbian principality centred in Belgrade, eight thousand Hungarian Serbs met at Sremski Karlovci (Karlóca in Hungarian) and proclaimed an autonomous province, Voivodina, under an elected executive committee, the Glavni Odbor, and a prince (voivoda), Stevan Šupljikac, a colonel from the border regiments. Like Croatia, Voivodina recognised the ultimate sovereignty of the Habsburg Emperor, but not the authority of the Hungarian government. Yet, when the Serbs also restored the Orthodox see of Karlovci and proclaimed Metropolitan Josip Rajačić to be its Patriarch, the imperial government refused to recognise both. The Glavni Odbor also began to enforce its authority in southern Hungary by inciting Serbian peasants against Magyar landlords and Hungarian, Romanian and Saxon farmers alike. The crisis developed into open war between Hungary and the Voivodina Serbs, with both sides claiming their loyalty to the Emperor. The Serbs, supported by their own troops from the border regiments, held their own against the Hungarians, fighting off an attack on Sremski Karlovci on 12 June. In the Banat (a mixed Serb, Romanian and German region in southern Hungary), the Serbs and the Romanians nearly came to blows since the Romanian majority struggled for recognition of their own separate Orthodox Church as against the Serbs, who recognised Rajačić as their metropolitan.

Unsurprisingly, therefore (and unlike their fellow countrymen in Transylvania), the Banat Romanians, led by Eftimie Murgu, expressed their loyalty to Hungary and asked permission for their own separate congress, which the Hungarian authorities, seeking to counterbalance the Serbs, willingly granted. The Romanian Orthodox congress was held in Lugoj on 27 June, where the ten thousand delegates emphasised that the Banat was not a Serbian province, but its official language and church would be Romanian, while remaining within the Kingdom of Hungary.[82]

For Jelačić, the challenge was how to extend his authority over Serbian insurgents and then harness their energies for his purposes. Some of the Serbian border regiments certainly rallied to the ban, but others preferred to back the Glavni Odbor. Meanwhile, the Hungarian war minister, Hrabovszky, armed with formal military authority, was urging the borderers back to obedience. Consequently, the Serbian section of the Military Frontier was torn between three centres of power. The waters were muddied further when the Croatian Sabor opened in Zagreb on 5 June and, in deference to the Illyrian ideal, voted to invite a delegation from Voivodina. It was a move that could only provoke the Hungarians, which was precisely why Jelačić himself encouraged such behaviour. At the opening of the parliament, he took his oath from none other than Metropolitan Rajačić. As a Croat, Jelačić then took Catholic Mass, but he also held a service of thanksgiving in Zagreb's Orthodox church. All this publicly underlined his support for the idea that the Serbs and Croats were a 'single-blooded nation of two faiths'.[83]

Both sides – Magyar and south Slav – now dashed to gain the imperial blessing for their conflicting claims. When the Sabor sent a deputation to Emperor Ferdinand, they arrived at Innsbruck to find that Batthyány had beaten them to it. On 10 June an imperial decree deposed Jelačić, confirmed Hrabovszky's powers, and gave Latour a slap on the wrist, reminding the Austrian war minister that control of the Military Frontier fell to Budapest, not Vienna. None the less, through the summer, Latour continued to send money quite openly to the Military Frontier's treasury. He may have had good reasons to do so, since the Hungarians were understandably reluctant to provide the Croats with money and supplies, while Austrians needed the Croats not necessarily against Hungary, but as reliable recruits for the war in Italy.[84] In any case, the dismissal of Jelačić did nothing to curb the resistance of the southern Slavs: Jelačić, determined to prove his loyalty to the Habsburgs, had begun to concentrate his forces on the Drava and, already aroused by Magyar pressure, the Sabor closed ranks in support of the ban. The Magyars now faced the very real possibility of a full-blown invasion from Croatia.[85] Yet the imperial government was still unwilling to countenance such a drastic means of restoring Habsburg authority because it was already fighting in northern Italy.

IV

The early days of the Italian revolutions were dark for the Austrians, but exhilarating for Italian liberals. By April the Austrians had been pushed back to the four fortresses of the Quadrilateral in the north, while further south Pope Pius IX still seemed to be fulfilling his early liberal promise and offering his leadership to a rejuvenating Italy. Having proposed a customs union in November 1847, Pius now suggested some form of defensive league for the Italian states, to which Tuscany and Naples immediately subscribed. Meanwhile, there was a widespread popular movement across Italy to join the war against Austria, putting Pius under intense pressure to commit to the anti-Austrian conflict. The moderate liberal Pellegrino Rossi, who shared Vincenzo Gioberti's vision of an Italian confederation under the Pope, but no supporter of the war, declared that 'the national sentiment and the enthusiasm for war are a sword, a weapon, a powerful force; either Pius IX will grasp it firmly in his hand, or the hostile factions will take it and turn it against him and against the Papacy'.[86] Alexander Herzen, in Rome with his family at the time, was even blunter: Pius, he remarked, 'must either withdraw from rising events or ingloriously hit the ground and be crushed or be dragged along against his will'.[87] In fact, privately Pius viewed the early defeats of the

Austrians as providential, but the papacy had a moral and religious obligation not to go to war unless in self-defence. So he hedged his bets, hoping that Austria would be thoroughly defeated before he had to commit any papal troops into action against what was, after all, a Catholic monarchy.[88] The Pope's dilemma explains the ambiguity of his orders to the Piedmontese general Giacomo Durando, whom he had invited to command his soldiers. These men – seven thousand in all – were marched to the northern frontier of the Papal States, from where they were to offer the Piedmontese invasion under King Charles Albert their support – but to what extent and how were left deliberately unclear.

Patriotic enthusiasm in Rome was kept on the boil by a popular radical leader, the wholesale merchant Angelo Brunetti, better known by his moniker Ciceruacchio, and by the tall, dark and fiery figure of Father Alessandro Gavazzi. A Barnabite monk, the latter had been criss-crossing the country like a medieval mendicant friar, electrifying his audiences with his rallying cry: *'Fuori i barbari!'* ('Out with the barbarians!'). When the news of Milan's Five Glorious Days arrived in Rome, Gavazzi and Ciceruacchio presided over a ceremony in the Colosseum, in a scene described by Herzen: 'the setting sun came through the arches in bright strips. The innumerable crowd filled the centre; on the arches, on the walls, in the half-ruined loges people crowded – people sat, stood, or lay everywhere. In one of the prominent loges was Pater Gavazzi, tired, pouring sweat, but ready to speak again.' Gavazzi, who offered his services as chaplain to the Roman legion that was now being formed, declared that the Christian cross and the Italian tricolour stood side by side in this struggle: it was a holy war. Below one of the arches bedecked with the Italian and Lombard flags, young men signed up to join the legion. 'It grew dark in the courtyard, and torches burned near this strange *recruits' levy*; the people remained in semi-darkness, the wind shook the flags, and frightened birds, unaccustomed to such visitors, circled overhead, and all this was embraced by the gigantic frame of the Colosseum.' Two days later Herzen saw the first volunteer detachments setting out and, revolutionary though he was, wondered how many of these fresh-faced young men would not return: 'War is a savage, disgusting proof of human folly, generalized brigandage, justified murder, the apotheosis of violence – and mankind still has to fight before there is a possibility of peace!'[89]

The Roman volunteers, nicknamed *crociati* (crusaders) left Rome on 25–6 March: comprising ten thousand raw recruits and civic guards under the republican Colonel Andrea Ferrari, they boosted the papacy's contribution to the war to seventeen thousand men.[90] In Tuscany moderates like Baron Bettino Ricasoli joined the Florentine democrats in criticising Grand Duke Leopold's premier, the Marchese Ridolfi, for his lukewarm attitude towards the war. At a great public meeting in Florence on 26 March, watched by Leopold himself, Ricasoli whipped up popular passions for the 'crusade' and Leopold had to cool tempers by agreeing to send a force of some 7,770 men to join the Piedmontese campaign in Lombardy.[91] Southern Italy made a contribution, too: even the fractious Sicilians, who wanted independence from Naples before they wanted to be any part of a unified Italy, sent a symbolic force of a hundred men northwards.[92] In Naples the patriotic Princess Cristina di Belgiojoso, herself from Lombardy, hired a steamer to carry her back to northern Italy, but found her lodgings besieged by Neapolitans clamouring to go with her to join the fighting. On 29 March, with the princess bearing the Italian tricolour, her ship steamed out of port, passing through waters crammed with smaller craft saluting her and the 184 volunteers bound for the war.[93] They were to be joined by a much larger, regular Neapolitan force under the command of the Napoleonic veteran and former revolutionary exile General Guglielmo Pepe. Now sixty-eight years old, Pepe wore a cocked hat topped with a towering white feather and at his side clanked an enormous sabre that was a relic of his younger days.[94] Amnestied by King Ferdinand of Naples, he returned from exile on the day of Belgiojoso's departure and was initially invited to form a government by the monarch, keen to quiet liberal demands by appointing one of their own. Pepe, however, made demands that were far too radical for the King's taste, including the immediate departure of the army for Lombardy.

Ferdinand managed to force Pepe to resign, but he could not withstand the popular pressure to go to war against Austria. On 7 April he formally joined the conflict, now asking Pepe to command his forty-thousand-strong army. Pepe accepted, but found his efforts to organise his forces hampered at every turn: the foot-dragging King, he claimed later, 'was determined to do all he could to ensure that the army remained numerically weak, lacking in everything, and incapable, in all, of lending powerful support to the Italian cause'. Ferdinand was certainly reluctant to commit troops to a war that, for one, would primarily help to aggrandise his great rival, Charles Albert, while also diverting Neapolitan energies from the more urgent task of destroying Sicilian separatism. These troops none the less sailed three weeks later, disembarking at Ancona for the march northwards.[95] Having accomplished this task, the Neapolitan squadron, consisting of seven frigates, five of steam and two of sail, and two brigs, then set course for Venice to help raise the Austrian naval blockade. The vessels dropped anchor in the lagoon on 16 May, to a rapturous welcome.[96] Yet on land progress was less promising. On 3 May, the day he joined his troops, the exasperated Pepe received an order from the King's new war minister telling him that when he reached the south bank of the River Po, which marked the northern frontier of the Papal States, he was to wait for further orders. Pepe exploded with rage: what sort of general, he asked, could possibly sit on one side of a river while, on the other, the Piedmontese and Venetians were sacrificing themselves for Italy's honour? Worse was to come, for when Pepe's troops reached the Po, they numbered only fourteen thousand, not the full forty thousand he had expected.[97]

Yet papal and Neapolitan hesitancy was not as immediately alarming for Italian patriots as the ambiguous intentions of King Charles Albert of Piedmont himself. Publicly, the King peppered his words with the tantalising spice of Italian unity. His declaration of war on Austria on 23 March proclaimed his 'feelings of Italian brotherhood' and that his troops were 'to carry the Cross of Savoy [his dynastic emblem] imposed on the tricolour flag of Italy'.[98] The monarch's decision for war, however, was not driven by the lofty aim of Italian unification. Rather, Charles Albert's energies were sustained by a muddier soup of domestic political pressures and his own dynastic ambition.

At home, there was a real danger of a republican backlash in Piedmont if the King failed to assume the leadership of the anti-Austrian struggle. The stirring news of Milan's Five Glorious Days had galvanised the democratic movement in Turin and Genoa: followers of Giuseppe Mazzini, protesting against the limitations of the constitution of 4 March, were mustering in the great port city, and across Piedmont anti-clerical crowds attacked Jesuit houses. The prime minister, the cautious moderate Cesare Balbo, warned the King that not to act would almost certainly drive public opinion away from the monarchy and into the arms of the republicans. Moreover, without a Piedmontese military presence, there was a real danger that neighbouring Lombardy and Venetia would become hives of republicanism under Cattaneo and Manin. With revolutions sweeping along the duchies of Parma and Modena too, Charles Albert was persuaded that an invasion of Lombardy would stem what he saw as an alarming tide of republicanism. After all, it had been moderates like Milan's mayor, Casati, who had pleaded for Piedmontese intervention not only to defeat the Austrians but to prevent the republicans from assuming power.

The King also had personal ambitions: to expand his state by annexing Lombardy and Venetia, creating a northern Italian kingdom under his dynasty. His battle cry, 'Italia farà da sé' ('Italy will do it herself'), was not just an empty nationalist slogan: it was a warning to Italian republicans not to appeal for French intervention, which would certainly weaken his own cause. A war of dynastic expansion would curtail and then choke the incipient nationalist movement. Yet, for now, Charles Albert was buoyed by outspoken and enthusiastic public support for his intervention. On 23 March even the shrewd political fox, the moderate Piedmontese liberal Count Camillo Benso di Cavour, got carried away in his newspaper, *Il Risorgimento*:

The supreme hour for the Sardinian monarchy has struck . . . In the face of the events in Lombardy and Vienna, hesitation, doubt,

delays are not possible; they would be the most lamentable of policies. We are cool-headed men, accustomed to listening to the
dictates of reason rather than the impulses of the heart, and having
pondered our every word we must now in conscience declare that
there is only one path open for the Nation, for the Government, for
the King. War! . . . Woe to us if . . . we do not arrive in time![99]

Unsurprisingly, Italian republicans approached the King with suspicion bordering on open hostility. Mazzini, who was hastening to
Italy via France and Switzerland from his exile in London, wrote to
an English friend on 28 March, 'my countrymen in Lombardy have
done wonders; but, as soon as they have nearly conquered, Ch.
Albert goes in and will gather the fruits grown up through Italian
blood. I do not know what I will do.'[100]

The republican dilemma was that the Piedmontese had the military strength to finish off the job of expelling the Austrians, but
accepting such aid meant bowing to Charles Albert's monarchist
ambitions. The Milanese revolutionaries had all agreed to put off
the political debate between monarchists and republicans *a causa
vinta*, and Mazzini, despite his private misgivings, agreed. While
passing through Paris on 31 March, he issued a proclamation to the
Lombards in the name of the Italian National Association (itself an
organisation aimed at unifying the different strands of exile opinion):

> Faithful to the programme put forward, the National Association
> does not claim the authority to give advice regarding the type of
> political order which would conform best to your traditions and to
> European trends. But choose freely, as is worthy of those who have
> triumphed with no other help than their own strength; thought-
> fully, as expected from those who are masters of their own
> destinies.[101]

Yet Mazzini could not resist giving a thinly veiled warning to beware
of the monarchists: the powerful, he cautioned, had a habit of
wresting the rights from those who were too compliant or too reck-

less. The Lombards should not yield their rights to the mighty; to do so would be to surrender the entire national cause. Still, Mazzini accepted the political truce because the Piedmontese army was the means by which the first step towards national unity would be achieved. Independence and unification should come first, while a republic and democracy (words which Mazzini studiously avoided in the proclamation) could wait if they would compromise the struggle against the Austrians. The republicans could unleash their political campaign for democracy once the war was won.[102]

This political truce played into the hands of the monarchists. The Lombards at large were spellbound by word that 23,000 Piedmontese troops had crossed the River Ticino on 25 March. The next day, in pouring rain, their advance guard marched into Milan, hemmed in by cheering crowds. Mazzini arrived on 7 April and for the next two nights he was cheered by crowds who gathered outside his window. He may have been inspired by this display of support, but the republicans were all too aware that they were in a minority. They could count among their core supporters radical students and urban artisans, but the challenge was to reach the peasantry, who would play a vital role in the political decisions to come.

That any compromise between the republicans and the monarchists would be almost impossible to sustain was emphasised on 11 April when Charles Albert invited Mazzini to accept the monarchy in return for a role in drafting a democratic constitution for northern Italy. Mazzini rebuffed this overture with impossible demands of his own: 'let Ch. Albert break openly every diplomatic tie, every connection with other princes: let him sign a proclamation to Italy for *absolute* unity, with Rome as a metropolis, and for an overthrow of all other Italian princes: we shall be soldiers under his banner: *se no, no* [if not, then no]'.[103] Mazzini's adherence to the political truce was bitterly opposed by other republicans, including a repentant Cattaneo, who regarded Charles Albert as a reactionary, religious bigot whose impulses were even more oppressive than those of the Austrians. In a fit of frustration, Cattaneo went so far as to say that if he had to choose between Austrian and Piedmontese rule, he would opt for the former. The essential difference between

Mazzini and Cattaneo lay in their priorities. Mazzini was willing to secure national unity even if that meant delaying the creation of a democratic republic. Cattaneo's loyalties were essentially to Lombardy, so he put winning political liberty there above the dream of national unity.[104]

While the republican opposition was weakened by infighting, the monarchists broke the political truce. The Piedmontese began to turn the screw on the Lombard moderates. On 16 April Count Di Castagnetto of the court of Turin wrote to Casati with a stern warning that the King was far from pleased with the republican shenanigans in Milan: 'This, my dear Casati, is too much. The only talk at Milan apparently is of a republic; and they even want Genoa to go republican too. Bad faith comes into this, and so does foreign intrigue and foreign money.' He appealed to Casati to 'save your country and mine! Save it a second time, for this danger is no less than that you overcame a month ago.'[105] How the Lombard liberals were meant to save their country was becoming clear: it was expected that they were to put the question of 'fusion' with Piedmont to a plebiscite. It was easily done: Milan's war committee had disbanded at the end of March and was replaced by a Lombard provisional government that included precious few republicans. On 12 May it hastily declared that a referendum would be held over the next seventeen days – and the question posed was simply over the timing of 'fusion' – whether it should take place immediately or at the end of the war. No other option – be it a federation or a republic – was offered. The one concession that the republicans managed to wring from the provisional government was a promise that a constituent assembly would meet to discuss changes to the Piedmontese constitution – but even this promise angered the court in Turin. Mazzini, whose new newspaper *Italia del Popolo* rolled off the press for the first time on 13 May, immediately and roundly condemned both the breach of the political truce and the idea of a northern Italian kingdom.[106] Such protests availed the republicans nothing. When the question was put to the Lombard peasantry, there seemed to be little choice: one observer wrote that the 'fusionists' went among the peasants, the tradesmen and all the simple people, announcing the choice to be between Charles Albert and the Austrians; either to give themselves to Piedmont immediately, or to return to Austrian rule. I heard them with my own ears. Naturally the simple people, faced with such an alternative, put their names or crosses where the government and the provincial committees wanted.[107]

As the voting drew towards a close, a despairing Cattaneo begged Mazzini to join him and other republicans in toppling Lombardy's provisional government. Mazzini, stubbornly true to the principles of legality, refused. On 29 May, the last day of voting, desperate Milanese democrats invaded the municipal chambers, but the civic guard stood firm. *Italia del Popolo* denounced the uprising: force, Mazzini urged, was no substitute for freedom of speech and persuasion and should not 'interrupt the course of our pacific evangelism'.[108] The result of the referendum was almost a foregone conclusion: since a vote against fusion would provoke a Piedmontese withdrawal from the war and expose Lombardy to the vengeance of the Austrians, most Lombards – including, if the voting figures are to be believed, many republicans – felt they had no choice but to fall into the immediate embrace of the Savoyard monarchy. With an overwhelming turnout of some 84 per cent of eligible voters, the results were unquestionably impressive: some 560,000 votes in favour of immediate fusion to fewer than 700 against. Milan was soon joined by the duchies of Parma and Modena in voting for annexation by Piedmont. Northern Italians now awaited the decision of Venice.[109]

The early decision by Milan to accept Charles Albert's support left Daniele Manin's Venice politically isolated. Rather than joining arms with a sister republic in Lombardy, the newly proclaimed Venetian republic was sitting uneasily alongside a region that had unambiguously declared for the Piedmontese monarchy. Manin tried to delay Venetia's decision by adopting the policy of *a causa vinta*, putting off political discussions until after the war. He hoped that this would encourage all the Italian states to stand shoulder to shoulder until the Austrians were expelled – and Venetia was very much in the front line of the fighting. He was bitterly opposed by his colleague and rival Nicolò Tommaseo, who, like Manin, did not trust Charles Albert, but who also had a firm faith in the sincerity of Pius IX and the promise of troops from the south. Yet the Neapolitan, Tuscan and papal troops were still a long way off, making their painfully slow marches northwards. Meanwhile, immediate military assistance was urgently required. Manin was virtual dictator of a state that had no army of its own and so required time to recruit and train its citizens. Meanwhile, as early as the end of March, there were reports of Austrian forces building up along the eastern border, under Count Laval Nugent. If Nugent managed to cut through rural Venetia and link up with Radetzky, who was licking his wounds in the Quadrilateral, then the Austrians could crush the Venetian republic with overwhelming force. Manin was therefore almost bound to swallow his republican scruples and go on bended knee to the Piedmontese, who were making their ponderous advance across Lombardy, heading for the Quadrilateral. If the Piedmontese could flush Radetzky out of Italy, then they could face Nugent separately and drive his rather hastily assembled, rag-tag army back into Croatia. It was therefore a race between Charles Albert and Nugent for the Quadrilateral. The latter began his advance on 17 April, reaching Udine after five days. This town was important for its command of the roads fanning out through the sparsely defended countryside of Venetia. When it capitulated after a nighttime bombardment, Manin was finally pushed into making a frantic appeal to Charles Albert: 'In the name of Italy, of humanity, of justice, we demand immediate assistance.'[110]

The best hope now for the Venetian republicans was that a united Italy would be a loose confederation in which Venice could coexist with the monarchical states, but it was highly unlikely that Charles Albert would accept such an outcome: the Piedmontese wanted nothing less than to annex successively Lombardy and then Venice as 'another leaf of the Italian artichoke'.[111] To Venetian delegates who appeared at the King's headquarters, the Piedmontese minister of war bluntly declared that 'Piedmont cannot be inspired by a purely chivalrous spirit and awaits some recompense for its great sacrifices'. The minister did not spell out what such compensation should be, but it was made obvious that the price was to be 'fusion'. Manin initially baulked at this heavy cost, but as news of one military setback followed another, monarchist propaganda began to hit home. Believing that Manin's republican intransigence was jeopardising the promise of Piedmontese help, the people of the *terra firma* began to turn against the city itself. In Padua anti-Venetian slogans were painted on walls, while the provincial committee in Rovigo refused to send taxes to Venice because the great city was 'isolating itself from the rest of Italy'. While the poorer sections of the city supported Manin, the mass of the middle classes and the nobility leaned towards Charles Albert, both for his promise of troops and in the hope that he would prevent further revolution at the hands of the republicans. Some provincial committees in the region spontaneously held their own local plebiscites for fusion, which Manin desperately tried to counter by sending republican speakers out to the countryside to dissuade the locals from taking such a drastic step. But the republicans were ignored, and province after province voted in favour of fusion. By 5 June the advancing Austrian army and the provinces acquiescing to annexation by Piedmont had together reduced Manin's republic to Venice itself and its lagoon. On 4 July the Venetian Constituent assembly, elected on 9–10 June, also agreed to the 'fusion'. Nominally, at least, all of northern Italy was now a united kingdom.[112]

This Piedmontese stripping of the artichoke excited the jealousy and animosity of other Italian princes. Shortly before Charles Albert decided on war, Piedmont's putative allies, the Tuscans, sent in troops to seize a strip of territory linking the Duchy of Modena to the sea, as well as the small, formerly independent state of Massa and Carrara. Charles Albert had clearly been eyeing these lands hungrily himself, for the Tuscan volunteers skirmished with Piedmontese troops. In a later incident, when Tuscany and Piedmont were theoretically on the same side, the Piedmontese refused to assist a small Tuscan unit that had been overwhelmed by the Austrians.[113]

Throughout the peninsula, the movement for unification itself proved to be fragile, and it began to fragment as different states pursued their own interests rather than the goal of national unity. Moreover, not all revolutionaries envisaged an Italy forged into a single, unitary state along the lines imagined by Mazzini. Cattaneo fought above all for a republic in Lombardy, while even the Piedmontese, who stood to gain most from the war, worried that their capital, Turin, would lose its pre-eminence to Milan. Venice was accused of putting its local republicanism above the Italian cause: Manin himself unfurled the banner of the Venetian republic because he knew the revolution would receive wider support among Venetians if he evoked the ancient 'Republic of Saint Mark', which – to Manin's regret – had been the main battle cry of the Venetian revolutionaries in the March days. The Sicilians, too, were more concerned for their local autonomy than for the national struggle. The parliament that opened in Palermo on 25 March proclaimed that the ancient rights of the island were restored, but that it would be willing to form part of an Italian federation. In the end the islanders had to devote more energy to their struggle to defend their independence from Naples than to the wider fight for unification. Italian patriots later accused Sicily of waging a separatist 'civil war' while the cause of Italian unity floundered.

But the first significant blow to the struggle for independence was the Pope's withdrawal from the conflict. Pius rapidly regretted his decision to send troops against the devoutly Catholic Habsburgs, an action that might have caused a schism within the Church. He was shoved decisively against the war on 5 April when Durando issued an order that left him with little choice but to act as pontiff rather than as an Italian patriot. In a tactless proclamation penned by Massimo d'Azeglio, Durando summoned his men to nothing less than a holy war: Pius, he shockingly declared, 'has blessed your swords which . . . are to exterminate the enemies of God and of Italy . . . Such a war is not merely national, but highly Christian.'[114] The intoxicating blend of religion and nationalism was an inspiring, lethal and insidious cocktail. It was more than Pius could stomach. He had carefully avoided any formal declaration of war (which would have run against his role as Pope), yet now Durando had not only openly proclaimed war on Austria, making the Pope appear to be the aggressor, but had shouted from the rooftops that Catholic Austria and its Catholic soldiers were 'enemies of God'. Pius soon heard that the German bishops were reacting angrily and the feared schism seemed to be looming. After more than a fortnight of angry debate, Durando, disobeying orders, crossed the frontier on 22 April. The Pope could not stop him, but he could disavow him. On 29 April Pius issued an 'allocution' in which he repudiated 'the treacherous advice . . . of those who would have the Roman Pontiff to be the head and to preside over the formation of some sort of novel republic of the whole Italian people'.[115] He also informed the other princes that he was abandoning his project for a league of Italian states. The 'liberal' Pope had set off on a path that would lead him to repudiate unification and liberalism altogether: it was a parting of ways between Italian nationalism and Roman Catholicism that would endure until the twentieth century. The reaction in Rome was one of stunned disbelief giving way slowly to anger: one flabbergasted republican growled that 'the Papacy is unchangeable, it is the chief enemy of Italy, and Rome must not suffer it any longer'.[116]

The outrage so galvanised the Roman democrats that on 1 May Pius was forced to appoint a new cabinet led by the left-wing liberal Count Terenzio Mamiani, who was popular for his support of the war and his belief that the new constitution had to be 'enlarged' — that is, parliament had to have more power vis-à-vis the Pope – and that the state had a role in guaranteeing the means of subsistence to its poorest citizens. But he was no Mazzinian: he feared the 'extremists' as much as he disliked the ultra-conservatives among the clergy. Meanwhile, Durando's regular troops had already crossed the papal frontier and put themselves under Piedmontese orders. By contrast, few of Pepe's Neapolitans reached the battlefield. This was because, on 15 May, the revolution in Naples was crushed by King Ferdinand II.

The liberalised regime in the Kingdom of Naples had never

managed to achieve the essential for its own survival: to restore order and social stability to both the city and the countryside. The collapse of royal power at the beginning of the year left a vacuum in which radicals and moderates jostled with each other. In Naples democratic political clubs called for the abolition of the upper house and for an extension of the suffrage, meaning that the liberals, who had initially focused their energies on simply ensuring that the King honoured his promises, were now fighting a war on two fronts for the defence of the constitution. To add to this political conflict, the liberals – whose backbone was provided by the non-noble landowners in the countryside and the merchants and manufacturers in the cities – also confronted social unrest. Urban artisans and apprentices, facing redundancy because of the introduction of new technology, rampaged through workshops in Naples and Salerno, smashing machinery. Far more serious was the uprising in the countryside: peasants occupied land that they claimed was theirs, particularly common land that had been enclosed by wealthier landowners. Radicals, including a 'red' priest near Salerno, preached that the great landed estates should be broken up and the spoils shared among the people. The landlords found protection in the new National Guard, but the divisions between liberals and democrats formed a yawning chasm that weakened the revolution and gave King Ferdinand his opportunity. The moderate prime minister, Carlo Troya, a historian more at home with his books than with the storm-tossed world of revolutionary politics, was out of his depth. While his government and the National Guard were unequal to the task of keeping the spectre of social revolution at bay, his support for the war allowed conservatives at court, in the army officer corps and the clergy to spread the word that the liberals wanted to deliver Italy into the hands of the hated Piedmontese. Now, with Pius's allocution, priests and friars could add religion to the counter-revolutionary arsenal: the liberals, they claimed, were also defying the Pope.

Given this poisonous atmosphere, it is scarcely surprising that when the parliamentary elections were held, only a fifth of all eligible voters turned out. The opening of parliament was to take place on 15 May and the majority of deputies who arrived to take their seats in Naples were moderates, with a vocal minority of radicals and a rump of conservatives. Many of them suspected the King's sincerity as a constitutional monarch. Radical determination was steeled by the arrival in the city of provincial supporters, including democratic elements from the National Guard. When the King demanded an oath from parliament that it would maintain the existing constitution and concentrated some twelve thousand troops in the centre, barricades were thrown up in the city. Despairing moderates tried in vain to persuade the radicals to stand down, but by now the King was set on crushing the revolution by over-whelming force.[117]

In the morning of 15 May, the first shots were fired, the red flag of martial law flew from Saint Elmo's Fortress and Ferdinand's troops – including Swiss Guards and artillery units – advanced down the Toledo. In grisly hand-to-hand fighting, with the Swiss leading the charge, the soldiers blew apart the barricades with cannon fire before killing or driving the insurgents back with bayonets. They broke into the houses on either side of the avenue and cleared the rooms and rooftops. At three o'clock, a committee of seventy deputies tried to organise resistance from the seat of the municipal government in the Monteoliveto District. The troops smashed their way through the barricades in this quarter, taking the city chambers by seven o'clock in the evening. Lord Napier, the British consul, witnessed the fighting and reported that some two hundred soldiers were killed and four hundred wounded, with the Swiss bearing the brunt of the casualties. No death toll was available on the insurgents' side, but some six or seven hundred were taken prisoner and, Napier wrote,

> no doubt a number of innocent persons, and even some women and children fell, victims to the soldiers on their first irruption into the interior of the houses. The Neapolitan troops, during the course of the evening and night, committed great excesses, extorting sums of money by threats of personal violence, and even wantonly wounding and insulting inoffensive persons.

Some prisoners were summarily shot and, in the wake of the royal troops came the dreaded urban poor – the *lazzaroni*. Having stood aside as royal authority collapsed in January, they now took full advantage of the devastation to loot the bullet-riddled houses. They also reasserted their loyalty to the King, disarming the National Guards, parading in the streets waving the Bourbon white flag and crying, 'Long live the King!' and – in an unambiguous rejection of Italian unity – 'Death to the nation!' On 17 May, using the excuse that a number of deputies had formed a 'committee of public safety' to throw the country into civil war, Ferdinand dissolved the parliament.[118]

The reaction in Naples had serious implications for the southern Italian contribution to the war of independence. General Pepe, his forces strung out on the road to the River Po, was in Bologna when he learned of the counter-revolution of 15 May. He received orders from the Neapolitan government to return to Naples. The squadron that had sailed into Venice obeyed, but Pepe, bristling at the obvious pleasure with which his superior, General Statella, delivered this message, resigned his command, leaving Statella to carry out the unpalatable orders. The patriots of Bologna soon got wind of the imminent Neapolitan withdrawal and the city's National Guard flocked around Pepe. Putting their hands on their hilts, they pledged: 'This sword is for you, Italian General.' Moved, Pepe grasped his own sword and cried, 'This one will be for Italy for as long as I am alive!' With Bologna in uproar, Pepe resumed his command; Statella, having yielded, felt honour bound to resign. The latter tried to return to Naples via Tuscany, but there an angry crowd stopped his coach and burned it to ash, with its hapless passenger still inside. Pepe countermanded the order to withdraw but, in the end, only two thousand of his original force were willing to disobey the King's orders. It was with this small force that, on 17 June, the intrepid general finally crossed the Po and began the march to relieve Venice.[119]

For all the enthusiasm of Italian patriots, however, the war had been going badly. The Piedmontese drove the Austrians back in the first battle at Goito on 8 April, crossing the River Mincio and penetrating the region held by the Quadrilateral. This victory was soured a little when the Austrian garrison downstream in nearby Mantua refused to capitulate, but Charles Albert laid siege to one of the other fortresses, Peschiera, on 29 April, while the rest of his troops drove on to dislodge Radetzky from Verona. A further victory followed at Pastrengo at the end of the month, but then the Piedmontese finally hit the rocks of Austrian resistance. Falsely informed that the population of Verona was ready to rise up, Charles Albert sent his troops to take that fortress, where Radetzky himself had his headquarters. They attacked on 6 May but were driven back by determined Austrian counter-attacks. The King settled down for the siege of Peschiera, but this was probably a mistake, for the war would now be decided by whether Nugent could join forces with Radetzky: blocking the former's way may have been a more judicious use of Piedmontese energies.

The only forces that could now stop Nugent were the papal divisions marching from the south under Durando and Ferrari. These soldiers did move quickly, reaching the River Piave in the nick of time, burning a bridge just before Nugent's vanguard arrived on 30 April. Nugent, however, cunningly left his baggage and one division as a decoy and then force-marched with the rest of his men northwards, moving around the Roman forces. His grittily determined Austrians then fell on Ferrari's volunteers at Cornuda on 9 May: the amateurs fought stubbornly all day, with the promise that Durando was on his way 'at the double', but the reinforcements never arrived. The dispirited volunteers began to melt away, but Durando's professionals, including the Swiss, embarked by train to Vicenza in an effort to catch Nugent again. This south-westwards manoeuvre left nothing between the Austrians and Venice. By 25 May Nugent's forces, some 18,000 strong, had reinforced Radetzky's 51,000 in Verona. Durando's determination to hold on to Vicenza threatened to harass the Austrian communications, but Radetzky resolved to ignore the problem and strike directly at Charles Albert. He fell first on the King's brave Tuscan allies, who fought bitterly at Curtatone and Montanara on 29 May: one volunteer was Giuseppe Montanelli, a bearded, diminutive but fiercely patriotic professor at

Pisa University who stood alongside his students. He battled on until shot through the shoulder by Croats, who mockingly yelled, '*Viva Pio Nono!*' ('Long live Pius IX!'). These two engagements knocked the Tuscans out of the war.

Radetzky was held off by the Piedmontese at the second battle of Goito on the following day, whereupon the exhausted garrison at Peschiera surrendered. None the less, Radetzky simply pulled his troops back to Mantua, rested them for a few days and then turned some of his forces eastwards to eliminate Durando at Vicenza. On 10 June the Austrians stormed the city and, after hours of fierce fighting (in which Massimo d'Azeglio was wounded in the leg), Durando capitulated. His men were allowed to march out of Vicenza with full military honours, but they had to withdraw south of the Po and promise not to fight for another three months. The Austrians could now concentrate on reducing Venice and defeating the Piedmontese.[120] The tide seemed to be turning Austria's way.

Then a figure who would soon become talismanic arrived on the scene: Giuseppe Garibaldi, who had been fighting in the service of republican causes in South America. On hearing the news of the revolutions in Italy, he and sixty-three other Italian revolutionaries set sail from the River Plate on 15 April, arriving in Nice (then part of the Kingdom of Sardinia and Garibaldi's birthplace) on 23 June, where he joined his Uruguayan wife, Anita Ribeiro da Silva, and their children. Moving on to Genoa, Garibaldi's plans were to join the forces of Charles Albert – the very man who had condemned him to death in 1834 – and to fight for what the republican sailor-turned-soldier saw as the common national cause. However,

> I made my way to Roverbella, which was then his headquarters, to offer him my services and those of my comrades. I met him and saw the distrust with which he received me; the hesitancy and indecision of the man to whom Italy's destiny had been entrusted made me grieve. I would have obeyed the King's orders as readily as I would have done in a republic . . . Carlo Alberto's position as King, the circumstances of the time, and the wish of the majority of Italians – all called on him to lead the war of redemption, a role for which he was

found wanting. He did not know how to use the immense forces under his command; he was indeed the principal cause of their destruction.[121]

The King certainly had his faults as a commander, but Garibaldi's judgement here is too harsh. The campaign was also undone by the skill and determination of the Austrian counter-attack, for which the old fox Radetzky could claim much of the credit. He was hampered early on by the lack of clear direction coming from Vienna. The political crisis in the imperial capital and uncertainty over the future of the rest of the empire initially made the government reluctant to commit itself to a full-scale campaign in Italy. There were also some ministers who believed that the Habsburgs should abandon Italy altogether, as they regarded the region as a strategic weak-point. Count Ficquelmont and the majority, however, were less keen on such a retreat. In April Vienna therefore chose to pursue a dual policy: diplomacy with Lombardy, with offers of autonomy in return for recognition of the Habsburg crown, while reconquering Venice. By early summer, Radetzky was still labouring under the burden of political uncertainty in Vienna. On 11 June Baron Johann Wessenberg, the Austrian foreign minister, sent orders to Radetzky to 'end the costly war in Italy' by negotiating a ceasefire on the basis of independence for Lombardy, though not Venetia, most of which had been recaptured. Radetzky, though, was now more confident that the situation on the ground was shifting in his favour: Nugent had arrived at Verona and Piedmont's allies had received severe maulings. He admitted that the position was still bad, but stressed that it was not so desperate that they had to concede to Italian rebels: 'We have sunk low, but by God, not yet so low that we should take orders from Casati.'[122] Thus, Radetzky disobeyed orders: he stubbornly refused to negotiate and eventually gained the support of some 'hawks' in Vienna, including Latour, the minister of war. Radetzky's arguments and Latour's backing swung the government, which at the end of June ordered the field marshal to move rapidly, expel Charles Albert from Lombardy and force their rebellious northern Italian subjects to submit.

V

One of the central problems with nationalism in 1848 – as in more recent times – was that it posed difficult questions about the relationships between nationalities and about the relationship between national aspirations and political liberties. Where these two questions fused was in the issue of Jewish emancipation. Many European nationalist ideologies had little difficulty in accommodating (on paper at least) a Jewish minority into their visions of new, liberal states. Indeed, a good rejoinder to those interpretations that see modern German history as a current flowing inexorably towards the Nazi gas chambers is that, for all its flagrant expansionism and sometimes illiberal undercurrents, in 1848 German nationalism gave rise to little anti-Semitism. Many German states had given Jews full civil rights several decades before (Prussia in 1812). The fact that both Heinrich von Gagern's successor as president of the Frankfurt parliament, Eduard Simson, and its vice-president, Gabriel Riesser, were Jewish (or of Jewish origin) attests to the prevailing lack of prejudice among the deputies; and Riesser was a vocal advocate of Jewish rights. German Jews from Bohemia also distinguished themselves by standing up for German interests in Bohemia against the Czechs: Ignaz Kuranda was editor of the *Grenzboten*, a newspaper that was particularly strident in its expressions of German nationalism.[123] Article 13 of the Basic Rights in the German constitution abolished religious requirements for civic rights, which essentially enfranchised the Jews. In the debate on this article, one liberal, Moritz Mohl, certainly tapped into classic anti-Semitic currents when he fretted that because of the international connections of the Jews, they could never be fully assimilated into the German people. While they should not be denied political rights, Mohl argued, the new Reich should have powers to pass laws that regulated their economic activities and encouraged Jews away from 'usury' into agriculture and other wholesome occupations. Significantly however, Mohl's speech was interrupted by hissing from all sides of the chamber and his motion received very little support. When Riesser (who sat on the centre-left) rose to reply immediately, he was supported by a Catholic centre-right deputy from Prussia, a Catholic jurist from Hesse and the Protestant spokesman for the parliament's constitutional committee. This was no aberration: support for Jewish emancipation cut across confessional and political divisions.[124]

This is not to say that anti-Semitism was unknown in German society; far from it. The half-million-strong Jewish population in Germany had been subjected to violence at the hands of rioting workers and peasants, their motives a coarse mix of religious prejudice and economic distress: in eighty towns across southern Germany, Jewish businesses were attacked,[125] since Jews were thought to cheat consumers with high prices (though, of course, the agrarian crisis was the real cause) and to be money-lenders who ruined impecunious peasants with punitive interest rates. This violence, however, was not supported by liberal opinion in Frankfurt. Indeed, one of the reservations expressed in the parliament about Article 13 was not that it was wrong in itself, but rather a concern over how it would go down among the wider, less enlightened populace. Yet the deputy who raised this anxiety – a Catholic priest named Georg Kautzer – still applauded the article and claimed that Jewish emancipation would start a process whereby popular prejudices would be eroded.[126]

In the Habsburg monarchy, Jews had been subject to discriminatory legislation, including the obligation to pay a special tax in return for being 'tolerated' in the empire and a ban on holding landed property. In Vienna only resident Jews could engage in business: others were allowed to stay in the capital for only three days at a time. Perhaps unsurprisingly, therefore, many Jews took the lead in the revolution in the capital: the young doctor whose inspirational speech had fired up the Viennese crowd on 13 March, Adolf Fischhof, was Jewish, and he emerged as one of the leaders of the revolution, becoming president of the Committee of Safety established after the 15 May uprising. Yet the revolutionary efforts of his co-religionists were often mocked by the Viennese, many of whom still regarded the Jews as usurers and petty tradesmen.

Pamphleteers offered anti-Semitic counter-blasts to Jewish petitions for emancipation. In the outburst of working-class violence
that set the industrial suburbs ablaze in the March revolution,
Jewish businesses were attacked. In other towns Jewish lives were
physically threatened: only the timely arrival of the student militia prevented a full-blooded pogrom in Raab. In Prague the
collapse of censorship brought anti-Semitic propaganda flooding
on to the streets, which encouraged workers' attacks on Jewish
retailers through the spring, climaxing on 1–2 May, when rioting
was unleashed against Jewish shopkeepers accused of overcharging
for their wares.[127] Understandably then, when Prague's June
insurrection came, the residents of the Jewish quarter barricaded
their streets not to support the uprising but to protect Jewish
neutrality in the struggle between the revolution and the counter-
revolution.

Such were the openly visceral currents of anti-Semitism in the
Austrian Empire that when Baron Franz Pillersdorf's original draft
of the constitution of 25 April guaranteed freedom of religion to all
people he was urged by the Lower Austrian Estates to limit this provision only to Christian denominations, 'not on principle, but on
account of popular feeling'.[128] It was to be left to the parliament
itself to decide on the rights of non-Christians, but that proved to
be too short-lived to address the issue. When the constitution was
torn up after the reaction, the provisions guaranteeing religious toleration were retained, but they still excluded the Jews, who had to
wait until 1868 before they were liberated from all restrictions in
Austria.

In Hungary the April Laws failed to enfranchise the Jewish population, reflecting elite anxieties over a dark wave of popular
anti-Semitism that swept the country in the spring of 1848 – and
much of the violence was committed by workers against Jewish
premises, forcing the authorities to bring out the National Guard
to protect their owners. The spark was the proposal in the
Hungarian Diet on 21 March to give the franchise in municipal
elections to anyone who was sufficiently wealthy, regardless of religion. Anti-Semitic violence was unleashed in Pressburg, where

Jews were beaten up and their shops smashed. The rioting then spread to other towns, climaxing in early April. The consequence was that most liberals in the Diet reluctantly agreed – over Kossuth's protests – that to pacify this popular rage the enfranchisement of the Jews should be delayed.[129] There were, however, further outbreaks soon afterwards: in Budapest on 19 April (miraculously) no one was reported killed, though plenty were wounded when 'the lower classes of the people armed with sticks, knives and axes' fell on the city's Jews, with the apparent aim of expelling them from the city. In Pressburg some ten Jews were lynched and a further forty wounded. Although both Batthyány and Kossuth were horrified, they also felt that further concessions to the mob would save lives: as Kossuth put it, any more pressure for emancipation would send Hungarian Jews to the slaughterhouse. On 25 April, therefore, Jews were 'excused' from military service – in other words, their services were not required for the National Guard. This was a reversal of the more radical Budapest Committee of Public Safety's rejection on 18 March of an anti-Semitic petition demanding that Jews be expelled from the militia. Led by Petőfi, the radicals simply formed a special battalion for Jews. They accused the Germans (the 'the blind tools of the overthrown regime') and the dregs of the working class of being behind the anti-Semitic violence. These were judgements prompted by embarrassment and a strong sense that the pogroms were casting the revolution into disrepute; or, as Petőfi put it, throwing 'mud at the virgin flag of 15 March'.[130] While it is true that Germans did take the lead in some of the violence, there is no evidence that the anti-Semitism was motivated by counter-revolution or that it was merely carried out by an underclass of the urban poor. Rather, it was economically motivated and committed by otherwise respectable members of the artisanal guilds who resented the quiet immigration of Jews into the towns, setting up shop alongside and in competition with their Magyar and German-speaking rivals. Jews would in fact prove to be fiercely loyal to the liberal regime in Hungary – so much so that Slavs for years afterwards would equate Jews with rampant Magyar nationalism.

Ultimately, in 1849, while Jews were among those fighting for Hungarian independence, the Diet would be true to its own ideals and fully emancipate them. Kossuth saw the Jews no differently from the other ethnic minorities of Hungary: they would be content with their status as free citizens in a state where they shared exactly the same rights as all the others. In such circumstances, they would have no need of special treatment as a separate national or religious group. As Kossuth put it, the Jews themselves must prepare for their own emancipation by agreeing that living under separate institutions governed by Mosaic law was not, after all, an essential part of their identity.[131] This was much the same as the German liberal view, but Jewish emancipation and assimilation into the liberal state created something of a crisis within their own communities, where more traditionally minded Jews feared that their separate sense of identity would be gradually erased.[132]

The year 1848 in Central Europe therefore posited one of the great dilemmas of the modern, liberal state: should ethnic or religious minorities be obliged to assimilate fully into the political order, effacing in public life any sense of identity other than that of being a citizen, or should the state rest on pluralism (or multiculturalism), which allows all groups to express their own sense of separateness fully, but within a consensus that is supposed to guarantee mutual respect and the rule of law? There is no easy answer: the first option threatens to ride roughshod over religious and ethnic sensibilities; the second raises the spectre of a fragmented civic order. French republicans, however, had no doubts: since Jews had been fully emancipated in 1791, they were also citizens of the new republic. Nevertheless, one of the traditional flashpoints of anti-Semitism – Alsace – still flared up. This region was exceptional in France for this type of violence in 1848; it arose due to the peasants and workers identifying Jews with usury and economic competition. As a frontier province, it was also an area where people were on a particularly short fuse during the economic distress because they witnessed the ease with which food was still being exported[133] – and Jews were unfairly blamed for that. In early March peasants in upper Alsace ransacked and burned Jewish homes and synagogues, forcing their occupants to take refuge in Switzerland. In Altkirch there was evidence that the local elites turned a blind eye and even actively encouraged the violence. According to one of the Jewish leaders, the root cause was

> straightforward religious prejudice and resentment of usury, yet in the village of Oberdorf, peasants fell on the Jews, even though they were almost all indigent there . . . moreover, everywhere the attacks began with the synagogues, yet the synagogues have nothing to do with commerce or usury. For the greater part of the inhabitants here, all issues can be reduced to a matter of religion: people here are Catholic or Protestant rather than Republicans, Philippistes [i.e., Orléanists], or Legitimists.

A cluster of Jewish refugees in Porrentruy appealed, successfully, to the republican values of the new regime: 'If there was ever a time for tolerance and legal protection for all religions, as well as respect for people and for property . . . it is certainly at the present time, now that the Nation has just constituted itself freely and spontaneously as a Republic.' Adolphe Crémieux, now minister of justice and religions, promised material help to the Jewish refugees and to pursue the authors of 'those savage assaults'. To the provisional government's commissioner in Colmar, he wrote: 'I am stupefied to learn that in France, in old Alsace, in a country so full of patriotism, that there should be enough miserable people who can attack citizens whose only crime is to be Jewish.' To the Jews, he promised that they would find justice in the law courts, but the government also sent in the army, for 'the government has no greater desire, no more pressing interest, than in protecting the property and lives of citizens'. The column that repressed the anti-Semitic violence in Altkirch was led by a certain Louis Eugène Cavaignac, a general who had impeccably republican credentials but who in the summer would gain some notoriety.[134]

While most of the revolutions, with varying degrees of success, sought to grant civil equality to the Jews, they also went some way to emancipation in the colonial empires. The most important measure was the definitive abolition of slavery in the French Empire. Slavery had been decreed illegal once before – by the First Republic in 1794 – but Napoleon Bonaparte had bowed to planter interests in the French Caribbean colonies and tried to reimpose it in 1802. He was successful in the islands of Guadeloupe and Martinique, but signally failed in Haiti, where the emancipated slaves fought victoriously for their independence. With the revolutionary example of Haiti (and that of the British islands, where slavery had been abolished in 1833), the persistence of the institution in the remaining French colonies was harder to justify to its opponents. Under the July Monarchy, which upheld slavery as a 'property right', republicans like Victor Schoelcher and Ledru-Rollin had made anti-slavery one of their causes. The former wrote eloquently against the institution, while the latter delivered a thunderous speech in favour of abolition in April 1847. Schoelcher became the Second Republic's minister of the navy and, through that, had responsibility for the overseas colonies. On 27 April he carried the decree freeing the slaves in the French Empire: 87,000 on Guadeloupe, 74,000 in Martinique. These people joined the colonial elites, which included the whites and the free blacks (who, though educated and relatively prosperous, still faced racial discrimination), in formally becoming French citizens, with the right to vote. In the first elections Schoelcher would lead the list of candidates on both islands – and be elected in all six seats.[135]

The Danes and the Swedes also abolished slavery in their Caribbean islands (the Swedes still held Saint Barthélemy in 1848). Yet there was no serious talk of abandoning empire itself: the Dutch parliament certainly asserted some control over the Netherlands' overseas colonies, but the commerce itself remained a monopoly of the crown. Algeria remained a French colony (it was first invaded in 1830 in a desperate attempt by the last Bourbon king, Charles X, to curry popularity with an overseas adventure), and while the European colonists were given the right to vote, the indigenous population was not.

Another serious limitation to the 'Springtime of Peoples' was that it did little to emancipate women. Nowhere in Europe did they receive the right to vote, primarily because there was a persistent prejudice against it not only among most men but among many women, who had internalised the prevailing views of gender difference. Mid-nineteenth-century European society generally held that women were naturally predisposed to the domestic sphere: they were the nurturer of their children, the virtuous wife and the 'angel of the hearth'. They were thought to be best protected by being under male authority, be it their father or their husband. Politics were best left to men, who were deemed to be more rational than women and so were naturally attuned to public life, an arena into which women were not meant to stray. Typical of even the left-wing revolutionaries in this respect was the Mainz democrat Ludwig Bamberger, who spoke out against women's 'perfumed slavery' but asked, 'Who wants to eradicate differences which are present in nature?' Either sex, he argued, should get involved only 'as is appropriate to its nature'.[136] Even those rare voices that supported women's emancipation could not always be said to be full-blown supporters of gender equality: a Hessian democrat declared that depriving women of the vote was akin to denying them the pleasures of 'cooking, sewing, knitting, darning, dancing and playing'.[137]

Yet women did participate in the politics of the revolution in different ways; and, in the process, they challenged the limits to emancipation in 1848. Women almost everywhere (and of almost all social backgrounds) took part – usually in various supporting roles – in the street-fighting in the revolutions of February–March. Working-class women would also participate in later insurrections: in June in Paris and Prague, and in the radical uprisings in the Rhineland in 1849. In Paris women helped to build the barricades, and they carried food, messages and ammunition to the fighters – often by hiding these items in hollowed-out bread or in the bottom of milk canisters. The iconography of French women bearing flags on the barricades is no myth: two *parisiennes* were cut down by the National Guard as they did just that on 23 June 1848. The women of the barricades in Prague left a deep impression on posterity, as symbols of the heroism and sacrifice of Slav women.

Women were also important observers of the events, offering

influential commentary on the revolutions: to cite but a few examples, under the pseudonym of Daniel Stern, Marie d'Agoult wrote a history of the 1848 revolution in France that remains an important source; in Germany, Fanny Lewald penned a series of influential letters on the revolution; in Italy, the American journalist Margaret Fuller became, in effect, the United States' first war correspondent when she reported on the events in Rome for Horace Greeley's *New York Tribune*.[138] In Paris the socialist Eugénie Niboyet established a feminist newspaper called the *Voice of Women*. The Czech writer Božena Němcová sympathised with the plight of the poor, deplored anti-Semitism, opposed German nationalism and urged women's emancipation through education: 'We women have remained far behind the age, behind the banner of freedom and culture. Let us confess this, let us not be ashamed, for the fault is not with us, but with those who have completely neglected the education of people, and left the guidance of the female sex utterly to chance.'[139] Such voices were those of the politically engaged writer, not the detached observer.

. Women also formed, or joined, political clubs. In Paris the 'Fraternal Association of Both Sexes' admitted men and women as equals, while the Club of the Emancipation of Women and the Union of Women pressed for women's rights – generally not to political enfranchisement, but to education, divorce, a control over their own property – and for a system of national workshops that provided work for unemployed women as well as for men. Meanwhile, radical clubs, such as the Montagnard Club and Adolphe Blanqui's Central Republican Society, also admitted women, although most socialist clubs allowed women to attend but not to speak. In 1849–51 women played a role in distributing radical propaganda across the French countryside – by allowing their homes to be used as meeting places for the radicals and by reading left-wing newspapers aloud to the illiterate. Thousands of German women collected money for the popular cause of a German navy, while women's clubs were established in cities such as Berlin, Mannheim and Mainz. In the Rhineland women were admitted to some democratic clubs from the summer of 1848, while mass meetings held in rural areas were well attended by them. In Mainz Kathinka Zitz-Halein created the Humania Association in May 1849 because Bamberger's Democratic Association did not allow women to speak. Its purpose was to support 'needy patriots' with money, clothing, bandages and nursing during the radical insurrection that summer. Similar organisations appeared in Saxony, Nassau, Frankfurt and Heidelberg. The middle-class women of Prague founded the Club of Slavic Women to promote women's education; it organised two public meetings in August 1848 to protest against the Austrian military occupation of the city. The second of these sent a delegation to Vienna which secured the release of some political prisoners who had been held since the insurrection in June. While, to modern eyes, such activities seem scarcely to have scratched the surface of inequality, to conservatives they were viewed as especially dangerous. On 17 March 1849 the Austrian government handed down a law on associations, banning women's political activities of all kinds in the Habsburg Empire. It was even to be illegal for women to join political meetings as quiet observers.

Some women went so far as to try to stand in elections. In Paris in May 1849 Jeanne Déroin attempted to stand as a socialist candidate. The government declared her candidacy unconstitutional, warning that none of her votes would be counted. Her supporters among the left-wing republicans therefore backtracked, but it was an important symbolic moment in French politics. The great writer George Sand took a more Fabian approach to women's political enfranchisement: she argued in April 1848 that women would some day participate in politics, but society had to change first. Until that happened, women would be too dependent upon marriage and too subjugated by laws that reinforced male authority within the family to act truly independently in politics. She therefore distanced herself from her admirers who proposed her candidacy for the upcoming elections. The task of the Second Republic was not to give women the right to vote, she argued, but to improve women's status within the family first.[140] This was a curious argument from someone who worked closely with Ledru-Rollin, the Republic's minister of the interior.

VI

The events of 1848 appeared to provide an unprecedented opportunity for European liberals to realise their long-nurtured goals for national unity or independence. Moreover, the sudden collapse of the old governments offered some nationalities the chance to give political expression to their identities for the very first time. Yet the various nationalisms were riven by both internal divisions and conflicts with one another. The former problem was perhaps most glaring in Italy, where many patriots fought less for national unity than for the liberties of their own state: Venice, Lombardy, Tuscany, Sicily and so on. Loyalties could be even more localised than that: the inhabitants of the small towns and cities of the *terra firma* in Venetia regarded the preponderance of Venice itself with suspicion and even hostility. In Tuscany the port city of Livorno resented the capital, Florence, which provoked instability later. Civic pride – *campanilismo* (love of one's own *campanile*, or bell-tower) – still had a deep and widespread appeal; by comparison a sense of a wider, 'Italian' identity seemed too abstract. Moreover, the existing rulers of the Italian states were reluctant to countenance any form of unification that undermined their own dynastic interests, and they held the trump cards: their armed forces, which allowed Charles Albert to dictate terms to the revolutionaries and which other rulers provided and withdrew according to their own interests. At times, Mazzini must have felt like tearing out his hair and beard. To cite another example, the Polish radicals, who in exile had formulated a vision of a unitary, democratic Polish state, came up against the more pragmatic but less ambitious provincialism of the patriotic movement on the ground in Poznania and Galicia. The Polish elites who provided the local leadership of the national movement had their own social interests to defend and felt that their cause would be best served by working first with their Prussian and Austrian rulers for reform, before trying to piece Poland together again. Even in Germany, where nationalism had spread more broadly among the population, the liberals had little or no experience of working within a national framework. Respect for the individual states was still deep-rooted throughout German society, and the revolutionaries carried with them a complex baggage of state and regional loyalties, religious denomination and economic interests, all of which coloured their opinions on the bigger national issues of 1848.[141]

The 'Forty-Eighters' were also confronted with the fact that their own national aspirations conflicted with those of other ethnic groups, whether they were neighbouring peoples or minorities within the presumptive state. When they responded, the revolutionaries found it very hard to look at the 'national question' from any perspective other than that of their own national interests. Even Friedrich Engels, Karl Marx's intellectual partner, argued in 1852 that Bohemia 'could only exist henceforth, as a portion of Germany', dismissing the very idea of Czech nationality as 'dying according to every fact known in history for the last four hundred years'.[142] Engels was driven by the sense that the Slavs of the Austrian Empire were essentially counter-revolutionaries, since, when their national interests conflicted with those of the Germans and Hungarians, they turned to the Habsburgs for support. He was sympathetic to the Poles, and in the same article he denounced the travesty inflicted on them by the Prussians in 1848, but the apostle of communism had little sympathy for 'those numerous small relics of peoples which, after having figured for a longer or shorter period on the stage of history, were finally absorbed as integral portions into one or the other of those more powerful nations'. Yet precisely those nationalities were giving political expression to their aspirations in 1848, sometimes for the first time. For Engels, some nationalities were doomed by history to be subject peoples, since they had neither the culture nor the strength to survive independently. This intellectual position – a version of the 'threshold principle' of nationality, which argues that a particular ethnic group becomes a 'nation' when it is large and powerful enough to sustain itself – allowed Engels to support German national interests against the Czechs and even to demand the restoration of Poland, but only if it was at the expense of the peoples further to the east – Lithuanians, Belarussians and Ukrainians – not the Germans.[143]

One of the tragedies of 1848 was therefore that it marked the moment when European liberalism explicitly surrendered itself to its darker, nationalist impulses. This was primarily because, when the conflicting strategic and territorial interests of competing national aspirations became clear, most liberals threw their weight behind the desires or needs of their own nationality. They rarely admitted the perspective of the other ethnic groups, since that would have meant implicitly recognising that there was some good reason behind these rival aspirations. So, instead, the liberals generally preferred to deny to other peoples the very rights and freedoms that they claimed for themselves. The conflicts that thus arose had long-term consequences for the development of nationalism in Europe. Experts frequently distinguish between 'civic' and 'ethnic' forms of national identity. The 'civic' type defines the nation politically, as a matter of explicit or implicit choice by its individual citizens to live together as a nation: as the French scholar Ernest Renan famously declared in 1882, the nation is a tacit 'daily plebiscite'.[144] The nation here is simply a political community: one's nationality is defined by one's desire to share equal political and civil rights with other citizens and to live under the same laws that govern that particular state. This form of nationalism has the capacity, of course, to absorb as fully fledged citizens different ethnic groups, whose new nationality is meant to transcend, if not efface altogether, their original identity. 'Ethnic' nationalism glories in the shared cultural roots and heritage of a people enjoying a common descent from a particular ancestry, real or mythical. One remained 'organically' part of a particular nation, whatever one did and wherever one went. Ties of 'blood' and 'culture' are often invoked to justify or explain this immutable sense of belonging. In this definition foreigners who lived within the boundaries of the state but could not claim to share the same ethnicity or 'race' as the indigenous people could never be full citizens. As authorities such as Anne-Marie Thiesse and Anthony D. Smith have suggested, all European national identities in practice have elements of both the civic and ethnic forms of nationalism, albeit in different combinations. As Smith puts it, the two forms represent 'the profound dualism at the heart of every nationalism'.[145]

This point is well illustrated by the case of liberal Hungarian nationalism in 1848, which initially made its territorial claims through a form of civic nationalism, but ultimately assumed an ethnic, more exclusively Magyar form of identity. Liberals like Kossuth tried to argue that the non-Magyar nationalities should be satisfied with enjoying equal rights as citizens of the new order, rather than claim any special national status within it. This was, in other words, an attempt to resolve the problem of national minorities with an appeal to civic nationalism, a call for the non-Magyar groups to choose to be Hungarian citizens. But beneath this was an assumption that the Magyars would dominate the liberal state and that the non-Magyars would assimilate into it. In the long run it was even hoped that these nationalities might eventually adopt the Magyar language and identity. Consequently, assimilation into the liberal order in Hungary therefore assumed the superiority of Magyar identity and the eventual lapse of other forms of national identity within the historic 'Crownlands of Saint Stephen'. Since the promise of equal rights as individuals was understandably wholly inadequate for most Romanian and Slav nationalists, who had little faith that their own national identities would be sufficiently protected, they reacted by emphasising their own, distinct ethnic identities, which in turn prompted a reaction among Magyars. This process led ethnic definitions of nationalism to be ever more firmly embedded. In effect it represented the failure of the emerging constitutional order to resolve the problem of the national minorities within it.

French nationalism is usually regarded as a model of the civic type, and it may be viewed as an exception in 1848, in that it was not pushed towards a more ethnic position. This may have been due largely to circumstances, since France – despite the pressure of radicals – remained within its existing boundaries and did not face any serious ethnic challenges within its territory. Republicans universally condemned attacks on the Jews, who by virtue of the revolution of 1789 were deemed to be citizens like everyone else. It is also true that French republicans – particularly those on the left – never lost their zeal in 1848–9 to liberate all the subjugated peoples of Europe. Even so, this messianic dream assumed the superiority of the French model of democracy and national self-determination. Moreover, lurking behind this cosmopolitanism were the old territorial pretensions to France's 'natural frontiers', lost in 1815, which involved absorbing Belgium and the Rhineland. Such annexations would necessarily have posed the problem of assimilating the Flemish- and German-speaking inhabitants of those territories and may have created for the Second Republic difficulties of a similar type to those faced by liberal Hungary. Fortunately, in 1848 there was no new war of French revolutionary expansion, so French republican nationalism was able to hold fast to its civic impulses, offering equal rights to all its citizens regardless of confessional or (in the case of the Bretons and an ever-increasing immigrant population from the nineteenth century onwards) ethnic origins. The two cases of Hungarian and French nationalism in 1848 suggest that all expressions of nationalism, whether 'ethnic' or 'civic', were potentially aggressive and exclusive. This 'civic' ideal was rooted firmly in the assumption that nationality was a matter of choice – a decision by the individual citizen to live under a particular state and obey its laws, but in return to enjoy the civil and political rights of citizenship. The price of this assimilation into the civic order was that, in their relationship with the state (as voters, as soldiers, as officials, as pupils in state schools, for instance), individuals had to put their identity as citizens of the whole country first. Their sense of belonging in religious, class, provincial and even ethnic terms had to come second – and preferably a distant second – behind that. These other forms of identity, which threatened to fragment the civic order, had to be relegated to the citizens' private lives.

It was different in Central and Eastern Europe, where nationalism became based on a more exclusive 'ethnic' or 'cultural' sense of identity, rooted variously in a common language, religion and historic claims to ties of 'blood' or 'race'. This – almost inevitably – involved denying the rights of citizenship to those people who lived within the boundaries of the putative state, but who were not held to be part of the same ethnic group – like Jews in Hungary until 1849. Otherwise – as with Hungarian nationalism in 1848 in relation to the Romanians and the Slavs – it insisted that in practice those people had to accept the privileged position of the language and culture of the politically and socially dominant nationality. This development, which can be seen at work in 1848, did not occur because Eastern and Central Europeans were more bigoted than their Western contemporaries. Rather, it happened because of the historical and political circumstances, which were also clearly exerting their influence during the revolutions of that year. While Western European states like France, Britain and Spain have had (more or less in the case of the first) stable territorial boundaries for the last two centuries, those countries in the East and Centre have not. In 1848 nationalists there were faced with the thorny task of carving new states out of multi-national empires. The boundaries of their presumptive countries were not set and where there were historical memories of long-lost borders, these could now be challenged by other national groups. With the fluidity of the frontiers and the overlapping claims of rival nationalities to the same territory, the inhabitants of these regions faced an uncertain political future. In 1848 a Transylvanian Romanian, for example, was politically a subject of the Habsburg Emperor, but was at the same time claimed as a Hungarian citizen by the Magyar liberals and hailed as a fellow citizen by the Romanian revolutionaries in Moldavia and Wallachia, who were in turn technically subjects of the Turkish sultan. The Romanians of 1848 were, in short, a stateless nation, like the Poles, the Ruthenians and the various other Slav peoples of the Habsburg monarchy. In the absence of a state of their own, which might have ruled over a clearly defined territory with settled political boundaries, the thread of continuity in the life of the nation – running through all the changes in foreign overlordship and conquest – became the culture of the people, its language, its religion, its shared history and its sense of common bloodlines. The germs of this idea, however, would bear its bitter fruit right up to the late twentieth century and, in the Balkans at least, it might continue to do so unless a 'post-national' solution is found to the problems posed by the emergence of new nation-states there. The brutality of the Second World War in Eastern Europe and the ethnic cleansing witnessed in the fragmenting Yugoslavia in the 1990s were distant but horribly resonant echoes of the darker side of the nationalism of 1848.

The Springtime of Peoples crystallised and sharpened national differences. The conflicts that constantly arose would dog attempts at European nation-building deep into the twentieth century. They also split the European liberal revolutions of 1848, eventually giving the counter-revolution the opportunity it needed to set them against one another. These ethnic conflicts were all the sharper where, as was often the case in Eastern Europe, the national tensions coincided with social divisions: the Ukrainians of Galicia could be turned by the Habsburgs against the Poles not only (or even primarily) because of ethic differences but because the latter were landlords while the former were frequently their serfs. The national conflicts alone presented the liberal revolutions with a gargantuan obstacle to overcome in the construction of a constitutional order. Yet, adding to the pressure, they were also beset by internal political and social challenges that threatened to polarise politics and poison social relations. Almost tangible fears of a renewed revolution, this time social rather than political in nature, grew more intense as spring gave way to summer. In those middle months of the year the liberal revolutions were contorted in an agony of social conflict from which they would never recover.

4

THE RED SUMMER

At 11 a.m. on 15 May, up to twenty thousand members of the radical clubs of Paris set off from the Place de la Bastille towards the National Assembly. They were led by Aloysius Huber, the president of the central coordinating body of the radical organisations, the Club des Clubs. The demonstration was on behalf of Poland, whose revolution had just been snuffed out in Poznania and on the streets of Kraków. Huber and most of the steering committee had insisted on a peaceful demonstration. The Executive Commission, the new government chosen by the recently elected National Assembly, was well aware of the plans. It chose not to provoke a confrontation by a strong demonstration of force, although the legislature itself would be defended by the militia. This restraint probably ensured that the day turned out to be bloodless. It could so easily have been different. When the marchers reached the Palais Bourbon, where the legislature met, some three thousand club members poured into the chamber. 'I could never have imagined that such a mass of human voices could make such an immense noise,' wrote an astounded Tocqueville, who was sitting in his deputy's seat.[1] Lamartine strode up and down as he made a futile effort to parley with the invaders. As the crowd's discipline evaporated, Alexandre Raspail – whose fiery petition had been hastily adopted by the demonstration because Huber had absent-mindedly left the official one behind – strode into the chamber and read out his address. He could scarcely be heard above the din.

The situation went from bad to worse when the pallid revolutionary socialist Louis-Auguste Blanqui rose to the tribune. Blanqui had been one of the most dedicated of republican conspirators: along with Armand Barbès, he had been sentenced to death after the abortive uprising in 1839. This was commuted to life imprisonment after a public outcry, in which Lamartine and Victor Hugo had taken the lead. Blanqui (who at his death in 1881 had spent a grand total of thirty-three years in captivity, earning the nickname 'l'Enfermé', or 'the Incarcerated') was under house arrest in Blois when the revolution broke out. On his release, he returned to Paris, where he established the Central Republican Society, with the aim of pressing for an insurrection that would bring about a social revolution. Tocqueville, who was seeing him for his first and only time, wrote that Blanqui had 'gaunt and withered cheeks, white lips . . . a dirty pallor, a mildewed appearance, no visible white linen, an old frock-coat stuck to his pockmarked and emaciated limbs; he seemed to have been living in a sewer and just come out of it'.[2] Given Blanqui's politics and character – uncompromising, austere, violent, sometimes sarcastic, socialist and revolutionary – it is scarcely surprising that moderates should have recoiled. Yet he had good cause to have a sinister appearance: his wife had died while he was in prison, and ever since he had worn black from head to toe, without even a white shirt to diminish his mourning; even his hands were sheathed in black gloves. Blanqui had political talents that gained him fervent admirers on the left: 'his incisive, penetrating and reflective words . . . cut clinically like the blade of a knife'.[3] The loyalty that he could inspire among his supporters had been tested in April, however, when the journalist Jules Taschereau (one of the moderates who in February had moved the banquet away from the 12th Arrondissement) published a document that purported to show that Blanqui had betrayed his comrades back in 1839. Barbès, who had fallen out with Blanqui during the uprising of that year and had thrown his weight behind the provisional government, readily accepted Blanqui's guilt. The latter hit back with a fervent denial – 'you are attacking me for my revolutionary inflexibility and my single-minded devotion to my ideals'[4] – which sold a hundred thousand copies. His club rallied around him: some six hundred members gathered outside his home and carried him triumphantly back to their meeting-place with shouts of 'Down with the *National!*' How genuine the Taschereau document was has never been firmly established. And while it certainly damaged Blanqui's reputation, it clearly did not shake the loyalty of his hard-core supporters. Armed with this, he continued to inspire fear among his opponents.

Now, on 15 May, he demanded that Poland be restored, but when he had said his piece, he was, according to one eyewitness, surrounded by 'many men with sinister faces' who shook their fists and yelled, 'Rouen! Rouen! Speak of Rouen!'[5] – a reference to a massacre of workers at the hands of the authorities in the Norman city in April. The chaos then descended into full-blown anarchy, as speakers including Barbès demanded, variously: immediate war on behalf of Poland; the outlawing of those who were 'traitors' to the fatherland; the sacking of the new, conservative ministers; and the creation of a special committee to oversee the new government. As the National Guard finally arrived to clear the chamber of the invaders, a demonstrator impulsively threatened to kill the president of the National Assembly unless the militia withdrew. Huber, losing his cool in the heat of the moment, forgot his earlier efforts to ensure that the demonstration would be peaceful and shook his fist at the president, shouting that the National Assembly had betrayed the people and was thereby 'dissolved'. This left an opening for the demonstrators to declare a new government made up of the republican left, including Barbès, Louis Blanc, Ledru-Rollin, Caussidière and Albert. When the chamber was cleared by the National Guards, some three to four hundred people led by Barbès moved on to the Hôtel de Ville and began issuing decrees. When, at last, the National Guards finally arrived, Barbès told them that he was too busy to be arrested since he was now a government minister. Unimpressed, the

Guards marched him off to the château at Vincennes, where he was imprisoned along with Albert, Raspail and Huber. Blanqui managed to give the police the slip and remained at large until 26 May. The *journée* of 15 May was over: what had started as an orderly demonstration had degenerated into a near riot that may have been a clumsy attempt at a *coup d'état*. It finished as a farce, but a farce that would have tragic repercussions for the Second Republic.[6]

If there was any single day that was a European-wide turning point in 1848, it was 15 May. Besides this 'red' surge in Paris, the day saw the *Stürmpetition* in Vienna, and in both cases the radicals had tried to push the revolution further to the left, but merely succeeded in provoking a conservative backlash. The other event of that day – the counter-revolution in Naples – had also been provoked by fear of radicalism. Lurking beneath this fear were deep-rooted anxieties that the revolution would not stop at its political victories, but would slide into the terror of social conflict. The March days in Vienna had seen workers burning down factories and plundering shops. In Prague Czech liberals were still haunted by the working-class riots of 1844, in which the authorities lost control of entire districts for a week. The most politically militant workers in Europe were usually the skilled craftsmen of the artisan workshops, rather than the proletariat of the factories or railways, because the former had greater literacy, their own trade organisations and traditions of social and even political behaviour. Their independence was also threatened by the rise of industrial technology, the factory system and new, cheaper ways of organising production. In 1848 workers' demands for protection from these forms of competition were beginning to be coupled with more forward-looking elements drawn from socialist ideas. In France cities such as Paris, Lyon, Rouen and Limoges were replete with such politically conscious workers, but they were also active in Germany, particularly in Saxony, Württemberg, Prussia, Frankfurt and the Rhineland. In Italian cities artisans and craftsmen provided a fertile ground not so much for new socialist ideas as for Mazzini's republican propaganda. In Vienna the workers had not developed their own political programme, but by following the lead of students and journalists, they provided the proletarian muscle behind the middle-class radical movement.

Working-class militancy and the radical left seemed to endanger not only the nobles and well-heeled bourgeois, but anyone who had property, including the landowning peasantry and the more prosperous artisans. Tocqueville, who in mid-March returned to his native Normandy to campaign for election to the Constituent Assembly, found that among his rural constituents 'fear, which initially was confined to the upper reaches of society, descended into the depths of the popular classes, and a universal terror took hold of the entire region'.[7] The spectre of social revolution piqued the innate conservatism of those who had gained in different ways from the February and March revolutions, but for whom the time had come for stability. Yet, in the end, it proved impossible at one and the same time to preserve the political gains of the 1848 revolutions and to restore 'order'. Terror (in many places, the word is not too strong) of further revolutionary violence, of social upheaval and of 'socialism' itself proved to be stronger than attachment to the liberal victories of the spring. When faced with the choice between holding on to their new political liberties or conserving their lives, their property and their communities against 'anarchy' or 'communism', most people chose to sacrifice their freedom for the sake of security. The social fear provoked by left-wing activism therefore played into the hands of conservatives, as liberals, moderates and the uncommitted abandoned much of the middle ground and sought to repress the danger of a second revolution by resorting to more authoritarian methods. The 'red summer' polarised the revolution between left and right, creating an irreparable fracture that gave the conservatives the chance to strike back.

I

In Paris the moderate republicans had willingly recognised the 'popular' nature of the February revolution and congratulated themselves and the Parisian workers for keeping good order in the city. Yet socialist ideas had come frothing to the surface. Workers organised themselves into political clubs, led by the radical republicans and socialists. This popular movement was determined not to see a repeat of the 1830 revolution, from which they had drawn no benefits. There was, consequently, an explosion of working-class political participation in clubs that aimed to influence the progress of the revolution. The Paris area alone in March and April counted some two hundred such 'popular societies',[8] in which workers debated the 'democratic and social republic' – a new regime that would not only give them political liberties but would take an active role in ordering society so that poverty and the harsh realities of working-class life would be eliminated. Thus, the republican left rapidly took on the label 'democratic socialist' – they were the *démoc-socs*. On 25 February, a petition to the provisional government had demanded 'a guaranteed right to work', 'an assured minimum for the worker and his family in case of sickness' and the 'organisation of labour',[9] by which was generally meant the state-sponsored reform of working conditions, wages and industrial relations and the creation of workshops run by the workers themselves. To nineteenth-century liberals soaked in laissez-faire economics, these demands seemed dangerously socialist and economically counter-productive. As the owner of the moderate newspaper *Le Constitutionnel* recalled, 'the day following the February Revolution, the bourgeois of Paris trembled for his head, and, once he was sure of retaining it, he trembled for his purse'.[10]

The provisional government had applied some practical solutions to ease the workers' economic desperation, but the answers proved insufficient to meet either the depth of misery or the more ambitious aspirations of the left. Although not intended to be controversial, the decision that would end in the greatest bitterness of all was the establishment, on 25 February, of the National Workshops, promising to 'guarantee work for all citizens' by providing employment in (often tedious) public works for the poor. It was the most obvious solution to a government whose composition would neither permit a radical, socialist response to the problem of unemployment nor allow the free market to take its own course. In response to a workers' protest on 28 February, the government also established a labour commission in the old Chamber of Peers at the Luxembourg Palace, presided over by Blanc and Albert. Consisting of delegates from the various trades, the 'Luxembourg Commission' was meant to address the concerns of workers and artisans, so it became their forum and rallying point. In fact, most of their demands showed little evidence of socialism, but rather reflected the familiar concerns of artisans beleaguered by the accelerating rate of social and economic change: higher wages, a minimum rate for goods produced, better working conditions, the right to organise unions, the creation of an arbitration system for industrial relations, the abolition of *marchandage* (or subcontracting, which was exploitative because the subcontractor maximised his profits by paying lower salaries to his workers), the restriction of the use of machinery and of competition from women and unskilled workers (who commanded lower wages), the creation of National Workshops for each profession and state support for industry. On the first day that the commission met – and with the agreement of employers' representatives – it banned *marchandage* and reduced the working day from an average of fifteen hours to ten in Paris and eleven in the provinces. An arbitration committee of ten workers and ten employers was also created to deal with industrial disputes.

Underlying the government's difficulties was a budget crisis that had catastrophic effects on tax revenue. The new regime was determined, for the sake of financial stability, to honour the deficit. It quickly paid the interest owed, but could do so only by increasing direct taxation by 45 per cent – which was immediately dubbed the 'forty-five centimes'. This, of course, angered much of the property-owning population, who were already struggling in the harsh economic climate. While the government had compelling fiscal reasons for the surtax, it seemed to those hit by it that they were paying for the National Workshops. Combined with the fear of social revolution, the resentment set the battle lines for the collision between the radicals and the moderates.

The Parisian 'insurrection' of 15 May was the catalyst for the final descent towards a bloody confrontation. Republican sympathies for Poland ('the France of the North') were sincere, but it was also a cause that could mobilise popular support in an attempt to inject new life into the revolutionary left. The *démoc-socs* certainly needed a good dose of restorative adrenaline, for they had taken a battering at the polls in the elections of 23 April. Of 900 seats, no more than 150 were left-leaning. A central block of around 500 were moderate republicans, while on the right were 250 who were either Legitimists (royalists who supported the old Bourbon dynasty) or Orléanists. Since the elections were based on universal male suffrage, the vast majority of voters were peasants. The results therefore partially reflected the continued influence of the landed elites: on election day, Tocqueville led some 170 of 'his' Norman villagers to the polls, where, as he noted coyly, 'I have reason to believe that they almost all voted for the same candidate.'[11] Many peasants supported their local worthies, but their votes went beyond simple deference, reflecting their deep resentment at the 'forty-five centimes'. One rural newspaper declared that the hard-pressed rural folk were 'tired of nourishing . . . lazy men who . . . make a trade of avoiding work'.[12] The vote also expressed widespread anxieties over disorder, which naturally led men to vote for moderates or conservatives rather than those who promised even more social upheaval. It was therefore indicative of the failure of the radical republicans to reach out to the wider population – and the fact that the elections were held only two months after the February revolution ensured that they had little time in which to win converts.

The election results dealt a serious blow to left-wing hopes for a democratic and social republic. The unemployed urban workers also feared, with good reason, for the existence of the National Workshops. When it became clear that the conservatives were winning the poll in Limoges, the prefecture was invaded by workers, who, armed with picks, pikes, sticks and staffs, swept aside the National Guard and tore up the records of the electoral count. For two weeks from the end of April, the workers controlled the city:

groups of them carrying axes and batons patrolled the streets and guarded all the strategic points.[13] Tempers eventually cooled and the insurgents handed control back to the legal authorities. In Rouen matters were much more serious. This Norman textile city was suffering particularly badly from unemployment, and workers demonstrated noisily against the election results on 26 April. They were confronted by the National Guard, whose cavalry charged into the crowd. In the mêlée a protester was mortally wounded, which provoked a full-scale insurrection. The workers tore up paving stones to build barricades and armed themselves with iron bars and machine tools. The next day, the militia brought up artillery and blasted apart the defences, taking twenty-three lives with them.

These events in the provinces led to uproar in Paris. Blanqui's Central Republican Society condemned the slaughter as a 'Saint Bartholomew's massacre of workers'. It did not help that the magistrate charged with investigating the events was the same prosecutor who had secured Blanqui's death penalty in 1839. The Society of the Rights of Man warned its members that 'if today reactionaries rise up in arms in Rouen, tomorrow it will be the turn of Paris'.[14] The moderately oriented National Assembly first met in this feverish atmosphere on 4 May.

The intensity of post-electoral feeling drove the demonstration eleven days later, although the precise motives of the organisers remain unclear. Blanqui had opposed the whole protest, believing that the earlier marches had alienated public opinion and that a fresh show of strength would prevent popular sympathies from returning to the revolutionary left.[15] None of the main organisers seems to have planned on an insurrection. The socialist Prefect of Police Caussidière's second-in-command, Joseph Sobrier, explained to the socialist Victor Considérant on 12 May that, while the legislature could not afford to offend 'public sentiments' (meaning the demonstrators), 'their dignity imperiously commands that they do not appear to give in to the pressure of the People'. They would rather have to show their unity with the marchers in 'a spontaneous, magnificent momentum of patriotism, a solemn commission of Peoples, a great triumph carried off by democracy'.[16] In other words, the aim was to put the moderate republicans under intense moral pressure to unite with the radicals and to respect their aspirations, while resisting the authoritarian blandishments of the conservatives.

Yet, with the disastrous turn of events on 15 May, the *démoc-socs* were badly compromised. Their most recognisable leaders were arrested, and Caussidière – the only socialist still clinging on to a position of power since the April elections – lost his job at the Prefecture of Police because his militia had done nothing to stop the invasion of the National Assembly. His men, loyal to Caussidière to the end, barricaded themselves into the Prefecture, but they gave up after a brief siege laid by General Bedeau. The radicals' hot-headed behaviour allowed conservatives to cast a shadow of suspicion over even the more cautious wing of the *Réforme* tendency, who had not participated in the insurrection and who wished to work within the democratic framework of the Republic. Blanc and Ledru-Rollin, who had nothing to do with the planning or execution of the insurrection, were immediately put under intense pressure. The former, who had been manhandled by the protesters on 15 May, none the less only narrowly avoided arrest, and he was indicted by a parliamentary commission, though he survived the final vote in the Assembly. Ledru-Rollin's gifted female assistant, the cigar-smoking, trouser-wearing feminist George Sand, who had helped edit his official *Bulletin de la République* when he was minister of the interior, was so disenchanted that she left Paris and took refuge in the provinces. The political middle ground was crumbling beneath the feet of those republicans who wanted peaceful social reform: compromise between 'order' and the 'social republic' was becoming dangerously elusive. On 5 June the National Assembly passed a law cracking down on public gatherings. The political clubs limped on, but the arrests had deprived them of their high-profile leaders: the revolutionary left had effectively been 'decapitated'.

The greatest tragedy of the French revolution of 1848 then followed. The build-up to the agony of the June days began when the Executive Commission closed down the Luxembourg Commission, which had, it was alleged, 'spread the poison of their theories'[17] among the unemployed in the public works. Preparations were then made to disband the National Workshops: they were put under investigation from 20 May. A committee of inquiry found that they employed a hair-raising 115,000 people and argued that they were a threat to social order, an assumption given some weight by the fact that three-quarters of the demonstrators on 15 May were National Workshop employees. The royalist Comte de Falloux, a member of the commission, concluded that the public works were 'from the perspective of industry, nothing less than a permanent strike costing 170,000 francs a day . . . from a political point of view, the active source of menacing agitation'.[18] In what was widely regarded as a first step towards closing them down, their manager, Émile Thomas, was dismissed on 27 May. The moderates seemed to be ready for a final reckoning with the radical left. The new prefect of police reported that 'all the citizens who have industrial or commercial interests prefer a violent confrontation to letting things drag on . . . It is said that, when faced with all the various abuses resulting from the National Workshops, the government should have taken decisive steps.'[19] On 20 June the National Assembly finally took the widely anticipated and much-feared step and dissolved the National Workshops, ordering that the workers be either drafted into the army, or sent to drain marshes in the Sologne.

The response of the unemployed was immediate: 'Work,' wrote the foremen of the workshops, 'who will give it to us if not the state at a time when industry has everywhere closed its workshops, shops and factories?'[20] There were demonstrations every night on the boulevards, demanding not only the 'right to work' but a democratic and social republic. They also called for the shady figure of Louis-Napoleon Bonaparte. These protests gathered momentum until Thursday 22 June, when two columns of protesters – totalling eight hundred people – marched through Paris. They shouted that they would not be sent to the Sologne and would take up arms against the National Assembly. From their chants, it was clear that they expected support from the Mobile Guard (*garde mobile*), which was recruited from young, unemployed men shortly after the February revolution, partly to counterbalance Caussidière's well-drilled police force. There were also cries of 'Napoleon forever! We won't go!' After midday, the two crowds dispersed, but they agreed to reassemble on the square outside the Panthéon at 6 p.m. Within an hour of the appointed time, the space was crammed with some five thousand agitated workers, who set off, again in two columns, to rally the working-class suburbs of the Faubourg Saint-Marcel to the south and the Faubourg Saint-Antoine across the river to the east. By nine o'clock, police estimated that the latter column alone numbered between eight and ten thousand people. This over-whelming mass of protesters then regrouped once more at the Panthéon. Flaubert's friend Maxime du Camp was walking home that night when he heard an ominous noise 'from the depths of the rue Saint-Jacques, drowned in darkness':

> it was a sort of muffled chant which always repeated the same grave, low, incomparably sad notes. Anxious people came out of their houses and, like me, tried to see into the thick shadows which enveloped the lower end of the street, from which that strange murmur came. Our uncertainty soon vanished. A band of men – two thousand at least – marched three by three, climbing the steep windings of the rue Saint-Jacques. As they passed, all the shops closed up and alarmed faces appeared at the windows; they ignored them. They advanced in good order, leaning forward a little, with-out weapons, and keeping in step. All of them, neither shouting nor clamouring, repeated the same phrase, dismally in hushed tones: 'Bread or lead! Bread or lead!' It was sinister and truly startling.[21]

The social fear shrouded the city. The massive crowd gathered below the darkened dome of the Panthéon and listened to delegates from the National Workshops, including one named Louis Pujol – who told them to prepare for the following day. By 11 p.m., the workers had dispersed, but only to gather their strength for the collision to come.[22]

The authorities were well aware that the protests were gathering pace, but they did little to stop them. Caussidière went so far as to ask: 'did they allow the riot to grow in order to destroy the worker insurgents in one blow?'[23] None other than Karl Marx, writing shortly after the events, claimed that, after the insurrection of 15 May, the National Assembly was bent on a final resolution: '*Il faut en finir!* This situation must end! With this cry the National Assembly gave vent to its determination to force the proletariat into a decisive struggle.' For Marx, the Assembly's decisions regarding the workers were deliberately provocative.[24] It does seem that the decree dissolving the National Workshops was hasty: even the liberal monarchist newspaper *Le Constitutionnel* – no great supporter of the public works – baldly stated on 23 June that 'more effort could have been made . . . to prepare opinion for the announcement; more prudence could have been shown'. It specifically criticised the government for issuing the decree without any attempt to reassure those affected.[25]

It is true, as Caussidière and Marx suggested, that the insurrection was given time and space to develop. But this was probably not due to any desire to have a bloody collision with the left. Although there were certainly plenty of conservatives who relished the prospect of settling scores, when the insurrection gathered momentum the most outspoken opponent of the workshops, the Comte de Falloux, tried to rush through parliament a package of welfare reforms; hardly the action of a man hell-bent on confrontation.[26] Rather, the initial space given to the uprising was the price of the authorities' strategy for dealing with the anticipated protests. The lessons of February 1848 had been that when troops or militia were used as police – dispersed in small detachments to keep order on the streets and prevent the construction of barricades – the insurgents easily isolated and disarmed them. The minister of war, General Louis Eugène Cavaignac, who had put the Paris military garrison on a state of alert at noon on 22 June, therefore intended to deal with any insurrection by concentrating his forces in three strong columns, each with infantry, artillery, National Guards and the Mobile Guard. These would smash their way into the heartlands of the uprising from the outside. All this may have made sense from a military perspective, but, as Alexander Herzen later despairingly cried, 'At that moment everything could still have been prevented – the republic saved – and with it the freedom of Europe; there was still time to make peace . . . But the stupid and clumsy government did not know how to do this.'[27]

Early in the morning of 23 June, some seven to eight thousand workers marched unopposed on to the Place de la Bastille, where Pujol, seizing on the symbolism of the location, called on the workers to bare their heads and kneel 'at the tomb of the first martyrs of liberty'. His stern voice carried across the respectful silence: 'The revolution is to begin anew,' he told the sea of bowed heads. 'Friends, our cause is that of our fathers. They carried on their banners these words: Liberty or Death. – Friends! *Liberty or Death!*'[28] The crowd arose and thundered back: 'Liberty or death!' Pujol solemnly led the crowd to begin its work of building barricades. 'I can still see the gloomy faces of the men dragging stones; women and children were helping them,' wrote Herzen later. He passed by some workers joining a student in singing 'The Marseillaise': 'the chorus of the great song, resounding from behind the stones of the barricades, gripped one's soul', but, ominously, the Russian socialist could also hear the clatter of artillery being moved across the river. He saw General Bedeau scanning the 'enemy' positions with his field-glasses.[29]

By the end of the day, almost all of eastern Paris was held by the insurgents, whose numbers have been estimated at somewhere between 40,000 and 50,000, as against 25,000 regular troops and the 15,000-strong Mobile Guard. Many of the members of this latter militia were pitifully green – some no more than sixteen years old. As it was recruited from among the same unemployed workers as the insurgents themselves, few people believed that it would be reliable. The National Guard, democratised under the Second Republic, had been swollen to an impressive 237,000, but the thoroughly frightened rank and file proved less than courageous in their response to the call to arms.[30] Maxime du Camp was one of the few who joined his battalion: many of his comrades, he charitably put it years later, 'pushed prudence to excess'.[31] In fact, the more middle-class units (which tended to be based in the westernmost districts of the city) were the most likely to see their members respond to the drum beat. The units from the central districts, with their substantial population of master-craftsmen and shopkeepers, were severely thinned by an 'excess of prudence'. Their reluctance to fight did not indicate cowardice but rather reflected their social position: this lower middle class had been severely affected by the economic crisis and, while having a stake in law and order, it had no desire to get enmeshed in a struggle against people who were often their customers, employees and neighbours. Of 64,000 National Guards from the central arrondissements, only 4,000 turned out. Meanwhile, thousands of men from the legions of the working-class eastern districts actually defected to the insurgents. Of the 7,000 National Guards in Belleville, 3,000 joined the uprising. The balance, therefore, was not necessarily tipped in the government's favour.

There were last-ditch efforts at mediation. François Arago stood before the barricade on the rue Soufflot near the Panthéon, trying to persuade the insurgents to stand down. The bitter reply showed that the barricade was not just a military fortification but could symbolise the great social division within the republican movement: 'Monsieur Arago, we are full of respect for you, but you have no right to reproach us. You have never been hungry. You don't know what poverty is.'[32] Arago sadly withdrew, convinced that 'force must decide'.

The first deaths came at noon on 23 June, when the barricade at the Porte Saint-Denis was attacked by National Guards. It is said that two beautiful prostitutes hoisted up their skirts and, taunting the troops with obscenities, dared them to fire. They were immediately cut down in a hail of bullets.[33] The National Guards managed to overcome the defences, but only after losing thirty men in some bitter fighting.

In the end the government prevailed over the insurrection because it had superior firepower. Lamartine, who joined the fighting at twilight, saw the cannon sent by Cavaignac levelling the fortifications in the north-eastern Faubourg du Temple. He counted 'four hundred brave men, killed or mutilated, [who] strewed the faubourg'. It was carnage. Cavaignac himself supervised the successful attack on one particularly stubborn barricade on the rue Saint-Maur. In his absence none other than Ledru-Rollin – no socialist, but certainly a left-wing republican – had telegraphed the provinces on his behalf asking for the help of their National Guard units against the uprising. This was ample illustration of how sharply the republicans were divided over the June days and how isolated the insurgents were even from those who might have sympathised with their plight. Ledru-Rollin's appeal would be met with an instant and enthusiastic response. The opportunity – if any ever really existed – for conciliation had rapidly passed. When the socialists Louis Blanc and Victor Considérant proposed appealing to the rebels to put down their weapons, they were silenced by a deputy who roared: 'One doesn't reason with insurgents, one defeats them!'[34] That night, many deputies slept fitfully in the chamber, where Cavaignac also established his headquarters.

When the National Assembly reconvened at 8 a.m., some of these bleary-eyed and shaken politicians suggested a withdrawal of the legislature to the suburban palace of Saint-Cloud. The more pusillanimous – or alarmist – deputies even suggested a wholesale flight to Bourges. The foreign minister, Jules Bastide, confided to the British ambassador, the Marquis of Normanby, that no member of the government could be sure that they would live to see the end of this day. Tocqueville hastily scribbled a note to his wife, advising her to leave the city.[35] In this atmosphere of near panic significant numbers of deputies – republican and monarchist alike – agreed that strong government was needed to weather the crisis. Cavaignac was the obvious candidate. An experienced soldier of impeccably republican credentials of the *National* ilk, he was seen by his fellow moderates as a saviour who would protect the republic against the double-headed serpent of social revolution and royalism.

Even the monarchist deputies, assembled in their club on the rue de Poitiers, backed the general, perhaps seeing in authoritarianism the prelude to the destruction of the Second Republic and the first step towards bringing back the monarchy. At 10 a.m., the thoroughly frightened Assembly – after a mere twenty-five minutes of debate – invested Cavaignac with executive power. This meant he had absolute military authority in the capital, but he was also virtual dictator of France. Preoccupied with the insurrection, though, he kept on the existing ministers, although the Executive Commission was dissolved and a state of siege declared in Paris. Maxime du Camp recalled the deep impression that this last decree made: 'we sensed that we were about to follow a serious, unique and determined direction'. The normally jostling Paris boulevards were now 'a desert . . . here and there several stray dogs ran off, as if they themselves were frightened by so much solitude'.[36]

The government forces, supported by cannon, pressed on with the grim work of reducing the barricades to splinter and rubble. Du Camp's National Guard unit was hurled against a barricade in the northern suburb of the Faubourg Poissonnière through a maelstrom of spinning metal: 'bullets fell so thickly around us, and with such a repeated, shrill noise, that I remember stopping and looking at the ground . . . the paving stones were marked with brilliant, blue, metallic spots, traces of lead which grazed them as they drew new momentum'. In this hornets' nest du Camp shuddered with 'a violent shock to my leg, as if I had been hit with a thick whalebone cane'. His lower leg had been splintered and his boot filled with blood. With masterful understatement, he recalled that it made him feel 'melancholic'.[37]

It is harder to piece together the experience of the struggle from the insurgents' perspective. In the first place, many of them were killed – in both the fighting and the repression that followed – while others simply wanted to escape the brutal retribution that came after and, having managed to melt away, kept quiet. Those insurgents whose voices were heard were mostly recorded in the distinctly unsympathetic surroundings of magistracy interrogation cells. Unsurprisingly, most of the captive insurgents were coy about their role in the uprising and their political commitment. One accused claimed that, having been plied with drink, he was led to a barricade by the insurgents and told to shoot. 'Hell,' the insurgent claimed to have replied, 'who at?' When asked why he eventually fired at the forces of order, he pleaded, 'I was carried away, like lots of others. The ones who wouldn't go along with them got called idlers and were maltreated . . . A man like me up from the country, who had never heard these things talked about, had never seen anything, and who couldn't read or write – a man like me is easily led astray.'[38]

It is, of course, entirely plausible that some insurgents were press-ganged or misled, but such testimony should be treated with caution. Those captured faced the possibility of death, transportation or imprisonment – reason enough to play down one's commitment to the uprising. The leadership of the insurrection, meanwhile, was unabashed in giving political reasons for its inception. One leader, who had been imprisoned under the July Monarchy for his political activities, explained bluntly to his interrogators what he meant by a 'social Republic': 'I mean a republic with social reforms . . . free and compulsory education and the organisation of work through association; . . . that the worker receives the product of his labour, a proportion of which is at present taken away from him by the man who provides the capital.'[39] The rank and file did not lack political influences, either. After 15 May delegates from the abolished Luxembourg Commission had made contact with the elected representatives of the National Workshops and, along with the clubs, they held a common ideology in the call for a 'democratic and social republic'.[40] It was just that, among the mass of the insurgents, the meaning of the term was far from clear. Furthermore, many still cried out for Louis-Napoleon Bonaparte, Napoleon's enigmatic heir, who had been elected to the National Assembly on 4 June and was regarded by some as the people's champion.

The insurgents were well aware of republican and socialist rhetoric, but they often used it only loosely to give expression to their far deeper social distress. This was illustrated by the interrogation of Louis Bocquet, an unemployed hat-maker who had found sustenance in the National Workshops. He had been captured while wielding a sabre on a barricade near the Pont Saint-Michel (agonisingly close to the Palais de Justice, which probably explains the prosecutor's zeal in questioning him). While he admitted only that he had once attended a political club, he made no bones about the fact that he and others planned to 'raise and defend the barricades in order to name [parliamentary] representatives who would perhaps be nobler or who might have done their duty better'. Having admitted this much – which was already enough to condemn him, as the prosecutor certainly thought – one might have expected him then to expand defiantly on his *démoc-soc* motives, but he revealed little else other than stating simply that 'our rights [were] being repressed'. When pushed, Bocquet's main concern appeared to have been that 'the workers should not leave Paris and it was a result of that resolution . . . that I did all that I could to prevent them from going'.[41] For many workers, the National Workshops comprised one of the few meaningful gains of the February revolution, and these were torn from them: it was this, rather than any fully developed *démoc-soc* ideology which gave the uprising its rather blunt political edge. In his memoirs, Caussidière hit the mark when he called the June days 'that insurrection of despair'.[42] The insurgents were drawn not only from those workers disbanded from the National Workshops but from among those fifty or sixty thousand who had arrived in Paris seeking to learn a trade or, failing that, to find assistance in the public works, but who had been turned away from both, the first because of the economic downturn, the second because of the rules that no migrants from the provinces were to be admitted. Their participation in the uprising was an expression of their desperation and resentment. The strong presence among the insurgents of these poorest and most deprived of all workers also explains why so many of those arrested had addresses in the worst slums. This bleak landscape of social despair is compounded by the fact that a large number of those who joined the uprising were married, older workers with children, whose families would suffer enormously if they lost a husband or father to death, prison or exile. Their presence on the barricades indicated the depth of distress.[43]

Moreover, the uprising did not secure political leadership from sympathisers within the institutions of the Second Republic. Neither the clubs (under pressure since 15 May) nor the parliamentary leadership of the republican left (many of whom had already been arrested or cowed) put themselves at the head of the uprising. So while there were some sympathetic noises coming from the radical politicians, no one who was either close to the centre of power or at the forefront of the radical revolutionary movement was willing to make sincere efforts on the insurgents' behalf. On the contrary, on 23 June, Louis Blanc tried to persuade them to stand down: 'the counter-revolution has been sighing for an opportunity to crush [the Second Republic] . . . defeat is almost certain; nothing is primed for success'.[44] He later stated that the political clubs were thrown into utter confusion and that among the socialist newspapers there 'reigned a poignant uncertainty'.[45] In fact, much of the left was caught off guard. Among them was Pierre-Joseph Proudhon, one of the great anarchist thinkers (and later a friend and associate of Herzen), who had just been voted into the National Assembly (in the same round of by-elections in which Louis-Napoleon Bonaparte and Victor Hugo secured their seats), largely thanks to working-class Parisian votes. But the June days, from which he remained aloof, showed how out of touch Proudhon was with his constituents. 'No, Monsieur Sénard', he frankly declaimed later to the president of the National Assembly, 'I was not a coward in June, as you have said in insulting me in front of the Assembly; I was, like you and so many others, an imbecile.'[46] Blanc probably expressed the views of most of the socialist politicians when he wrote: 'I was consternated. What side should I take? I thought the best thing to do was go to the Assembly, where I could at least be of some use in opposing violent measures which by their nature would aggravate or complicate the situation.'[47] This was the furthest that most socialist politicians dared go.

The fighting continued into Sunday 25 June. A tragic casualty that day was Monseigneur Affre, the archbishop of Paris, who tried to intercede: he courageously stood in front of the barricade that blocked the entrance to the rue du Faubourg Saint-Antoine, clutching copies of a conciliatory proclamation that Cavaignac, at the urging of both Caussidière and Sénard in the National Assembly, had drafted that morning. As Affre spoke, firing inexplicably erupted, and a bullet from the government side tore through his body. As he died, he uttered, 'May my blood be the last to be shed', then passed from this world into conservative iconography as a martyr, a victim of revolutionary brutality. Atrocities were certainly committed: as he tried to dislodge the last resistance centred on a formidable barricade on the Place d'Italie, General Jean de Bréa tried to parley, but he was seized and taken prisoner by the insurgents. When asked for advice on how to deal with this particular crisis, Cavaignac's chilling response was: 'The Republic cannot be sacrificed for the life of an imprudent general.'[48] While the barricade was stormed, nothing could save Bréa's life: the insurgents had heard rumours (which were only too true) that the Mobile Guards were executing prisoners and, in retaliation, they had already shot the general and his aide-de-camp dead.

The newspapers multiplied the scale and magnified the horror of such atrocities. The liberal, monarchist *Constitutionnel* told its readers that

> rather than release their prisoners, the [insurgents] cowardly murdered them by cutting off their heads . . . hanged prisoners, cut off the heads of four officers of the Mobile Guard on a block with a hacking-knife, sawed another in half and wanted to burn alive several soldiers of that unit . . . Corpses were desecrated. It is true that they were not actually eaten; but, patience, that will come, if they continue to listen to the socialists.[49]

Provincial newspapers, which drew much of their information from the Parisian broadsheets, reprinted these stories as fact. That such tales were widely believed illustrated the depth of the divisions that had opened up in French society: between rich and poor, moderate and radical, Parisian and provincial. It was but a short step from demonising the insurgents to arguing that the street-fighting was nothing less than a struggle between 'anarchy' and 'civilisation'. On 29 June, *Le*

National gave its verdict: 'on one side there stood order, liberty, civilisation, the decent Republic, France; and on the other, barbarians, desperados emerging from their lairs for massacre and looting'.[50]

Yet, while the insurgents certainly committed some atrocities, the forces of order similarly killed captured rebels in cold blood or (to use the official parlance) while the prisoners were 'attempting to escape'.[51] Estimates of those summarily slaughtered range from a conservative 150 to a socialist 3,000 (the guess of Karl Marx): the truth probably lies somewhere in between. Most of these killings were by the vengeful civilian militias, the Mobile Guard and the National Guard, rather than the regular army, whose officers did their best to protect the prisoners. Unlike the mass executions that followed the Communard uprising of 1871, they do not seem to have been official policy. Rather, Marx claimed that 'the bourgeoisie compensated itself for the mortal anguish it underwent by unheard of brutality'.[52] One of Flaubert's characters, old Monsieur Roque, volunteering with the provincial National Guard, relishes his sentry duty outside the lock-up that lay beneath the riverside terrace of the Tuileries. The prisoners, 'packed together chaotically in the filth, black with powder and coagulated blood, shaking with fever and shouting with rage', beg for bread. Roque's response is to fire his musket into the seething mass of humanity.[53]

At least 1,500 workers lay dead and some 11,727 more were arrested and held in hastily improvised jails while awaiting transportation or imprisonment. Some 6,000 were released within a few days, others were freed in a trickle over the next couple of years, and 468 were eventually deported to Algeria. Paris hospitals admitted 2,529 wounded people, but there were probably considerably more men and women who tried to tend to their wounds at home, for fear of capture. On the government side, the army, the National Guard and Mobile Guard lost over nine hundred men. For those on the left, the June days were the 'victory of reaction'. Caussidière bristled at the 'theatrical' celebrations of the moderates in the National Assembly 'while they were gathering the dead in the Faubourg Saint-Antoine'.[54] The insurrection gave the left its martyrs. In the evening of 26 June Herzen and his friends heard the sound of gunfire at short regular intervals . . . We glanced at one another, our faces looked green. 'The firing squads' we all said with one voice and turned away from each other. I pressed my forehead to the windowpane. Moments like these make one hate for a whole decade, seek revenge all one's life. *Woe to those who forgive such moments!*[55]

In this antagonistic climate it was natural for onlookers, some fearfully, others hopefully, to see the June days as a class conflict. Tocqueville later wrote:

> I had suspected . . . that the whole of the working class was engaged in the fight, either physically or morally . . . In fact the spirit of insurrection circulated from one end to the other of that vast class and in all its parts, like blood in a single body . . . it had penetrated into our houses, around, above, below us. Even the places where we thought we were the masters were crawling with domestic enemies; it was as if an atmosphere of civil war enveloped the whole of Paris.[56]

He claimed that the June insurrection was different from all other uprisings since 1789 because 'its aim was not to change the form of government, but to alter the social order. It was not, in truth, a political struggle . . . but a class conflict, a sort of "servile war".'[57] From the other side, Marx – naturally – agreed that the June days amounted to a class struggle: it was 'the tremendous insurrection in which the first great battle was joined between the two classes that split modern society. It was a fight for the preservation or annihilation of the bourgeois order.'[58] It is true that one of the main consequences of the June days was to sharpen antagonisms, but not necessarily those that existed between strictly defined 'proletarian' and 'bourgeois' classes. The insurgents were mostly craft workers in the small-scale, artisan trades such as tailoring, shoemaking, furniture-making and metalworking, but there were also clerks and shopkeepers – a lower middle class that made up some 10 per cent of those arrested. Large numbers of unskilled workers and builders fought too, as did some workers from modern industrial plants, such as railway workshops. The wide social base of the revolt indicates the extent of the economic distress that was shared by so many people in the mid-century crisis.[59]

On the other side the troops deployed by Cavaignac certainly included well-to-do 'bourgeois' among the units of the National Guard from the prosperous western districts of the capital, but they also numbered shopkeepers and workers who believed that they were defending their neighbourhoods from 'anarchy'. Although the Mobile Guards came from the same unemployed masses as the insurgents they confounded all expectations by fighting ferociously for the government. Workers in other cities stirred – there was violence in Lyon and some tension in other manufacturing towns, such as Limoges – but the rural population generally supported the government, holding church services to remember the soldiers who had died 'defending the republic'. In some small towns rumours flew that insurgents from Paris were pillaging the countryside. The struggle itself, therefore, was less one of bourgeois against worker than a broader antagonism between urban workers and a much wider cross-section of the French population. However, while the nineteenth-century rhetoric of class conflict obscures the complexities, the antipathy and the social fear were real enough. All those in the French population who felt that they had something to lose were alarmed at the prospect of social disintegration. Widespread dread of what the Parisian insurgents might do led to a dramatic response from the provinces. Cavaignac's call for provincial help on 23 June was answered enthusiastically: in the end, some hundred thousand volunteers travelled to the capital, mostly too late to take part in the fighting and mostly by train – the first time in France that this form of transport was used for military purposes.

The legacy of bitterness and anger left by the June days permanently split the supporters of the Second Republic between leftists and moderates. Among the former, Blanc and Caussidière, politically isolated and now under blistering attack in the National Assembly, thought it best to leave for exile in London. 'The more I see of the representatives of the people,' Lamartine is said to have remarked about his colleagues, 'the more I like my dogs.' Paris was officially under a state of siege until October, with fifty thousand men under arms tramping through its streets, or waiting in barracks. In August a new law forced the closure of several newspapers by reimposing the hated Stamp Tax and the payment of a deposit as a security against prosecution. The polarisation of left and right opened a wide gap into which stepped Louis-Napoleon Bonaparte, who would prove to be the nemesis of the Second Republic.

II

Plenty of observers saw the Parisian June days as a crucial European moment. If Paris, with its great revolutionary traditions, could be brought to heel, then so too could Milan, Venice, Vienna, Budapest and Berlin. The young German democratic journalist Ludwig Bamberger was sitting in a tavern with some of his associates in Frankfurt when he heard the news of the insurrection. 'We felt that a great decision would fall there, which had to change the course of the French revolution and with it the whole European situation. We had a clear premonition that a turning point had set in for the whole course of future political development.'[60] Bamberger's German contemporaries, Karl Marx and Friedrich Engels, agreed that the June days represented a turning point: 'immediately, all over Europe', wrote Engels, 'the new and old Conservatives and Counter-Revolutionists raised their heads with an effrontery that showed how well they understood the importance of that event'.[61] For Bamberger, who was no socialist, the great weakness of the Parisian workers was that they knew what they wanted (social justice), but they had no realistic way of achieving it. A principle, he argued, could be 'right' only if it was morally sound and could be applied in practice. By this time, Marx and Engels had already stepped forward to provide the 'proletariat' with a rational and clear prognosis for the future. The 'Communist League' was the name given in June 1847, at Marx's urging, to an underground socialist organisation that had adherents in France, Switzerland and

Germany. Its motto was internationalist – 'Workers of the World Unite!' – which appeared on all of its proclamations. Its aims were penned by Marx: 'The overthrow of the bourgeoisie, rule by the proletariat, the abolition of the old bourgeois society based on class conflicts, and the establishment of a new society, without classes and without private property.'[62] *The Communist Manifesto*, written by Marx and Engels, appeared early in 1848. It envisaged a class struggle between the bourgeoisie and the proletariat as the driving force that would lead modern society through the crucible of a social revolution. This struggle would establish the 'dictatorship of the proletariat', which would forge an egalitarian society. The theory rested on the presumed existence of a class-conscious, forward-looking and cohesive proletariat that would take on and destroy bourgeois capitalism in the next revolution. Therein lay both the long-term strength of *The Communist Manifesto* and its short-term weakness in 1848. The potency of the argument lay in the fact that it offered a vision of the future that saw the ailments and inequalities of industrialising society as part of a historical process towards socialism. This process would be painful but necessary, because out of it the proletariat would emerge triumphant in the final reckoning of the inevitable revolution. History was therefore on the side of the working class. *The Communist Manifesto* offered not so much an analysis of society in 1848 as of developments to come. Yet the industrialisation that would create a proletariat was still far from its peak in 1848, and this was one of the reasons why the Communist League had so little immediate influence in Germany, or even in France: there was no cohesive, politically knowledgeable and class-conscious proletariat to carry out the new revolution. German and French workers were not factory hands but artisans and craftsmen labouring in small workshops – and they wanted to keep it that way. They were skilled, with aspirations to independence, and, as such, were fighting tooth-and-nail against industrialisation. They wanted to *avoid* becoming part of the industrialised proletariat, that growing mass of unskilled or semi-skilled workers whose only asset for sale was their labour in the service of the relentless factory machine and steam engine. The craft workers sought to defend their interests not in a class war but through traditional methods, such as guilds and confraternities of workers, which traditionally upheld craft standards, governed admission to the trade and created a sense of solidarity among the artisans. Consequently, articulate and literate workers found little in *The Communist Manifesto* that was immediately relevant to their circumstances.

One of Marx's associates, Stephan Born, understood this because he himself had worked as a typesetter in a Berlin printing shop. Elected head of the printers' union, he organised a successful strike for better wages and shorter hours, and his example was followed elsewhere in Germany. When confronted with the realities of organising German workers, he therefore shed the rhetoric of class conflict and concentrated on their immediate concerns. Thereafter, he felt ill at ease when facing his intellectual masters, Marx and Engels: 'They would have laughed in my face or pitied me if I had presented myself as a communist. I was no longer one.'[63]

The Communist League did have some German adherents, particularly in the Rhineland, to where Marx moved from his London exile in 1848. He settled in Cologne, where he and Engels established their newspaper, the *Neue Rheinische Zeitung*. The Communist League also had strong cells in Hamburg, Breslau and Nuremberg, and their agents were active across Germany in 1849, spreading propaganda produced by the league's central committee in London. Yet in 1848 most Communists found that they had to water down their programme to appeal to the majority of German workers. One of them, Wilhelm Weitling, found his more extreme demands rejected by the German Workers' Congress in Berlin in the summer of 1848 and thereafter he studiously avoided talk of class war. Marx and Engels themselves rapidly grasped that the full-blooded *Communist Manifesto* could not be applied convincingly to the Germany of the time: the 'Demands of the Communist Party in Germany', issued in Paris at the beginning of March, stopped far short of the root-and-branch egalitarianism envisaged for the future, calling instead (among other things) for 'an aid for the organisation of labour', national workshops, the abolition of all remaining feudal dues for the peasantry and a progressive income tax. Otherwise, the

programme echoed the political demands of the German democrats: Germany would be a single republic with universal male
suffrage, a citizens' army, separation of Church and state, and universal and free education.[64] But even this watered-down social
programme still went too far for most German craftsmen. An
attempt by Marx to create a central organisation of all the emergent
workers' associations in Mainz was rejected in April. He and Engels
then changed their focus, devoting most of their energies to supporting the German republican movement.

It was not easy to tie the essentially economic concerns of the
workers to the political struggle of the democrats, as Marx himself
discovered when he tried to reshape the Cologne Workers'
Association. With eight thousand members by the summer, this
organisation's founder and first leader, the socialist Andreas
Gottschalk, actively sought to steer the workers away from political
action, concentrating on the more prosaic problems of social and
working conditions. Gottschalk believed that the association's main
goal was to put moral pressure on the bourgeoisie, primarily
through its newspaper. Ultimately, Gottschalk believed, the employers would be so worried by the chaos caused by the economic crisis
that, recognising the willingness of so many unemployed people to
work, they would be persuaded to take the side of the workers and,
in a peaceful transition, would see the wisdom of a socialist society.
Jonathan Sperber, the historian of the democratic movement in the
Rhineland, argues that Gottschalk's efforts to raise a politically passive brand of class consciousness had a special appeal among the
poorest workers, 'schooled to passivity, to living from charity, by
decades of un- and underemployment'.[65] Marx at first joined the
more political Cologne Democratic Society. Unlike Gottschalk's
organisation, which attracted journeymen and labourers, the society
drew its members mainly from the more educated master-craftsmen
and artisans. The differences between the two organisations were
such that Marx and the democrats accused Gottschalk of being a
reactionary stooge, 'bribed by the government and the bourgeoisie
to mislead the workers with pretty sounding words until the reaction was able to regain its strength'.[66] The authorities themselves

disagreed and arrested Gottschalk in early July, allowing Marx and his associates to take over the association and transform it into a harness by which the mass of poorer workers could be bound to the democratic movement. Yet, precisely because it no longer answered the needs of its members (and because it started to levy membership dues), the association withered. By the autumn, it counted its members in the hundreds, rather than the thousands.

Bamberger, who was in Frankfurt during a congress of democratic organisations (representing eighty-nine associations from sixty-six towns) between 14 and 17 June, noted the grave difficulties in reconciling the republicans and the socialists: 'Here for the first time, I realized the sharp difference which separated the . . . radical republican views from the purely socialistic and was to continue to separate them for the future . . . I still recall quite clearly the ill feeling with which it filled me.' For Bamberger, the dispute was whether to give priority to political or to social issues: while he accepted that Marx, Gottschalk and others may have had some valid points, it was necessary to put them forward subtly and in moderation. At the congress he listened aghast as Gottschalk expounded baldly on socialism. This put off much of his audience, who started to drift out of the hall. Bamberger and other democrats did not want to base their movement on any particular class, but hoped to forge a political movement that transcended social differences. He sadly watched as ever more delegates deserted the congress: this, he felt, was no way to nurture a still fragile and incipient movement for democracy.[67]

Yet, some hot-heads aside, the German workers' movement remained generally moderate in its social programme. On 15 July, artisans sent delegates to the Congress of Craftsmen and Tradesmen in Frankfurt which was led by Karl Georg Winkelblech, nicknamed 'Marlo', a teacher at a Kassel trades school. Their demands blended a nostalgic desire to return to pre-industrial days with a progressive impulse for social reform. The congress wished to avoid both the overbearing dominance of big business and the bitterness of social conflict. It hoped to protect the independence of the hard-pressed master-craftsmen by restoring the guilds, which the separate

German states had progressively abolished, but also wanted a state-sponsored 'organisation of work', whereby the government, cooperating with the guilds, would control production. This mix of retrograde and progressive demands mirrored the fact that German society was in the midst of the transition from a pre-industrial to an industrialising age.[68]

When the master artisans, eschewing any notion of social solidarity, refused to give seats or votes at this congress to their journeymen, the latter broke away to form their own German General Worker Congress and to join the General German Workers' Fraternity, which began the process of adopting more modern forms of political identity: they now rejected the 'antithesis between masters and journeymen' as antiquated. Instead, workers should accept the 'modern social antithesis between capitalists and workers'.[69] Here, at last, Marxism had some impact, for forty-eight of the leading officials of the Fraternity were also members of the Communist League. With this early expression of class consciousness, it is no wonder that 1848 is usually regarded as the birth date of the German labour movement.

The Fraternity had sprung, however, from the hard work of Stephan Born, who was not preparing for a class war but who dreamed more prosaically of forging all German workers into a wider political association, beginning with the Berlin Central Committee. Its demands reflected traditional artisan concerns, such as that a fair share of government contracts would go to smaller workshops and that cheap credit would be provided to invest in small-scale technology. In addition, there should be a progressive income tax, pensions and the right to work to ensure that everyone could provide for himself. The Berlin Central Committee demanded free education for all, so that eventually working-class candidates could be elected to parliament. It also proposed a commission of both workers and employers to prevent labour disputes. There was no talk of nationalisation, or of attacking private property: rather, this programme was the cry of the craft worker against industrialisation, a protest against the deskilling of the artisan, forced by economic pressures to abandon his trade and submit to the factory, the discipline of the relentless pace of the machine or to the new rhythms of work imposed by the entrepreneurs.[70]

Born organised the Fraternity at a workers' congress in Berlin – representing thirty-one associations across twenty-five cities – between 23 August and 3 September. The fraternity's resolutions included a ten-hour day, the abolition of taxes on consumption (which hit the poor proportionately harder), free public education, the reduction of the voting age and the division of large landed estates. The Frankfurt parliament was also to be asked to establish a 'social chamber', a German form of the Luxembourg Commission, which would draft legislation on social and economic matters for parliamentary debate. The Fraternity was based in Leipzig with district committees in twenty-seven German cities, creating a nationwide network for German workers. These regional branches acted quite pragmatically to help the beleaguered craft workers: some formed cartels of artisans who would buy their raw materials in bulk; others established job agencies and provided money for journeymen travelling in search of work. The Berlin branch created an insurance scheme for disability, which attracted some twenty thousand subscribers. So, despite its occasionally fiery class rhetoric, the Fraternity emphasised that stolidly liberal value – self-help. To realise this tenet, it offered a programme of education: if they so chose, workers could be edified by lectures on topics as diverse as religion, morality, the 1789 French revolution, geography and political economy.[71] All this was perfectly respectable and posed no direct challenge to the emerging liberal order: indeed, the demand for a 'social chamber' to be appended to the Frankfurt parliament was a strong signal that the Fraternity wanted to work with, not against, the new regime. The journeymen's workers' congress in Frankfurt, whose members joined the Fraternity in droves, rallied not around a red flag but around a green banner with a golden oak wreath. 'The long-term aim', writes Wolfram Siemann, 'was the integration of the workers into political democracy.'[72] Marx later scoffed that if German revolutionaries ever stormed a railway station, they would buy a platform ticket.

The essential moderation of the German labour movement did not prevent displays of working-class strength from stirring middle-class anxieties. On 4 June a massive demonstration of Berlin's democratic clubs marched down Unter den Linten, waving the red–black–gold of German unity: artisans, civic guards and the wives and daughters of the (exclusively) male members of the clubs marched with them. Fanny Lewald, still clinging to her hope of a new era of peace, commented that 'it would be bad if we could still not find a different argument for the truth than the thunder of cannons and the blade of the guillotine'. Yet the demonstration graphically illustrated the social divisions within German urban society. After the established artisans, who bore the banners of their old guilds, came the unemployed, the impoverished craft workers and journeymen marching behind the Fraternity's green banner, which was emblazoned with a slogan – a plea, as much as a threat: 'The Workers without Bread!' Lewald shuddered: 'the workers will be justified in fighting for a place in society and for the enjoyment of life, if we do not find peaceful means to do enough for them.'[73] As if heeding this plea, the primarily middle-class and artisan Democratic Club worked hard to feed three hundred unemployed labourers a week. Yet since the March revolution no fewer than seventy thousand people had fled Berlin out of fear for their safety. Events in June seemed to prove them right, while delivering a body-blow to liberal hopes of a conciliatory, peaceful progress towards a new Prussia.

The elections for the Prussian Diet had taken place on the basis of indirect, but universal, male suffrage in May, returning a mixture of peasants, nobles, artisans, shopkeepers, plenty of civil servants, but (surprisingly) few lawyers and no workers. The parliament met for the first time on 22 May and there was a strong left-wing showing, with some 120 democratic delegates out of 395, including some republicans on the fringes. It was a composition that astounded contemporaries – not least the government itself. Frederick William IV had retained the moderate Rhenish liberal Ludolf Camphausen as his minister-president. The latter was no revolutionary, believing that only close cooperation between the

Prussian state and reformers would prevent what he called the *Kommunistencliquen* from running riot.[74] Lewald understood that 'he wants conciliatory transitions', but the strain could be read on his face: 'sorrowful sleepless nights and the hours of struggle are evident on his pale features'.[75] It was clear that Camphausen could neither command a majority in the parliament nor control the Berlin democrats. When the King handed down a draft constitution when he opened parliament on 22 May, it was rejected out of hand, and a parliamentary commission was established to produce its own version. The left again flexed its muscles on 8 June by putting forward a motion which, in effect, asked the representatives to approve the principle of popular sovereignty and to legitimise the revolution against royal power: the Diet was to declare that those insurgents who fought in the March revolution 'had rendered outstanding services to the Fatherland'.[76] Camphausen managed to muster enough votes to defeat this highly charged motion, but the left still seemed to be running amok.

The defeat of the motion provoked an insurrection six days later, aimed at arming a democratic citizens' militia, which would not be limited to students and men of property. The leader of the uprising, Friedrich Held, was neither an orthodox socialist nor a democrat: a former lieutenant in the Prussian army and one-time actor and writer, he used his bitter pen and sharp tongue to galvanise the crowds in the Zelten. His granite core of support lay among the railway workers as he was the editor of their newspaper, *Die Lokomotive*. He had a vision of an authoritarian and populist mix of socialism, militarism and royal power – a precursor of modern, extreme right-wing ideologies that would combine social revolution with iron rule. Held exploited a widespread fear that the army was preparing to attack the city, and on 14 June his supporters crammed into the small square in front of the royal armoury, clamouring for arms. As the crowd pressed forward, the soldiers protecting the building fired, killing two demonstrators. The predictable riot followed, in which the guards were overwhelmed and the armoury plundered. The affair raised the political excitement in Berlin to fever-pitch. Moderate democrats, such as Born, tried to distance

themselves from the insurrection (he called Held's locomotive workers 'plunderers' while the left-leaning Fanny Lewald condemned
the attack as 'criminal'), but the affair was a gift to the conservatives,
who could now plausibly claim that Berlin was endangered by
armed workers. A despairing Lewald noted at the end of the month
that 'the tone of the opposing parties is becoming more violent on
both sides. Even the remembrance of the terrible street fighting in
Paris seems to arouse the fury of the contesting factions instead of
calming and exhorting them to peace.' Like French observers of the
Parisian tragedy, Lewald saw the gathering crisis in Berlin in social
terms: 'This battle of the "have-nots" against the "haves" was something that seemed a certain eventuality to me long before this
present revolution came upon our horizon. Now it has broken out
and one does not know how to deal with it except with the power
of the bayonet and with cannon balls.'[77] The liberals, meanwhile,
were caught in the middle, having to choose between the authoritarian urge to restore order and the desire to preserve the hard-won
freedoms that now seemed to be encouraging the 'reds'. No one,
not even the conservatives, was ready to contemplate a full-blown
counter-revolution, but Camphausen's resignation on 20 June – he
was unwilling to call troops, the instrument of the old absolute
monarchy, into the city to protect parliament – convinced many
people that the extreme left was out of control. Many anxious liberals began to swing towards the conservatives. One of them, a
philosopher named David Strauss, now candidly admitted that 'to
a nature like mine it was much better under the old police state,
when we had quiet in the streets and were not always meeting with
excited people, new-fashioned slouch hats, and beards' (radicals,
labelled the 'wild reds', distinguished themselves by wearing fur
caps and long beards).[78] Strauss was almost certainly representative
of Berliners who wanted peace and order. The former enemies, the
royal troops, were now greeted cheerfully on the streets as the pro-
tectors of law-abiding citizens.

All this was grist to the conservative mill, which was beginning to
crank into action. Frederick William, shaken by the revolution,
had withdrawn to the peaceful surroundings of the palace of Sans

Souci. 'Shame and self-reproach lie heavy upon him,' wrote a Hessian diplomat. 'His weariness is actually visible.'[79] Yet, travelling to Berlin for only a few hours at a time to consult with liberal ministers in whom he had little confidence, the King had given himself the space to become the figurehead for such conservatives as Leopold von Gerlach, who was later described by Otto von Bismarck as 'a noble and unselfish character, and a loyal servant of the King'.[80] Gerlach urged his royal master to resist the revolution and 'not to deviate by a hair's breadth'.[81] Frederick William was all ears: privately, he thought that the revolution was a sin. His royal mission was to reconnect with his 'true' people, who really loved him. Among the men who appeared at the court to offer their services was Bismarck, who spent time reassuring the King that his power still rested on firm foundations.[82]

While Frederick William was rebuilding his confidence, the conservatives in parliament, sensing that public opinion was turning away from the revolution in disgust at the disorder, finally made a stand. The occasion was the presentation of the draft constitution on 26 July. The chair of the constitutional committee was held by Benedikt Waldeck, an elderly judge from Westphalia, whose combination of stern virtue, Catholic faith and awareness of the travails of everyday life made him a convinced republican. The 'Charte Waldeck', as the draft became jocularly known, was a dagger aimed at the heart of Prussia's monarchical, military and Junker traditions. It assigned to parliament control of a people's militia and broad powers of executive oversight (including the right to approve diplomatic treaties); it gave the King a suspensive rather than an absolute veto; it abolished aristocratic titles and the remnants of seigneurial privilege. Up to the summer, the conservatives in parliament had at least paid lip-service to the idea of a constitutional monarchy, but now they were strident in their denunciations of the 'republican' articles. After fourteen people demonstrating in favour of the citizens' militia were mowed down by regular troops in the small Silesian town of Schweidnitz on 31 July, parliament passed a decree on 9 August demanding that all soldiers swear an oath of loyalty to the constitution and 'distance themselves from all reactionary efforts'.[83] It was a desperate attempt to ensure the fidelity of the army, but at the same time it was a tacit admission of just how weak the nascent liberal order was when confronted with the Prussian military.

Similar vulnerabilities were exposed in Frankfurt, where the German parliament met for the first time on 18 May. The precise mode of election had been left to the separate states. The guidelines issued on 7 April had declared that voters must be adult males who were 'independent', but the term was not defined. Most of the German governments were therefore able to restrict the franchise to those who owned property, paid certain types or levels of tax, or were not dependent on wages alone for their existence.[84] The vast majority of states also made voting indirect, which gave disproportionate influence to local worthies, since they were usually chosen to fill the electoral colleges. Nevertheless, across Germany, it has been estimated that some three-quarters of all adult males had the right to vote, and turnout was generally high. Significantly, those states with broader franchises, like Prussia, tended to return constitutional monarchist or even conservative deputies, while those states with a more confined electorate, like Baden and Saxony, chose democratic delegates. Like most of the European peasantry, the predominantly rural population of Germany was conservative and monarchist. The radicals appealed mostly to the small-town urban middle classes, so republican candidates did better wherever their votes were not diluted by a wider, rural electorate.[85] Few truly blue-blooded conservatives were elected, since most of them had disdainfully shunned the elections altogether, so popular support for monarchy was expressed in the strong showing that the liberal, constitutional monarchists enjoyed in the 585-seat parliament, accounting for half of the deputies, although they were split between moderates and leftists. There was also a vocal group of radicals, making up 15 per cent of the deputies. They were divided equally between the likes of Robert Blum who, for tactical reasons, were willing to work with the constitutional monarchists, and the more fiery democrats who wanted to brook no compromise with the remnants of the old regime. The Assembly was dubbed the 'Parliament of Professors' because the vast majority of its deputies were middle class and university educated. But this epithet also implied that the politicians were full of pedantic hot air, with no practical solutions to meet the challenges of the day.

Ultimately though, the deputies had no chance of taking shelter in an ivory tower. While they tried to hammer out a constitution for a united Germany, they were confronted by an international crisis that would rebound severely on the emergent liberal order. In May, under diplomatic pressure from Britain, Russia and Sweden, the war in Schleswig-Holstein came to an uneasy truce. The Prussians were forced to sign an armistice at Malmö on 26 August. By this agreement, the German and Danish troops alike were to withdraw and the German provisional government in Schleswig was to be disbanded and replaced by a joint Danish–Prussian administration. There was an immediate storm of protest across Germany. It was also clear that the provisional central government appointed by the parliament, under the popular Habsburg Archduke John, was powerless to stop Prussia from signing the armistice, regardless of public opinion. Real power obviously still lay with the old order, not with the brave new world of a federal Germany. One of the right-wing liberals, the historian Friedrich Dahlmann, exploded in parliament, exclaiming that the effect of the armistice had been 'to nip the new German authority in the bud'. In bowing to international pressure, he warned, 'then, gentlemen, you will *never* again be able to hold up your proud heads! Consider these my words: *never!*'[86] At the other end of the political spectrum, Robert Blum warned prophetically that to ratify the armistice would be to spark an insurrection. The delegates, quaking indignantly with wounded national pride and/or trembling from fear of a left-wing uprising, voted to reject the armistice. Archduke John's liberal ministers, who understood that this vote was tantamount to a decision to continue the war against Denmark – and possibly invite British and Russian intervention – resigned. These dangerous implications finally sunk in on 16 September, and the parliament reversed its vote (even Dahlmann had changed his mind). Prussian power was simply too strong, and the possibility of European war too great, for the parliament to wish to provoke either.

In Frankfurt, this volte-face produced a tragedy. The following day, a public meeting of twelve thousand people listened to calls from members of the extreme left of the parliament for a second revolution. It was agreed that there would be a mass protest, declaring that those who had voted for the armistice were traitors to Germany and proclaiming their mandates revoked. Archduke John's new first minister, the sharp Austrian Anton von Schmerling, moved quickly to confront this challenge. He called for troops from Hesse-Darmstadt, Austria and Prussia to protect the parliament. Two thousand soldiers were marched in early the following morning. On 18 September, the great crowd swarmed on the square around the Saint Paul's Church, and some of the demonstrators found an unguarded back entrance to the parliament. As fists and axes smashed through the door, Heinrich von Gagern stepped forward and thundered: 'I declare every transgressor against this holy place a traitor to the Fatherland!'[87] His courage stopped the assailants cold and they withdrew immediately. The rest of the session continued behind the barred doors of the church. The square outside was swept by the troops and barricades that had been thrown up in the city centre were stormed by Hessians. Gagern's children, being spirited out of the city in a carriage, could hear the rattle of musket fire in the distance. In all, sixty insurgents and soldiers were killed – as were two conservative delegates to the parliament, Hans von Auerswald and Felix Lichnowsky. They were out investigating the insurrection when they were trapped by a posse of rebels, who killed Auerswald on the spot. Lichnowsky, one of the more outspoken and therefore hated conservative deputies, was slaughtered in a more agonising and barbaric way: his bones were shattered with repeated blows, the word 'Outlaw' was posted around his neck, then his broken body was tied to a tree and used for target practice.

The shockwaves were felt across Germany, but it was in long-suffering Baden that, on 22 September, the incorrigible Gustav Struve marched across the frontier from Switzerland with other republicans, including the young Wilhelm Liebknecht, later a leader of the German Social Democratic Party. They seized the town hall of Lörrach, proclaimed a German republic, promised social reforms and started to confiscate the property of known monarchists, alarming liberals and conservatives alike. They also succeeded in gathering an army – numbering ten thousand by Struve's probably overoptimistic estimate – but it was poorly equipped, with only two casks of gunpowder, one of which turned out to be useless. So when they were met by the Grand Duke's troops at Staufen four days later, they were crushed in just two hours of fighting. Struve narrowly escaped being torn apart by an angry, loyalist crowd before he and his wife (an active democrat in her own right) were arrested.

The September crisis set the German revolution on an almost irrevocably conservative course. Frankfurt was now under martial law. Carl Schurz passed through the city shortly after the bloody events:

> the victorious soldiery still bivouacked on the streets around their burning camp-fires, the barricades had not yet been removed, the pavement was still stained with blood, and everywhere the heavy tramp of military patrols was heard . . . The royal Prussian government had successfully defied the National Parliament, which represented the sovereignty of the German nation. Those who called themselves 'the people' had made a hostile attempt upon the embodiment of popular sovereignty resulting from the revolution, and this embodiment of popular sovereignty had been obliged to call upon the armed forces of the princes for protection against the hatred of 'the people'. Thus the backbone of the revolution begun in March, 1848, was substantially broken.[88]

It was clearer than ever that real power lay not with the Frankfurt parliament and the liberal administration but with the separate states – and the monarchs – who could still command the obedience of their armed forces.

Meanwhile, the revolution was tearing itself apart. As in France,

German politics became increasingly polarised as liberals were more willing to look to authoritarian solutions for the defence of law and order. On the left, the reasonable, patient Blum despairingly wrote to his wife that, were it not for the disgrace of abandoning his fellow democrats, he would be inclined to withdraw from politics altogether and watch events unfold from a comfortable distance. Schurz commented that the right-wing deputies sat in parliament 'with smiles of triumph on their lips'.[89] Although some of the radicals had been willing to assume leadership of the Frankfurt uprising, the majority of their colleagues had tried to persuade the crowd to disperse and, once the fighting started, worked hard to find a peaceful settlement. It availed them little: like their French counterparts, they were blamed for the violence. Fanny Lewald, visiting Frankfurt and watching the proceedings of the parliament a month later, noted the strength of 'party hatred', and she was saddened by how the politicians 'are without faith, how they call the others bad and irresponsible and deny each other any political insight'. She also noted that conservatives coldly spoke of the 'bullet solution'.[90] Clotilde Koch-Gontard, a daughter of one of Frankfurt's leading industrialists, who hosted salons and dinners for the moderate liberal deputies, wrote on 23 September that she was disillusioned with the revolution. She condemned the liberals and conservatives for their 'German stubbornness and pettiness', but was convinced that the left was looking for trouble: 'The armistice was only a pretext. Even without it, civil war would have broken out, and we have it, so much must be clear to us. This Left cannot justify its sins against Germany.'[91]

III

Social fear also played into conservative hands in Austria. After the flight of the royal family on 17 May and the backlash of ordinary Austrians against the Viennese radicals, Baron Pillersdorf's government sensed that it was time to strike back. A new press law punished with imprisonment treasonable writings, insults against the Emperor and attempts to corrupt public morals. On 25 May the government went so far as to strike at the mainspring of Viennese radicalism, the student movement, by ordering the disbandment of the Academic Legion and the closure of the university. But the authorities had overplayed their hand, because they were still too weak to confront the inevitable resistance from the students and their working-class allies. The very next day students protested and workers armed with machine tools marched into the city centre. One hundred and sixty barricades were constructed, using weighty granite paving-stones heaved out of the roads. They rose 'as high, in many places, as the second stories of the houses . . . over them waved either the red or black flag, those certain emblems of blood and death'.[92] Yet there was no fighting: the government, well aware of its inability to assert its authority, yielded on 27 May, promising to entrust the security of the city to the Academic Legion and the National Guard, under the command of the 'Security Committee', which had been created after the Emperor's flight.

The insurrection of 26 May, such as it was, was to be the high tide of the revolution in Vienna. Events had moved too far and too fast for most Austrians. As the American diplomat William Stiles put it, the moderate supporters of the constitution were fighting a 'double conflict . . . first, that of the people against the old form of government; secondly, that of the new form of government against the Radicals, or enemies of all government'. He was left in little doubt that, when faced with a choice between the old system and more upheaval, they would choose the former as the lesser of two evils.[93] Many Austrians were alarmed by radical militancy in support of German unity, which threatened to reduce the once-mighty Austrian monarchy to a mere appendage of a greater Germany, which, moreover, was potentially a republican state and, even worse, would be dominated by the hated Prussians.[94] There were social anxieties as well, which were intensified by an acute consciousness of the poverty borne by the Austrian workers.

Over the summer of 1848 the economic hardship worsened in Vienna, aggravated by the political uncertainty and a downturn in demand caused by a steady flight of the well-to-do from the city.

Viennese workers initially demonstrated little political consciousness, retaining faith in the students to whom they often looked for
help in their disputes with employers. Radical journalists, however,
soon started making an impact with appeals for proletarian unity,
verbal attacks on the rich and demands that the government do
more for the poor. Workers had been excluded from the new liberal
order in two important ways: first, they were denied membership of
the National Guard, which therefore remained essentially a middle-
class militia dedicated to protecting property; second, until the
Stürmpetition of 15 May, the suffrage had been denied to those who
earned a daily or weekly wage, servants and those who took charity.

Some effort had been made to tackle the distress of the city's sixteen thousand workers. In the spring the government had lowered,
or abolished altogether, taxes on certain types of food; and it had
established public works, including, among other projects, shoring
up the river banks along the Danube. This was not enough to help
the growing army of unemployed who were still suffering in the
economic crisis. Over the summer, calls for lower rents, or for no
rents at all, were heard at public meetings, while for the first time
Viennese workers paraded in the streets, forcing some employers to
grant ten-hour days and pay increases. The tailors held an assembly
to demand that women (who undercut men's wages) be banned
from making dresses and mantillas. The workshop of a French lady
milliner was ransacked. To deal with this working-class militancy,
the Security Committee set up a labour committee that was charged
with providing food and further public works for the unemployed,
while preventing non-Viennese from drifting into the city. Some
workers were given the task of repairing the machines that had
been wrecked and rebuilding the factories that had been torched
during the March days. Yet, despite all efforts to stop them, impoverished outsiders desperate for help continued to trickle into the
city, swelling those working on the public projects into a veritable
army. The government began to fret over this potential threat to
order and the cost to an already dangerously depleted city budget.

The elections to the Austrian parliament were held in this atmosphere of political tension and social fear. Consequently, voters

returned a majority of conservatives or moderate liberals, although there was also a significant minority of left-wingers who would become important later. For now, however, the centrist 'law and order' group, which backed the ministry and the constitution of 25 April, dominated. The parliament opened on 22 July and, by then, a new cabinet had been appointed under Baron Johann Philipp von Wessenberg, a former servant of the old regime who could – when the time came – orientate policy on to a more monarchist tack. Among his ministers was the repentant liberal lawyer Alexander Bach, whose abhorrence of the instability and violence of the revolution was fast pushing him towards a conversion to conservatism. As the summer blazed on, the government's grip on the situation grew tighter, with the crushing of the Czech revolution in June, the overpowering of the Piedmontese in northern Italy in July and the slow but sure gathering of Croatian forces against the Hungarians. By August, the ministry was looking to reassert imperial power closer to home.

For now, however, Vienna was feverish. Count Alexander von Hübner had been released from his imprisonment in Milan and had made his way back to Austria, taking in a leisurely holiday in Switzerland *en route*. When he finally arrived home, he was stunned by the tableau presented by the imperial capital:

> I no longer recognised my good old town of Vienna ... In the streets one meets only slovenly students, national guards struggling with their sabres, proletarians and low-class whores. The good people, those with self-respect, the *Black-Yellows*, the *Kaiserlics*, who formed the immense majority and who shut themselves up at home or took refuge outside the city wished for the Emperor and trembled together with their families.[95]

Stiles noted that the city was transformed from a garden of hedonistic delights to an arena of dreary political activities: 'constant spectacles, processions, consecrations of flags, festivities of fraternity'. He also noted that the flight of the court and the nobility had severely reduced spending in the capital, crippling the city's artisans who produced luxury items – an assessment with which Engels agreed. It was therefore more than just the middle class that joined in the 'shout for a return to a regular system of government, and for a return of the Court'.[96] When, on 12 August, Emperor Ferdinand finally returned after being persuaded of his safety by a deputation from the parliament, he was greeted joyfully, with girls scattering flowers in the imperial family's path as they stepped off the Danube steamer. Watching the procession, Hübner was impressed by one of the royals, the eighteen-year-old Franz Joseph, nephew of the Emperor, who was wearing a military uniform: 'his cold demeanour, the severity of his look, betrayed the emotions which were agitating him. It was sadness, but not discouragement: I would almost say that it was anger being contained with difficulty. For me, it was a revelation and a hope.'[97]

The radicals responded to Ferdinand's return by holding a stormy mass meeting of ten thousand members of the democratic clubs at the Odeon Hall, where they declared their adherence to the extreme left of the Frankfurt parliament. This provoked an outcry among the more moderate Viennese, who accused the Academic Legion and the radicals of nurturing republicanism. There remained, meanwhile, the economic crisis, and the issue of the public works. The government, mindful of the example of the June days in Paris, was reluctant to shut down the projects altogether. Instead, it announced a reduction in pay, which provoked the crisis. On 21 August, there were street demonstrations, with women in the lead, in the suburbs. The following day, the workers built an effigy of the public works minister and gave him a mock-funeral, saying that he had choked to death on the money he had extracted from the unemployed. When the National Guard tried to disperse the protesters, there were clashes, which escalated on 23 August. The Academic Legion, though refusing to join in the repression, was reluctant to side with the insurgents and stood back, a mere spectator to what followed. Lacking the support of the very people whom they regarded as their leaders, the workers stood no chance. Demonstrators were beaten with the flats of sabres, bayoneted and shot. Between 6 and 18 workers were killed, and between 36 and 152 seriously wounded (depending upon whether one believes government or radical counts). When the fighting was over, women from the more prosperous quarters of the city garlanded the National Guards' bayonets with flowers.

As with the Parisian June days, the workers' protests had been spontaneous, owing little to radical political leadership. Yet one conclusion seemed inescapable: the conservative *Wiener Zeitung* declared that 'the workers have seen the contrast between their defenceless poverty and armed property. And at this moment there came into being a proletariat that formerly did not exist.'[98] Middle-class radicals tried to deny the existence of a social schism. The Democratic Club shouted down Marx, who was then visiting Vienna, when he tried to argue that the violence was a class struggle between the proletariat and the bourgeoisie. For Engels, 23 August was the moment when the middle class abandoned the cause of the people: 'thus the unity and strength of the revolutionary force was broken; the class-struggle had come in Vienna, too, to a bloody outbreak, and the counter-revolutionary *camarilla* saw the day approaching on which it might strike its grand blow'.[99] But Marx found that it was not only the middle class who were deserting the revolution; there was little sympathy for his ideas even when he addressed workers' meetings. On 7 September, he left Vienna, grumbling at the stubborn refusal of the workers to see that they should be waging a class war against the bourgeoisie. However, the social fear was very real, even if it was not always expressed in the class-conscious terms that Marx would have liked, and these social tensions would help tear apart the liberal order.

The reaction began slowly at first: the public works were suspended, but they were replaced by a 'Committee for the Assistance of Destitute Tradesmen', which attempted to find work for the unemployed. In other words there was no more direct state intervention, but the committee at least set about its task enthusiastically, consulting with the guilds as to how the government could improve economic conditions. The National Guard was placed under the direct command of the Interior Ministry, which also assumed responsibility for law and order. This signalled the end for the Security Committee, whose moderate members carried a motion for its own dissolution on 25 August.[100]

In Vienna, the tide was beginning to turn back towards the conservatives. In Prague the counter-revolution was by then already complete. Social tensions in the Czech cities were complicated by the additional layer of ethnic strife between Czechs and Germans. The precise relationship between the social and national conflicts was complex. Workers formed a tiny segment of the population of the Czech lands, but memories of their destructive capacities in 1844 ensured that, four years later, there were palpable fears of a 'communist uprising'.[101] Yet little was done to address the root cause of their distress (although, in Prague, the prices of certain foods were reduced, relief funds were collected and the unemployed were set to work on public projects). Meanwhile, the best advice that a liberal newspaper, *Bohemia*, could offer was to await the drafting of a constitution, which would surely bring a brighter future for all. Yet the workers were effectively excluded from the new political order: they were denied the vote, first by the Moravian Diet in Brno in April and then by the National Committee when it drafted the electoral law for Bohemia on 28 May. The National Guard had, like elsewhere, been established to safeguard property and to keep the workers in check. The failure to enfranchise the latter came as supplies of raw materials (such as cotton from the United States) were choked off for lack of credit, so mills closed and unemployment continued to increase unabated. This was accompanied by a sharp rise in prices. It was small wonder that the workers remained restless, while the collapse of Austrian authority gave them the confidence to express their distress in acts of violence. They took to the streets of Prague in early May. There were strikes in Ostrava and Brno. Yet, while in Vienna the workers found spokesmen among the students and the democratic press, in Prague they were left with little voice. The call for the 'organisation of work and wages' in the earlier March petitions had been quietly shelved by the National Committee. Czech students' focus on political and national issues did not begin to address the workers' bread-and-butter anxieties. There was, moreover, no evidence of any socialist-style class consciousness: Czech workers took out their anger and despair on more traditional scapegoats, not least the Jews. When the textile workers marched in a demonstration demanding better working conditions on 3 June, they were easily dispersed by the army, and the city authorities castigated the protesters for their 'blind stubbornness'.[102]

None the less, the Czech workers did emerge as a political force in June 1848. As in so many other European cities, this played into conservative hands by arousing the fears of almost everyone else. The evidence is sketchy, but it appears that the imperial war minister, Count Theodor Latour, had thought of Radetzky's forces in Italy as a 'southern army' that was to be complemented by the efforts of a 'northern' force.[103] This implied that some ministers, at least, had a strategic vision for the defeat of the revolutions in the Habsburg Empire. While Radetzky pressed forward in Italy, the fiery Alfred Windischgrätz would be sent to Prague to take command of the imperial forces in Bohemia. There could have been no better choice for the leadership of the counter-revolution in the north: the marshal had been bitterly opposed to the concessions made in March and he drew no distinction between moderates and radicals, who were all rebels to him, equally worthy of a dose of hot lead. It was he who had crushed the Prague workers' insurrection of 1844, so his return to the city seemed to presage a new ruthlessness in the way in which Vienna proposed to deal with the Czechs.

People immediately noticed a new vigour in the military presence: patrols were doubled, the size of Prague's garrison was increased and artillery was placed on the heights of Vyšehrad and Petřín, which dominated the city centre. The radical press appealed to the soldiers not to become the instruments of reaction and demanded that arms, artillery and ammunition be given to the National Guard and the Academic Legion, a request that, of course, Windischgrätz had no intention of granting. Strangely, a Slavonic-themed ball was held on 10 June, to which the Czech liberals, Windischgrätz and the governor of Bohemia, Leo Thun, had all been invited. Although the revellers hissed when the marshal entered the ballroom, there was no other aggravation.

Windischgrätz had read the situation on the streets well: the students and their allies in the more militant companies of the National Guard could command at most three thousand rifles, while in time the marshal could muster close to ten thousand troops. He could also rely on the National Guards from more conservative and German-speaking districts. The odds were therefore stacked enormously against the liberals, but with both sides refusing to concede, a clash was almost inevitable. The spark in this tinderbox came on 12 June when, after hearing Mass beneath the statue of Saint Wenceslas, a large crowd of students, National Guards, members of Svornost (the exclusively Czech militia) and unemployed workers (some 2,500 of them, largely at the urging of radical students) marched in protest against Windischgrätz. This demonstration blundered into a delegation from the German Association, which had just met the marshal and promised him their support. The ensuing scuffles degenerated into full-scale running battles between workers, National Guards and soldiers. There were also stand-offs between Czech and German militia companies. With violence erupting spontaneously across the city, barricades were erected and six days of violence followed. Any hopes of an end to the fighting evaporated when, first, the insurgents took Governor Thun hostage and, second, when Windischgrätz's wife was killed by a stray bullet.

The revolutionaries had placed most of their four hundred barricades poorly: the marshal reckoned that he had to take only fifteen of them to keep communications open between the old and the new town. The flimsy fortifications were built hastily, and by end of the first day, the Austrian forces, led by grenadiers who acted as shock troops but backed by loyal units of the National Guard, had secured the city's main arteries. When the insurgents, led by Karel Havlíček, issued their demands, they were in the circumstances rather tame: the dismissal of Windischgrätz, the withdrawal of the troops and the establishment of a new provisional government. During a lull in the combat in the small hours of 15 June, Windischgrätz pulled his troops back from the barricades. It was an ominous sign. Shells then rained down on the city centre from the heights above: ten people were killed, three others later died of their wounds and some thirty mangled corpses were found among the rubble only after the fighting. By 17 June it was all over and martial law was declared. This was the first major victory of the counter-revolution in the Habsburg Empire since Kraków at the end of April.[104]

Windischgrätz established a dubious commission of inquiry to investigate those responsible for the insurrection. He more or less told it to 'discover' that it was the fruit of a vast Slavic conspiracy to undermine and destroy the Habsburg monarchy. The evidence for this was found in the coincidental fact that the Slav Congress was meeting in Prague at the time. This had been convened by the Czechs to keep up the momentum from Palacký's rebuke to Frankfurt and rally all Slavs against German pretensions. For this reason it was originally planned to coincide with the opening of the German parliament in May. In the event, the 385 delegates gathered in Prague under Palacký's presidency on 2 June. Similar ideas for a congress had come from other Slavs with their own agendas, namely Slovaks like Ľudovít Štúr, the Polish National Committee in Poznania (which had good reason to fear German nationalism) and southern Slav adherents of the 'Illyrian ideal'.[105] The congress therefore had a broad agenda. It was to discuss possibilities for the unification of all the Slav peoples of the Habsburg Empire, the relations between those Slavs and the other nationalities of the monarchy, links between the Austrian Slavs and the other Slav peoples and the relationship between all Slavs and the rest of Europe. Problems immediately arose with even the loosest notion of Slav unity: the Poles and the Ukrainians quarrelled over the question of Galicia. The Russians were conspicuous by their near absence: the congress was determined that neither the Germans nor the Magyars could accuse them of being tools of tsarist reaction. Of the seven Russian delegates, one was Mikhail Bakunin, an anarchist thinker who was scarcely representative of Russian opinion. The Czechs feared the Germans; but, for the Slovaks, the Magyars were the real worry. The Poles, who sympathised with the Magyars (for they were both anti-German and anti-Russian), wanted to mediate between the southern Slavs and the Magyars, rather than fully support the former.[106] Bakunin criticised the congress for focusing primarily on the Austrian Slavs, and so ignoring the plight of those who lived under the Ottoman and Russian empires.[107] Precisely because of these contradictory pressures the Slav Congress was, as Lewis Namier puts it, 'a seed-plot of history',[108] since it revealed the conflicts of aspirations, hopes and interests among the peoples who would emerge as the 'successor states' to the East European empires after 1918.

It is clear from all this that the congress could not possibly have been at the centre of a great conspiracy to dismember the Habsburg monarchy. When fighting broke out in Prague on 12 June, Austrian soldiers stormed the Czech National Museum, where the congress was meeting, fully expecting to find the Slavic hordes armed to the teeth. All they discovered was the museum's meek librarian. This did not stop Windischgrätz from arresting some of the leading delegates and expelling them from the city. Palacký and the other organisers were faced with little choice but to suspend the congress indefinitely. The historian himself, though plainly a moderate, was now kept under close watch by the police, while (with more reason) Havlíček was arrested on 3 July and the offices of his newspaper, Národní Noviny, were raided for evidence of the 'conspiracy'. The incarceration of this popular Czech journalist merely ensured that he was elected to the Austrian parliament in five different constituencies. Although Windischgrätz's final report predictably accused the congress of treason, it prompted a strong protest from the Slav members of the parliament, including Palacký. The sham investigation became an embarrassment to the imperial government, and most of those arrested in the wake of the June days had been amnestied by mid-September.[109]

The uprising had sharpened ethnic divisions. It is true that there were plenty of Czechs who were alarmed at the prospect of a working-class rebellion in Prague: those National Guard units that suppressed the June insurrection were not all German-speaking companies, although they were predominantly so. For some Czechs, therefore, anxieties over social revolution were more pressing than any national claims they may have had. Yet it is also true that most of the German citizens of Prague, many of whom had no love of Windischgrätz, either stood aside from the uprising or took an active role in suppressing it. Consequently, the insurgents overwhelmingly comprised Czech students and workers, so that, for the German-speaking elites, the social strife coincided with ethnic friction. Beyond Bohemia, German nationalists had little doubt: the fighting in Prague was a conflict of nationalities. The radical *Volksfreund* spat venomously at 'the insane or corrupt Slav party of the Czechs, which . . . has designs on turning . . . Austria into a Slav empire, at the expense of the Germans and Hungarians'. It shortsightedly saluted the marshal's victory as 'a joyful event. A victory for German concerns in Bohemia and in the monarchy can never be a misfortune, for the Germans bring humanity and freedom to the conquered.'[110] In Frankfurt a parliamentary committee on 1 July agreed that the Prague uprising was part of a grand design to create a Slav empire and proposed that German forces be sent to Bohemia to support Windischgrätz. Only Engels was perceptive enough to realise that the Czechs were neither the instruments of Russia nor the tools of anti-German reaction.

IV

In Hungary social tensions coincided powerfully with ethnic divisions, but Hungarian industrial workers were less numerous than their Czech counterparts, since the country was not so heavily industrialised as Bohemia and Moravia. Consequently, ethnic conflicts occurred most seriously in the Hungarian countryside, where there were tense relations between the predominantly Magyar landlords and the peasantry, who were frequently of a different ethnic group. Yet the workers of Hungary did offer a potential source of strength to the urban-based radical movement. In Budapest, in a population of 160,000 there were approximately 10,000 day labourers, 8,000 apprentices and a mere 1,000 factory workers. Moreover, they tended to be Germans and Czechs, which isolated them from the bulk of the Magyar population. Their demands, from mid-March to July, included those familiar to their counterparts elsewhere in Europe: better conditions, the reduction of working hours, higher rates for their goods and the legalisation of unions. Workers in Budapest and miners in northern Hungary agitated for these changes, and the liberal government made some concessions: it could do so with few misgivings primarily because, as Magyar nobles, its ministers had little in common with the usually German, middle-class employers. None the less, strikes, which arose in Budapest for higher wages and better conditions in April and May, were treated as a threat to public order and were broken with force.

Yet the radicals failed to mobilise the workers because they offered little in the way of a social programme. Hungarian radicalism rested on the Twelve Points proclaimed in the March days, so, except for peasant emancipation, its goals were primarily political. Petőfi wrote a few lines of sympathy for the plight of the patriotic poor, but poetry (no matter how well written) did nothing to address their material needs. However, the workers themselves had not yet drunk from the well of new, socialist ideas. When four thousand apprentices marched on the Café Pilvax, the beating heart of Budapest radicalism, to ask Pál Vasvári, Petőfi and others to be their spokesmen, the young artisans did not demand, in unison with their French and Czech counterparts, the 'organisation of work'; rather, they wanted to 'burn the tyrannical guild laws'. Dramatic as this rhetoric sounds, it was merely a demand to make entry into the guilds easier – and without paying high fees. Vasvári recognised the insurrectionary potential of the artisans, but even he suggested that they should take their requests to the government. The social gulf was simply far too great between the workers and the radicals, most of whose leadership had sprung from the Magyar gentry. Strikes went unreported in the main radical organ, *March Fifteenth*, and when, on 22 April, posters appeared demanding fixed food prices, the distribution of church land among the peasants and the abolition of the guilds, the radicals took fright and dismissed these dangerous notions at a public meeting.[111]

The core support for Hungarian radicalism therefore remained the students, intellectuals, professionals, government officials and clerks concerned about the continuing dominance of the landed elites in Hungarian politics. This was far too narrow a base for the radicals to score any resounding successes in the elections held between late June and mid-July. Most enfranchised Hungarians voted for the familiar political elites of the country: some 72 per cent of the new parliament were landed nobles, leaving *March Fifteenth* to declare sulkily that 'the people' wanted 'to serve the noble gentlemen'. The vast majority of the rest were drawn from the urban middle classes, mostly lawyers and government officials. The results are partially explained by the stubborn persistence of deference, but the system was also stacked in favour of the aristocracy, since the rural electoral committees were almost universally filled with estate owners, while in the towns they consisted primarily of the established burghers. Moreover, the radical programme itself had little appeal beyond the confines of its urban middle-class supporters. While Hungarian radicalism showed far more concern for the peasantry than it did for the workers, most of the poorer country dwellers could not vote. Meanwhile, the avowed anti-monarchism of many radicals, including Petőfi, ensured that they were rejected at the polls by most Hungarians, for whom the King was still sacrosanct. The poet, in a clumsy volte-face, wrote articles trying to dilute his earlier republicanism, but it availed him nothing: he failed to gain election and, to add injury to insult, he was nearly lynched by a drunken mob. In the end, of 414 members of the lower house, perhaps 50 adhered to the Twelve Points.[112]

The radicals therefore had to rely on extra-parliamentary pressure. They developed sophisticated organisations to coordinate policy and to bind the left-wing rump of deputies to the broader movement. In mid-July a 'Society for Equality' was created, with a journal entitled the *Radical Democrat*. Taking the French Jacobin clubs of the 1790s as its model, the society sought to forge a nationwide network, to rally patriotic, democratic opinion into a great pressure group – perhaps in readiness for a second revolution. The radicals may not have had much in the way of a social programme, but they potentially possessed a great weapon in Magyar nationalism, which was stewing in the capital. Suspicion of the Viennese court and Batthyány's willingness to compromise with it for the sake of stability stirred patriotic Magyar angst. One of the central issues here was the question of who controlled the armed forces. In May it emerged that the commander of the garrison at Budapest, Baron Ignaz Lederer, had refused to hand out arms to the National Guard, despite ominous signs that the country was about to be attacked by the Croats. When a government commission found that some fourteen thousand rifles were available, a crowd of two thousand, organised by the radical March Club, marched to beating drums on to Lederer's residence. Imperial soldiers reacted by charging with bayonets fixed, killing one protester and seriously wounding twenty. Petőfi seized on this incident to demand a change of ministry, the punishment of the troops involved and the withdrawal of all Hungarian forces from the imperial army in Italy. Batthyány, however, was working hard to put the April Laws on solid foundations and had no intention of provoking the Viennese court.

The issue of Hungarian troops in imperial service was now a hot topic. Moderates like Batthyány and Széchenyi were determined to serve the country's best interests (as they saw them) by soothing Hungary's relations with Austria. So when, on 11 July, the Austrian government sent a request for Hungarian troops to bolster Radetzky's Italian campaign, Batthyány told his fellow ministers that they should voluntarily offer 40,000 out of the 200,000 troops proposed for the entire Hungarian army. This would give the Magyars political leverage with Vienna and compel the Croatian Ban Jelačić to tread carefully. Even Kossuth agreed to this plan, although this meant reversing the earlier position whereby the Hungarians had steadfastly refused to support the suppression of another European people.[113] The about-turn infuriated the radical left. One of their most eloquent spokesmen, Count László Teleki, went straight for the jugular by pointing out (correctly, as it would prove) that the government had put its faith in a court that would never force the Croatian ban to back down. While the Italians were fighting for freedom, Teleki baldly declared, Jelačić most certainly was not.[114] Nevertheless, the government won the final vote overwhelmingly on 22 July. Although in practice fresh Hungarian troops were never sent to Italy, the government's victory illustrated once again that the European liberals of 1848 put their own national interests above the cosmopolitan ideals of universal liberty and self-determination.

The storm that would break over Hungary in September was now gathering, both in Transylvania and along the Military Frontier. Tensions in the former became increasingly strained when the Magyars brushed off the Blaj programme and when Transylvania was declared part of the Kingdom of Hungary. The Transylvanians were left with a tough choice: they could push for union with Moldavia and Wallachia, but this would spark a conflict with the Sultan, the principalities' ultimate sovereign, or with the Tsar, who was their 'protector'; alternatively, they could declare their loyalty to the Habsburgs and in return secure a separate Romanian crown within the Austrian Empire. This latter choice had been mooted by the three Hurmuzaki brothers in Bukovina, a territory that bordered on Hungary but was ruled directly from Vienna. Yet, for now, this idea had no mass support and it fell on deaf ears.[115] In the summer of 1848 the more attractive option was union with the two Danubian principalities. Moreover, it seemed viable – briefly – because in June a revolution in Bucharest had toppled the ruling Wallachian prince, Gheorgiu Bibescu, and established a liberal provisional government. On 7 August, one of the leaders of the Romanian movement in Transylvania, Dimitrie Golescu 'the Black', mused over a map of all the Romanian lands, from the Black Sea to the fringes of Transylvania: 'You know, they might make a handsome little kingdom, of nice round shape, which nature itself seems to have designed . . . I do not know why I believe that this idea, which last year would have seemed utopian, to-day looks within our reach.'[116] Weeks earlier, the reason had been the revolution in Bucharest. There, Romanian liberals, all of them from noble (*boier*) families, and many of them Paris-educated, aspired to national freedom and unity and seethed at Russian dominance. The more radical among them had also launched a critique of the society in which they lived. Many felt that the *boiers* exploited the peasantry (who were mostly enserfed) in order to live a life of 'sensualism, vice, and egoism' (as Golescu's cousin, Alexandru, put it).[117] In 1843 such critics, like Constantin Rosetti and Ion Brătianu, had established an organisation named *Frăţa* (Brotherhood) in Bucharest to coordinate the activities of liberal intellectuals and revolutionary conspirators in the army. Its ultimate aim was to be ready for the revolution, whenever it came. Its very secrecy – and the close surveillance of the authorities – prevented it from flourishing, but its members would emerge as the liberal leadership in 1848. Meanwhile, the *boiers* themselves had grievances, particularly in Moldavia, where they resented the dictatorial ways of the ruling prince, Mihail Sturdza, while merchants and manufacturers groaned under his onerous taxation. In Wallachia the *boiers* sought to persuade Prince Bibescu of the need for political and social reform, including the abolition of serfdom, driven as they were by an acute awareness that the countryside was becoming restless. During the 'Hungry Forties', peasants dragged their feet over their obligations to their landlords. By 1848 they were refusing outright to perform their labour services. Rural riots erupted more frequently and increasing numbers of serfs fled to freedom across the frontiers.[118]

In the Moldavian capital, Iaşi, at the end of March 1848, the liberal opposition, led by Alexandru Cuza, petitioned Sturdza for moderate reforms to boost the economy – they did not even demand the abolition of serfdom – and for a parliament with more power than the existing General Assembly currently enjoyed. When Sturdza accepted most but not all of the petition, the liberals confronted the prince at his palace and tried to cajole him. Steeled by the Russian consul's assurance of military support – and profoundly irritated by the swaggering behaviour of one of the liberal delegates, who ostentatiously took out his watch and informed the prince that he had half an hour to make his decision – Sturdza left the palace, called out the army and crushed the opposition, killing several people and arresting over two hundred people. Their hands tied behind their backs, the liberal leadership was dragged through the streets and 'beaten like dogs'. They were then hauled to the frontier town of Galaţi and expelled into Turkey.[119]

With Moldavia firmly pressed under Sturdza's iron heel, the revolution gathered momentum in Wallachia. In March, the liberals, including Rosetti, Golescu the Black and Ion Ghica, established a revolutionary committee to plan an uprising. There was to be no mild-mannered petition here because, unlike in Moldavia, the opposition could rely on an important middling strata of *boiers* and a large commercial middle class, who were resentful of their social superiors and frustrated by government policy. Still, while hotter heads wanted to rise up immediately, the calmer spirits prevailed to prepare the ground first. Prince Bibescu's determination to resist revolution, meanwhile, was being bolstered by a thinly veiled warning from the Russian government that it was 'in the interests of Wallachia as well as your own' to prevent any outbreaks of 'the plague that is now afflicting Europe'.[120] The Russians sent General Duhamel to advise Bibescu, but – fearing a permanent Russian military presence – the Prince rejected the offer of twenty thousand troops. By the beginning of June the revolutionary committee was ready. Curious 'wedding invitations' were sent out to liberal-minded *boiers* informing them of a 'celebration' at Islaz, a frontier town on the Danube, in the province of Oltenia. There, on 9 June, Orthodox priests, resplendent in their heavy robes, celebrated Mass before a proclamation was read out to units of the Wallachian army and an excited crowd of townsfolk and peasants. They were, said one of the priests, 'tailoring the garments of freedom'.

The 'Islaz Constitution' included the classic demands of European liberalism: the abolition of censorship, equal civil rights, fair taxation, the extension of the franchise and the election of the ruling prince for a five-year term, free education for all (boys and girls), the abolition of serfdom (with land being given to the freed peasants, while compensating the landlords), freedom for all gypsies (who were enslaved), the emancipation of the Jews, and the abolition of the nobility. A constituent assembly would meet to draft a constitution based on these principles. A Wallachian provisional government was proclaimed, but the Islaz programme did not demand full Romanian independence. Instead, it called for an end to Russian 'protection' and autonomy with ties to the Ottoman Sultan: throughout the summer, the Romanian revolutionaries worked hard to win the blessing of Constantinople. They were shrewd enough to understand that, wedged between the three great empires of Austria, Russia and Turkey, their incipient state would need the support of at least one if it were to survive.

News of the uprising in Oltenia was the electrical charge that jolted the Bucharest revolutionaries into action. The original insurrection had been planned for 10 June, but Prince Bibescu had struck first and pre-emptively arrested some of the revolutionary committee. Yet the loyalty of the army was in doubt: many officers had swallowed liberal ideas and there were rumours that the revolutionary forces from Oltenia were already marching on the capital. On 11 June the pealing of church bells brought the city's population flooding on to the streets and converging on the palace, some brandishing copies of the Islaz programme. As expected, the army stood aside, while the liberal leaders who had escaped arrest were allowed to enter the palace and thrust the new 'constitution' under Bibescu's nose. Powerless to resist, the Prince signed the document and grudgingly appointed a new provisional government. When he asked who was to be the new police minister, Brătianu pointedly told him that it was to be Rosetti, 'the one who's in jail'. A bristling Bibescu abdicated two days later and fled with other conservative *boiers* to Braşov, just across the border in Transylvania. On 15 June a massive public assembly on the Field of Liberty outside Bucharest acclaimed the new constitution. Elections were to be held for a parliament that was to meet on 6 September. The new government promised to abolish serfdom within three months, provided that the peasants ensured – for one last time – that the harvest on the landlords' fields was collected. The result was rural chaos, as the peasants immediately refused to perform any more services. Tragically, the Romanian revolution was crushed before the abolition of serfdom could get off the ground.[121]

Tsar Nicholas and the Ottoman Sultan Abdülmecid were both

anxiously watching these developments. The former was actually playing a double-game: while hostile to the revolution and determined to pulverise liberalism, he also saw an opportunity to strengthen the Russian presence in the principalities. The Russians had long harboured ambitions to secure the Bosphorus, which would provide them with a secure and certain outlet into the Eastern Mediterranean. That meant pushing Russian power southwards through the Black Sea region, and the anti-Russian tenor of the Romanian revolution had thrown down the gauntlet to these strategic interests. The Russians even sent a disingenuous proposal to Bibescu in his Transylvanian refuge, outlining a new constitution for Moldavia and Wallachia, on condition that the Tsar's son would be proclaimed King, which would effectively eliminate Turkish influence. Bibescu was also none too subtly told that, if he refused this generous offer, the Russians would impose it by '100,000 bayonets'.[122] Faced with the very real prospect of a Russian invasion, the Romanian revolutionaries sought salvation through diplomacy: the provisional government sent diplomatic agents across Europe to gain the recognition of the great powers. Ion Ghica went to Constantinople armed with a Romanian promise to honour all obligations to the Sultan in return for Turkish support. But in 1848 there was not much the other European governments could offer against Russian military might.

On 7 July, Russian forces tramped into Moldavia. The Wallachian government was so alarmed by this invasion of the neighbouring principality that it fled into the mountains, allowing power in Bucharest to fall back into the hands of the counter-revolutionaries. Only Brătianu's energetic efforts to raise the population prevented them from holding on to power for more than a couple of days. At this stage, the Tsar's move was intended to pressure the Ottoman government into rejecting the overtures of the Romanian revolutionaries. For now, the Russians left Wallachia alone, so the provisional government returned to Bucharest, shaken, more than a little embarrassed, but still intact. The Turks, however, responded to the Russian gambit by sending their own forces across the Danube at the end of the month, while the Sultan's envoy Suleiman

Pasha travelled to Bucharest to negotiate with the Romanians over the terms of their autonomy. The result was the creation of a short-lived 'princely lieutenancy', with a liberal cabinet but owing theoretical loyalty to the Sultan. With this agreement, Suleiman made a triumphant entry into Bucharest at the head of two hundred Turkish cavalrymen, cheered by a crowd waving both Romanian and Turkish flags.[123]

At the very moment of the liberals' apparent salvation, however, Abdülmecid bent to Russian diplomatic pressure and to the whispers of conservative *boiers* who had made their way to Constantinople. He repudiated Suleiman at the beginning of September, replacing him with the conservative martinet Fuad Pasha, who left for Wallachia with more Turkish troops, but their task this time was not merely protective. On 13 September, Ottoman forces battered their way into Bucharest, which was stubbornly defended by all the forces that the provisional government could muster, including the city's fire brigade. After ferocious fighting, the liberal government capitulated and the Turks imposed a conservative *boier* as the new ruling prince. A few days later, the remaining revolutionary forces in Oltenia, facing overwhelming numbers, also surrendered. The Tsar, however, had little faith in the Sultan's ability to suppress the revolution effectively. On 15 September, therefore, Russian troops poured into Wallachia, sweeping aside the Ottoman army and entering Bucharest. The administration was thoroughly purged and the frontier with Transylvania – where the revolution still had energy – was sealed by a cordon sanitaire of Russian troops.[124]

So, by the time Dimitrie Golescu had pondered the aesthetically pleasing shape of a united Romania, its fate had already been sealed, at least in 1848. Yet the revolution had at least made unification seem possible and, in the process, it had raised the stakes considerably across the Carpathians – in Transylvania. Early in June the Austrian government discussed ways in which not only the southern Slavs but the Romanians could be mobilised against Hungarian nationalism. War Minister Latour mooted the possibility of an alliance with the Romanians, which might eventually allow the

Austrian Empire to extend its influence as far as the Black Sea, while also counterbalancing Magyar power in Central Europe. For now, however, his colleagues felt that the government's position was too weak for such an adventure, which explains its rejection of Transylvanian Romanian demands later that month. None the less, with the revolution in the principalities on the verge of being extinguished, the only realistic hope left for the Transylvanian Romanians was an alliance with the Habsburg dynasty against the Magyars. Unless the Hungarians came to terms themselves (which at this stage remained a possibility, if a forlorn one), the Romanians might have been rewarded for their loyalty to Austria with autonomy inside the empire. By September, when the Austrian government felt stronger vis-à-vis its opponents elsewhere, it was ready to provide the Romanians with military backing against the Magyars, who were all too aware that trouble was brewing in Transylvania.

The Hungarians also faced a threat along the Military Border, where the southern Slavs were marshalling their forces. The determined Jelačić paid little heed to his formal dismissal as ban of the region on 10 June and was determined to prove his worth to the Habsburgs as well as to his own people. Only five days previously, resplendent in a red overcoat and carrying a scimitar, he had told the opening session of the Croatian parliament, or Sabor, that 'in the unhappy case that the Hungarians continue to prove themselves to act not as brothers . . . but as oppressors, let them know . . . that we are ready with sword in hand!'[125] Meanwhile the 'hawks' in the Austrian government continued to back him. On 24 June Latour – blithely shrugging off the reprimand he had earlier received for sending weapons to the Croats – sent money to Jelačić, since Kossuth, as Hungarian finance minister, had bluntly refused to provide him with funds: 'I would merit to be spat upon by the nation, if I had given money to the enemy,' he said.[126] Baron Franz Kulmer, who was the Sabor's representative at the imperial court, quietly wrote to Jelačić reassuring him that 'everybody here is in your favour. The June 10 decree is null and void because it was not countersigned by any of the ministers.'[127]

Yet the first victim of Jelačić's determination to serve Habsburg interests was Croatian liberalism. On 9 July he prorogued the Sabor. At the end of the month, the Habsburg Archduke John attempted to prevent the outbreak of war between the Hungarians and the Croats by mediation. Nothing came of the resulting meeting between Batthyány and Jelačić, but the latter made the most of the opportunity to make firmer arrangements with the imperial army command in Vienna. The Hungarian government made a shrewd attempt to woo the Croatian borderers away from Jelačić by promising them land reform, whereupon he trumped them with reforms of his own, including the right to dissolve the *zadruga* and to parcel out the land privately. He also raised more units for the army, redeploying forces from civil Croatia and the Ottoman frontier. The Hungarian efforts at compromise were not entirely disingenuous: since the spring, Batthyány's ministers had privately agreed that they should work hard to avoid giving Jelačić any pretext for a full break with Hungary. As late as the end of August, even Kossuth was willing to allow Croatia to secede *provided* (and here was the crucial point) Jelačić and the Croats were working 'in the spirit of nationalism and not reaction . . . if they want to secede let them go ahead, let them be free and happy, but let them not bring blood and misfortune on the two countries for a foreign, reactionary power'.[128]

Jelačić had been appointed, however, precisely because he was a loyal Habsburg instrument. He allegedly told Batthyány at their fruitless meeting in Vienna that 'you want Hungary to be a free and independent Hungary and I pledged myself to support the political unity of the Austrian empire. If you do not agree to that, only the sword can decide between us.'[129] Meanwhile, he gathered his forces. After his victory over the Piedmontese at Custozza, Radetzky released some of his Croatian units in Italy for service with Jelačić, so by early September the latter had fifty thousand men under arms. In Vienna Latour ordered Austrian military depots in Styria to be given extra supplies. Meanwhile, the Serbs had sent plea after plea to Jelačić to come to their aid against the Hungarians, so the pressure was mounting on him to take the offensive. He never received any clear order to do so from the Emperor: the court was still publicly trying to stop the war between Croats and Hungarians. It may have been that, while the Emperor's supporters wanted Jelačić to destroy the revolution in Hungary, they were also worried that he might grow too powerful if he did so. Some Croatian historians have suggested that the Habsburgs wanted both sides to wear themselves out, making it easier for the court to restore its authority later.[130] In the end Jelačić needed no signal: while Batthyány and Ferenc Deák (the Hungarian justice minister) were still in Vienna trying to prevent a final breach with Austria, the imperial government issued a formal manifesto that declared the Emperor's opposition to Hungarian independence: a 'Hungarian Kingdom separate from the Austrian Empire was a political impossibility'.[131] On 4 September, Ferdinand formally reinstated Jelačić to all his former powers. This was a sufficient nod of support and, on 11 September, the ban's army crossed the Drava: Hungary and Croatia were now at war.

While Jelačić and the Viennese government were making their complex manoeuvres, the government in Budapest worked feverishly to organise the Hungarian army. The immediate spur was the Serbian insurrection in Voivodina, to which Batthyány reacted by forming 'regular' or 'mobile' National Guard units on 16 May, to be recruited from volunteers serving for three years. The advantage of this new force was that it was unambiguously under Hungarian government control, unlike the regiments of the imperial–royal army, which continued to receive orders from Vienna. The new mobile National Guard battalions were to be recruited from all men aged between eighteen and forty, without property qualifications, so this was to be no bourgeois militia aimed at protecting property, but a true citizens' army, with an oath to 'defend the homeland, the royal throne and the constitution'. Their official name was soon supplanted by the more popular term *honvéd*, meaning 'defender of the homeland'. As prime minister, Batthyány was commander-in-chief of the new force, which allowed him to side-step the imperial command structure. By mid-August, the government had recruited close to ten thousand into the Honvéd batallions.[132] Yet the summer left many Hungarians with a dark sense of foreboding. Petőfi, fretting that government preparations to meet the gathering threat were too feeble, penned the gloomy lines:

> Let us paint our flags black and red
> Because mourning and blood
> Will be the fate of the Hungarian nation.[133]

At the other end of the political spectrum, Széchenyi had an apocalyptic vision of the future. On 18 July, while watching progress on his beloved chain bridge, a heavy steel cable broke free and lashed down on to the temporary pontoon bridge. No one was killed, but Széchneyi and many of the hundreds of other spectators were hurled into the Danube. The count (who was already struggling with depression) swam to shore but fell into black despair: 'We are lost, sunk back into barbarism . . . We are being ruined not by Kossuth and his associates . . . but by a greater power, by Nemesis.'[134]

V

Liberal Hungary's nemesis was certainly gathering strength. A week after the chain bridge accident, the reaction triumphed again, this time in Italy. In June Field Marshal Radetzky had at last convinced the Austrian government that the war was winnable. The cabinet had been rather stung by the old fox's recent sharp remarks, such as, in a letter to Latour on 21 June, 'I only wish . . . that the Minister [Pillersdorf] could have as much success in battle against the intelligentsia of our time . . . as I am now having, despite being in the minority, in battles and skirmishes with the King of Sardinia.' Six days later, Latour gave Radetzky the order he sought: to gamble Austrian power in Italy on one decisive battle.[135] The omens were good. Charles Albert had divided his forces, with 28,000 in front of Verona and 42,000 laying siege to Mantua. Radetzky now had 74,000 troops. He planned to ram a wedge between the Piedmontese by driving those in front of Verona back on to Peschiera.

The attack began on 22 July, and on the following day Radetzky smashed his way through the very centre of the Piedmontese line, which defended a series of hill-top villages north of the settlement that gave this epic encounter its name: Custozza. Charles Albert tried to counter-attack in the broiling heat of 24 July – and, at one stage, the King saw Italian tricolours being waved triumphantly on the heights – but in the small hours of the next day, Radetzky brought the full weight of his forces to bear on the parched, exhausted Italian units and swept them back off the slopes.[136]

Charles Albert's forces fell back on Milan, which turned out to be a mere staging-post in a general Piedmontese withdrawal from the war. In the Lombard capital power now slipped out of the hands of discredited monarchists and into those of the republicans, who, advised by Mazzini, prepared to resist the Austrians by throwing up earthworks, building barricades and collecting what money, ammunition and provisions could be had at such short notice. Food and ammunition were scarce and most of the available artillery was in Piacenza. While Charles Albert assured the populace on 5 August that he intended to fight, he was already negotiating terms with Radetzky. It was agreed that the Piedmontese would march out of Milan on 6 August and then have a day in which to withdraw altogether from Lombardy, taking with them all those who had 'compromised' themselves in the revolution. Radetzky would enter the city the following day. When word of this deal leaked out in the night of 5–6 August, an enraged crowd surged around the Greppi Palace, where Charles Albert was staying. The King had to be extricated by his troops, who were already beginning their evacuation.[137] 'The city of Milan is ours', wrote a triumphant Radetzky twenty-four hours later: 'no enemy remains on Lombard soil'.[138] On 9 August, the Piedmontese General Salasco signed an armistice.

Radetzky's grit – he had, after all, bullishly refused to follow earlier government orders to negotiate – and his military skills had retrieved Austrian power in Italy. By significantly easing the pressure on the Viennese government, he also contributed immensely to the survival of the Habsburg Empire itself in 1848. For the Italians,

Custozza was not just a military disaster but a political bombshell: faith in Charles Albert and in the monarchist leadership of the liberation of Italy was shattered. Republicans sensed that their moment had come. There were widespread cries for a *costituente*, an elected constitutional assembly for the whole of Italy that would forge a unitary state over the heads of the ruling monarchs. Carlo Cattaneo, always sceptical of Piedmontese motives, declared (no doubt with some bravado), 'Now we are our own masters,'[139] but he still fled Milan on 8 August for the safety of Paris, where he arrived on the 16th. There, he wrote and published *L'Insurrection de Milan en 1848*, aimed at countering the efforts of Charles Albert's agents, who were trying to blame the republicans for the disasters of the summer. The book turned out to be a bestseller.[140]

Meanwhile, Mazzini had grabbed a musket and left Milan on 3 August, joining Garibaldi's volunteers, who after being snubbed by the Piedmontese had placed themselves in Lombard service. They were not yet wearing their famous red shirts, but white linen jackets left behind by the retreating Austrians: one witness remarked that they looked 'like an army of cooks'.[141] With the news of Custozza, Garibaldi pulled back towards Milan to defend the city. While he was *en route*, he learned of the armistice. 'Armistice, surrender, flight – the news struck us down like successive bolts of lightning, spreading, in its wake, fear and demoralisation among the people and among the troops.'[142] Some of his men deserted, but the remnants of the force marched northwards to Como, from where Garibaldi hoped to wage a guerrilla war in the lakes and mountains. Mazzini, marching with his followers under the banner 'For God and the People', split off from Garibaldi at Como, entering Switzerland, from where he hoped to direct the resistance. With Cattaneo's agreement, he created an Italian National Committee at Lugano, which proclaimed that 'the royal war is over; the war of the people begins'.[143]

Ironically, Mazzini had fallen out with the one man who was continuing the fight – Garibaldi. 'I had made the mistake,' Garibaldi later explained, 'for which Mazzini never forgave me, of suggesting to him that it was wrong to win and keep the support of young men by holding out the prospect of a republic to them, at a time when the army and the volunteers were engaged in fighting the Austrians.'[144] When Italian unification was finally achieved in 1860, it was in no small part thanks to Garibaldi's willingness to compromise his republican principles to the cause of unity. The two men who would become the great figureheads of Italian unification also fell out over tactics. Garibaldi, still taking orders from Mazzini despite their differences, moved on to the idyllic Lake Maggiore, where he and his men commandeered two steamers and, cheered on by women and children waving tricolours from the balconies of lakeside villas, took Luino, where they repulsed an Austrian attack.[145] Mazzini had hoped that a small show of resistance would spark a wider insurrection in the mountains of Lombardy, but Garibaldi, seasoned from his guerrilla experience in South America, read the situation on the ground differently. 'For the first time', he wrote, disillusioned, 'I saw how little the national cause inspired the local inhabitants of the countryside.' Its strength sapped by desertion, his small band made its way by a night march over difficult mountain paths into Switzerland. By the time he crossed the border, Garibaldi had just thirty men left of the eight hundred who had taken Luino.[146]

Elsewhere in Italy, the republicans fared much better. The moderate, liberal governments which had cast their lot behind the monarchists' war were now under intense pressure. In Piedmont the ministry, which since its appointment in early July had been selected from across the putative northern Italian kingdom and had been led by the former mayor of Milan, Casati, fell in the public outcry against the armistice. There would be no fewer than six different governments between Piedmont's first loss at Custozza and its final defeat at Novara in 1849. Critics of the successive ministries, demanding that the war be rekindled, were supported by the clamouring of some 25,000 Lombard refugees. By the autumn, war fever was becoming almost irresistible, and democrats threatened a new revolution, particularly in the restive port of Genoa. To ease the pressure, in October the government increased the size of the army with a fresh levy of fifty thousand men.

Venice was now completely isolated in an Austrian sea. The news of Custozza and the armistice 'fell on Venice like a thunderbolt from a serene sky', as the American consul, Edmund Flagg, put it.[147] The Venetian vote for 'fusion' was now redundant, and Daniele Manin emerged from the crisis with great credit. The small, bespectacled republican had refused to be part of the monarchist provisional government that had been appointed on 5 July: 'I am and will remain a republican. In a monarchist state I can be nothing.'[148] As if to ram the point home, Manin put on his civic guard uniform and, with the rank of private, took his turns doing sentry duty – a simple citizen doing his best for his city. The monarchist 'July government' certainly had its work cut out, for the Austrians, commanded by Marshal Franz von Welden, had isolated the city from the *terra firma*. His forces, numbering some nine thousand, were now extended in a cordon around the lagoon. Yet many of these troops were shivering with malaria, and there was no immediately obvious way of striking at the city itself, which was defended by no fewer than fifty-four forts, only three of which were on *terra firma*. Command of the 22,000-strong Venetian forces (of whom 12,000 were Italian volunteers and regular troops who had converged on the city from all over Italy) had been given on 15 June to General Pepe, who had reached the city on a steamer from Chiogga with the remnants of his Neapolitan regiments.[149]

The population's hostility towards the monarchists was palpable: the provinces of the mainland had voted for fusion, not the great city itself. With news of Custozza, the anger in Venice boiled over. On 3 August, some 150 people, fired up with Mazzinian ideas, gathered in the Casino dei Cento and established the Italian Club, ostensibly to discuss the problems of the day, but in reality as an alternative, republican, centre of power. When the Piedmontese commissioners, who had been sent to Venice to assume authority in Charles Albert's name, arrived four days later, they were greeted with a storm of hostility. On 10 August, the leading republicans, including Manin and Tommaseo, signed a protest and demanded a meeting of the Venetian assembly. The government made itself remarkably unpopular when it tactlessly cited the old Austrian laws to try to silence its critics in the press and in the Italian Club. The following day, it yielded, agreeing to the creation of a committee of defence to be elected by the assembly. The Piedmontese commissioners resigned their powers, but they were still hounded on Saint Mark's Square, by a Venetian crowd baying for their blood.[150]

At this dangerous moment, Daniele Manin was busy browsing in a bookshop. This pleasant activity was interrupted when he was summoned to meet with the government and the commissioners. His very appearance on the balcony above the Piazza stilled the turbulence below. Manin promised them that the Venetian assembly would meet on 13 August and that, in the meantime, he would assume power. He called on all Venetians to defend their city. His audience, which moments before had been intent on murder, erupted into ecstatic cheering: 'Viva Manin! To the forts!' The mood of the city changed from one of anger and bewilderment to one of hope: the son of a leading republican later recalled 'with what confidence in saving the motherland we stayed up to watch the dawn breaking over the railway bridge and the battered vessels of our fleet!' Manin had carried off a coup, and not just against the monarchists: he had also stolen a march on the Mazzinians, who had hoped to seize power themselves. Manin had always feared the dangers of mob rule. To him, Mazzini's ideas of revolution seemed to pose just such a threat, and one of his tasks, as he saw it, was to prevent 'anarchy'. He viewed the June days in Paris as precisely the kind of bloody social chaos into which Venice could easily sink unless its leaders made law and order their priority.[151]

Nevertheless, the more urgent problem was the war against Austria, which Venice was now bearing virtually alone. When the assembly met on 13 August, Manin agreed to share power with two military commanders, one from the army, Colonel Giovanni Cavedalis, the other from the navy, Admiral Leone Graziani. In order to ensure that the greatest possible unity would prevail, Manin went so far as to declare that Venice would not, once again, be proclaimed a republic. The government, he said, was provisional 'in every meaning of the term'. This was another slap in Mazzinian faces, who were capable of mounting a serious challenge to the new triumvirate, since they had a great deal of support among the non-Venetian volunteers and troops. But Manin's popularity with the wider population was greater still, and he had the backing of the commander-in-chief, Pepe. So it was that, until the autumn, Manin successfully resisted the pressure from the Italian Club (and from Mazzini himself) to transform Venice into the hard kernel of Italian republicanism, from which the rest of the country could be revolutionised.[152]

In Tuscany the reaction to Custozza was maybe even more dramatic than it was in Venice. Cosimo Ridolfi's government, a coalition of conservatives and moderates, had long been castigated by the centre-left liberal opposition under Bettino Ricasoli for its lukewarm support for the war. Ridolfi's cabinet resigned when the news of the battle provoked rioting: Florence jostled with the unemployed, with deserters, with demoralised soldiers and volunteers still keen to fight, while radical political clubs shrilly demanded a Mazzinian war of the people. Eventually, the moderate liberal Gino Capponi stepped up to take the poisoned chalice and became prime minister. He promised to continue Tuscany's war effort if the armistice between Austria and Piedmont were to collapse. The real drama occurred in Livorno, which was always prickly about Florentine pre-eminence and where the dockers, in particular, were stricken by unemployment in the economic downturn. The Livornese democrats were roused by Father Gavazzi, the fire-breathing friar and preacher of holy war, who, ignoring a ban imposed by the government, had stepped ashore in the port. When he was arrested, Livorno rose up on 23 August: the crowd tore up the railway lines and occupied the arsenal. With the port threatening to become virtually an independent city-state, Capponi, in desperation, sent the popular radical Francesco Guerrazzi to try to calm Livornese spirits. Guerrazzi had himself been arrested in January for leading an insurrection in the city, but now he was afraid of the prospect of social upheaval. He had to exercise all his moral authority – and some physical force – to prevent the radicals from proclaiming a republic. But despite his work in restoring some semblance of order, Capponi disliked him and replaced him with a democrat and fervent advocate of a *costituente*, Professor Giuseppe Montanelli, who had been lionised as a hero for his valour at the battle of Curtatone. Yet even he struggled to master the situation in the city. Ultimately, the only way for the Grand Duke to prevent more violence was to yield to the democrats and appoint a radical ministry. In October he chose Montanelli, who refused to serve without Guerrazzi, so the two radicals assumed power together.[153]

In Rome, Prime Minister Mamiani had tried ease the Pope into the role of constitutional monarch, but it was a part which Pius IX filled only with difficulty. Mamiani swallowed his own radical liberalism after the newly elected parliament opened on 5 June, expressing support for the Italian national cause, but insisting that it must take the form of an Italian league, with the Pope acting as peacemaker. For this, he was blasted by the radical minority in parliament, led by the Prince of Canino, a member of the Bonaparte clan, and Doctor Pietro Sterbini. Outside parliament, Ciceruacchio could raise the working-class quarter of Trastevere and the teeming, impoverished districts immediately surrounding it. When the Austrians counter-attacked in northern Italy in July and spilled over into the Papal States, briefly reoccupying Ferrara on 14 July, the radicals mobilised the Roman crowd through the clubs, or *circoli*, which followed Canino's lead in demanding that the government declare both a state of emergency and war. Mamiani refused to budge, but when the crowd invaded the lower house of parliament, howling for arms to defend the city, it was clear that the government could do little to control the democrats. Custozza was the political *coup de grâce* and Mamiani resigned on 3 August. The Pope wanted to appoint the gifted and shrewd Pellegrino Rossi, but there was too much popular opposition to that, because Rossi was a very moderate breed of liberal, so for now Pius had to make do with a six-week caretaker ministry. Meanwhile, to stem the flow of determined Italian volunteers from making their way to help defend Venice, Austrian troops tried to occupy Bologna. The white-coated forces reached the gates of the city on 8 August, but the citizens put up a determined resistance: the urban poor, students, shopkeepers, artisans and bourgeois stood their ground under bombardment by field-guns and managed to cut off a company that had penetrated the town's defences. Within three hours, the Austrians withdrew, leaving behind a city feverish with revolution and patriotic fervour.[154]

In southern Italy the nascent liberal order in the Kingdom of Naples had been slowly strangled in its cradle since King Ferdinand had reasserted royal authority with cannon, musket-ball and bayonet on 15 May. Yet, for as long as the Piedmontese continued to challenge Austria in the north, the Neapolitan reactionaries did not feel strong enough to tighten the screws: no Italian government would dare to betray constitutionalism as long as there was the possibility that the liberal cause would triumph by force of arms. Moreover, Sicily was still fighting for its independence and much of the countryside on the mainland was in open revolt, with an uprising in the Abruzzo and a major insurrection in Calabria. Times were not yet propitious for Ferdinand to destroy all that he had promised his subjects in January: there was therefore no full-blooded censorship; and fresh elections, which were held on 15 June (albeit on an even narrower franchise than before), returned a parliament with a strong liberal showing. The old order none the less began to reassert itself in significant ways: the Jesuits were let back into the kingdom; the old royal police reappeared on the streets; and there was a ban on public meetings. The political currents were slowly beginning to run back in Ferdinand's favour, while the radicals failed to channel the peasant uprisings towards political objectives. A force of six hundred Sicilians sent to support the Calabrian uprising fractiously refused to have much to do with the peasants. The insurrection was brought to heel by the end of July, when the eight thousand troops sent by the King made their presence felt. In any case many of the insurgents were more than happy to turn their scythes back to their original use, for the harvest had to be brought in. Even parliament, though the lower house was still dominated by the liberals, had little in the way of teeth. The upper house was full of conservative peers and the King's prime minister Bozzelli pointedly and repeatedly failed to show up to parliamentary debates.

With word of Custozza, the King knew that the time to reassert his authority in full was fast approaching. His main concern was to bring Sicily under control. The liberal leadership of the rebellious island had been on the cusp of accepting a restoration of the constitution of 1812 early in March, when news of the February revolution in Paris arrived. The Sicilian parliament, which first met on 25 March, then raised the stakes by demanding a constitution whereby the island would be virtually independent, its only link with Naples being its shared royal dynasty, the Bourbons. When the Neapolitan government rebutted Sicilian pretensions, on 13 April the parliament at Palermo – mainly lawyers, intellectuals and liberal nobles – decreed the monarchy deposed: 'Sicily does not demand new institutions,' it haughtily declared, 'but the restoration of rights which have been hers for centuries.'[155] Sicily was, for a few months, truly an independent state: it did not even adopt the Italian tricolour as its flag, but the three-legged symbol of the island. Such separatism allowed the snubbed Neapolitans to accuse the Sicilians of waging a 'civil war' against a united Italy. Though there was a radical, republican minority, including Francesco Crispi, most Sicilian revolutionaries were constitutional monarchists, and the parliament voted for the respected liberal veteran Ruggiero Settimo to act as president until a new royal dynasty could be elected.

Beyond the rarefied confines of the Sicilian legislature, the island was slipping into anarchy. What police remained were being murdered by the *squadre*, who now not only controlled large areas of the countryside but enjoyed influence within Palermo itself. With the collapse of Bourbon power, they had seized control of their own villages and marched 'their' people into the capital, enjoying the awe and fear that they inspired among the Palermitans. The government created a National Guard to defend the property and lives of Sicilian citizens, who were liable to be kidnapped or threatened until they parted with their money. In April this militia, drawn from the propertied elites, came to blows with the *squadre*, one of whose groups was led by the trouser-wearing, pistol-wielding Testa Di Lana, a formidable woman who had graduated from herding goats to killing policemen.

In all the chaos the government could do little to raise an army strong enough to defend Sicily against any Neapolitan counter-attack. By September, the island could depend upon perhaps six thousand troops, including two regular battalions, with the rest made up of poorly trained National Guards, in addition to the hardened street-brawlers of the great cities and the unpredictable but undoubtedly violent *squadre*. They were no match for the Neapolitan regular army. In August Ferdinand mustered a ten-thousand-strong expeditionary force on the Calabrian coast, across the Straits of Messina. Seeking to free his hands of all political interference during his reconquest of Sicily, he also prorogued the Neapolitan parliament. The police set the *lazzaroni* on to the radical artisans who tried to defend the legislature on 5 September. The National Guard was severely reduced and liberal officials and judges were dismissed or harassed. By this time, the campaign to retake Sicily had already begun: the expeditionary force came to the rescue of the royal garrison in Messina's citadel, the one bridgehead that the Neapolitans had clung on to since the start of the revolution. After a relentless bombardment from the guns of the fortress between 1 and 6 September, the troops advanced, confronted only with the city's rough-and-ready civic guards and the urban crowd. The royal forces grimly set about retaking Messina street by burning street. When the fighting was over, some two-thirds of the city lay in smouldering ruins. Ferdinand was henceforth known to Sicilians by a new epithet: *Bomba.* A six-month armistice brokered by the appalled British and French on 11 September led to a lull in the fighting, but the Neapolitan reconquest of Sicily had begun with a royal vengeance.[156]

In 1847 the German writer A. von Haxthausen graphically warned his readers of the possible calamity to come:

> Pauperism and proletariat are the suppurating ulcers which have sprung from the organism of the modern state. Can they be healed? The communist doctors propose the complete destruction and annihilation of the existing organism ... One thing is certain, if

these men gain the power to act, there will be not a political but a social revolution, a war against all property, a complete anarchy.[157]

Though a conservative who was writing (with some sympathy) about Russia, Haxthausen expressed the deep-rooted fears of a much wider spectrum of European opinion about the dangers posed by the 'social question' of poverty and the painful economic transition of the nineteenth century. The liberals shared his fear that, after the political triumphs of the first months of 1848, radicals would seek to exploit the widespread distress and kill the new liberal order at the very moment of its birth, by pushing for a second, social revolution.

The moderates were right to be worried. The poverty of the urban workers was one of the most important factors in the ultimate collapse of the liberal regimes of 1848. The workers' demands were not always revolutionary, but they were social. In no country were they anywhere near a majority of the population, but because they were urban based, they could directly threaten the central institutions of the new order. Liberals, content with the constitutional liberties and governments in the making, were reluctant to concede to the workers much more than certain civil and political rights, along with some public works projects to ease the immediate economic misery. In the long run, they hoped, economic recovery and the new freedom to associate and to pursue any trade would take the sting out of labour militancy. But in 1848–9 there was little sign of economic recovery (undoubtedly the political uncertainties of those years contributed to this problem) and the measures promoted by liberal regimes to combat poverty were mere palliatives, sticking plasters barely covering the deep wounds of social despair. So even when workers' own demands were moderate, or rooted in social distress rather than political militancy, radicals were frequently able to exploit their grievances and channel them towards political goals. At the same time, it was all too easy for conservatives to point to the fearsome power of working-class demonstrations, the June days in Paris, the August uprising in Vienna or the September insurrection in Frankfurt, to claim that the workers were intent on destroying social order, or even civilisation itself. Most liberals and middle-class people were now sufficiently shocked to agree and consequently were willing to sacrifice some of their hard-won political freedoms if that would ensure a return to social order. In these circumstances, with liberals falling in line with the forces of authority and the workers becoming increasingly associated with radicals, the politics of the 1848 revolutions were fatally polarised. Yet more dangerous still to the liberal order were those social divisions that more or less coincided with ethnic differences. This lethal cocktail was particularly potent among the peasantry of Central and Eastern Europe – and it was the rural population that in 1848 lent its considerable support to the counter-revolution.

5

THE COUNTER-REVOLUTIONARY
AUTUMN

In June 1848 a young Prussian nobleman had an audience with
Frederick William IV in the King's palatial refuge at Sans Souci.
The thirty-three-year-old Junker advised the monarch that the
struggle against the revolution was simply a 'war . . . of self-defence'
for the conservative order, but 'I could not induce the King to
share my conviction that his doubts as to his power were without
foundation' and to resist the 'usurpations' of the Prussian parliament.[1] The nobleman was Otto von Bismarck, who as yet had
little influence with the King, but who would famously rise
to become one of Germany's greatest, albeit one of its more
Machiavellian, statesmen. In fact, Bismarck had also despaired over
the collapse of absolutism: 'The past is buried . . . no human power
is able to bring it back to life, now that the Crown itself has cast
earth on the coffin.'[2] Yet the Junker soon rediscovered his mettle.
He had already come to the notice of court conservatives before
the revolution. In the United Diet in 1847 his speeches distinguished him as an earnest supporter of the King, and Leopold von
Gerlach – one of the reactionaries who had Frederick William's ear –
took note. The King was not inclined to listen to Bismarck in the

summer of 1848, but by the autumn the situation had been transformed and Frederick William was ready to strike back against the revolutionaries.

Throughout Europe conservatives were steadily recovering their nerve – and with it the political initiative. There were several reasons for this. The first was that the events of the summer had shaken the liberals to the core. The threat of social revolution and working-class disorder allowed conservatives to feed on the widespread public fear of social disintegration. Anyone who had anything to lose from further chaos was drawn progressively away from the political centre to support the forces of law and order. The liberals generally fell increasingly – if often reluctantly – into line with their old enemies, the conservatives, in their desperate attempts to achieve social stability. In this way the persistence of the economic and social crisis and the attempts of both conservatives and radicals to assert themselves tore apart the revolutionaries, pushing the liberals closer to the reactionaries and drawing from them the same repressive measures that they had once opposed. This polarisation between left and right brought victory for the conservatives, because they still had the strength – and were clawing back the popular support – which the liberals lacked.

The 1848 revolutions also left many of the old state institutions intact. Since the revolutionary leadership in most parts of Europe were committed to constitutional monarchy and legality, the ruling monarch was left in control of ministerial appointments, even if those ministers were now responsible to a legislature. This was especially striking in Austria, where the essential structures of the empire were untouched: the Emperor, the court, the council of ministers, the state bureaucracy and the army all remained.[3] This meant that, unless the old regime had been totally overthrown, as it had in France and in Austria's northern Italian provinces, there was a good deal of continuity in personnel, many of whom were more willing to do the bidding of their monarch rather than the liberal upstarts, or else the monarch could appoint his own supporters. In the Habsburg Empire provincial governors, such as Stadion in Galicia and Thun in Bohemia, remained powerful figures who could use reforms such as the abolition of serfdom to gather popular support for the monarchy. In Croatia Ban Jelačić had ordered all his subordinates to obey the Emperor, rather than the Hungarian government, to which they were nominally subject. The liberal regimes, then, could never be entirely sure of the loyalty of local administrators and jurists. This was true even of France, where the provisional government sent commissioners into the provinces to replace monarchist prefects and sub-prefects with republicans and to dismiss the existing town councils. But this purge of local administration was not as thorough as one might expect. Certainly, in areas like the south-east, where there was already a deep-rooted tradition of rural radicalism, almost all the authorities were replaced, down to the mayor of the smallest village. However, in other regions, the existing officials simply declared a new loyalty to the republic and so retained their positions. These were the so-called 'republicans of the day after' – the pragmatic converts who swathed themselves in republican colours while frequently hiding monarchist clothes underneath.[4] A similar process took place in Hungary, Italy and Germany, where officials demonstrated their (questionable) loyalty to the new order by displaying the national rather than the dynastic colours.[5]

Control of the armed forces was, of course, crucial. In France the army adhered to the evolving tradition of service to the French 'state', an entity held to be above the frequent political swings between democracy, monarchy and dictatorship, which provided national continuity through these vicissitudes of revolution and counter-revolution. None the less, under the Second Republic, the president turned out to be Louis-Napoleon Bonaparte, so that even the French army became an instrument of authoritarianism. Elsewhere, the armed forces remained firmly in royal hands: Pope Pius IX and King Ferdinand of Naples could both order their troops to pull out of the conflict with Austria. The latter also used them to crush, successively, the Neapolitan revolution and Sicilian independence. In the Austrian Empire Radetzky, Windischgrätz and Jelačić were able to gather their forces and unleash them in the name of the Emperor, whose conservative ministers remained in command. In Germany the armed forces were still controlled by the governments of the separate states, which meant their princes. Consequently, while German liberals applauded the crushing of the republican movement in Baden, the destruction of Polish hopes in Poznania and the fight against Danish nationalism in Schleswig-Holstein, they were playing with fire. The fact that these troops were deployed not only under the command of the old regime rulers but at the request of the old German Confederation showed, first, that real power still rested with the separate states – and especially mighty Prussia – and, second, that the Bund, hated by the liberals as a relic of Metternich's conservative order, still had considerable vitality as an institution. When Bismarck told Frederick William that his position was far stronger than he realised, it was because the army was still his instrument. 'That I was right', Bismarck later recalled, 'was immediately proved by the fact that every military order . . . was carried out zealously and without scruple.'[6] Hungary was the exception, because its liberal leadership was drawn from the landed, political elite of the country, so it controlled the apparatus of the state, right down to county level, as well as much (but by no means all) of the Magyar officer corps.

Elsewhere, the revolutions barely scratched the surface of conservative strength. Once they started to regain their confidence, conservatives adopted some of the methods of their liberal opponents, including the press and networks, to mobilise and organise opinion for the fightback. Conservative newspapers and political organisations burgeoned over the summer, buoyed by the first successes of the counter-revolution. In Austria new journals appeared, including the *Wiener Kirchenzeitung*, which stood up in defence of the Catholic Church, while the scurrilous *Geissel* ('Scourge') outdid even the most foaming-at-the-mouth revolutionary journals in abuse and vilification. In mid-September the latter's acerbic editor, J. F. Böhringer, flew the imperial black-and-gold banner from the journal's offices and had to be rescued from an angry Viennese mob by the National Guard – an irony that surely did not escape even him. By then, Austrian conservatives had finally organised their own political society, the Constitutional Club. As its name suggests, it did not seek to drag Austria back to the absolutist days of Metternich, but it attempted to defend the liberal, parliamentary order against 'every bold encroachment in the direction of republicanism', which it saw as 'treason to the Fatherland and to constitutional freedom'.[7] In practice this was the only social organisation (outside the Catholic Church) that could rally anyone who feared the radicals and their influence in Vienna. It therefore attracted a following whose main concerns were not for the constitution, but for law and order. Within days, it had somewhere between 22,000 and 30,000 members. Count Hübner remarked that the success of the club was 'certainly a good symptom'.[8]

In trying to mobilise the population, the conservatives had a great moral weapon at their disposal – religion – which in some areas of Europe was *the* decisive factor in keeping the population loyal to the old order. There were some notable radical or 'red' priests, to be sure, like Father Gavazzi in Italy and, in France, the towering intellect of Abbé Félicité Robert de Lamennais. The latter's democratic-socialist convictions flowed directly from his religious faith: his bestselling *Paroles d'un croyant* depicted Jesus as a friend to the poor, while he believed that God spoke through 'the people' – *vox popoli, vox dei*. His newspaper, *L'Avenir* (*The Future*) had been banned by the Pope back in 1832. Elected to the National Assembly in 1848, he sat with the left and was one of the few voices to speak out in defence of the June days. Tocqueville, who worked with the Abbé on the draft of the Second Republic's constitution, noted that he may well have worn a yellow waistcoat underneath a green frock-coat, but Lamennais still moved with modesty and some awkwardness, as if he had just left the sacristy.[9] Religion, however, usually lent its moral force to conservatism. In Protestant Prussia Lutheran pastors played a leading role in the conservative 'King and Fatherland' associations. In Catholic Europe regions like the Tyrol in Austria, the Abruzzi in the Kingdom of Naples and Brittany in France were both Catholic and conservative strong-holds.[10] In Rennes in Brittany the 'Tree of Liberty' planted with such solemnity in April was sawn down by anonymous hands two months later. A notice was pasted on the stump: 'Thus perishes the infamous Republic!' The authorities claimed that this sacrilege was encouraged by the fact that the royalist candidate in the by-election of early June had been openly supported by the clergy.[11] In some countries religious conviction was channelled not only by the clergy from the pulpit but by new organisations. In Germany the first 'Pius Associations' sprang up as early as March 1848. Named after the Pope, they claimed to defend the Catholic Church against liberal secularism. By the end of October, there were four hundred such societies across Germany, with a staggering hundred thousand members. The pressure that these organisations exerted on the German parliament ensured that the Jesuits (who were then the bogeymen of all liberal-minded people) were not banned from Germany, while the Church retained its right to supervise religious education in state schools.[12] Religion was one of the forces that seduced the peasantry back to their innate loyalty and deference to the traditional order (if they really ever abandoned it at all). And the quiescence of the rural masses was an ace in the conservative hand.

I

The European peasantry had played an important part in the revolutions in the first three months of 1848. They had hastened the collapse of the old order by rising up: in the East against serfdom; in the West against taxation, low wages, indebtedness and the surviving manorial rights of the landlords and over rights of access to forests and pasture. Politicians of all political hues produced newspapers aimed at a peasant readership – in many places for the very first time. In Hungary the radical Mihály Táncsics – who had been a peasant before becoming a tailor and then a schoolteacher – began to publish the *Workers' Newspaper* at the end of March. Its title referred not to urban journeymen but to rural labourers: it backed universal male suffrage and demanded the abolition of all the remnants of 'feudalism' that the Hungarian liberals had left intact. The newspaper was distributed free to peasants on market days, which ensured that Táncsics was one of the few radicals to be elected to the new Hungarian parliament.[13] Elsewhere, the revolutions brought the ballot box to the peasantry for the first time. It is not clear that they understood the nuances of modern political concepts: for example, Czech peasants understood the word 'constitution' merely as freedom from compulsory labour service. The liberal press complained that Czech peasants also did not understand such terms as 'democrat', 'reactionary', 'despotism' and 'hierarchy', though one can surely forgive them for finding the slippery notion of 'sovereignty' hard to grasp. The claim that they did not know what 'aristocrat' meant seems somehow less credible.[14] Still, peasants across Central Europe voted for the first time and some of them were elected as deputies. The Austrian parliament, which first convened on 22 July, had 383 delegates, of whom 92 were peasants. The Moravian assembly, which met on 31 May, boasted 97 peasant deputies out of 247 – enough to have it dubbed the 'Peasant Diet'.

The revolutions of 1848 were therefore not restricted to the urban crucibles, but politicised the peasantry on an unprecedented scale. Yet, understandably, this development only went so far as the dictates of the peasants' own interests. Once those were met the rural population could fall back into detached neutrality. If (as in France) peasant proprietors felt threatened by the further radicalisation of the revolution, or if (as in Hungary and much of Italy) the liberal regimes did not entirely live up to the peasants' hopes, the peasantry were open to the blandishments of opponents of the new order. Sometimes these were radical, but more often they were conservative. The liberals were either landowners themselves or believed strongly in the rights of property, which did not incline them to radical measures that would satisfy the peasantry entirely. For example, where serfdom was abolished, the landlords received compensation, some of the costs of which were borne by the peasantry themselves, which saddled them with debts for a generation or so. Rural ire therefore focused on the liberal regimes that had apparently failed to deliver on their early promise. Moreover, after the initial disorders of the spring, traditional habits of deference could also creep back, when the peasants, still faced with the overwhelming economic crisis and the uncertainties of the revolution, sought security in obedience to their landlords and above all in submission to their sovereign. Where elections were held on the basis of universal or a broad male suffrage, this conservatism of the countryside counted heavily against the liberals. And almost everywhere, it was one of the pillars – or perhaps the very keystone – of the counter-revolution.

The impact of the revolutions on the countryside was most dramatic in Central and Eastern Europe, because there the peasants suffered under many heavy obligations to the state and to their landlords, including serfdom. Their counterparts in the West aimed primarily at wiping out the last relics of the old seigneurial (sometimes called 'feudal') system, which had already been eroded or all but levelled since the eighteenth century. In 1848 the fear of a *jacquerie* – an uncontrollable, unfathomable peasant uprising against landlords, government officials and other figures of hate – hastened the abolition of servile status in Central and Eastern Europe. Mindful of the slaughter of the Polish nobles of Galicia by Ukrainian peasants in 1846, European landlords were naturally jumpy over the prospect of an uprising of their serfs and tenants. In the spring of 1848 peasants almost everywhere in Eastern and Central Europe refused to perform their services or to pay dues, while the government's weakness meant that landlords also could not depend upon the state to enforce them or to protect their own lives and property from peasant violence. Consequently, the only way to restore order was to give the rural insurgents what they wanted and abolish all seigneurial obligations and, where it existed, to end serfdom. Yet the latter policy also meant that landlords would have to make material sacrifices, since they would lose their free supply of labour. Moreover, since the serfs did not own the estates on which they toiled, freeing them without giving them land would create an impoverished, restless and potentially rebellious social group. On the other hand, to give the freed peasants land meant taking property from the landlords, who could claim (on the basis of the liberals' own principles) that this was a violation of property rights. Consequently, it was argued, the owners would have to be compensated both for the loss of peasant labour services and for any grants of land that went along with emancipation. It was virtually impossible to find a solution that would satisfy everybody.

In Austria, on 11 April, the government issued a manifesto promising to free the peasantry from all enforced services and dues on 1 January 1849. In fact, Vienna had already begun the process of emancipating the peasants wherever there was greater urgency. In Bohemia in March peasants meted out 'people's justice', including acts of murder, as a groundswell of anger against the landlords rose in Czech villages. No fewer than 580 peasant petitions, representing over 1,200 villages, were stacked on the National Committee's table in Prague – and they kept coming until the counter-revolution in June. The thoroughly alarmed nobles demanded an immediate government response to the rural crisis. On 28 March 1848 the hated *robot* – the labour obligation enforced on the peasants – was abolished in Bohemia, with effect from 31 March 1849. The Moravian 'Peasant Diet' unsurprisingly showed even less patience, making the abolition of the *robot* and other impositions effective from 1 July 1848.[15] In Austria serfdom itself came before the imperial parliament on 24 July. A young Silesian deputy, Hans Kudlich, who was the son of a peasant, introduced a bill for the abolition of 'all servile relationships together with rights and obligations coming therefrom'.[16] While freeing the peasants did not present a problem, the issue of compensation burned on through the summer, splitting the revolutionaries between the radicals (who argued fervently against) and the government, the conservatives and the liberals, who all insisted that some indemnity was due. The peasant deputies were, of course, bitterly opposed to compensation: one Galician peasant delegate complained that in his community peasants had to doff their hats within three hundred paces of a nobleman's home and that the landlords refused to receive peasants at home because they stank and were dirty: 'For such mistreatment, we should now give compensation?'[17] The debate was resolved by the decree of 7 September, a compromise in which compensation would be paid for those dues that stemmed from property ownership, but not for any obligations that implied personal servitude. The precise details took until 1853 to elaborate, whereupon the state and the peasants each paid a third of the indemnity, while the remaining third was deducted from the total compensation as a tax, on the grounds that the state had taken over from the landlords the tasks of administration, justice and policing of the peasants.

In the short term, the landlords suffered a marked loss in income from these measures. They now had to pay those who worked on their land. They had to buy horses and oxen for ploughing and transport, whereas in the past the peasants had used their own when performing the *robot*. The peasants were emancipated with land, but the value of the compensation was fixed at far below the market value. The irascible Windischgrätz stormed about the emancipation: 'the most outstanding of Communists has not yet dared to demand that which Your Majesty's government has carried through'.[18] The marshal's exaggeration actually touched on one of the government's ulterior motives, for freeing the peasantry was not just a panicked reaction to the disorder in the countryside. It was clear very early on almost everywhere in Europe that whoever succeeded in winning over the peasant masses had a good chance of triumphing in the revolutionary struggles of 1848. It was for this reason that serfdom was swept away suddenly in Galicia on 22 April – months before it was abolished elsewhere in Austria. The governor, Franz Stadion, announced the immediate emancipation in order to pre-empt similar efforts by the Polish nationalists. For R. John Rath, freeing the peasants 'was one of the shrewdest moves made by the government during the course of the revolution'.[19] The Emperor could bask in peasant adulation, taking direct credit for meeting the most urgent of all their demands. His name appeared above the emancipation decrees of 11 April and 7 September, so after the rural disturbances of March, by and large the country dwellers settled down to enjoy the fruits of their

Victims at a barricade in Paris, the June days, 1848, by Louis Adolphe Hervier. (Bridgeman Art Library)

M. Thibault's remarkable daguerreotype of barricades on the Rue Saint-Maur, Paris, soon after the attack of government forces in June 1848. (Bridgeman Art Library)

The spectre of social revolution in Vienna: led by a young whippersnapper from the Academic Legion, armed railway workers march into Vienna on 26 May. Watercolour by Franz Gaul. (akg-images)

The Czech revolution bombarded into submission: Prague under fire from Windischgrätz's artillery in June. (akg-images)

THE COUNTER-REVOLUTION

The heroes of the Habsburg counter-revolution: Jelačić, Windischgrätz and Radetzky:

Ban Josip Jelačić. (akg-images)

Prince Alfred Windischgrätz, an unsigned wood engraving from 1848.

(akg-images)

Marshal Joseph Radetzky in 1850. (akg-images)

The siege and bombardment of Vienna, 28 October 1848. (Bridgeman Art Library)

Louis-Napoleon Bonaparte taking the oath to the Constitution of the Second French Republic in 1848. He was committing perjury.

(Bridgeman Art Library)

A motley bunch of German republicans in Baden in May 1849, by Ernst Schalk. Two months later, the city was much less relaxed. (akg-images)

The Scuola dei Morti is ablaze as Venice is bombarded by the Austrians from 29 June 1849, by Luigi Querena. (akg-images)

Habsburg retribution in Hungary: the execution of Hungarian officers at Arad, 6 October 1849, by Janos Thorme. (Bridgeman Art Library)

new freedom and took no further part in revolutionary outbreaks in 1848. While on 24 September Austrian peasants joined a twenty-thousand-strong celebration of the abolition of 'feudalism', they did not then meekly follow the Viennese radicals who had pressed their interests in parliament. They now sought to defend their gains, their religion and their beloved Emperor by siding with the forces of order. In Vienna's final revolutionary torment in October, the hapless radicals, including Hans Kudlich, the original author of the emancipation bill, travelled into the countryside to rally support among the peasantry. The country folk, however, held them at the point of their pitchforks and fowling-pieces and handed them over to the authorities.

In the long run the terms of the emancipation also reinforced the conservative order in the countryside. While the compensation that estate owners received was two-thirds the amount originally set, they were now free of direct responsibility for the peasantry, with all the costs and time that involved. The indemnity allowed them to introduce technological changes to agriculture, making their farms far more competitive than those of the emancipated small-holding peasants, who were now faced with paying indemnities, albeit in small instalments, over two decades.[20] In Galicia the government undertook to pay the landlords outright, but still the peasants would, in turn, repay the state through an interest-bearing loan in smaller instalments, but over a lengthy fifty years. The resulting indebtedness left the former serfs heavily dependent upon their landlords for access to further land, for work and for credit. A Czech radical, J. V. Frič, would later 'congratulate' the parliament of 1848 for having solved the issue of emancipation 'in the interests of the nobility and not of the people'.[21]

On the outbreak of the revolution in Hungary, Kossuth rammed through a bill freeing the peasantry on 18 March. Rumours of the impending emancipation stirred the excited peasantry into action: they invaded seigneurial land, stopped paying rents and dues, ignored the special rights of the landlords, killed their game, pilfered the forests and destroyed manorial records. The Hungarian Diet's abolition of labour services, tithes and other seigneurial rights and dues was enshrined in the April Laws. In practice, however, peasants found that there were limits to their emancipation. The urbarial peasants – those who held land from which they could not be evicted, but which they could neither pass on to their heirs nor legally sell without landlord interference – gained the most. They were granted absolute ownership of their tenures and they shed all their labour obligations. The majority, though, the landless cottagers, benefited less.[22] While free of dues to their landlords, they still had to perform labour services to their county, and their taxes did not change. The Hungarian peasantry therefore pushed for more far-reaching reforms by further rioting, which became so severe that on 21 June the minister of the interior, Bertalan Szemere, declared the entire kingdom under a state of siege, sent the army and National Guard into the countryside and had the peasant leaders arrested. At least ten people were executed before rural peace was restored.

Meanwhile, the landlords were compensated for the loss of services. Peasants were still not allowed to own the lucrative vineyards. Nobles still enjoyed exclusive rights (*regalia*) to sell wine, hold fairs, keep birds (which picked at the peasants' seeds), hunt and fish. So while the nobleman Count Charles Leiningen-Westerburg one day warned his wife that they would have to 'retrench our expenses considerably', he soon afterwards judged that the initial loss of income could be made up considerably by exploiting other rights, such as tolls and ferry dues on their estates.[23] The limits of reform, and the persistence of the belief that the Emperor, not the nobility, was the true protector of the peasants, meant that their reaction to liberal Hungary's grave crisis in the autumn of 1848 was mixed. While some saw in the counter-revolution the threat of being reshackled as serfs, others welcomed the imperial forces as liberators.

This was especially true in those parts of Central and Eastern Europe where the social chasm between lord and peasant coincided with ethnic differences. The Habsburg court, exploiting the monarchy's reputation as the protector of the rural folk, enlisted the support of the Slav and Romanian peasantry against their Magyar landlords. In southern Hungary most of the Slav peasantry pro-claimed their loyalty to the Habsburgs and attacked Magyar and German proprietors. In Transylvania the Romanian peasants – prodded by Habsburg officials – would rise up against the Magyars in what would become one of the most protracted and bloody ethnic conflicts in 1848–9. In Galicia the deep anger of the Ukrainian peasants towards their Polish landlords – and the knowl-edge that it was the Austrian governor who had emancipated them on 22 April – combined violently in a visceral sense of national feel-ing. In the Austrian parliament, the Ukrainian peasant deputies would stare menacingly at their Polish counterparts: 'The only feeling that governed them, aside from their loyalty to the emperor, was a passionate hatred for the Polish nobles. Even in the parlia-ment there were moments when one could read in their eyes that they were ready to let loose against [them] and bash their skulls in.'[24]

Although rural life was ordered in a very different way in Western Europe, peasant action during the revolutions often followed the same course as in Eastern Europe, beginning with insurrection and finishing in counter-revolution. Western peasants found specific outlets for protest against the pressures exerted by changes in the agrarian economy (and in Germany against the remnants of seigneurialism). The small-scale, independent peasant farmers depended on free access to woods and common land for fuel, food and the grazing of animals. This was being endangered by the devel-opment of large-scale market farming and by the enclosure by wealthier farmers and landowners of forests and commons. Peasants therefore targeted the homes and property of the rich, which included both nobles and the well-to-do peasantry. In western Germany peasants occupied land, burned down manor houses and consigned tax registers to bonfires. In France, where the Forest Code of 1827 regulated access to woods, peasants chased away foresters protecting state-owned or communal forests and invaded privately owned, but disputed, woodlands. Such acts were also widespread in western Germany and northern Italy. In many places this behaviour was driven by misery: the public prosecutor in

Toulouse in south-western France explained that the poor people of the mountains who lived in the midst of an abundance of trees were none the less obliged to burn their own furniture for fuel because they could not afford to pay for logs – or else they bundled themselves up in bed during harsh weather.[25]

Against these early protests and the peasants' initially high expectations, the 1848 revolutions offered them little. In France the property-owning peasantry were immediately crushed by the 'forty-five centimes' tax, which they resented as a subsidy to the workers. Some simply could not pay the tax anyway, as the economic crisis was too severe. Country people also feared the militancy of the 'red' urban masses, whose demands for a social republic seemed bent on expropriating their land. The fear inspired by the June days simply increased the hostility of all property-owners towards the workers and pushed them firmly into the camp of those who insisted on 'order' and spoke of defending 'civilisation'. As we have seen, the provincial response to the June insurrection was striking, with National Guard units from no fewer than fifty-three departments, many of them including peasants, travelling to Paris with the intention of crushing the radicals. Afraid of socialism and resentful of the workers, the peasants, while not necessarily hostile to the Second Republic itself, were instrumental in pushing it into reaction. Disappointed and fearful, they felt that they had few alternatives but to turn back to their traditional patrons, the rural notables, openly to resist those measures that they resented, or, ominously, to look for new political solutions. In areas such as the south-west, where the fall in agricultural prices bit deeply into their livelihoods, peasants took up arms against the tax collectors and government enforcers who dared to try to collect the 'forty-five centimes'. In September the public prosecutor in Pau reported that some eighteen thousand peasants had taken up arms against the tax and managed to cut the town off from military reinforcements. In a village near Agen in November a tax official was bound with a rope and threatened with being thrown off a crag, or burned alive, but the peasants contented themselves with incinerating his papers instead. Further north, in the Charente-Inférieure, protesters were heard to yell ominously, 'Down with the forty-five centimes! Long live the Emperor! Down with the Republic!' Slowly, but surely, the figure of Louis-Napoleon Bonaparte was emerging from the shadows.[26]

In Germany peasants saw in the March revolutions the chance to throw off their remaining seigneurial burdens and to protest against the taxes demanded by the state. In East Prussia, where serfdom had been abolished but where indebted peasants were still dependent on the aristocratic landowners and suffered acutely from the economic crisis, they rioted throughout the spring. In response the law courts and the police powers of the Junkers were removed by the liberal government. The worst of the violence occurred precisely in those areas where privately owned estates were most concentrated – in the region between Tilsit and Ermland – and so where the long-term effects of the 1807 reform of serfdom proved to be socially and economically the most disruptive for peasants. In eastern areas, where state-owned land was prevalent, there was less disorder. In western Germany much of the violence was aimed at the *Grundherren*, nobles who still held many legal rights over the land and its inhabitants. It was largely a protest against the fact that, although seigneurialism had been abolished more than a generation ago, peasants were still weighed down by redemption payments.[27] In the constitutional states of south-western Germany peasants showed signs of politicisation. In Nassau, for example, they marched on Wiesbaden, demanding that royal estates be nationalised and distributed amongst them. They also took control of local government by establishing committees in defiance of flabbergasted government officials. The new liberal regimes naturally disapproved of attacks on property, but they were ideologically opposed to 'feudalism' and, in order to mollify the peasants, willingly abolished the remaining dues. Apart from Baden, where the republicans encouraged the peasants to hold on to the land occupied during the March revolutions, and in Rhein-Hessen, where a sympathetic middle class living in towns combined with deep social grievances among the villagers, these concessions were usually enough to persuade the peasants to settle down. This, in turn, gave the German princes the advantage of having peace in the country-side when they struck back against the liberals. In East Prussia, virulent as the violence had been in the spring, peasants kept a deep-rooted faith in the King, if not in their immediate landlords and state officials. In the elections to the Prussian parliament some even wrote 'Frederick William IV' on their ballot papers.[28] In such circumstances, it was easy for the conservatives to recruit the peasants into the cause of the 'King and Fatherland'. Bismarck could reassure Frederick William, *almost* in complete honesty, that 'he was master of the country parts'.[29]

In Italy Neapolitan peasants occupied estate lands on the outbreak of the revolution. They were supported by a handful of radicals, but their action alarmed the moderates, who watched with relief as the National Guard was deployed to restore order. This meant that the peasant insurrection and the liberal, middle-class opposition to the monarchy were not only acting on different levels, but pulling in opposite directions. It was this that allowed Ferdinand to seize his chance with the coup on 15 May. Henceforth, the moderates, who were more terrified of social revolution than of a return to absolutism, were dependent on the monarchy (or, more precisely, the King's soldiers) for law and order. In the north the revolutionaries made little headway in persuading the peasants to support their cause. The Lombard peasantry had rallied to the insurrection in Milan in March and liberal landlords helped the hard-up peasants by providing bread. Ultimately, however, the economic crisis, aggravated by the closure of the Austrian market for the export of raw silk, combined with the introduction of conscription, a forced loan and Piedmontese requisitioning to alienate the peasantry from the revolution. By July they were actively opposed to a war that they believed to be for the benefit of their liberal landlords. Some were even heard to cheer 'Viva Radetzky!' Lombard liberals, like Stefano Jacini, began to think that an Austrian restoration would be preferable to the 'evils of anarchy' that would be unleashed by a peasant insurrection. In neighbouring Venetia peasants were initially enthusiastic for the revolution, fired up by their loyalty to the Pope – affectionately called 'Pio Nono' –

and zealous in their hatred for the Austrian tax collectors, who seemed to personify Habsburg rule. Daniele Manin won over rural hearts early on by abolishing the head tax altogether and by reducing the imposition on salt. Yet the peasants were soon calling for much more than these fiscal concessions: in a wave of protests over the spring, they demanded access to forests and grazing rights on lands that they claimed were commons. Manin did very little to satisfy these demands, because he had no desire to alienate the local landlords, upon whom the reborn Venetian republic was, to some extent, financially dependent. By the summer, therefore, peasant enthusiasm had dissipated. As the tide in the war turned in favour of the Austrians, they shrewdly promised not to restore the head tax. This meant that the peasants now had little to lose in the event of an Austrian resurgence.[30]

II

When the counter-revolution struck first in Vienna and soon thereafter in Berlin, the implications for Germany as a whole were severe. The Austrian imperial government's hand, already stronger after the crushing of the workers' insurrection in August, was strengthened further in the wake of riots on 11–13 September. Small investors in a 'people's bank' established by a clock-maker, August Swoboda, had discovered that the whole business was a swindle. Artisans, shopkeepers, students and master-craftsmen gathered to protest and to convince both the minister of the interior, Baron Anton Doblhoff-Dier, and the Vienna city council that the state should bail them out. When the authorities refused, the crowds became angry, and student radicals used the demonstrations to demand the re-establishment of the Security Committee and the arrest of certain government ministers. On 12 September, Doblhoff-Dier's offices were raided, but the minister made good his escape as the crowd swarmed through the building, smashing windows and doors as they went. The next day, the government called out the entire National Guard and, for good measure, brought in regular troops.

However, the more radical suburban units of the militia went over to the Academic Legion in support of the demonstrators. Vienna looked set to witness yet another bloody collision, but the situation was retrieved by the parliament, which coolly voted to make the considerable sum of two million florins available to help small Viennese businesses (which suffered most from the scandal) in the form of interest-free loans, and to underwrite 20 per cent of the shareholders' losses. At the same time, it ordered the withdrawal of the regular troops. In this way the deputies shrewdly took the sting out of the demonstrations without conceding any of the radicals' demands.

There was to be one last great upheaval, in which the radicals finished by fighting for the survival of the very liberal order that they had done so much to undermine. The immediate spark for the Viennese insurrection in October was the outbreak of open conflict between the Habsburg monarchy and Hungary. When the Emperor formally declared war on 3 October, the Viennese radicals immediately opposed it: Magyar resistance represented the strongest shield against the forces of reaction anywhere in the empire. Moreover, from the German perspective, the Magyars pursued the wholesome occupation of keeping the empire's troublesome Slavs in their place. Workers and suburban National Guards appeared before the students, assuring the Academic Legion of their unqualified support in trying to regain the revolutionary initiative. Meanwhile, Austrians wearing the Habsburg black–gold cockade were beaten up in the streets. There were attacks on property by angry workers, sometimes with radical endorsement. The atmosphere became poisonous with suspicion and hostility. 'A dark cloud hung over the city,' wrote Stiles. 'It daily grew more ominous. All saw and felt that it must soon burst upon their devoted heads, and yet, spell-bound, no one attempted to avert or prevent the catastrophe.'[31]

When Latour, the hated conservative war minister, ordered troops to board trains for the Hungarian frontier in the small hours of the morning of 6 October, workers, students and National Guards prevented them from leaving. A grenadier battalion mutinied and smashed up all the furniture in its barracks in the

Gumpendorf, one of the working-class suburbs. In response Latour called out more troops, who forced the grenadiers towards the railway station. Progress was fitful, since the National Guard made repeated efforts to block the way, while the grenadiers defiantly beat their drums to rally the people in their support. And rally they did: soon a huge crowd had gathered at the railway depot and had torn up the rails. Undeterred, the officers prodded the reluctant soldiers across the Tabor Bridge towards the first station. Yet several arches had been torn apart and the lumber used to build a barricade. When General Hugo von Bredy, the imperial commander, brought up sappers to destroy the obstacle and restore the bridge, there was a stand-off during which some workers tried to seize one of the army's cannon. This was too much for Bredy, who ordered his troops to fire as the gleeful insurgents were dragging off the gun. When the Academic Legion returned a volley, Bredy fell mortally wounded from his horse. There followed a murderous exchange of fire, in which some thirty mutinying grenadiers were cut down in the relentless hail of government musketry. Numerical superiority on the part of the insurgents soon told, however, and the military fell back. The revolutionaries marched jubilantly into the city, pulling two captured cannon and the grim trophies of Bredy's hat and sabre.[32]

By now, imperial troops were being attacked everywhere in Vienna by the National Guard, by the students and the workers. Moderate units of the National Guard were forced to barricade themselves into Saint Stephen's Cathedral by their radical comrades until its doors were battered down and the officer in charge was killed. Parliament and government alike called for calm, but by now barricades had risen around the city centre. Left with minimal protection, the ministries were exposed to the vengeance of the crowd. Latour was protected by a cordon of soldiers outside the War Ministry, but the government, seeking to stop the bloodshed, ordered the military to retreat. This left the minister horribly vulnerable to an angry mob bearing axes, pikes and iron bars. They smashed at the immense doors of the ministry, shouting, 'Where is Latour? He must die!' A deputation from the parliament rushed to the scene to intercede, while Latour took shelter in the attic of the building. The crowd jeered at the deputies and streamed through the ministry, looking for their prey. When they found Latour, the parliamentarians tried to shield him from their fury, but they were pushed aside. The minister was then battered to death, his head caved in with a hammer and cleaved with a sabre before a bayonet sliced into his heart. He was then set upon with a grisly array of weapons until his mangled, limp body was dragged to the square of Am Hof. There the broken corpse was left dangling from a lamp-post for fourteen hours before it was finally cut down.[33]

Meanwhile, the arsenal had been taken by the insurgents, but only after the troops guarding it had swept the streets with grapeshot and inflicted terrible casualties. The revolutionaries had then bombarded the building with captured Congreve rockets and it burst into flames. Thousands of muskets were seized, however, and some insurgents were seen leaving the arsenal wearing breastplates and medieval helmets and bearing a range of other historical artefacts, including Turkish scimitars. In comparison with this sight, sniffed Stiles, 'Falstaff's regiment would have appeared a noble guard.'[34]

The imperial government pulled its forces out of the city, leaving Vienna to the revolutionaries. The victorious radicals then issued their demands, including the reversal of the declaration of war against Hungary, the deposition of Ban Jelačić and the appointment of a 'new and popular government'. The only person who had the authority to issue these orders was the Emperor, but the imperial family was soon taking flight once more, leaving the palace at Schönbrunn, under heavy military escort, and heading to the great Moravian fortress at Olmütz. Before long, most of the remaining government ministers had joined them. Foreign Minister Wessenberg escaped only because no one recognised him as he slipped through the Viennese crowds. Hübner also stole away, disguised in a worker's blouse with his short-cropped hair hidden underneath a hat borrowed from a servant.[35] These refugees were joined by the moderate members of parliament, who no longer felt safe in the capital. The assembly was now in the hands of a left-wing rump and, since the exodus included the large phalanx of Czechs, what remained of the parliament was also dominated by Germans. But there was a range of other political organisations that could try to fill the political vacuum – including the city council, the students' committee and the radical clubs (which were now coordinated by a central committee) – and the result was governmental paralysis, although lower-ranking officials soldiered on bravely. The parliament established a permanent committee to deal with the crisis. Though it was meant to get the legislature's approval for all its measures, in the emergency it was able to issue orders freely.[36]

Its main task was the defence of the city: on 8 October, the Emperor authorised a build-up of troops outside Vienna, to add to the twelve-thousand-strong garrison under Count Maximilien Auersperg, which was encamped just outside the city. Facing them was the National Guard, but the imperial commander wanted to be sure of his victory by amassing overwhelming force. One of Auersperg's couriers rode through the night to Jelačić, who was then taking advantage of a truce with the Magyars and pulling his troops towards Vienna, where he felt he was needed most. When he received Auersperg's appeal for help, he immediately detached a small section of his army to move rapidly on to the imperial capital and ordered the rest of his troops to follow. Thanks to a forced march, he was two hours away from the city with twelve thousand men by 9 October. The Hungarians were in hot pursuit, though, so for the Habsburgs time was now of the essence: the imperial forces had to crush the Viennese revolution before the Magyars arrived to save it. The Hungarian parliament had already offered military assistance to the Viennese, but the Austrian parliament was in an invidious position. On the one hand, since it claimed to be the legal, constitutional authority in Austria, it had to send assurances to Ferdinand of its loyalty and urged him to return to Vienna and withdraw his troops. On the other, most deputies were realistic enough to know that they could not depend upon the Emperor's goodwill, so an appeal to the Hungarians was now the only real hope for the survival of liberal Austria. Since no one was willing to grasp this particular nettle, there was a game of political tennis, in which the parliament and the city council kept returning the question of Magyar assistance to each other. The students and the radicals sent a deputation to Budapest to make their own appeal to the Magyars, but the latter – now poised on the Austrian border – would respond only to a request from the legal authorities in Vienna, which meant the parliament.[37]

Meanwhile, the Emperor rebuffed the parliamentary committee's plea for him to withdraw his troops. This meant that the middle, constitutional road was no longer an option: there could now be victory only for either the revolution or the monarchy. To make matters worse, on the evening of 10 October, Jelačić's approaching Croats were spotted by lookouts perched in the steeple of Saint Stephen's Cathedral. Viennese fear was palpable: the streets were deserted except for companies of the civic militia and National Guards, the Academic Legion and the new Mobile Guard (set up with funds made available by parliament), who tramped through the streets in ominous silence. Watch-fires burned through the night along the city walls. Everyone knew that the only good chance of victory would be provided by the timely arrival of the Hungarians. From Frankfurt, Archduke John sent two German delegates to mediate between the court and the city, but the imperial government was now determined to crush the revolution and gave them a frosty reception. Meanwhile, after their motion to send help to Vienna was voted down by the Frankfurt parliament, the German radical deputies sent two of their colleagues, Robert Blum and Julius Fröbel, to Vienna to offer moral support. They arrived on 17 October.[38]

Meanwhile, the Habsburg forces were still mustering around the city: on 16 October, Ferdinand confided the command to Windischgrätz, who was also given full powers to restore order. By 20 October, the field marshal's thirty thousand men in Bohemia were on the road to Vienna. In a proclamation written by Hübner, the Emperor warned that measures would be taken to curb the press, freedom of assembly and the militias, although these laws would be drafted with parliamentary collaboration. Alarmed, some of the Czech deputies at Olmütz persuaded him to offer reassurances that a constitution would still be drafted.[39] For this purpose, on 22 October, Ferdinand ordered the parliament to leave Vienna and move to Kroměříž (Kremsier) in Moravia (not far, but a safe enough distance, from the imperial court) by 15 November – an order that the left-wing deputies disobeyed.[40]

By 23 October, all of Windischgrätz's troops were in position, surrounding the city with 70,000 men; Jelačić's Croats held the eastern front. The Magyars were now twenty-eight miles away, on the Hungarian–Austrian border, waiting for the rump Austrian parliament to make a formal request for aid: 'We are not entitled', declared Kossuth, 'to force our aid upon people who do not express their willingness to accept it.'[41] In Vienna, which was now entirely cut off from the outside world (even its water and gas supplies were severed), there were hopeful rumours that Magyar pickets had been spotted close to the city. Windischgrätz was all too aware that time was pressing, so he demanded the city's capitulation within forty-eight hours. The defiant response of the defenders was to make a sortie, in the small hours of the following day, against the imperial outposts. The field marshal's ultimatum expired on 26 October, when the attack began. The revolutionary outposts were driven back into the city, while an artillery battery dug into the Schmeltz cemetery just outside the first ring of the Viennese entrenchments was bombarded and then taken by storm. The main assault, however, was led by Jelačić, whose men, after twelve hours of fighting, managed to advance by midnight into the city's eastern suburbs. Even at this late stage, there were honest efforts to broker peace: Baron Pillersdorf, now a member of the Austrian parliament, asked Windischgrätz to offer some concessions in return for a Viennese surrender. The old soldier gruffly brushed off this suggestion. 'Well then,' sighed Pillersdorf, 'may the responsibility of all the blood shed fall on your head', to which the unfazed field marshal replied, 'I accept the responsibility.'[42]

After a lull on 27 October, every battery around the city opened fire on the entrenchments outside. At 9 a.m., Windischgrätz himself led his troops from Schönbrunn and broke into the industrial suburbs, while Jelačić consolidated his grip on the eastern outskirts. Led by the fearsome Montenegrins – wrapped in their fiery red cloaks with their curved blades clamped in their mouths while they clambered on to the fortifications – the southern Slavs cleared some thirty barricades in hand-to-hand fighting. By evening, imperial troops stood in front of the walls of the inner city. The suburbs were bursting with flame, set alight by grenades, shells and Congreve rockets 'tracing their brilliant curves across the night sky'.[43] The bombardment continued all night, ending only in the morning when Windischgrätz decided to give the Viennese time to reconsider their defiance. Sure enough, a delegation from the city council made its way to the field marshal's headquarters at Schönbrunn to offer Vienna's unconditional surrender. But while the majority of Viennese were certainly desperate to see an end to the fighting, many of the revolutionaries were now far too compromised to throw down their arms without some guarantees: they were, as Stiles put it, 'fighting with halters around their necks'.[44] Nevertheless, being so short of food and munitions, even those Viennese who wanted to continue the battle could not hold out for much longer.

At this point, the commander of the National Guard, General Wenzel Messenhauser, who had spent two uninterrupted days in the cathedral tower watching the fighting and scanning the horizon hopefully, at last spotted the long-awaited approach of the Hungarians. Kossuth, who had joined the Magyar army with 12,000 volunteers on 28 October (bringing its total strength up to 25,000), had seen the flames of Vienna shooting into the night sky and decided that the time for legal niceties was over. 'Vienna still stands,' he declared. 'The courage of her inhabitants, our most faithful allies against the attacks of the reactionary generals, is still unshaken.'[45] When the Hungarians crossed into Austria, the Viennese could hear their guns booming. The Viennese radicals, the National Guard, the students and the workers repudiated the city council's peace overtures and took up the fight once again. Windischgrätz detached Jelačić and Auersperg with 28,000 men to meet the Hungarians. On 30 October, the Magyars were a few tantalising miles from the city. At one of the most finely balanced moments in Austria's history, they marched straight towards the waiting mouths of sixty Austrian cannon, which were lurking behind the heights of Schwechat. When the Habsburg artillery opened fire, it was, according to Colonel Arthur Görgey, 'truly murderous at so short a distance'. The Hungarian regulars plodded doggedly onwards through the hail of shrapnel, but it was too much for the Honvéd, who broke and ran. By the next day, they had fallen back 'like a scared flock' across the frontier.[46] Despairing Viennese revolutionaries could hear and see this drama unfolding from the towers of the city: with the Hungarian defeat, the last hope of the Austrian revolution died.

Subjected to a further bombardment – in the light of which Saint Stephen's Cathedral was bathed in pink, scarlet and crimson[47] – the city capitulated on 31 October. The city council sent a delegation to Windischgrätz, explaining that most Viennese wanted to surrender, but that they were being prevented from doing so because the desperate radical students, democratic clubs and workers were terrorising them.[48] White flags now flapped from the city's towers and spires, but there were still pockets of stubborn resistance: when the field marshal's troops had to blast their way through the great Burg Gate, the adjacent imperial palace caught fire, destroying much of the Emperor's library. By the following day, though, the soldiers were in control, and Windischgrätz and Jelačić formally entered the city.

Two thousand people had died in the fighting. Since Vienna had broken the terms of its first surrender, the field marshal was in no mood for kindness: he declared a state of siege, with cordons of troops preventing people from entering or leaving without written permission. Some two thousand revolutionaries were arrested, the Academic Legion and National Guard were both disbanded, and censorship was imposed. Twenty-five revolutionaries were tried by court martial and executed. Among the victims were Messenhauser and Blum. By his public speeches, the latter was held to have encouraged the Viennese into rebellion. While it is true that, in his final days, Blum had succumbed to the radical

temptation to be sanguinary in his rhetoric, his moderation in
Frankfurt suggests that he did not deserve such a terrible fate. He
was executed, 'by powder and ball' (Austrian military jargon for
death by firing squad), after a summary court martial on 9
November. His colleague Fröbel was also found guilty, but was
pardoned and then expelled from Austria. His life was spared
because (by his own testimony), he had published a pamphlet
entitled 'Vienna, Germany and Europe', in which he argued that
the 'German question' should not be resolved by partitioning the
Austrian Empire. After the death sentence had been passed at his
court martial and he was being led away, he shrewdly dropped the
pamphlet on the table in the room. It was picked up and read by
Windischgrätz, who was presiding over the tribunal. The commander was impressed enough to sign the pardon a couple of
hours later.[49] Messenhauser was shot in the city moat, having
refused a blindfold and exerting his privilege, as a former officer, to
give the order to fire himself.[50]

With the Habsburg black–gold now fluttering everywhere in the
capital, the forty-eight-year-old Prince Felix zu Schwarzenberg was
asked to form a new government on 19 November. He was
Windischgrätz's brother-in-law: it was his sister who had been killed
in Prague's June days. Earlier in 1848 he had been in Italy, first as
ambassador to Naples and then with Radetzky's army. Unlike
Radetzky and Windischgrätz, however, Schwarzenberg was no reactionary: when, in mid-October, it had looked like the Emperor
was about to dissolve parliament altogether, it was his influence
that had ensured that it was ordered to reconvene at Kremsier
instead.[51] Yet, in the end, he believed in the traditional Habsburg
way of reform, from above: 'Democracy must be fought and its
excesses must be challenged but in the absence of other means of
help that can only be done by the government itself.'[52]

He wanted to restore Habsburg authority, centralise the monarchy and, to some extent, Germanise it. The cabinet that he
appointed therefore included some who had been associated with
the liberal governments of 1848, namely Franz Stadion, who would
soon set about drafting a new imperial constitution, and Alexander

Bach, the one-time democrat. Before 1848, Bach had been one of the stalwarts of the liberal Legal-Political Reading Club and he was one of the more radical leaders of the March revolution; but during the summer, he grew more alarmed by the radical tide, declaring privately that he wanted 'progress, but not upheaval'. Elected to the Austrian parliament and then appointed justice minister in the Doblhoff government in July, he saw, as Hübner (who got to know and respect him) put it, 'the abyss which was opening beneath his feet'. Bach's definitive break with the left came in September, when he argued strenuously in favour of the imperial veto on parliamentary legislation. The murder of Latour in October merely confirmed Bach's entry into the conservative camp: 'he had lost the faith in which he had been raised' and for this he was castigated by his former left-wing allies as an apostate.[53] On 2 December, Schwarzenberg's government persuaded Ferdinand to abdicate, then replaced him with his nephew, the eighteen-year-old Franz Joseph. The new emperor had no associations with the liberal concessions made that year, so he could not be bound by them.[54]

The events of 1848 had taught Franz Joseph that the two great pillars of the Habsburg monarchy were the army and its subjects' loyalty to the dynasty. None the less, the Constituent Assembly was for now maintained, reconvening a little later than initially instructed, on 22 November, as a rump in Kremsier, primarily as a means of gathering support in the final reckoning with the Magyars. For now, the imperial parliament was allowed to produce its own version of a liberal constitution, but the government acted as if this document did not exist. On 4 March 1849, it foisted three acts on to the empire: its own bill of rights; a law on compensation for landlords for their losses from the abolition of serfdom; and a constitution 'granted' by Franz Joseph. This last document was Stadion's work, and it was top-heavy in the sense that the Emperor held all the meaningful power, including legislative initiative and the appointment of ministers, who would be responsible to the sovereign, not to parliament. The Emperor was to make all decisions on matters affecting the empire, and since the whole monarchy was henceforth to be regarded as a unitary, centralised state, that meant virtually every area of policy. Some important traces of 1848 remained, including the abolition of serfdom and seigneurial obligations; the constitution recognised civil rights (including the equality of all subjects before the law); and, of course, it retained a parliament – of sorts. None the less, the government followed all this up by restricting freedom of the press and of association on 13 March. All nationalities were henceforth to be equal, but effectively that meant that no nationality was to have the right to its own separate political identity, since the empire was now divided into uniform provinces. The Kingdom of Hungary was thus to be erased. The nationality question in the Habsburg Empire was to be effaced by administrative uniformity and centralisation; this was no 'federal' solution to the problem, but rather an 'a-national' one.

III

Events in Vienna gave Frederick William IV of Prussia the final shot of courage to take the revolutionary bull by the horns. In the autumn Prussian politics was still on the path towards constitutional government, but it was a rocky one. The Prussian parliamentary decree of 9 August requiring all soldiers to cooperate 'respectfully and devotedly in the achievement of a constitutional legal situation'[55] was taken at the court to be an outrageous assault on royal control of the army. The liberal ministry under Rudolf von Auerswald resigned on 8 September rather than force the military to swallow this order. By now, reassured of popular support – some of it expressed in petitions imploring the King to save the country from radicalism – the camarilla at Sans Souci was beginning to draft plans for a *Streik* against the National Assembly, but these were not set in stone. Frederick William appointed Ernst von Pfuel as a stop-gap minister, and he worked hard to heal the rift between court and parliament. He tried in vain to enforce a softer version of the 9 August decree, arguing that if order were to be restored, it should be done within a legal framework. In early October

he permitted parliament to debate Prussia's draft constitution, but
his attempts to mollify the legislature failed to steer the King and
the National Assembly off their collision course. Conservatives were
revolted by the proposals to expunge from the royal title the words
'by the Grace of God' and to abolish noble titles and the death
penalty.

These counter-revolutionaries were gathering their forces.
Leopold von Gerlach's brother, Ernst, had created the Association
for King and Fatherland in early July. This organisation aimed at
rolling back the revolutionary gains of March 1848, dissolving
parliament and restoring royal power. The only representative
institutions would be the provincial estates – dominated, of course,
by the landed nobility. The 'Fatherland', too, meant Prussia, not
Germany, for the conservatives knew that a distinctly *Prussian* patriotism still lingered among the masses. During parades in honour of
Archduke John – the regent of the new Germany – on 6 August,
some thousand peasants showed up pointedly waving the Prussian
black–white banner rather than Germany's black–red–gold. Many
Prussians feared that merging into Germany would obscure the
kingdom's own sense of identity, diluting its greatness among the
weakling states and threatening its Protestantism by too close an
association with southern Catholics.[56] Gerlach also founded an
ultra-conservative newspaper, the *Neue Preussische Zeitung*, which
was rapidly dubbed the *Kreuzzeitung* because of the iron cross motif
on its front page – a patriotic symbol dating from the 'War of
Liberation' against Napoleon. Its appeal lay in the fact that it combined wit, political discussion and polemic with hard facts:
Bismarck, one of its most important contributors, understood that
a newspaper would be influential beyond its natural constituency if
it was useful as a source of actual news, not just opinion. This did
not prevent him, however, from writing some brutal pieces against
the conservatives' opponents.[57] The Association for King and
Fatherland rapidly spread across Prussia, where local organisations
affiliated to it. By the autumn, there were some one hundred of
these societies, and by the following spring as many as three
hundred, boasting a total membership of sixty thousand, showing

that this was not merely a movement of irascibly reactionary country squires.[58]

Enlisting the support of the masses was for some members of the old social elites a leap into the dark that they took with some trepidation. A generation gap may have come into play here: old-style conservatives like the Gerlachs idealised the hierarchical, deferential society that was meant to have existed before the revolution. Thrusting young men like Bismarck, however, took a much more pragmatic view of the popular role. The principles of a newer form of conservatism were hammered out in the *Kreuzzeitung* and among the members of the Association for the Protection of the Interests of Landed Property, established by Bismarck and his allies in order to unite the Prussian Junkers and to rally the peasantry behind them. For this reason, the association added to its name 'and for the Maintenance of the Prosperity of All Classes of the People' – as if the original title was somehow too catchy. Four hundred people attended its general assembly in Berlin on 18–19 August, which its opponents scornfully dubbed the 'Junker Parliament'. For Bismarck, it was not enough simply to expect that the masses would tug their forelocks and follow the lead of their social 'superiors', as traditionalists hoped. Instead, the old nobility had to stress that they shared the same material interests as the rest of the population. Liberalism, Bismarck argued, was the ideology solely of the propertied, urban middle class – a narrow social group. Anyone else who supported it – peasants, artisans, retailers and delusional Prussian noblemen – were betraying their own best social and economic interests. Bismarck's brand of conservatism therefore offered not a return to an ossified past, but rather a combination of measures that would serve the peasants and the lower middle class well, such as confirmation of the abolition of the last remnants of 'feudalism' for the peasants and tariffs to protect small businesses. Popular support would thus be enrolled behind the traditional elites, an alliance that would be invincible against liberalism and radicalism.[59]

In September, Frederick William had appointed the outright reactionary General Friedrich von Wrangel to command the army

around Berlin. Coarse and rather eccentric, Wrangel (who habitu-
ally sported a well-polished cavalry breastplate) soon appeared in
Berlin, where he gave a clumsy speech assuring the locals of his
desire not to have to shoot them. On 21 September, Helmuth von
Moltke, then a junior staff officer but destined to become one of
Prussia's great generals, wrote to his brother:

> We now have 40,000 men in and around Berlin; the critical point
> of the whole German question lies there. Order in Berlin, and we
> shall have order in the country . . . They now have the power in
> their hands and a perfect right to use it. If they don't do it this time,
> then I am ready to emigrate with you to Adelaide.[60]

As if to emphasise the point, a new uprising took place in Berlin in
mid-October. The excitement generated by the constitutional battle
allowed the radicals to mobilise large numbers of people in political
clubs such as the Linden and Friedrich Held's Democratic Club.
What was more, since March, anyone was allowed to bear arms,
and, alongside the official civic guard, there were 'mobile associations' of workers, students and artisans. On 13 October, the
National Assembly – trying desperately to cling to the subsiding
middle ground – decided that it was time to disarm the radicals and
voted to declare the primarily middle-class civic guard the only
legitimate police force in the capital. The liberals and the democrats
now came to direct blows. Radical protests erupted in the city and,
on 16 October, the canal workers seized the opportunity to riot
against the steam pumps that they saw as a threat to their livelihoods. The civic guard drew up and shot dead eleven of them.
Further pressure was brought to bear on the Assembly when the
radical Democratic Congress and the 'anti-parliament', intended to
be a counterweight to the more moderate German Assembly in
Frankfurt, met in Berlin at the end of the month. Among its par-
ticipants was Franz Zitz – one of the instigators of the September
crisis in Frankfurt – and Johann Jacoby, who called on Prussia to
send troops to help the Viennese in their struggle against the
Habsburg reaction. This demand was presented beneath streaming

red flags by a one-thousand-strong protest march on the Prussian National Assembly on 31 October. When a parliamentary majority rejected the petition, the crowd outside roared angrily. One deputy was struck in the face by a flaming torch when he tried to leave the chamber. His colleagues were forced to escape through a side door, clambering through storerooms and over ladders to get to it. As they emerged into the street, a shot was fired and pandemonium erupted as club-wielding civic guards and workers swinging torches struck at each other. The locomotive workers arrived and broke up the fighting, but in the confusion the civic guard had turned its weapons on them, too.[61]

The incident showed that there was an unbridgeable gap between the moderates and the radical left, which provided the conservatives with their opportunity. Pfuel resigned, his efforts at compromise in tatters. The King sensed that the divisions between the liberals and the democrats were so irreconcilable that he could at last strike, but even now he wavered: should he, he asked a friend, 'continue with the constitutional comedy . . . or suddenly march in with Wrangel and then, as conqueror, fulfil the letter of my promises'?[62] This last phrase was telling: it suggested that the King was not set on an outright reaction, but wanted to impose a 'revolution from above'; that is, reform, but on the monarchy's own terms. A constitution of 'the most liberal sort' was being considered, but it was one which, when the moment was right, would later be reformed to the monarch's satisfaction. On 1 November, he heeded Bismarck's advice and appointed the conservative Count von Brandenburg as prime minister. The situation then went from extremely bad to irretrievable. Frederick William snubbed a parliamentary delegation desperately trying to fend off a *coup d'état* (one of its members was an exasperated Jacoby, who exclaimed, 'That's the trouble with kings: they don't want to hear the truth!'). This provoked fifteen hundred protesters to take to the streets in a show of radical defiance, which they called 'a last fight for the fatherland and right and freedom'. On the other side of the political divide, the shrieks for an end to 'anarchy' and 'lawlessness' from the conservative press became shriller. Fanny Lewald returned to her city on 7 November to find the mood extremely depressing and the political bitterness harsher than before, learning that the 'stable friends of order' were waiting impatiently for the 'verdict by shrapnel'.[63]

Two days later, Count Brandenburg appeared before the National Assembly and read a royal proclamation explaining that, for their own protection, the deputies were to be dismissed until the end of the month, when they would reconvene in Brandenburg. The majority in the Assembly rose in support of its president when he declared that such an act was illegal. It was only now that liberals and radicals rediscovered their common ground and talked about combining their forces – the democratic clubs and the civic guard – to defend the parliament, but it was too late. All that remained was passive resistance – the commander of the civic guard refused to use his men against the Assembly – but this merely provided the government with the pretext to send thirteen thousand of Wrangel's troops, supported by sixty cannon, into Berlin on 10 November.

Now, though, came perhaps the National Assembly's finest hour. Protected by the civic guard drawn up outside (with Wrangel's men only two hundred paces away), and watched in respectful silence by supporters in the public galleries, the deputies went on with their business as the sky darkened and the lamps were lit. They discussed such matters as the abolition of the taxes on quill pens, dog biscuits and the feed for a peasant's 'house cow'. 'They debated very calmly', explained Lewald, 'because they found themselves on the firm ground of true law.' At one stage during the evening's proceedings, the president sent a polite letter to Wrangel, asking how long his troops intended to stand outside, since their presence was not needed. Wrangel, his coarseness not attuned to such subtle humour, replied bluntly that he would not budge, since he recognised neither the National Assembly nor its president.[64] Sitting casually on a chair in front of his troops, looking pointedly at his watch, the general gave the Assembly fifteen minutes to adjourn. In the end the parliamentarians meekly dispersed and the civic guard allowed itself to be disarmed. Even the backbone of the popular movement, the locomotive workers, who had gathered angrily in front of the royal palace, had no stomach for a fight against Wrangel's well-drilled soldiers. They abandoned the square with only a formal protest.[65]

A sizeable proportion of the deputies hastily reassembled in the Berlin sharpshooters' club (members of the same society had wreaked havoc on the army during the March revolution), where they voted in favour of a radical proposal to call on Prussian citizens to go on tax strike. Yet Brandenburg was not finished: on 12 November, he declared martial law and Wrangel's artillery was wheeled ominously into positions around the city. The civic guard was disarmed, the democratic clubs were scattered and newspapers were closed down. Berlin was full of soldiers tramping the streets in their hob-nailed boots, or lounging in stairwells. The museum was turned into a barracks, where rifles were propped up against statues and helmets were piled on antiques. Streets were periodically sealed off as patrols searched houses for weapons.[66] The tax strike had little impact, since the people who paid the most were precisely those who wanted a return to order. None the less, the conservatives avoided a complete reaction. On 5 December Prussia 'received' a constitution that had been 'granted' by Frederick William (over the protests of outright reactionaries like Brandenburg). There was to be a two-chamber parliament, with a lower house elected by universal male suffrage. Parliamentary controls over the machinery of the Prussian state were, though, swept aside: the King had full executive powers, including command of the armed forces. Soldiers and officials had to swear an oath to obey the King, not parliament; and on 30 May 1849, when he felt strong enough to do so, Frederick William handed down a revised electoral law, which divided each constituency into three classes of taxpayer, to ensure that the wealthiest voters elected one-third of all the delegates. He also confirmed the emancipation of the peasants from their remaining obligations, along with the abolition of noble tax privileges and of the local policing and judicial powers of the Junkers. Some artisans were satisfied with the restoration of the guilds in seventy trades, but the revolution in Prussia was well and truly over.[67]

The victory of conservatism in Austria and Prussia endangered the liberal regimes elsewhere in Germany. Some moderates who had been profoundly worried by the rising tide of radicalism welcomed Frederick William's bloodless coup in Berlin: Gustav Mevissen hailed the 'bold move' and called on all men of courage 'to place themselves on the basis of the new legal order and fight the impending anarchy'.[68] After all, Prussia still had a constitution, which was an important fact. First, it showed that, while the revolution had been smashed by the instruments of the Prussian state, in the process the monarchy had accepted some of the opposition's concepts of law and rights. Second, it meant that Prussia could remain the focus of German national aspirations, because it gave the kingdom some credentials for leadership of a united, constitutional Germany. However, other Frankfurt delegates made loud protests against the royal *coup d'état*. The entire German left at last rediscovered the unity that had been shattered in the spring. The moderate left-wing delegates established the Central March Association, aimed at uniting all shades of opinion in support of the revolutionary achievements against the gathering forces of reaction. It was an impressive network, boasting some half a million members in 950 affiliated clubs, which dwarfed the efforts of the more radical democrats who had been behind the troublesome Democratic Congress in Berlin in October (which counted 260 affiliated clubs). Meanwhile, the Frankfurt parliament soldiered on in its task of hammering out a German constitution.

One of the central issues exercising the deputies was the question of whether German-speaking Austria should be included in the united German Reich. As the moderate Friedrich Dahlmann put it succinctly, there were two choices: dissolving the Habsburg Empire and binding its German parts to the united German state; and keeping the empire intact, which meant excluding Austria from Germany. The parliament debated this issue in October, as news was filtering through of the fighting in Vienna. The deputies were split between two different German visions, which cut across the political divisions of left and right. In the early, heady days of the revolution those who supported the inclusion of Austria (the

'Greater German' or *Grossdeutsch*) solution were in the majority. They included Catholics who feared that, without Austria, the northern German Protestants would predominate, since they would make up two-thirds of the population. Democrats, who saw no sense in a German nation-state without the German-speaking Austrians, wanted a unitary, centralised and democratic Germany: to leave the Austrians out of it would mean that a substantial proportion of the German people would be left vulnerable to the other non-German peoples of the Habsburg Empire. As Tübingen radical Ludwig Uhland put it, the Austrian parliament already showed that the Slavs, with their mass of population, would dominate politically, so where would that leave the Austro-German minority? Austria's mission was to be 'a beating artery in the heart of Germany'.[69]

The *Kleindeutsch* (or 'Smaller German') solution opposed the inclusion of Austria. Its proponents included moderate liberals like Heinrich von Gagern, who could see no other practical way of creating a united German state. Alongside the parliament's mandate to give the 'whole German nation' a constitution, Gagern argued, the deputies had to 'take account of the circum-stances, the facts . . . if we intend to create a viable constitution'. The *Grossdeutsch* idea would effectively dismember the Austrian Empire, which for Gagern was neither morally right ('we have an obligation . . . when civil war has broken out in a federal state, when the fire is blazing, not to add more fuel to the con-flagration') nor in the interests of the new Germany, as it would leave the future stability and security of all Central Europe in doubt.[70] Since they had no desire to assail the dynastic rights of the Habsburgs, such moderates believed that the simplest solution was to forge a smaller German state in the north, but loosely tied in a confederation with Austria and its non-German nationalities. As the *Kleindeutsch* solution excluded conserva-tive, Catholic and protectionist Austria, its supporters tended to be northern, Protestant liberals who admired constitutional and free-trading Prussia. Wilhelm Wichmann spoke for many when he blasted:

Austria is the only state capable of placing real obstacles in the path of German unification and, in fact, has already done so. The other German states will have to merge into Germany or they will sink into it and into history. But Austria contains many anti-German elements, whose opposition and awakening could be a serious obstacle to the German movement which has been building up.[71]

By excluding Austria, the *Kleindeutsch* solution would also have pre-empted the problem over how far the non-German nationalities in the Habsburg Empire were to be included. For Wichmann, to include those peoples would be downright dangerous: Germany could stand as the equal of others 'only if we keep our nationality as pure as possible, if we emerge from the great crystallization of nations about to take place in Europe as an unblemished crystal excluding as many foreign elements as at all possible'.[72] By contrast, at its extremes, the *Grossdeutsch* solution envisaged an enormous state that included all of Germany and the entire Habsburg Empire. This was a view proposed strongly by those deputies who represented the more beleaguered German populations in non-German Habsburg territories. 'Our aim', declared Count Friedrich von Deym from Bohemia, 'is to establish a giant state of 70, or even if possible of 80 or 100 millions.' This idea, which would become known as the *Mitteleuropäisch* (Middle European) solution, would ensure that German influence would reach all the way into south-eastern Europe, while acting as a massive bulwark against other empires, particularly the Russian. This huge state would 'stand in arms against east and west, against the Slav and Latin peoples, to wrest control of the sea from the English, to become the greatest most powerful nation on the globe – that is Germany's future!'[73] This vision of *Mitteleuropa* would lead – though by no means intentionally in 1848 – to Europe's darkest years in the twentieth century. It should be said that the *Kleindeutsch* proponents were no shrinking violets when it came to the idea of 'colonising' south-eastern Europe, either. Together, according to Gagern, Germany and Austria had a mission to spread 'German culture, language, and way of life along the Danube to the Black Sea'.[74]

The parliament was still debating this thorny issue and all its prickly ramifications when the counter-revolution struck in Austria. Days before Windischgrätz's troops battered their way into Vienna, the parliament agreed on the first three articles of the German constitution, which declared that the German Empire would consist of the entire territory of the old confederation (though leaving the problems of Poznan and Schleswig-Holstein to future debate); that no part of the empire may form a state with non-German lands; and that any German country that shares a head of state with a non-German one should have a purely personal, dynastic union with the latter.[75] In other words the Constitution proclaimed the *Grossdeutsch* solution just as it was becoming practically impossible. The Habsburg court and the imperial government had never been enthusiastic about German unification, since it would reduce Austria to being a mere 'province' in the Greater Germany. Symbolic of this reluctance was the fact that the ill-fated Latour had permitted the Austrian armed forces to fly the black–red–gold colours for only a single day, before ordering a return to the imperial black–yellow. While Vienna was still being hammered into submission, Baron Wessenberg, the Austrian minister-president, wrote to all Austrian diplomats in Germany that 'the revolution has covered itself with a German mantle; the German colours have become the ensign of the party of overthrow'.[76] When Robert Blum and Julius Fröbel were sentenced to death, some conservatives worried that, since they were members of the Frankfurt parliament, there would be repercussions in Germany. Schwarzenberg was unimpressed, bluntly telling Windischgrätz that their parliamentary privileges 'have no legal force in Austria. The only privilege they can claim is that of martial law.'[77] There cannot have been many more decisive ways of expressing the Austrian rejection of German unification than by shooting two of its representatives. On 27 November, Schwarzenberg declared that the Habsburg monarchy was a unitary state, a statement that was reinforced by the imperial constitution imposed by the Emperor in March 1849. The Greater German solution was therefore an impossibility, as it would mean tearing the German organs out of the body of the Habsburg monarchy. On 9 March, Schwarzenberg facetiously made a counter-proposal: a

'Greater Austrian' solution in which the entire Habsburg Empire would join Germany in a huge Central European confederation. As this would include a vast array of non-German peoples, it was clearly unacceptable to the majority in the Frankfurt parliament. Still, the advocates of neither the *Kleindeutsch* nor the *Grossdeutsch* solution had a majority in Frankfurt. Even with the unequivocal Austrian rejection of German unification, the *Kleindeutsch* idea would win the final vote only after some parliamentary horse-trading. The Austrian government's uncompromising position was a statement of its new-found strength, now that it had destroyed the revolution in Prague in June 1848, crushed the Italians at Custozza in July and defeated the Viennese radicals in October. Yet, even in the spring of 1849, the empire still faced two major challenges: the first was finding a way to defeat the Hungarians; the second was to bring Italy well and truly to heel.

IV

Prodded by some of the Habsburg court, Jelačić had crossed the Drava with his forces and invaded Hungary on 11 September 1848: his declaration promised to deliver Hungary 'from the yoke of an incapable, odious, and rebel Government'.[78] Against his enormous army of some fifty thousand men, the Hungarians had a skeletal force of five thousand, mostly raw recruits and National Guards commanded by Count Ádám Teleki, an aristocratic career soldier who was squeamish about fighting a fellow commander who had sworn an oath to the Emperor. He pulled his forces back towards Budapest, declaring on 15 September that he felt morally bound not to fight the Croats. In response the Hungarian government (still clinging to its desire for legality) asked – more in hope than expectation – the palatine, Archduke Stephen, to command Hungary's forces, but he refused, since Emperor Ferdinand had ordered him not to resist Jelačić. So the Croats advanced on to Budapest virtually unopposed, visiting the horrors of war on the countryside. One of Jelačić's officers wrote:

In four days' time we will be before Pesth, and God help the town, for the Frontiersmen [Jelačić's troops] are so embittered and angry that they will be awful to manage. Already, they can't be kept from excesses, and rob and steal frightfully. We order a thousand floggings to be administered every day; but it is no sort of use: not even a god, much less an officer, can hold them back. We are received by the peasants quite kindly, but every evening come the complaints, sometimes dreadful ones. I am driven desperate by this robber train and feel no better than a brigand myself.[79]

The invasion provoked a political crisis in Budapest, but its outcome was quite remarkable. Radical unease with Batthyány's government and the 'treachery' of Palatine Stephen had been rumbling since the summer. By early September, the newspaper *March Fifteenth* and the Society for Equality were talking openly about a second revolution. Following the French example, the club organised a massive banquet, scheduled for 8 September, to put pressure on the government and force the resignation of the ministers, excluding Kossuth and Minister of the Interior Szemere. Yet Kossuth himself rose in parliament on 2 September and persuaded the radicals to postpone the gathering. The great and popular orator explained that the government was currently engaged in delicate negotiations in Vienna, trying hard to avert open war. There was also the fear that a second revolution in Budapest would provide the pretext for Palatine Stephen to bring in imperial forces and crush the entire liberal order. This, as it turned out, was not idle speculation, for on 29 August Stephen had written to the Austrian garrison commander in the fortress of Komárom upstream from Budapest and told him to be ready to move on the capital against 'the planned machinations of the unruly party'. Yet such troops could also have been used in a counter-revolutionary coup against the government itself.[80] Fortunately, the radicals – albeit after some heated debate – agreed to Kossuth's request. Their press even accepted that the last-ditch negotiations with the Emperor were a valid attempt at 'saving our country'. The government itself, explained the *Radical Democrat*, was raising 'the holy standard of the principles of the revolution', so it called on everyone to support its efforts to ward off the crisis.[81] The Society of Equality had also organised a thousand-strong 'national defence' force, aimed ostensibly at defending the country when diplomacy failed, but in reality forming a revolutionary militia that could seize power should Batthyány's government fall on the outbreak of war. But even this paramilitary organisation voluntarily disbanded on 12 September.

By then, the Croats had invaded and, as expected, the Hungarian government – its efforts at diplomacy in ruins – stood down. So, for two crucial weeks, Hungary had no central government. Although Palatine Stephen asked Batthyány to form a new cabinet, the dogged prime minister's nominations were repeatedly knocked back by the imperial court, even though the candidates were men with impeccably moderate credentials. In these days it was parliament that effectively governed Hungary, and there Kossuth pushed through a bill that urgently organised the new army decreed in August. The volunteers were mustered into Honvéd battalions and all soldiers in the regular units of the imperial army were urged to join these new units. Those who obeyed tore off their black–yellow flashes and assumed the Hungarian tricolour instead; some went so far as to trim their long coats in order to differentiate themselves from the Austrians, who were known as 'swallow-tails' for the shape of their long, white coats. Siding with the radicals, who were now calling for him to be appointed prime minister or even dictator for the duration of the crisis, Kossuth began to show his revolutionary colours, having adhered for so long to the constitution. What was the point, he asked, of following legality if Ferdinand did not feel bound by it himself? There was no greater form of tyranny, he declared, than that which used the very principle of legality to destroy the constitution.[82]

Kossuth's lifelong opponent Count István Széchenyi disagreed, but it was also clear that the imperial court regarded *everything* achieved in Hungary since the March revolution as null and void. The moderate (and hypersensitive) count was therefore confronted with the theoretical possibility that all his work in 1848 had been 'illegal' and that, in the process, he had brought his beloved country to the brink of disaster. Emotionally drained, Széchenyi slid towards psychological collapse. Until now, he had blamed Kossuth's intransigence for provoking the crisis with Austria; now it seemed that even his own, most conservative style of reformism had also angered the imperial court. He passed sleepless night after sleepless night, attending cabinet meetings during the day in a silence of despair. After one such session on 3 September, he burst into a friend's home and released his torment in a flood: 'Blood and blood everywhere! Brother will slay brother and nation nation, in a frenzy. Houses will be marked with crosses of blood for burning. Pest is lost.' He heaped most of the blame on his own tired shoulders, scratching his pen deeply into the pages of his diary: 'I am to be blamed for it all!'[83] The final personal crisis came the following day, when Széchenyi's doctor urged him to retire to his country estate to recuperate. After saying a tearful farewell to his chain bridge, he set out for his home in Cenk. Two suicide attempts were foiled and he voluntarily committed himself to the asylum in Döbling, where he closed himself off from the world behind its great gates, living the life of a penitent.[84]

On 15 September, when Jelačić was a hair-raising forty miles from Budapest, and people were digging entrenchments outside the city, Kossuth rose to the challenge, proposing that a parliamentary committee be established to deal with confidential military affairs, since the responsibility was too much for Batthyány, who still had no cabinet. Parliament agreed over the prime minister's protests, and Kossuth joined with the radicals in taking control of this new 'Committee of National Defence': since no one knew how the crisis would turn, the initiative fell to those who were willing to risk bold measures. Meanwhile, Palatine Stephen resigned and left for Vienna on 23 September. In fact, if not in law, Hungary was at this moment a fully independent country. Shortly afterwards, Kossuth toured the central Hungarian plains, drumming up recruits, like 'a giant spirit who works the people up from their deathly dream', as an awe-inspired radical wrote. When he returned to Budapest, he claimed that some twelve thousand volunteers were now on their way to join the Hungarian colours.[85]

At this point the Austrian government made what was meant to be a conciliatory gesture, by appointing Count Ferenc Lamberg as royal commissioner and commander of all forces in Hungary on 25 September. Lamberg was a conservative, but he was no outright reactionary: a Hungarian who had earned Batthyány's respect, he had participated in the Magyar reform diet of 1847–8. As a soldier, the doves in the Austrian government hoped that Lamberg would be able to exert some authority on both the Croatian and the Magyar forces and broker an armistice. It seems odd that the imperial ministry should have sought a suspension of hostilities just as it looked like Jelačić was going to take Budapest. It may have been because the more moderate ministers, like Wessenberg, feared that an outright victory for Jelačić would either provoke further radical upheavals in the Austrian capital or strengthen the hands of reactionaries like Latour – or probably both. Wessenberg may not have liked the Viennese radicals, but, as a constitutional minister, he wanted to see at least some of the political gains of 1848 survive. On 21 September, he fretted to Ferdinand that a triumph for Jelačić 'would be likely to do away with the constitutional liberties'.[86]

Unfortunately, the Hungarians did not see Lamberg's appointment as an olive branch, not least because the Austrian government also named the conservative reformist Baron Miklós Vay as prime minister. In accordance with the April Laws, these appointments were both illegal, because they had not been approved by the Hungarian government in Budapest. On 27 September, the Hungarian parliament hit back with a resolution declaring its determination to uphold the constitution. When Lamberg arrived in Budapest the following day, his carriage was spotted crossing the pontoon bridge by a crowd of artisans, students and soldiers, who dragged him out and then bludgeoned and stabbed him to death. Only the late arrival of the National Guard prevented the mob from stringing up his torn, lifeless body.[87] The news of this horrific murder discredited moderate Austrian attempts at conciliation and played straight into the hands of the reactionaries in the government, which was now determined to join Jelačić in crushing the Hungarian revolution by force. War was duly declared on Hungary on 3 October.

Even now, Batthyány did not give up in his efforts for peace. Returning from a visit to the army facing the Croats, he sped to Vienna to plead one more time for reconciliation, but he was coolly received. In the absence of a proper government the Hungarian parliament took over. All too aware of the consequences of Lamberg's brutal death, it agreed to Kossuth's suggestion of condemning the deed and resolving to bring those responsible to justice. Then it converted the Committee of National Defence into an emergency executive government, with Kossuth as its president. Yet, at the very moment when the radicals gained power, they consciously shared it with the moderates. The committee's membership was expanded from six to twelve, with all the new members being drawn from the upper house of parliament and from among Batthyány's former cabinet. That the Hungarian radicals – unlike many of their hot-headed European counterparts – were so compliant (although during the September crisis an article in *March Fifteenth* did call for a gallows and a guillotine to be used on 'traitors') can be explained in at least four ways. First, they sought to show that the extraordinary government was not just working in the interests of a radical minority, but was genuinely a national executive. Second, it was in the radicals' own interests to join with the moderates in defending the constitution: their vision of a democratic Hungary could scarcely have survived if it were destroyed.[88] Third, the Society of Equality had only a thousand members nationwide and the elections that summer had shown that they did not enjoy mass support. If they were to govern alone in Budapest, then they would have to force their will on the rest of the country, igniting civil war at precisely the moment when Hungary faced invasion. Fourth, when the radicals surrendered their predominant political position, the military situation had just taken a turn for the better, since Hungarian forces had finally made a stand at the village of Pákozd, where they had defeated Jelačić.

The radicals had no desire to break apart the national unity that had now been forged. They were absorbed with the task of defending Hungary against foreign invasion: most of the radical leadership,

including Petőfi and Vasvári, went off to join the Honvéd units —
both would meet their deaths, killed in action, in 1849 — while those
in parliament supported the war effort in a variety of ways.
Hungary's September crisis therefore did not provoke a radical revolution. An emergency government which included radicals had
been established by parliamentary vote. For this reason, Istvan Deak
describes the events of 1848–9 in Hungary as a 'lawful revolution'.[89]

Nor did the crisis provoke a scurrying of the moderates away
from the political centre and towards the reactionaries, as occurred
elsewhere. One of the explanations for this was social: while the
landed elites in most other European countries were generally conservative or moderate, the Hungarian liberals and radicals alike
were magnates and landed gentry. For them, the national cause
coincided with entrenching and strengthening their political influence. This meant that even relatively conservative reformers like
Széchenyi were sucked into the revolutionary storm. Moreover,
since the main threat of insurrection against property came not
from radical artisans or workers but from the peasantry, which was
usually loyal to the Emperor, the Magyar nobles had much to fear
from a counter-revolution. So it was that Count Karl Leiningen-
Westerburg, a moderately liberal German magnate with large estates
in Voivodina and the Banat, had no difficulty in offering his sword
to the Hungarian revolution, since the Serbian insurgents had over-
run his land and burned his fields.[90] He was driven by an urgent
desire to see order restored to his province. He was also, as a
German born and bred, increasingly hostile to the Habsburgs,
whom he was coming to regard as a perfidious obstacle to the emergence of a federal German state. Moreover, it should be said, he had
a genuine love for his adopted country (and his wife, Lizzie, was
Magyar):

Let the devil fight against his own convictions, if he likes; I had
rather anything happen to me than that I should join hands with
thieves in warring against a nation that has hitherto been quite
peaceful. I cannot tell you how utterly I despise the machinations of
the Court party, and how ridiculous this Jellasich [Jelačić], who

thinks it is so easy to be a Napoleon, appears in my eyes! . . . The die is cast; my fate is bound up with that of Hungary . . . God cannot desert a just cause.[91]

Yet the variety of circumstances, the complexity of motives and the conflicting loyalties, particularly among aristocratic army officers who had taken an oath of loyalty to the Habsburg crown, meant that not all nobles rallied to the revolution. The war tore apart elite families. Leiningen's cousin, Christian, commanded a battalion at the fortress of Temesvár (or Timisoara in Romanian) and joined his fellow officers in declaring for the Habsburgs against the revolution and stirring up the Serb and Romanian peasants against the Magyars in the region. The radical Count László Teleki was brother to Ádám Teleki, the conservative general who resigned his commission rather than fight Jelačić

It was the day after Latour's murder that the Hungarians, under General János Móga, at last engaged with the Croats in battle. The strength of Jelačić's forces had been sapped because their looting – and perhaps some of the patriotic propaganda emanating from the Magyar revolutionaries – had incited the peasantry against them. Small skirmishes erupted, particularly in the rear of the Croatian army, but its numbers were still far greater than those mustered by the Hungarians, who on 29 September defeated them at Pákozd, only thirty miles from Budapest. Further east, a famished and bedraggled second Croatian army that had also been advancing on Budapest surrendered to the Hungarians at Ozora on 7 October. Immediately after Pákozd, Jelačić had asked for a three-day truce, which he used to withdraw his tired troops towards Vienna to support, he claimed, the Habsburg court. On 8 October, as he advanced on that city, he received the news of the radical uprising, which justified his decision retrospectively. Two days later, he was at the gates of Vienna, where he awaited the arrival of Windischgrätz's forces on the march from Prague. The Hungarian pursuit culminated in their force's defeat at Schwechat twenty days later.

With this new crisis, the National Defence Committee donned

the full panoply of its new powers to mobilise the resources of the country so that Hungary was (just) able to survive the crushing Austrian counter-attack. This had started not from Austria itself but in Transylvania. There, General Anton von Puchner, the commander of imperial forces in the province, gave the wink to the Romanian nationalists and – while carefully avoiding any hint that he supported Romanian independence – allowed them to hold a second great congress at Blaj at the end of September. When he received word of the Austrian declaration of war a few days later, he sensed that the time had come for a coup against the Magyar authorities in Transylvania and to assume executive powers in the name of the Emperor. Declaring the committee in Budapest illegal, he called on all loyal Transylvanians to 'rise to the last man, one for all and all for one'. When he made this declaration on 18 October, the Magyar Székely minority defiantly declared its loyalty to Hungary, and some thirty thousand of them, including the border regiments, took up arms. Puchner's appeals found an enthusiastic response among the Romanian peasants, who had been alarmed and enraged by the attempts of Hungarian officials to enrol them into the Honvéd battalions. (By contrast, Puchner endeared himself to the peasants by ordering an end to such recruitment.) The Romanian revolutionaries also backed Puchner: irked by Magyar nationalism, they now saw in Austrian help their best hope of securing at least some recognition of their Romanian aspirations. The peasant insurrection swamped Transylvania. Groups of villagers tracked down and slaughtered Magyar and German landlords and government officials. In retaliation the Székelys and Honvéd units chased after the peasants, mowing them down in mass executions. Hundreds of villages were razed to the ground.[92] This brutal conflict would prove to be one of the longest and bloodiest of all the ethnic struggles of 1848–9, with some 40,000 people killed and 230 villages set aflame.[93] Leiningen was with a Hungarian unit that was advancing on Temesvár after dispersing a band of armed peasants who had skirmished with the Magyars. His testimony mixed a sense of revulsion for the atrocities with the ethnic hatred that drove both sides:

Then began work which filled me with disgust. In a few moments the village was in flames at various points; and the men started pillaging and committed various other offences. We had the greatest difficulty in getting the flames under control. Yet these villainous Wallachians [i.e., Romanians] deserved the punishment they got, for they are daily threatening to murder the poor Hungarians who live among them. As I was slowly riding back out of the village, an officer brought 30 prisoners, truly deplorable wretches! As soon as they reached me, the officer shouted to them in Wallachian (so I was told afterwards) 'Down on your knees before that gentleman! Kiss the dust from off the hoofs of his horse!' Disgusted at the sight, I cast a look of derision at the officer and rode away.[94]

Meanwhile, Puchner's imperial troops and Romanian volunteers had swept across most of Transylvania by the end of November, with only a few pockets of stubborn Magyar resistance holding out. When they invaded Hungary proper, however, Puchner ran into a hastily assembled Hungarian army under the Polish exile General József Bem, who had fought in Vienna in October and fled when Windischgrätz took the city. Bem managed to drive out the Austro-Romanian forces and had reconquered most of Transylvania by the end of January. Imperial forces clung on in Sibiu and Braşov, but Bem's victory secured Hungary's eastern front as the main Austrian onslaught started in the west. As for the Romanians, they were now left weighing the pros and cons of securing Russian help. At Puchner's urging, the Romanian National Committee sent Bishop Andreiu Şaguna to Bucharest, where he met the commander of the Russian army occupying Wallachia. The general refused to offer Russian aid without the Tsar's approval, so the cleric then tried a new tack, travelling to meet the Emperor, whose court was still taking refuge at Olmütz. There, Şaguna presented the now modest Romanian national programme – in effect, it called for an autonomous Transylvanian duchy within the Habsburg Empire – but even that fell on unsympathetic ears in a court now in the grip of a counter-revolutionary fever.[95]

The horrors of ethnic strife in Transylvania were shared in neighbouring Voivodina and the Banat, where Serb (or 'Rascian') peasants had risen up against the Magyars and Germans in the summer. In October Leiningen had heard from his brother-in-law, Leopold ('Poldi') that after the Serbs were routed outside Besce (or Bečej, where the Serb inhabitants of the town joined the insurgents) 'the fury of the Magyars was terrible. For several hours there was an end of all discipline; and then ensued a horrible butchery. Poldi puts the number of those massacred at 250–300. It is awful to think of! That is what I call a real war of extermination.'[96] Later, as the winter began to bite in November, there were constant reminders of the brutalities of the ethnic conflict:

> Every day, several carts of Rascians (mostly women and children) approach our outposts; and the miserable wretches beg and pray to be taken prisoners, as to stay in the Rascian camp means starvation. Pale, reduced to mere skeletons, they ask the soldiers for a bit of bread, which they devour like so many ravenous wolves. The military commanders offer these poor fugitives refuge; but the civil authorities would exterminate them if they could. Innumerable Rascians have been hanged; three were executed to-day. It is no business of mine to inquire whether this is the best mode of subjugating them; for my part, the very sight of such measures is revolting.[97]

Through the winter, village after village taken by the Magyars was torched. It is hard to ascribe the atrocities to official policy, since it appears that on entering the settlements the soldiers acted spontaneously, out of rage and hatred. In a winter campaign lasting from mid-December to late February the Hungarians relentlessly pursued the Serbs. Leiningen himself was willing to justify the burning of villages where, as in Illancsa, the Serbs had allegedly turned on their Magyar neighbours and depopulated the surrounding Hungarian townships, or where the Serbs had proven to be 'treacherous', as in Jarkovácz, where they welcomed the Magyars before nearly catching them in a death-trap of musketry.[98] This was ethnic conflict at its most brutal and squalid.

The Hungarians may have meted out rough justice to the rebellious ethnic minorities, but they were less successful in stopping the main Austrian thrust under Windischgrätz, whose imperial forces invaded in mid-December. Kossuth had tried desperately to bring about an armistice during the winter months through the good offices of the US chargé d'affaires in Vienna, William Stiles. The American met Schwarzenberg on 3 December, but, as Stiles put it, the imperial government was now 'in the proud consciousness of its inexhaustible strength' and Schwarzenberg confidently rejected the Hungarian proposal. A week later, Kossuth asked Stiles to try his influence on Windischgrätz, but the field marshal gruffly told the American that 'I cannot treat with those who are in a state of rebellion.' Stiles noted that the new emperor, the young Franz Joseph, who had taken Ferdinand's throne only on 2 December, shared in the fresh bullishness of the Austrian government after the recent victories in Prague and Vienna. But, the diplomat also remarked darkly, those were fought against 'his own undisciplined and ill-armed subjects'.[99] Hungary, he implied, would offer a very different scenario. And so it proved.

The new Hungarian commander was Arthur Görgey, who was only thirty years old, but he had shown Kossuth that he was a fine tactician and strategist at Ozora, where he had played a key role in encircling the Croatian forces, and he had been one of the few commanders to emerge with some credit after the disaster at Schwechat. He came from an impoverished gentry family in northern Hungary, and had embarked on a military career in the imperial army at the age of nineteen. His lack of funds, however, meant that he struggled to live in the manner expected of an officer (in the early years of his career as a lieutenant, his breakfast consisted of a piece of bread and he never ate dinner) and he was refused permission to marry on account of this impoverishment. Frustrated, Görgey resigned his commission and took a degree in chemistry (his great academic interest), but 1848 found him enthusiastically enrolling in one of the new Honvéd battalions, where he received the rank of captain. Even his appearance distinguished him from his whiskered fellow officers: Leiningen, who was one of his admirers, described his 'oval face, with a high, noble forehead, blue eyes full of deep earnestness – yet sometimes merry and even wicked . . . his moustache and beard are not very thick, and close-cropped, like his hair; his chin is beardless'.[100]

His dizzying rise began in the summer when Batthyány, well aware of Hungary's shortage of munitions, ordered him to buy ammunition from abroad and to learn how percussion caps were made – a skill which, ironically, he duly studied at the imperial fireworks factory in Wiener-Neustadt.[101] By the time Jelačić attacked, he was already a major. Görgey owed his rapid promotion thereafter to his brilliance as a soldier and to his determination. He had proven his utter ruthlessness early in the war, when he had a conservative Hungarian magnate, Count Eugene Zichy, hanged for treason after he was arrested and found to be carrying copies of one of Jelačić's proclamations.[102] Görgey also publicly rejected the armistice that Jelačić signed with the Hungarians after his defeat at Pákozd.[103] Yet his politics would prove to be problematic for the Hungarians in the long run. He was a moderate constitutionalist who hoped that the conflict would end when the Emperor recognised the April Laws and accepted Hungary back as an autonomous kingdom in the Habsburg Empire. Unlike Kossuth, he placed his faith not in a massive 'people's war', but in the force of a well-trained, professional army. These differences would lead to a major political conflict between the two men, tainting Görgey's reputation for generations to come.[104]

With only 30,000 men and 80 guns against 52,000 Austrians and their 210 cannon, even Görgey's gritty genius could not stem Windischgrätz's steamrolling advance down the Danube. Görgey slowly pulled his troops back, fighting some delaying actions, but also complaining about civilian interference and lack of supplies and *matériel*. The troops were in a pitiful state: in the retreat from Austria, the army had lost its linen, so the soldiers were covered with lice and, if they wanted to wash their underclothes, 'they must wear their cloak all day long on their naked bodies',[105] which was not easy in the bitter winter. Kossuth (who would soon make strenuous efforts to ensure that the army was well supplied) retaliated by suggesting that Görgey was unwilling to stand and fight: a battle was needed if only for the sake of morale. The army's commander was therefore caught in the classic dilemma between military and political imperatives.[106]

Ultimately, Görgey read the military situation well: because Komárom, upstream from Budapest, was holding out against the Austrians, he calculated that, when Windischgrätz reached the Hungarian capital, he would be mindful of his supply lines and so would be reluctant to advance much further. Görgey could therefore pull back and marshal his forces for the counter-attack. He also knew that his command of the army was an important political weapon with which, if his military strategy worked, he could then force his own government to negotiate on the basis of imperial recognition of the April Laws. But his military plans did not satisfy the politicians, who at the end of the month sent General Perczel (the victor at Ozora) forward with a small force to engage Windischgrätz in battle. Perczel's army of six thousand was annihilated. With Budapest now open (since Görgey was determined to retreat deeper into Hungary), on 31 December Kossuth prevailed on both the National Defence Committee and the National Assembly (where a large peace party had emerged) to move to Debrecen, deep in eastern Hungary. A delegation led by Batthyány was also sent to Windischgrätz to discuss terms on 3 January, but the field marshal insisted on nothing less than unconditional surrender. Batthyány was allowed to return to his palace in Budapest, but when it fell to the Austrians two days later, he was arrested on Windischgrätz's orders. By then, Kossuth, the National Defence Committee, the parliament and the contents of the State Treasury had left the capital. The new railway worked poorly in the freezing weather, so those who were able continued the journey on foot, while others scrambled into peasant carts and bumped along the road to Debrecen, 140 miles to the east.[107] It was there – in a small provincial backwater with no street-lighting, pavements or sewers, where cattle roamed the streets – that the political leadership of liberal Hungary would cling on.

V

While the Habsburgs and their allies were turning the screws on Hungary, they were also trying to reduce the stubborn pocket of northern Italian resistance: Venice. In February 1849 Schwarzenberg would write that 'as long as the revolutionary government in Venice still stands as a living symbol of the subversive spirit which arouses Italy, . . . ideas of order will not be able to triumph in the rest of the peninsula'.[108] The city still had a lot of fight left in it, having been far from hermetically sealed by the Austrian naval blockade, because the Austrian fleet, based at Pula and Trieste, had few seaworthy ships and the loyalty of its largely Italian crews was doubtful. Moreover, the tides, sandbanks and channels in the lagoon required intimate local knowledge, which of course aided the Venetians. The Austrians could therefore mount only a loose guard on the entrances to the lagoon. The weakness of the Austrian naval presence, however, encouraged the Venetian naval command to do little to strengthen the city's existing fleet by arming more ships (the Austrians had spirited their own vessels away to Trieste at the outbreak of the revolution). The Venetian naval forces were bolstered by the return of the Piedmontese fleet, which Charles Albert, after withdrawing it as part of the armistice, now ordered back to the lagoon because he had been angered at the imperfect way in which the Austrians were honouring the ceasefire. Yet there were obvious dangers in relying on others to guard the lagoon, and the government's apparent lack of vigour gave the Mazzinian opposition in the Italian Club the grounds on which to launch its strident verbal attacks on Manin and his colleagues.

Facing inland, the Venetians were better prepared. By October, the Austrians had 21,000 troops on paper, but in reality a third of them were sick from malaria. Meanwhile, the Venetians still held both ends of the railway bridge, with the *terra firma* side protected by the Marghera fort. Pepe's Neapolitan soldiers worked as a hard professional core, training the mostly Venetian recruits, supervising the artillery and the construction of new defences. The government

had been assiduous in stockpiling provisions and there was no lack
of munitions, since the city controlled the arsenal. Finance was
trickier: the troops and the arsenal workers had to be paid, and
over the summer the governing triumvirate had imposed forced
loans and collected jewellery as a stop-gap. To survive the siege,
more funds were needed, so the government had to impose fresh
taxation on tobacco and beer – the former, of course, merely
replacing the hated Austrian levy that had been one of the sparks
of the revolution in the first place. Shares in the Milan–Venice railway were sold off and a new loan was raised on the security of
Venice's artworks and historic buildings (fortunately for the future,
after the war its wealthiest citizens paid off the debt, so the treas-
ures were saved for the city). In July, a savings bank had been
established, issuing Venice's own currency – 'patriotic' money. The
clergy, inspired still by Fathers Gavazzi and Ugo Bassi, steeled the
Venetian will to resist and appealed for donations. Pepe donated
his salary to the beleaguered state.

He also gave the Venetians a remarkable, though short-lived,
victory. On 27 October, a three-thousand-strong Italian force, personally led by Pepe and Giovanni Cavedalis (one of Manin's fellow
triumvirs) sortied from the Marghera fort. Emerging from a thick
early morning fog, they bayoneted the Austrian gunners who
guarded the road, before surprising and overwhelming the defenders of Mestre. Although the hand-to-hand fighting was bitter –
casualties on both sides may have reached a staggering 444 dead and
wounded (and Bassi risked his life to give spiritual comfort to the
fallen) – the Italians prevailed, taking 500 Austrian prisoners. They
could not hold on to the town, but it was clearer than ever to the
Austrian commander, Marshal Welden, that reducing the city's formidable defensive system of fifty-four forts and octagonal gun
batteries would be no easy task.[109]

In the autumn of 1848, however, Venice could not depend militarily on any other Italian state: the Austrian–Piedmontese armistice
was (just) holding, while the Papal States and Naples had withdrawn from the conflict. Its salvation lay in foreign intervention,
either diplomatic or military. When war broke out between

Hungary and Austria in October, the Venetians saluted the Magyars as allies, but the latter were struggling for their own survival. Pragmatically, Daniele Manin had set his hopes on a French invasion and on British mediation to secure the city's independence. Shortly after he had taken power in August, he had sent Nicolò Tommaseo to secure France's help, addressing a letter to the French foreign minister, Jules Bastide, poetically declaring that 'the life of a people who have contributed not a little to European civilisation now depends on the immediate assistance of the heroic French nation'.[110] The French had already come close to intervening after the disaster at Custozza, since they were truly alarmed by the prospect of the Austrians overrunning Piedmont, which would have brought Radetzky right up to the French frontier. Yet the French government also knew full well that the outbreak of war would give a shot of adrenaline to the French radicals, who were still cowed by the brutal repression of the June days. So in July Bastide had sought to end the war in Italy by proposing Franco-British mediation on the basis of Piedmont annexing Lombardy, while Venetia would stay under Austrian rule, albeit with some autonomy. This was scarcely a solution that would have been acceptable to Manin or Tommaseo. In any case the Austrian government now felt strong enough to resist any diplomatic pressure to negotiate and was prepared to drive for outright victory in Italy. This rejection of Franco-British mediation provoked a cabinet crisis in Paris, with half of the ministers now supporting armed intervention and the other half favouring peace. General Cavaignac was left with the casting vote, and in the end he chose peace. Manin's hope for salvation from the French had therefore been dashed by a single vote in Paris.[111]

Meanwhile, he faced vocal domestic opposition in the shape of the Italian Club established by followers of Mazzini. In early October the club and the radical press chastised the government for not being sufficiently energetic in its prosecution of the war. The danger for Manin was that, increasingly, the all-important cohort of non-Venetian troops, who had no particular loyalty to either the city or Manin, were being drawn into the club's orbit. At the same time, more conservative supporters of the triumvirate were becoming alarmed by the organisation's burgeoning influence, fearing, as one Venetian nobleman put it, that 'new ideas' were being disseminated among the people, 'especially the uneducated, ideas which are worse than those of the red republicans'.[112] Manin, though, had two trump cards: first, he knew that if it came down to street-fighting, he could still command the loyalty of most of his beloved Venetians; and second, General Pepe backed him. There was therefore no bloodbath when Manin struck against the opposition. On 2 October, the leaders of the Italian Club were arrested and deported. All soldiers were banned from joining political organisations. While some of the non-Venetian soldiers protested, Manin deftly sweetened his repressive pill by promising that on 11 October the Venetian assembly would meet to draft new electoral laws, implying that the large non-Venetian contingent defending the city would be enfranchised. Meanwhile, the Mazzinian pressure for a vigorous 'people's war' against Austria had been defused.[113] As in Hungary, the looming presence of the Austrian counter-revolution concentrated minds and hearts on the existing government and ensured that there was neither a stampede of moderates back to the conservative fold nor a second revolution.

This was not true of Rome, however, where new life was unexpectedly breathed into the Mazzinian cause. In late September Pope Pius IX – swimming against the radical tide of the streets – finally appointed a moderate, Count Pellegrino Rossi, to lead his government. A lawyer and teacher with a sharp intelligence and a sarcastic wit, Rossi was a capable politician. He had liberal credentials: on his appointment, one of the more progressive cardinals jokingly congratulated him by saying, 'I have known you extremely well, Sir, ever since you were burnt in effigy.'[114] Aged sixty-one in 1848, he had been exiled from Italy much earlier for supporting the Napoleonic regime. He eventually settled in France, where he entered the service of the July Monarchy as a diplomat. (His liberalism was of the conservative kind deemed acceptable by Guizot.) It was as an ambassador to Rome that he returned to his native land and where he won the trust of Pius IX. In 1848 he urged Pius to uphold the new constitution, but opposed any further political reform. Rossi's long-term vision for Italy was moderate, taking the shape of an Italian league led by the Papal States. He opposed Roman involvement in the war not only because it would galvanise the nationalists but because he saw that it would result in Piedmontese expansion.[115] He also feared that a second, republican revolution would bring about foreign military intervention and occupation by foreign powers.

Rossi therefore stood for the rule of law as enshrined in the papal constitution – and he would go no further. 'In a constitutional government such as ours,' he declared, 'everything would result in confusion and disorder, if the opinions and actions of the whole people did not . . . breathe a spirit of life into the law.'[116] His ideal reform was 'from above' – imposed by the government and primarily for the sake of administrative and fiscal efficiency. On taking office, he forged ahead with reforming the administration, putting the state's finances on a stable footing and restoring law and order. He planned to root out corrupt officials, he imposed fiscal policies at the expense of the clergy, and he planned railway lines and new telegraph services. He called on his friend General Carlo Zucchi, a veteran revolutionary who had served with Napoleon, to command the armed forces and restore discipline. He opened negotiations with other Italian states, namely Piedmont and Tuscany (with the door being left open to reticent, unpredictable Naples), on the formation of an Italian league. Yet Rossi's pursuit of this monarchist federation and his stout defence of the constitution earned him the inveterate hatred of the Roman radicals. His idea for an Italian league threw a great obstacle in the way of the democrats' aim of summoning a *costituente*, which the Tuscan radical Montanelli had been invoking. A liberal monarchist alternative – which Rossi also opposed because it was obviously a lever for Piedmontese influence – had been summoned at the same time by Charles Albert's prime minister, Vincenzo Gioberti, and this met in Turin between 10 and 30 October. With these alternatives and the multitude of aspirations as to how the *costituente* would function, the path to be followed towards Italian unification was still far from clear.[117]

The frustration of the radicals over the setbacks and disappointments of the year now concentrated on Rossi, and they were strengthened by demobbed soldiers, the *Reduci* ('the Returned'), and by Neapolitan refugees who had fled the reaction in the south. One attempt at raising the Roman populace against the Pope, led by the Neapolitan exile Vincenzo Carbonelli on 24–5 October, was foiled because among those involved were undercover police officers who kept the government informed. The news of the October revolution in Vienna and the Hungarian victory over Jelačić seemed to present a golden opportunity to renew the war against the Austrians in Italy – and King Charles Albert himself had rattled his sabre during Gioberti's *costituente*. In the painful fortnight before the first session of the Roman parliament on 15 November, Rossi bore the slings and arrows of an outrageous radical press with remarkable stoicism and courage. He was likened to Guizot and Metternich, lambasted as a man who sought to restore the old despotism. His aims, claimed the radical leader Sterbini later, were to 'tame democracy and to destroy, or indefinitely postpone, the conception of nationality'; he 'sneered at the War of Independence; ridiculed the idea of a *Costituente*'.[118] He received hate mail – all of it anonymous – but he brushed off these poisonous missives with contempt, although the comments must have hurt, for Rossi's own son had fought against the Austrians in Lombardy.

Rossi struck back with a vengeance on 12 November, when he arrested some of the leading Neapolitan troublemakers, including Carbonelli (who had been preparing to raise the standard of insurrection at Trajan's Column), and had them deported. Exactly what happened next is murky, but it appears that a radical cabal – possibly including Sterbini and Cicerruacchio's son, Luigi Brunetti – met in a tavern near the Piazza del Popolo on 13 November and discussed ways of ridding themselves of Rossi once and for all. In what must have been a tense, seething but hushed debate, it was apparently agreed that Rossi should be assassinated at the opening of parliament in two days' time. People across the city were, in any case, anticipating some great demonstration of radical force. The exile of the Neapolitans, who were conducted to the port at Civita

Vecchia on 14 November, and Rossi's show of strength – parading columns of *carabinieri* through the streets – increased the political temperature. Towards noon on 15 November, when Rossi arrived at the Chamber of Deputies, he had to alight from his carriage and walk through the great gate of the Cancelleria Palace and then some twenty yards along a passage that was lined with onlookers. The police had already noticed that clusters of *Reduci*, obvious in their grey tunics and blue trousers, had been ominously fingering their daggers and declaiming noisily against Rossi. Ten minutes before, they had cheered as Sterbini appeared to take his seat in parliament. When the prime minister's carriage approached, the crowd fell silent in an expectant hush. Rossi, the pallor of his complexion striking against his dark blue overcoat, made his way into the passageway. The onlookers closed around behind him, but Rossi pressed on towards the staircase at the end, wearing a defiantly contemptuous smile. He had just started up the steps when a young man struck him lightly on one side. When Rossi turned, another assailant – allegedly Luigi Brunetti – plunged a dagger into his throat, severing his carotid artery. Blood spurted out in a jet and the assassins escaped when the other *Reduci* around them also raised their daggers. Rossi, bleeding profusely, was lifted up by his friends and carried into a nearby house, where he died. 'Order had only one energetic and highly intelligent representative left at Rome,' wrote the Belgian ambassador. 'This representative was Monsieur Rossi, and that is exactly why he was killed.'[119]

The diplomat's remark was prescient, for the shellshocked authorities seemed utterly disarmed against the tide of popular republicanism that seeped through the city over the next few hours. Parliament suspended its session, although the radical aristocrat Canino scathingly shouted, 'What is all this fuss about? Is it the King of Rome who is dead?'[120] The Pope, in the Quirinal Palace, received the news of his friend's murder with stunned silence. Without Rossi's firm hand, the discipline of the *carabinieri* and the loyalty of the civic guard wavered: the former were already beginning to fraternise with the people, while even the commander of the regular forces warned that his men would be deeply reluctant to fire on the crowd. To pacify the gathering storm, Pius would have to appoint a ministry that supported at least the renewal of the war against Austria and the *costituente*. The radicals demanded more: that the constitution be revised. The government resigned, unable to defend itself yet unwilling to yield to the opposition. The hour of the republicans had come – and Sterbini, backed by the force of the Roman crowd that was mobilised by the Circolo Populare, the club of which he was president, was ready to seize the initiative. That night, a procession of clubbists and *Reduci* marched up the Corso cheering triumphantly, hailing Rossi's murderer as the new Brutus. With terrible cruelty, they stopped beneath the windows of Rossi's house, hurling up taunts and jibes at his bereaved wife, chanting 'Blessed be the hand that stabbed Rossi.'[121] A 'good many loathsome reptiles' had indeed emerged on to the streets.[122]

In the afternoon of the following day a crowd gathered on the Piazza del Popolo and marched on the Quirinal to press the radical demands. The palace was protected by a thin cordon of a hundred troops: a company of Swiss Guards, some loyal *carabinieri* and members of the elite Noble Guard. At three o'clock, the masses surged up to the locked gates of the palace, where two hapless Swiss sentries just managed to escape, one having broken his halberd over the head of an insurgent, the other having had his torn from his hands. The Pope confronted this desperate situation with stubborn courage and, though he had appointed the popular Giuseppe Galletti to lead a new government, he refused to give way any further. Acting as if he were oblivious to the thundering crowd outside, he ignored Galletti's entreaties to concede. Growing angry and impatient, the demonstrators started to chant, 'A democratic ministry or a republic!' By now, there were an estimated six thousand armed people in the piazza, including regular soldiers, civic guards and *carabinieri* who had gone over to the radicals. When some of the crowd tried to burn down a side entrance into the Quirinal, the first shots were fired: they were aimed into the air by the Swiss, but the tension now boiled over into violence. The insurgents climbed into nearby towers to fire back and one of the Pope's secretaries was killed when a bullet shattered the window of his office. When a cannon was wheeled up to blast open the main gate, even Pius was persuaded that the time for concessions had at last come. Protesting to the foreign ambassadors (who had gathered around him throughout this ordeal) that he was yielding under duress, the Pope appointed a new government which included Sterbini, Galletti and Mamiani.

The constitutional regime was now rapidly unravelling. Parliament was in an uproar and unable to function effectively. Conservatives and moderates were screamed down from the public galleries. And in any case the murder of Rossi had caused such fear that the lower chamber was denuded by resignations and absences. The Pope's friends and political allies visited him only furtively – one travelled to and from the Quirinal with a brace of pistols for his own protection. The last straw was the publication of the ministry's programme, which included a declaration of war and the summoning of a *costituente*. In the evening of 24 November Pius disguised himself in the cassock of a humble parish priest and climbed into a carriage. After a twelve-hour journey through the night, he crossed into the Kingdom of Naples, where he took refuge in the coastal town and fortress of Gaeta.

His flight turned the revolution in Rome into an international affair: Catholic Europe was now thoroughly shaken. While the government of the secular French republic would do nothing unless the Austrians used the overthrow of the Pope as a pretext for an invasion of central Italy, in December Spain declared that Pius was under the protection of all Catholic states and called for an international congress to resolve the matter. Naples, which was protecting the Pope in more than just theory, agreed. Austria, seeing the opportunity to kill off the ideal of Papal leadership of a united Italy once and for all, readily assented. For his part, Pius at first adamantly insisted from his refuge that he still honoured the *statuto*, the constitution that he had granted his subjects. Yet, increasingly, he fell under the conservative influence of both the Neapolitans and his own retinue, including the shadowy figure of Cardinal Antonelli. The latter spotted the conservatives' opportunity in the collapse of the liberal, constitutional experiment in Rome. He calculated that a head-on collision between the conservatives and the radicals would finish with the triumph of the former, particularly if Pius secured international help. The Pope therefore disavowed the new government in Rome, and in December he appealed to the new emperor, Franz Joseph, 'his very dear son', for assistance.[123]

The revolution in Rome gave all Italian radicals a fresh focus for their activities. In Tuscany Guerrazzi and Montanelli saw the opportunity of realising their plan of a democratic *costituente*, which could now convene in Rome itself. Garibaldi and his followers were also drawn towards Rome. They had undertaken a veritable odyssey since their retreat into Switzerland that summer. From there, Garibaldi had made his way to Genoa, where he received a formal invitation from the Sicilians to help them fight against the Neapolitans. He duly embarked on a French steamer with seventy-two followers – mostly officers – and they chugged southwards, bound for Palermo. Yet one of the ports of call was Livorno, and there the radical leadership convinced him that he would discover in Tuscany a fertile recruiting ground for his republican army. Garibaldi therefore offered his services to Guerrazzi and Montanelli, sending a telegram suggesting that he lead an army of Tuscan volunteers against the Neapolitan King. The message finished rather curtly: 'Yes or no – Garibaldi'.[124]

The answer, as it turned out, was a clear 'no'. In the first place the great campaigner had been misled: rural Tuscany, in particular, was loyal to the Grand Duke and resisted the republicans' blandishments. Second, Guerrazzi and Montanelli were not at all happy about Garibaldi's sudden appearance. They may have been radicals, and Guerrazzi may have been a demagogue, but now that both men were in power, they wanted to prove that they could maintain law and order. Moreover, their plan for a *costituente* was to be democratic, but it was not necessarily to be exclusively republican. As Montanelli later explained, they wanted a constituent assembly to persuade 'constitutionalists and republicans, federalists and unitarians to shake hands . . . in order to contribute jointly towards the task of enfranchising Italy'.[125] This willingness to involve the liberal monarchists did not please the more uncompromising republicans like Mazzini and Garibaldi. Moreover, the latter's force threatened to be a source of instability for a government which, while radical, was now trying to strengthen its position against the more hot-headed Tuscan democrats. 'They are like a plague of locusts', fretted Guerrazzi of Garibaldi's men. 'We must do all we can to get them away quickly.'[126] Consequently, the Tuscan reply to Garibaldi's proposal was 'evasive'; and, while the small band of Garibaldini received a tumultuous welcome from the Florentines, the government itself kept a stony silence and did not provide them with provisions for the onward march.[127] Garibaldi's small regiment had crossed the icy Apennines and reached the frontier with the Papal States at Filigare on 9 November. At that point, Rossi still had six days to live and General Zucchi had advanced from Bologna to Ferrara with four hundred Swiss troops to block the Garibaldini, who now numbered no more than one hundred. The republican force was in a terrible state: 'So we had left South America for this: to fight the snow in the Apennines,' Garibaldi later commented bitterly. 'It was distressing to see these worthy young lads in the mountains in such harsh weather: most were wearing only light clothes, some were in rags, all were hungry.'[128] It was while the Garibaldini were spending 'a few miserable days' in Filigare that the people of Bologna came to their rescue. With Zucchi absent, Father Gavazzi led a huge demonstration, cramming into the street below the windows of Zucchi's second-in-command: 'Either our brothers come here', they cried, 'or you come down from that balcony.'[129] Hearing of the protest, Zucchi, reluctant to provoke a full-blown uprising, agreed to a compromise: Garibaldi's force would be allowed to cross the Romagna, but it had to march to Ravenna, where it would embark for Venice to support Manin's defence of the city against the Austrians.

Rossi's assassination and the radical uprising in Rome gave the Garibaldini a new opportunity to march southwards. Garibaldi's verdict on the murder was virulently bloodthirsty: 'in getting rid of him the ancient metropolis of the world showed itself worthy of its illustrious past. A young Roman had wielded anew the sword of

Brutus and drowned the marble steps of the Capitol with the tyrant's blood!'[130] His recruiting efforts now bore fruit, so that when he left Ravenna at the end of November, he was riding at the head of five hundred men – mostly young middle-class townsmen, artisans, workers and students: 'fine-looking, polite, almost all the sons of cultivated families from the country's urban centres'.[131] Garibaldi planned to winter in Umbria, but he also rode on to Rome in mid-December, in order, as he expressed it, to 'put the legion's miserable and vagabond existence on a more organised footing' by getting the recognition of the new war minister, from whom he hoped to secure supplies.[132]

Garibaldi entered a turbulent city fractured by a confused and complex dispute between conflicting radical factions and the remnants of the moderates. Early in December, moderate arguments that the *costituente* should be along Vincenzo Gioberti's federal lines were fervently challenged by the democrats. The republican Mazzinians, having been defeated in Venice, had found in Rome a new theatre for their activities. Some, like Mazzini himself, believed pragmatically that it was too early to convene a full Italian *costituente* – it would never be accepted by the Piedmontese, among others – so the Papal States should be democratised first, becoming the nucleus of the future Italian republic. Other republicans disagreed and wanted to proceed immediately to all-Italian elections. Meanwhile, some members of the new government in Rome, like Mamiani, were not extremists and were well aware that much of the Roman population was reeling from both the moral and the economic effects of the Pope's sudden flight. There was a strong belief that, if Pius was willing to negotiate, he could return to Rome. While this possibility remained open, the ministers were reluctant to entertain any hard-line republicans – and once again Garibaldi found himself being snubbed. He spent the winter with his troops at Foligno in Umbria. Yet the pressure of the radical political clubs was soon too much to resist for the government, which faced the grim prospect of a fresh insurrection on the streets of Rome. In any case the Pope had repeatedly refused to return, so on 29 December there were few options left but to hold elections to a Roman

Constituent Assembly, which was the obvious prelude to the proclamation of a republic. Under further pressure from the clubs, on 16
January the Roman government also declared that the hundred
candidates who attracted the most votes to the Roman assembly
would represent Rome in the all-Italian *costituente*, wherever it
met.[133] Having had their cake, it seemed that the republicans would
be able to eat it as well.

VI

While Italian republicanism was suddenly breathing in fresh
oxygen, the French Second Republic was slowly being stifled to
death, although it lingered on painfully until the end of 1851. The
author of its agonising demise was an unlikely man who stood with
a slouch, was less than five feet six inches tall, and had a pronounced
hook nose, a long handlebar moustache and a pointed goatee beard.
His name was Louis-Napoleon Bonaparte. Born in 1808, he was
Napoleon Bonaparte's nephew, the son of Hortense de Beauharnais
(Empress Joséphine's daughter from her first marriage) and Louis
Bonaparte, Napoleon's brother, who was then King of Holland.
Louis-Napoleon was an enigmatic, strange and at times comical
figure. After the Napoleonic Empire unravelled in 1814, he and his
mother, who doted on him, spent his childhood in exile, finally set-
tling in the Swiss castle of Arenenberg on Lake Constance. There,
Hortense immersed Louis-Napoleon in his Bonapartist heritage.
At the time of the 1830 revolution, the immediate heir to Napoleon's
imperial throne was Napoleon II, Duke of Reichstadt, the son of
the Emperor and his second consort, Marie-Louise of Austria. He
had spent his life in the 'gilded cage' of the Habsburg palace of
Schönbrunn, but he died of consumption in 1832. Louis-Napoleon
regarded himself as the rightful heir. He envisaged Bonapartism as
a combination of the principle of popular sovereignty and authoritarianism: the Emperor would be the executor of the people's will,
which would be expressed by a parliament elected by universal,
though indirect, suffrage. It was a hauntingly modern blend of

political ideas – a dictatorship claiming its mandate from the 'people'. Yet the government, he wrote in *Napoleonic Ideas* (1839), must work for the benefit of society: it was to use the 'necessary means to open a smooth and easy road for advancing civilisation'.[134] By uniting authoritarianism, popular sovereignty and social progress Louis-Napoleon appealed to a wide range of people and, by emphasising different facets of his ideas according to his audience, he succeeded in being all things to all people. Later, after he had become Emperor Napoleon III, he exclaimed, referring to his closest associates, 'How do you expect the Empire to run smoothly? The Empress is a Legitimist, Morny is an Orléanist, my cousin Jérôme-Napoleon is a Republican; I am a socialist; only Persigny is a Bonapartist and he is mad.'[135] His ideas possessed such emotive force because they were presented in Napoleonic packaging – and the empire was remembered by many people not for dictatorship, not for the horrors of war, but for its 'glory' and its claim to the idealism of the 1789 revolution.

Armed with his usefully nebulous concept of Bonapartism, Louis-Napoleon made two botched attempts to provoke an uprising against the July Monarchy among French army garrisons – in 1836 at Strasbourg and in 1840 at Boulogne. After the first attempt, he was exiled to the United States but he soon returned to Europe. The second effort was the stuff of farce. Louis-Napoleon appeared in Boulogne with a paddle-steamer named (of all things) *The Edinburgh Castle*. Since the insurgents had no imperial eagle as a symbol, they made do with a tame vulture: the bemused bird was chained to the mast. As a result of Boulogne, Louis-Napoleon was sentenced to life imprisonment, serving his sentence in the fortress of Ham in northern France. There, he penned *The Extinction of Poverty* in 1844, in which he confronted the 'social question'. He criticised the free market economy, proposing instead a radical programme of state intervention to ease the plight of the poor. His ideas were far from socialist, but they allowed him later to appeal to the workers as their friend – and certainly some Parisian artisans had paid notice. Two years after writing this tract, he escaped from the prison when, during some restoration work, he dressed as a builder, nonchalantly picked up a plank of wood and walked out through the gates. In less than a day he had reached London.[136]

With the revolution in 1848, Louis-Napoleon travelled to Paris, but the provisional government, suspicious if not a little alarmed, rejected the offer of his services, and by early March he was back in London. There, he enrolled as a special constable against the Chartists on 10 April. In France this marked him out as a friend of order against the 'red' menace.[137] However, he remained inscrutably mysterious in the precise direction of his politics, although his name helped.

While he was still in London, Louis-Napoleon was entered as a candidate for the French by-elections that were held on 4 June. He was returned in four separate constituencies, including Paris. This success unleashed a political storm. On the one hand, groups of Parisians cheered the election of the man with the electrifying name: 'Bonaparte'. Workers gathered on the boulevards mixing democratic-socialist slogans with cries of 'Long live Poleon! We'll have Poleon!' They conflated in Louis-Napoleon the patriotic pride in the glorious days of his uncle with their aspirations for social reform. This magnetic appeal was precisely what alarmed the republicans. Proudhon warned in his newspaper that, 'eight days ago, Citizen Bonaparte was nothing but a black dot in a fiery sky; the day before yesterday, he was still only a smoke-filled ball; today he is a cloud carrying storm and tempest in its flanks'.[138] When the alarmed *démoc-soc* Club of the Revolution of 1793 debated its response to Louis-Napoleon's success, one speaker argued that it could be explained by their own failure not to have 'carried the banner of democracy widely enough'.[139] On 12 June in the National Assembly, Lamartine and Ledru-Rollin presented a bill barring Bonaparte from his seat, arguing that a 'pretender' who had twice tried to seize power illegally could not be a deputy. 'We will never allow . . . the republic to be sold, under any name, into the hands of a few fanatics!' proclaimed Lamartine.[140] Louis-Napoleon's supporters gathered on the Place de la Concorde, among them unemployed workers from the National Workshops. The cry '*Vive l'Empereur!*' resounded across the great square and carried over the river to the National Assembly, which, though protected by troops and National Guards, rejected the bill: 'one of its rare weaknesses', wrote Lamartine. D'Agoult explained this strange decision by the fact that, frightening though Bonaparte was, the republicans were more worried by their Legitimist and Orléanist opponents, who had a powerful presence in the Assembly.[141] None the less, Bonaparte himself defused the situation by resigning his seat on 16 June, insisting that he now stood for legality: 'I desire order and support a Republic which is wise, great and intelligent, but since I have been involuntarily the cause of disorder, I place my resignation in your hands, with my deep regrets.'[142]

It was a shrewd move. D'Agoult's judgement was as perceptive as ever:

> His moderation made him rise in public esteem, without stopping him from representing the very principle of national sovereignty which the representatives themselves seemed to mistrust . . . He incorporated . . . that ideal of revolutionary dictatorship which a still uncultured, turbulent, irrational and passionate democracy prefers to liberal government.[143]

The resignation was also a fortuitous masterstroke, for it meant that Louis-Napoleon was still in London when the June days erupted. He had no part in the vote to close the National Workshops and he missed having to make the tough political choice between sympathising with the insurgents and supporting the forces of order. His popularity and the sparkle of his name therefore remained undiminished. In the Yonne, one of the departments that had originally elected him, the public prosecutor was told to keep an eye on Bonapartist activity. On 2 July, the lawyer duly reported that he had discovered very little, but this did not mean that Louis-Napoleon's electoral success was a flash in the pan. Everywhere, people were saying things like:

> Louis-Napoleon is the only one who can save France from the financial crisis under which she is suffering. He is extremely rich: he will put his millions at the disposal of the country: no more 45 centimes!

Exemption for the countryside from all taxation for two years! To obtain these benefits, to ensure that agriculture, industry and commerce are set to work all at the same time, it is necessary to appoint Louis-Napoleon, first of all as a deputy, then as President of the Republic, then Emperor![144]

During the elections, there were posters everywhere with the slogan, 'Louis-Napoleon Bonaparte – Emperor!'

The lawyer's concerns seemed fully justified in the autumn. When he contested thirteen different seats during further by-elections in September, Louis-Napoleon was re-elected in five. In Paris, he came top of the list of deputies, but he carefully chose to represent the outlying department of the Yonne, arriving in the capital on 24 September. He took his place as the Assembly was hammering out the Second Republic's constitution (which was eventually ratified on 4 November). Louis-Napoleon's luck once again served him well, since the new constitution created a presidency, against the advice of those who feared that this would concentrate too much power in one pair of hands. Louis Blanc had even advised the Assembly that the simplest way of preventing Louis-Napoleon from becoming president was not to have a presidency.[145] Yet the parliamentary commission responsible for drafting the constitution did not argue about whether such an office should exist, but merely over how the president would be elected. Tocqueville, who was a member of the commission, argued that in a nation such as the United States, where executive power was weak, there was no harm in having the president elected by popular vote, because he would always be subject to the will of a strong legislature. Yet, he continued prophetically, in a country such as France, which had powerful monarchist currents and where political authority was traditionally very centralised, a popularly elected president would become dangerously powerful. The office, he warned, could serve only those who wanted to transform it into a throne. The great historian and political philosopher had delivered this argument on the day after the first election of Louis-Napoleon Bonaparte – and no one doubted whom he had in mind.[146] The alternative was to have the president elected by the National Assembly, which would virtually ensure that Bonaparte stood no chance in any contest for the office.

In the end, though, popular election won the day, with Cavaignac notably urging the commission to make the presidency elected by the people, not by parliament. Still riding high on the wave of conservative popularity in wake of the June days, Cavaignac was placing his own political future in the hands of a grateful electorate. Moreover, the republicans could see that the strong monarchist presence in the Assembly made election by parliament rather problematic from their perspective. On 7 October, when it appeared that the conservative majority was about to secure presidential election by the legislature, Lamartine rose and argued successfully for the popular vote, dismissing the Bonapartist danger as he did so. For a new dictatorship to arise, Lamartine claimed, would require the shocks of Terror and a charismatic military leader. And France had neither in 1848.[147] That day, the Assembly voted to have a president elected by universal male suffrage for a four-year term, after which he would be ineligible to stand for a second. On 9 October, taking no chances, an amendment was tabled by the moderate republican Antoine Thouret which barred members of former ruling dynasties from standing for the presidency. Louis-Napoleon rose to challenge this, but he spoke so poorly – and in a German accent acquired in his long years of exile – that he seemed to be a buffoon. 'What an idiot!' scoffed Ledru-Rollin gleefully. 'He is ruined.'[148] Thouret contemptuously withdrew his amendment.

In any case the vast majority of deputies believed that the republican hero of law and order, Cavaignac, would cruise home in the first presidential election, which was set for 10 December. Nevertheless, Louis-Napoleon announced his candidacy on 26 October. The contest, d'Agoult remarked, was one between 'authority', represented by the general, and 'dictatorship' in the shape of Louis-Napoleon Bonaparte.[149] The re-election of Louis-Napoleon in September had shown that, no matter how much contempt the political elites may have had for him, he was popular among the people. Those who voted for him in the by-elections in Paris and the suburbs came from the working-class districts. Even more importantly, his name would work its magic among the peasantry. The 'great' Napoleon remained, in popular memory, the 'people's emperor' who championed their interests: in Alsace, peasants remembered fondly that there was no Forest Code restricting access to woodlands during the empire. Moreover, as the peasants already had a poor opinion of the Second Republic, casting one's ballot for Louis-Napoleon was effectively a protest vote against both the regime and the rich, while also avoiding the pitfalls of socialism. So when Louis-Napoleon stood for president, he was a genuine contender against Cavaignac. Once it became clear that this was essentially a two-horse race, the left-wing radicals were willing to support Louis-Napoleon to prevent the 'butcher' of June from winning. Meanwhile, conservatives deserted their first hero and, albeit often grudgingly, supported Bonaparte. For them, the Napoleonic tradition meant strong, authoritarian government. Even monarchists were willing to back Louis-Napoleon in the hope that he would crush the left and then become a mere figurehead, a curtain behind which, ultimately, the way could be cleared for a restoration of the monarchy. Adolphe Thiers, a leading Orléanist, described Bonaparte as 'a cretin', but he appreciated his political uses and supported his candidacy. Cavaignac, by contrast, was too strong a character – and too republican – to be pliable.

Louis-Napoleon, then, offered many contradictory things to a wide variety of people. In the event, he won the election by a landslide, polling 5,400,000 votes against Cavaignac's 1,400,000. The heroes of the republican left, Ledru-Rollin and Raspail, did not even come close to offering a serious challenge, with 400,000 and 37,000 votes, respectively; Lamartine, to the poet's own shock and disgust, could muster only 8,000 votes. The latter could not face the Assembly when the results were announced, which was just as well, for when his derisory poll was declared, there was mocking laughter from the right-wing benches. The candidate of the Legitimists, General Changarnier, attracted the support of fewer than a thousand people.[150]

President Bonaparte took his oath of office on 20 December. When he swore to uphold the constitution, some of the parliamentary deputies present squirmed: was this, they wondered, a sincere conversion to the republic or were they witnessing perjury? One of Bonaparte's first acts was to appoint as his prime minister an Orléanist, Odilon Barrot. The message was clear: this was to be an undeniably anti-republican cabinet. The royalist Changarnier, who had performed so dismally as a politician, was given the consolation prize of command of the armed forces in Paris. The Second Republic was now set on a reactionary course.

6

1849: THE INDIAN SUMMER OF THE REVOLUTION

The crushing defeats of 1848 did not mean that the revolutionary momentum had entirely expired. The reaction had not triumphed equally everywhere and even when conservatives were back in control, they did not feel sufficiently strong to raze the new liberal institutions entirely to the ground: most governments, for example, still at the very least paid lip-service to the notion of having a constitution. Liberals may now have been less optimistic about applying their more libertarian ideals, but they were still determined to defend what was left of their achievements. European radicals, meanwhile, made renewed efforts either to push forward their democratic and social programmes or to make a belated defence of the liberal order. It was only when this second wave of revolutionary activity had been suppressed that the mid-century revolutions came to an end.

The German revolutionary experience in 1849 was driven by the democrats who (rather ironically) fought in support of the liberal constitution produced by the remnants of the united German parliament. In Italy and in Hungary the revolution was radicalised because of a military crisis. In France radicals took the fight from the cities, where in 1848 they had been comprehensively beaten, into the provinces and the countryside. The *démoc-socs* worked feverishly among the grass roots in rural France, converting grievances into votes and making enough electoral gains so that, by 1851, monarchists and moderate republicans alike were thoroughly alarmed by their new-found confidence.

I

In the New Year the German parliament was confronted with the uncomfortable fact that neither of the two great powers, Austria and Prussia, now paid it much heed. Without their cooperation, German unification would be a castle in the sand. The smaller German states still saw some use for the parliament and the government: as they were weak when they stood alone, they had always sheltered under a wider, pan-German political umbrella. So the parliamentarians forged on with the constitution. At the end of December 1848 they had published the Basic Rights (Grundrechte), which could not be infringed by subsequent legislation, be it federal or state. The Grundrechte guaranteed personal liberty, equality before the law and habeas corpus. Titles of nobility and all aristocratic privileges were abolished, including the manorial jurisdiction and the police powers of landlords over their peasants. There was to be no return to serfdom, but there was to be freedom of religion, education, opinion and the press. The death penalty, corporal punishment and the pillory were all to end. The secular ideals of the parliament emerged in the clause on marriage, which made the civil ceremony the legally binding act, and in the issue of education, which was removed from clerical hands. The separation of powers was guaranteed in that the judiciary was to be free from political influence. The national minorities were promised 'their national development, especially equality of the rights of their languages' in religion, education, law and local government. Other than upholding property rights, however, there were no social rights: the liberals firmly believed that free trade and open competition would ease the economic distress of the struggling poor. For this reason, all German citizens were to enjoy the full freedom to travel and live where they liked, to acquire property and to engage in any form of occupation. It was, in other words, a classically liberal document in every political sense of the word.

The Grundrechte were not universally accepted by all the German states. Some, like Württemberg, Baden and Hesse-Darmstadt, declared their immediate recognition of the Grundrechte, but others, like Prussia, Austria and Bavaria, refused to do so. Expressing startlingly modern-sounding anxieties, some governments objected that the freedom to travel would simply allow 'communists' to settle in their states, while others feared that armies of unemployed workers would roam across the country, with some complaining that 'all the efforts of every state and every community will be fruitlessly expended in providing work and necessary support in cases of want'. The guilds forcefully rejected freedom in choice of occupation, because that meant they would lose control over who entered their trade.[1]

The political arrangements for the German Empire included a two-chamber Reichstag. Half of the upper house, the House of States, was to be chosen by the parliaments of the separate German states and half was to be appointed by the governments. Thus, the constitution entrenched the federal principle. Moreover, all German states would be obliged to have a popularly elected assembly of their own, with ministers responsible to it. The lower chamber, the House of the People, was to be elected by popular vote. The extent of the franchise was a thorny issue: the left, of course, wanted universal male suffrage, while the liberals hoped to restrict it to those who were economically independent, excluding apprentices, factory workers, journeymen, farm labourers and domestic servants. Yet, with the definitive Austrian rejection of German unity, the liberals had to secure left-wing support for the *Kleindeutsch* solution, with the Prussian King as hereditary Emperor. The compromise was sealed and the Reich electoral law declared that 'every German of good repute who has completed his twenty-fifth year has the vote'. The secret ballot 'by voting paper without signature' was carried, though only with a wafer-thin majority. While this electoral law was never implemented because of the counter-revolution, it would live on thanks to an unlikely figure, Bismarck, who used it as the basis of the constitution of the unified German Reich in 1871.[2]

The constitution was adopted on 27 March 1849, and the following day King Frederick William IV of Prussia was elected hereditary Emperor, with the power to delay legislation with a suspensive veto. He now had to be persuaded to accept the crown, but he dithered for a month: not all his advisers were hostile to the idea of Prussian leadership in Germany, calculating that in return for Prussian agreement to the constitution they could secure some major revisions, including restrictions on the franchise. Meanwhile, the liberal governments of twenty-eight German states accepted the constitution, but it was a bad sign that the larger of the German middle states – Hanover, Bavaria and Saxony – all refused to do so. Nevertheless, the viability of the new political order depended, ultimately, on a positive Prussian response. Aware of this, in mid-April the twenty-eight signatory governments sent a joint note to Berlin, urging the Prussian government to follow their lead, although Frederick William suspected that their own acquiescence was far from willing. Meanwhile, the Frankfurt parliament had anxiously sent a thirty-two-man delegation led by Eduard Simson to meet the King. They had arrived on 2 April. Frederick William promised that they could always rely on 'the Prussian shield and sword' to defend German honour against foreign and (pointedly) domestic enemies, but he made no other promises. The *Kreuzzeitung* circle was closing around Frederick William and it was most definitely *Prussian* in outlook. Its members were deeply suspicious of blurring that identity in a less predictable *German* frame: Bismarck later wrote that his own hostility towards the imperial crown was driven primarily by an 'instinctive distrust' of the 1848 revolutions, but also by his sensitivity for 'the prestige of the Prussian crown and its wearer'.[3] The King hated the idea of being 'Emperor of the German People' – the formal imperial title, which suggested that he would owe his position not to God but to the unwashed multitudes. He joked with his courtiers, calling the imperial crown a 'sausage sandwich' and a gift from 'Master Butcher and Baker'.[4] In darker moments he scowled that the crown was 'the dog-collar with which people want to chain me to the 1848 revolution', a 'pig's crown' and a 'crown from the gutter'. Moreover, there was a diplomatic reason to reject the constitution: how would Russia react to a united Germany dominated by Prussia? The last straw came on 21 April, when both chambers of the new Prussian parliament accepted the German constitution and the lower house urged the King to do the same. Frederick William's reaction was immediate: he dissolved both chambers and, a week later, issued his formal rejection of the German crown. Ominously, he also promised military help to any government that chose to repudiate the constitution.

The decision shook the Frankfurt parliament to its core and sent shock waves through Germany. A member of the committee that had drafted the constitution, Karl Welcker, wrote fearfully: 'We had hoped that we were at the end of our great work. We had hoped that we would succeed in concluding the revolution . . . now it seems that an even larger, more terrible and difficult revolution than that of 1848 is presenting itself to us.'[5] During the long wait for Frederick William's decision, the political tensions had been stretched to the limit. Now, they snapped. On 4 May the deputies of the Frankfurt parliament issued a declaration demanding that all German governments accept the constitution and calling the elections for the lower house for 15 July. Should Frederick William continue to turn up his nose, then another ruler would be appointed Emperor in his place from one of the middle states. Prussia and the conservatives immediately latched on to this ultimatum, castigating it as a call for a further revolution. On 10 May, Heinrich von Gagern, who had desperately tried to find a compromise between the Frankfurt parliament and Frederick William, resigned as minister of the Reich when Archduke John refused to condemn the Prussian intervention in Saxony, where an insurrection in support of the constitution was crushed. Gagern was unwilling to countenance further revolutionary violence and, ten days later, he led sixty other deputies out of the parliament, claiming that to press the constitution on Germany would lead to civil war. This walkout was only one of several blows to the assembly. The Austrian delegates had been recalled by their government in April, the Prussians on 14 May, followed by two of the other states that had refused to recognise the constitution – Saxony and Hanover. As a national assembly, the German parliament was on the brink of collapse.

On 30 May the remaining deputies, now numbering only 104 and mostly of the left, withdrew to Stuttgart, in Württemberg, to distance themselves from the Austrian and Prussian troops who lurked menacingly in Mainz. The rump parliament was assured of a good reception in its new home, where a mass demonstration had taken place in support of the constitution on 16 April. The government was reluctant to crush the protests since it feared that its troops might go over to the side of the people, so King Wilhelm grudgingly accepted the constitution, although he then left Stuttgart and took up residence in Ludwigsburg. Two days later, in the King's absence, the Württemberg assembly formally agreed to the German constitution. When the remnants of the German parliament had assembled in his capital, Wilhelm refused in high dudgeon to return until they had left. Meanwhile, the Prussians noisily rattled their sabres, threatening to use force unless the parliamentarians were expelled. In these circumstances even the most determined German delegates recognised that their mission was now one of defiant symbolism, rather than one of constructive state-building. Johann Jacoby wrote to a friend: 'we cannot conceal from ourselves the fact that, with the apathy into which a large part of Germany has fallen, the prospect of success . . . is only slight, but we believe we are obliged for the honour of the nation . . . to make this last effort'.[6] The government in Stuttgart was enraged by the Prussian threats (the prime minister, Friedrich Römer, sarcastically described Berlin as Württemberg's new capital), but it also faced the real possibility of a Prussian invasion. It yielded to the pressure and this spelled the end for the German parliament. On 17 June royal troops sealed off all the roads out of Stuttgart, while the government ordered the parliament to have no more meetings. The following day, the city's streets echoed to the tramp of army boots. Soldiers smashed up the assembly's benches and tables and tore apart the German colours. A small group of deputies tried to gather at a hotel, but their dignified procession was blocked by cavalry. They were expelled from the state, but not before the deputy Adolf Schoder tried to console his colleagues: 'the National Assembly will disappear today; perhaps for a time, the German cause will be trodden in the dust; but its spirit, gentlemen, you will not tread its spirit in the dust, and it will soon break away for itself again, in spite of all bayonets'.[7]

Across Germany a wide spectrum of liberal and radical opinion at last rallied to the defence of the 1848 revolution in the shape of the half-million-strong Central March Association. This organisation gathered support for what became known as the 'campaign' or 'civil war' for the constitution. One of the boiling cauldrons of this movement was the Rhineland. In Cologne five different provincial congresses were held in a matter of three to four days from 6 May, two of them liberal, three of them democratic. Some democratic and workers' organisations seem to have been preparing for a full-blown insurrection in the Rhineland and the spark came when the Prussian government called out the Landwehr, the citizens' militia, in readiness for the anticipated uprising. The plethora of Rhenish political clubs and congresses appealed to the troops not to use force. When delegates from over three hundred town and village councils in the Prussian Rhineland met at one of the liberal congresses in Cologne on 8 May, they demanded that Frederick William accept the constitution, rescind the call to arms and dismiss the conservative Prussian ministry – or face the break-up of the Kingdom of Prussia as it then existed. When asked whether they were 'German' or 'Prussian', the councillors had only one answer: 'German! German! Secession from Prussia!'[8]

This seemed to be a real possibility, since the obedience of the local Landwehr to the government was doubtful. Carl Schurz witnessed a day-long protest of its members in Bonn, hearing calls to disobey the Prussian government and seeing its numbers swelling by the hour as militiamen from the surrounding countryside arrived.[9] A mass meeting of the Landwehr at Elberfeld on 3 May proclaimed its support for the constitution. The democrats also hoped, however, that by rising up they would be able to enforce those aspects of their programme that had been rejected by the Frankfurt parliament. Marx's *Neue Rheinische Zeitung*, however, urged its readers to stand aloof from the campaign for the constitution altogether, arguing that its leaders were not committed to the workers' revolution. Within the democratic clubs, there 'lurked betrayal and self-interest'.[10] Marx was warning that a premature revolution would merely expose the left to further repression for very little gain. His congress in Cologne was held primarily to make preparations for a national workers' convention in Leipzig in June.

Nevertheless, there were outbreaks of revolutionary violence in the Rhineland: militia around Elberfeld, Düsseldorf and Solingen all mutinied. A thousand of them gathered in an armed camp overlooking Elberfeld on 8 May before barricading the centre of the city itself, successfully resisting an attack by regular troops the following day. In Solingen the revolutionaries included red-scarved women wielding revolvers and daggers. Democrats built barricades in Düsseldorf, but these were blown to smithereens by mobile artillery. The uprising spread to the countryside, where village democrats had agreed to ring the church bells as a pre-arranged signal for an uprising. On 10 May, several thousand armed peasants marched on Düsseldorf to help the beleaguered democrats, only to find that they had already been repressed. While the insurgents melted away and returned home, the uprising had stretched the capabilities of the local authorities to keep order to breaking point. First Elberfeld, then Solingen fell into the hands of the democrats, who established 'committees of safety' to direct the insurrection. These committees tried to maintain as wide a consensus as possible, cooperating with the liberal, constitutional monarchists. When Marx's close collaborator Friedrich Engels joined the insurgents at Elberfeld, he was soon expelled because he was accused of trying to convert the revolution from a movement of the 'black–red–gold' (the constitution) into a purely 'red' (social, republican) uprising.

But the insurrection in the Prussian Rhineland soon fizzled out:

delegates sent to Berlin were too eager to believe government prom-ises that Frederick William wanted unity, and the insurgents dismantled the barricades, so that when the Prussian troops arrived, they met no opposition. Some ten to fifteen thousand people, how-ever, had taken up arms to defend the constitution in one of Frederick William's most prosperous provinces,[11] and there were also uprisings in Saxony, the Bavarian Palatinate and Baden. Women played an important role in these insurrections: they fought in Dresden (Saxony) in May, but more usually they formed organ-isations supporting the insurgents and offering help to those who were imprisoned or exiled after their defeat.

In Saxony the parliament (or Landtag) tried to force King Frederick Augustus II to accept the Frankfurt constitution. Assured of Prussian support, the King refused, and on 30 April he prorogued the parliament and appointed an ultra-conservative government. Alarmed by the news that the Prussians were massing their forces on the border in support of the King, workers and craftsmen took to the streets of Dresden. These protests turned violent on 3 May after troops fired on the crowds. The King fled and a provisional govern-ment, including radicals such as Stephan Born, the Russian anarchist Mikhail Bakunin and the composer Richard Wagner (who perhaps was biting the hand that fed him since he was Royal Kapellmeister), was established. Bakunin hoped that Dresden would inspire a Europe-wide revolutionary movement – and a conspiracy inspired by events in Dresden was certainly discovered in Prague, where the authorities swooped on students and intellectuals in a series of pre-emptive, night-time arrests to prevent an insurrection planned for 12 May.[12] In Dresden the revolution came to a more violent end. Prussian troops marched into the city on 5 May. Then, in four days of street and house-to-house fighting, they used new hand-guns that operated with modern firing-pins and inflicted terrible casualties. The opera house burst into flames. Wagner clambered up church towers, ringing their bells to rally the revolutionaries and reconnoitring Prussian troop movements. He was accompanied by a schoolmaster, with whom he passed the time discussing religion and philosophy, while bullets chipped the masonry around them.[13] Born applied his considerable talents for organisation to mobilise the workers, whom he used to keep communications open by smashing through the internal walls of houses, so that the insurgents could pass through the buildings without having to run the murderous gauntlet of enemy fire in the streets. When the end was near, Bakunin, who had been rather contemptuous of the 'amateurish' Saxon revolutionaries, calmly puffed on his cigar and coldly proposed that the town hall, the seat of the provisional government, should be packed with all the remaining munitions and detonated. His colleagues, however, were in no mood to immolate themselves. In all some 250 insurgents were killed and 400 wounded, and a further 869 people were arrested and interrogated, mostly workers. Six thousand others were prosecuted for their actions since the revolution of March 1848, with 727 of them given heavy prison sentences.[14] Born had managed to stage an orderly withdrawal from the battered city with two thousand of his supporters before striking out on his own, finally reaching the safety of Switzerland. Wagner, hidden in a friend's carriage, made his escape to Zürich.

In Bavaria King Maximilian II rejected the constitution after encouragement from Frederick William. In the Rhenish part of his kingdom a massive meeting of clubs and organisations of all shades of liberal and radical opinion held at Kaiserslautern on 2 May established a ten-member 'provisional defence committee' to act as a provisional government until the King came to his senses. The meeting also declared (in a rather neat if facetious inversion of conservative attitudes) that the Bavarian government was guilty of high treason against the constitution and that the King was therefore a rebel. This provisional government then appealed to all other parts of the kingdom to obey its decrees. With the forces of order weak in the Bavarian Palatinate, the revolution easily spread, with people arming themselves to defend the constitution. In each of the local demonstrations the well-organised radicals took the lead through the 'people's associations', in oath-taking, unfurling red flags and giving the uprising a strongly republican tone. Among those who joined the revolution here was Carl Schurz, who, with all his possessions in a knapsack, had made his way on foot to Kaiserslautern to join his friend and teacher, Gottfried Kinkel, who had found an outlet for his revolutionary energies as a secretary to the provisional defence committee. Schurz was made a lieutenant and was employed as a commissioner; his task was to mobilise the country-side in preparation for the royal counter-attack. By 17 May almost all of Bavaria west of the Rhine was in revolutionary hands. This success inspired the democrats of the neighbouring Rhine-Hessen to try to expel the Prussian garrison from Mainz and to march to the support of the republicans in Kaiserslautern. The revolutionar-ies also reached out to long-suffering Baden, which was undergoing its third revolution.

The strength of the Baden republicans lay in the support that they enjoyed among the rank and file of the forces, politicised by the democratic clubs which had proliferated across the grand duchy. The latest revolution began as an army mutiny in which the fortress of Rastatt was seized on 12 May. Grand Duke Leopold fled the cap-ital, Karlsruhe, in the night of 13–14 May and found safety across the French frontier. Baden was now a republic with a provisional government led by moderate democrats, including Franz Raveaux, a member of the German parliament who acted as a conduit between the Baden republic and the remnants of that assembly. He also worked hard to get the Badensian, Rhenish and Palatine repub-licans to coordinate their actions. They agreed on an attack along the Rhine towards Frankfurt, to protect the German parliament from Prussian troops, while a smaller Palatine effort would act as a diversion by invading Rhine-Hessen. The main Badensian attack – led by Franz Sigel, Friedrich Hecker's military adviser – was a dis-aster, but the Palatines captured Worms, holding it for four days (25–9 May) before the Hessian army bombarded the city, forcing the insurgents to withdraw.

Baden became the centre of democratic hopes in the early summer. The incompetent Sigel was replaced as commander of the ex-grand duchy forces by Ludwik Mierosławski, who had led the Polish insurgents against Prussia. The stubbornly persistent Gustav Struve, released from prison, re-emerged as well. He organised a rag-bag force of workers, students and returning republican exiles.

Schurz later wrote that 'the majority of our men not being uni-
formed, every soldier dressed more or less according to his fancy,
and this gave tempting scope to individual taste. Many of the men
evidently endeavoured to look very wild and terrible, which they
would have done had their faces not been so strikingly good-
natured.'[15] Among the battalions was a legion named after Robert
Blum and led by his daughter, who rode in front of its ranks wearing a velvet riding habit and a broad-rimmed slouch hat plumed
with a red feather, with a sabre and pistol clattering at her side and
bearing a red banner emblazoned with the words 'Revenge for
Robert Blum'.[16] It was hoped that Baden would become the
nucleus of a great German republic, but naturally no other German
state, however liberal, would be willing to let this happen. So, while
the Prussian army was the backbone of the counter-revolutionary
forces, the governments of Hesse, Nassau and Württemberg provided contingents. These forces dealt with the Palatine first, which
was invaded on 12 June. Schurz was with the republican forces that
retreated into Baden, and he recalled 'the dull rumble of the wheels
on the road, the rustle of the marching columns, the low snorting
of the horses, and the rattling of the sabers and scabbards in the
darkness'.[17]

The Prussians had reached Kaiserslautern on 14 June and, in hot
pursuit of the retreating democrats, crossed the Rhine on the 19th
to invade Baden. The population there was stirred by the sight of
the hated Prussians and some twenty thousand people put up resistance, fighting bravely against overwhelming odds at Waghäusel on
the 21st. Mierosławski manoeuvred his troops skilfully, scoring some
minor successes until his forces inevitably disintegrated under the
pressure; some two thousand of his men made their way to
Switzerland.

The final resistance of the German revolution of 1848–9 was
concentrated at Rastatt. This fortress held out for as long as its
defenders expected that Mierosławski's army would appear. When
they learned that it had evaporated, there was a fraught council of
war, in which some hot-heads spoke of fighting to the last man.
The majority, however, were determined to spare the town further

Prussian shelling and the horrors of a protracted siege and this view prevailed. The six thousand defenders surrendered on 23 July. The supreme commander of the Prussian forces was Prince William, now known pejoratively as the 'grapeshot prince' because he was rumoured to have given the order to fire on the Berliners on 18 March 1848. As if living up to this reputation, he overrode his subordinates' impulses in favour of clemency: one in every ten prisoners was shot and their bodies flung into mass graves. Others received heavy prison sentences. As a Prussian subject, Schurz was likely to be shot, but he escaped from the city through an underground drain, finding a hiding-place with two of his comrades in the loft of a shed. That building was soon taken over by Prussian cavalrymen, so that Schurz and his friends had to lie 'still like corpses', watching the enemy through the chinks in the wooden floorboards. After a couple of agonising days, they slipped out when the hussars caroused noisily beneath them. A sympathetic labourer guided them in their dash for the Rhine and the safety of France, where they told two bemused customs officers that they had nothing to declare.[18] Risking his own life, Schurz courageously returned to Germany in 1850 to help rescue his friend and mentor, Gottfried Kinkel, who had been captured outside Rastatt and was now being held in Spandau Prison. Schurz then sailed to the United States, where he joined some eighty thousand Badensians who emigrated to North America in the revolution's aftermath. Schurz embarked on a Successful political career in the United States, standing up for progressive causes: he fought as an officer in the Union army in the civil war, after which he was elected to the US Senate, before becoming secretary of the Interior. He died, at the ripe old age of seventy-seven, in 1906. The Prussian army left a deep impression on Baden, and memories of the repression persisted in a grim lullaby:

Sleep, my child, don't cry,
The Prussian's going by,
He killed your father at his door,
He made your wretched mother poor,

Keep very still, if you'd be wise,
Or he'll find ways to shut your eyes.
Sleep, my child, don't cry,
The Prussian's going by.[19]

II

When 1849 dawned in Italy, the radicals were already in power in Rome and Tuscany, while the Venetian republicans were still stubbornly resisting the Austrians. In the south, however, King Ferdinand II squeezed what life was left out of the liberal order in Naples while brutally throttling the separatist movement in Sicily. The monarch did not yet feel sufficiently secure to get rid of the Neapolitan parliament altogether, but he pointedly severed diplomatic relations with both Tuscany and Piedmont, while protecting Pius IX in Gaeta. When the war was rekindled between Piedmont and Austria in March, Ferdinand threw his lot in with the Habsburgs. He recalled the Austrian ambassador and dissolved parliament. The Piedmontese were routed at Novara, and with that the hopes of Italian patriots evaporated. Ferdinand now knew that he would have no more trouble from the national movement in Naples. The liberal parliamentary deputies were arrested and newspapers were closed down, their printing presses smashed. Sicily was then crushed under the same absolutist heel. When the armistice brokered by the French and British expired on 29 March, the Neapolitan forces sallied forth, faced only with a thinly spread army of seven thousand men under the ubiquitous Ludwik Mierosławski. It did not help that this Polish revolutionary could not speak Italian, but he was labouring against almost impossible odds anyway. His troops were green, disorganised and some were mutinous. Catania, on the east coast, fought desperately before it fell, but the sight of plumes of smoke rising from the city – and the fact that both sides executed prisoners – discouraged other towns from resisting, and Syracuse gave up without a fight. After Catania, Ferdinand's soldiers marched almost unopposed towards Palermo.

In the capital there was no great political will to resist: while Sicilian moderates loathed Ferdinand, they were also frightened by the war and by the instability that the revolution had brought. The *squadre* had temporarily suspended their criminal activities on the resumption of hostilities, but as the separatist movement collapsed they returned to type – looting and engaging in protection rackets. The Sicilian parliament was badly divided. In February Ferdinand had issued an ultimatum: in return for recognition of his dynasty, Sicily would have the constitution of 1812 restored, with its own parliament and government. The Sicilians had baulked at Ferdinand's demand for control of the armed forces and the right to dissolve parliament as he pleased. Now, to deflect the Neapolitan hammer blows, the Sicilian moderates were minded to accept these terms and sought French mediation in mid-April. Although the Sicilian forces were ordered to disengage from the enemy and the less compromising revolutionaries were expelled, this effort came too late. On 26 April the Neapolitan fleet appeared off Palermo. While the radicals wanted to resist, the bulk of the National Guard promised only to protect property from popular violence. Francesco Crispi, a radical determined to fight on, bitterly wrote that 'the moderates feared the victory of the people more than that of the Bourbon troops'.[20] Some barricades, draped with red flags, were built, but the fear of social revolution that this inspired merely spurred the moderates into negotiating with Ferdinand. Having agreed to surrender, some of the Sicilian liberal leadership helped to guide the royal troops into Palermo, although it should be added that this also gave them the opportunity to allow some of the more compromised revolutionaries to escape. By 11 May the Sicilian revolution was over. The island was once more under Bourbon rule after more than a year of independence.

While 'Bomba' was restoring his absolute authority over Naples and Sicily, Rome was sliding inexorably towards a republic. This was the result of the political polarisation that followed the Pope's flight. On the left, the radicals in the political clubs, the *carabinieri* and some battalions of the civic guard grew ever more uncompromising when it became clear that Pius was determined not to budge from his refuge at Gaeta. On the news that the original parliament had been dissolved on 26 December, Pius excommunicated in advance all those who would participate in the elections to the new Roman constituent assembly. The position of more moderate souls, who had wanted to negotiate the Pope's return to the city – provided that Pius promised to uphold the constitution – was now untenable. The interim government in Rome, pressed by further radical demonstrations, proclaimed universal male suffrage. The moderate, liberal vote collapsed in the elections held on 21 January. There was no violence or intimidation at the polls, but conservatives and liberals simply stayed away in disgust (or from fear of eternal damnation), handing the radicals an overwhelming victory. While most deputies were still landowners or middle-class professionals, their sympathies were democratic and even republican. Among the seven outsiders elected were Garibaldi and Mazzini.

The Constituent Assembly first met on 5 February. The question immediately arose as to what to do now that the Pope was clearly in the reactionary camp. The proclamation of a republic was not a foregone conclusion. The Assembly was regarded by enthusiastic Italian patriots as the lawgiving parliament not just for the Papal States but for all Italy: it was to be the long-awaited *costituente* itself. From Tuscany, Montanelli urged the Romans not to alienate Italian voters by deposing the Pope. Cooler heads in the Assembly, like Mamiani, worried that a Roman republic stood little chance of survival, since neither reactionary Naples nor monarchist Piedmont would tolerate it for long. Yet there seemed to be no alternative to a republic, since Pius would brook no compromise and the political uncertainty seemed to be pushing parts of the country into civil war: in the Romagna, violence was brewing between moderates and democrats. On 9 February, the Constituent Assembly therefore overwhelmingly proclaimed that Rome was now a 'pure democracy, and it will take the glorious name of The Roman Republic'. While 'the temporal government of the papacy in Rome is now at an end, in fact and in law', the Pope would have 'every guarantee needed for the independent exercise of his spiritual power'.[21] The wider, Italian role of the Assembly was yet to be determined. While Montanelli had wanted it to be a democratically elected assembly for all Italy, Mazzini was more realistic. He was still in his Swiss exile when he heard the electrifying news from Rome, and he travelled as fast as he could to the great city. On his arrival, he argued that neither Piedmont nor Naples would be persuaded to participate in a republican parliament. Instead, he argued, the Roman republic should be consolidated as the nucleus of the unified, democratic Italy of the future. And the first step should be the union of the Tuscan and Roman republics.

By suggesting this in Rome, Mazzini was ignoring what he had been told in Florence a few days earlier. There, his onetime friend, Guerrazzi, was fearful of Mazzini's popularity and saw him as a disruptive influence.[22] Guerrazzi worried that by taking a great leap into an uncertain republican future, the Italians would compromise social stability – and he saw stability as a vital precondition for the resumption of the war against Austria. He also feared that a democratic Tuscany would provoke Piedmontese intervention, so he had consistently stood firmly against universal male suffrage. One consequence of this had been rioting by the democrats during the Tuscan elections of 20 November 1848. Guerrazzi was now branded an opponent of the radical cause, and in Florence the ballot boxes were smashed and splintered by the rioters. When the Tuscan parliament met on 10 January, it was dominated by liberal moderates, but the news that a constituent assembly had been summoned in Rome gave new impetus to the democratic opposition. A demonstration of thirty thousand people in Florence forced the government to agree to the election of thirty-seven delegates to the Constituent Assembly in Rome on the basis of universal male suffrage. On 31 January, the day after voting finished, a fearful Grand Duke Leopold fled, first to Siena and then to the small port of Santo Stefano. As a Habsburg, he received a promise of military aid from Radetzky 'as soon as I have put down the demagogues of Piedmont'.[23] Within three weeks, Leopold would accept the warm invitation of King Ferdinand of Naples to join Pope Pius in exile in Gaeta.

Meanwhile, in Florence, the emblems of the Grand Duke were hacked down from buildings; and in radical Livorno, only the arrival of Mazzini – *en route* to Rome – prevented the city from proclaiming itself an independent city-republic there and then. In Florence, pressed by a massive crowd surging outside its meeting chamber in the Palazzo Vecchio, the Tuscan parliament vested power in a triumvirate: Guerrazzi, Montanelli and the democrat Giuseppe Mazzoni. Once these three had met Mazzini and assessed the continuing popular pressure, they took the next logical step on 18 February and proclaimed Tuscany a republic. Mazzini's suggestion of a union of between Tuscany and Rome now seemed viable, but Guerrazzi stood firm, adamant that Tuscany must remain independent. Mazzini left for Rome, bitterly disappointed that his unitary nationalism had failed to overcome old provincial loyalties.[24] On 5 March, fresh elections were held for a Tuscan constituent assembly, simultaneously with the choice of delegates to the Roman *costituente*. Yet Tuscany was now on the brink of civil war. Only 20 per cent of the electorate turned out: supporters of the triumvirate won a majority primarily because conservatives and moderates shunned the polls. Guerrazzi had to mobilise troops and civic guards to defend Florence from peasant insurgents marching in support of the Grand Duke and worried that a republican Tuscany meant war – with either Austria or Piedmont – and higher taxes. They were effortlessly stirred up by the clergy and landowners, whose position became almost unassailable when the country was, as feared, suddenly faced with an Austrian invasion.

That assault came as the aftershock of the war between Piedmont and Austria, which was rekindled in March. Charles Albert had many reasons for taking up the cudgel again. Domestically, he faced intense pressure from the democrats, who after Custozza appeared to be the only dedicated and persistent supporters of Italian independence. It was to calm the domestic political opposition, to salve his own bruised pride and to efface the humiliation of the previous year that, now supported even by moderates, he repudiated the armistice on 12 March. The British and French had tried to mediate and turn the truce into a lasting peace, but neither Austria nor

Piedmont was willing to relinquish its claims to Lombardy. On the outbreak of war, the fledgling Roman republic offered to place its fifteen-thousand-strong force under Charles Albert's orders, but the offer from a bunch of republican usurpers was turned down scornfully by the monarch. This was to be – more nakedly than in 1848 – a war of dynastic expansion. So hostile was the Piedmontese leadership to the republicans that some, such as the liberal politician Count Camillo di Cavour (who would become one of the central figures of nineteenth-century Italy), argued that an Austrian victory in the coming war would be preferable to a triumph in which the likes of Mazzini had a share of the spoils.[25]

Cavour should have been careful what he wished for. The campaign was embarrassingly brief. The Piedmontese had an army of eighty thousand, but many of the men had been hastily recruited and were still untrained. They were no match for the hardened, professional Austrians, nor for the steely Radetzky, who routed them at the battle of Novara on 23 March. As his dreams fell to dust around him, Charles Albert rode into the thick of the fighting, unsuccessfully trying to die heroically ('even death has cast me off', he bitterly observed). Back in Turin, he was threatened with the loss of his throne, because he was faced by the twin prospects of the Austrians overrunning his kingdom and a democratic uprising. There was an insurrection in Genoa (as fractious as ever), set off by the false rumour that Charles Albert had rejected the constitution and signed over the port to the Austrians. The revolt was crushed by the same army units that had retreated from Novara. They fought bitterly in the streets for two days and then bombarded the city, which capitulated on 10 April. The King chose to pre-empt any further disaster for his dynasty by abdicating in favour of his son, Victor Emmanuel II. After considerable debate in parliament, an armistice was accepted: the terms were fairly generous, not least because Radetzky had the desire neither to fan further the flames of Italian republicanism nor to provoke French intervention. In the final peace treaty Piedmontese territory was left intact, the Piedmontese had to pay a war indemnity of 75 million lire (the Austrians had initially demanded 230 million), and Victor Emmanuel promised to make no claim to territory outside his own kingdom. The Austrians agreed to amnesty all but a hundred of the most incorrigible Venetian and Lombard revolutionaries – a clause that the Piedmontese parliament, to its credit, tried to neuter by naturalising all those who were excluded from the amnesty.

The Piedmontese state therefore emerged from the crisis relatively unscathed. Most significantly, the new king promised his subjects that he would uphold the *statuto* granted by his father. This made the Sardinian monarchy unique in Italy in that it remained constitutional even after the revolutionary torrent had subsided. For the bruised Italian nationalists of the 1850s, this very fact would give Piedmont, already the premier military state in Italy, a strong claim to both moral and political leadership in Italian unification. Victor Emmanuel himself declared, 'I will hold the tricolour high and firm,' while Massimo D'Azeglio, his cerebral prime minister, appointed in May 1849, stated, 'I am Premier to save the independence of this fort of Italy'[26] – a reference to Piedmont as the putative nucleus of a united Italian kingdom.

With the Piedmontese disaster, Tuscany was suddenly left horribly exposed to the vengeance of the Habsburgs. Guerrazzi now knew that his only task was to save Tuscany from an Austrian invasion. On 27 March, he rose in the Constituent Assembly and openly renounced the earlier proclamation of the republic in an effort to prepare the ground for a peaceful restoration of the Grand Duke. Montanelli then had the Assembly elect Guerrazzi dictator before he himself wisely left the country. Guerrazzi used his powers to try to stamp order on the counter-revolution in the countryside and to prepare the country for the inevitable invasion, but he negotiated in vain with the moderates over the terms of Leopold's return. Matters came to a head on 11 April when the Florentines rioted outside the church of Santa Maria Novella against the swaggering, brutal behaviour of volunteers from Livorno brought into the city by Guerrazzi. The moderates harnessed the outpouring of popular anger and led the peasantry from the surrounding countryside into the city. The city council, which had remained in moderate hands, declared that it was now the Grand Duke's provisional government.

The Constituent Assembly was expelled from the Palazzo Vecchio. Guerrazzi, pursued by a crowd baying for his blood, surrendered himself to the protection of the new interim government. None of this saved Tuscany from invasion: on 26 April fifteen thousand Austrian troops streamed into the grand duchy. Leopold did not even return on their coat-tails, but pointedly took his time, waiting until July before resuming his place over his cowed subjects.

Novara galvanised the Roman republic, where Mazzini finally came to power. It would be his only practical experience of government, and it lasted only a hundred days.[27] He had arrived in Rome in early March 'with a deep sense of awe, almost of worship . . . I felt an electric thrill run through me – a spring of new life.'[28] Soon he relaunched his newspaper, *Italia del Popolo*, calling on all patriotic Italians, of whatever political stripe, to unite and confront their enemies. He was therefore dismayed to learn of the crushing of the Genoese insurrection by the Piedmontese army. The republicans in Rome had been preparing to wage war against Naples, in an attempt to spread their revolutionary message to the allegedly benighted population of the south. Now news of the Piedmontese rout forced the Romans to look anxiously northwards. The Constituent Assembly appointed a new emergency government, a triumvirate consisting of Mazzini, the lawyer Carlo Armellini and a Romagnol radical, Aurelio Saffi. Their wide mandate was to prepare for war against Austria and to secure the republic. Mazzini, in particular, exercised his power with considerable care: even his critics had to admit that he was moderate, hardworking and at times even wise. Unlike Rome's former rulers, he lived simply, unguarded in a single room, and remained accessible to all citizens: he ate in a local *trattoria* where he could be approached by all and sundry.

His actions were driven by a sense that the republic almost certainly would not survive, but that it had to be remembered for posterity. 'We must', he told the Constituent Assembly, 'act like men who have the enemy at their gates, and at the same time like men who are working for eternity.'[29] These sentiments seemed to run through the triumvir's actions during his hundred days in power. Religious belief and practice were protected in a republic which, in the circumstances, could have unleashed a wave of anti-clerical and anti-religious violence. There were certainly some horrifying murders, but they were not sponsored by the government – or even justified by it after the fact. When a particularly bloodthirsty extremist named Callimaco Zambianchi and his small gang of followers shot a friar and then slaughtered six residents of a convent in the slums of Trastevere, he was arrested by the authorities. In Ancona, where the violence was more widespread, the government's commissioner, Felice Orsini (later to gain notoriety – and be guillotined – for trying to assassinate Napoleon III with a bomb in 1858), cracked down hard (ironically enough) on the 'terrorists'. The Inquisition and censorship were abolished, the ecclesiastical courts were replaced by secular ones and the Church's grip on education was loosened. Some church property was confiscated to shelter the homeless and taxation was structured to help fund poor relief. All this was desperately needed, since after Rossi's murder many of Rome's wealthier families had fled, so the tradesmen and artisans whom they usually patronised suddenly faced unemployment. Yet Mazzini worked hard to protect Catholic sensibilities, ostentatiously attending Easter Mass in Saint Peter's, as the republic proclaimed religious toleration for all faiths.

For ordinary citizens, the streets of Rome felt safer now than they had been under the Pope – and this under a democratic regime that had just abolished the death penalty. None of this added up to the accusations of Mazzini being a 'communist' or (as Cavour put it) a latter-day Robespierre. 'No war of classes, no hostility to existing wealth . . . but a constant disposition to ameliorate the material condition of the classes least favoured by fortune' ran the triumvirate's programme of 5 April.[30] Those who met Mazzini in those days were impressed: the American consul, Lewis Cass, described him as 'a man of great integrity of character and of extensive intellectual acquirements'.[31] An astonished Ferdinand de Lesseps, the French envoy sent to Rome in May, noted that there were even plenty of devout Catholics who certainly wanted to see the Pope return to the Vatican, but only as a religious leader, not as an absolute monarch. Nevertheless, the republic would not last. It was destroyed not, as

initially expected, by an Austrian invasion, but by a French assault
on Rome. In a cruel twist, throughout 1848–9 the Italian republicans had yearned for French intervention to save them. Eventually
it arrived, but it was not on the side of the revolution.

The idea of a foreign invasion to restore the Pope had been
mooted almost from the moment when Pius had fled to Gaeta. In
February Cardinal Antonelli had proposed that the Catholic powers
of Naples, Spain and Austria, possibly joined by France, should
jointly occupy the Papal States. King Ferdinand, enthusiastic reactionary that he was, had already assembled his forces on his
northern frontier. The Austrians had retaken Ferrara and were con-
templating another assault on Bologna. Spain was marshalling a
seaborne expedition. The attitude of the French was uncertain. On
learning of Novara, President Louis-Napoleon Bonaparte at first
wanted to fight against the Austrians. Much as conservative opinion
in France sympathised with the Pope, it was still patriotic enough to
fear and despise Austrian power. At the end of March, the National
Assembly approved a six-thousand-strong French force under
General Nicolas Oudinot to occupy Rome's port, Civita Vecchia,
but not to march on the city itself unless he was certain that his
approach would not be received by hot lead. Ostensibly, the mission
was to protect Rome from an Austrian attack, but Bonaparte had
issued Oudinot with secret orders for the Roman republic to be
crushed. By doing this, the president was consolidating his conservative base by appealing to the sensibilities of the French Catholic
right. The French troops disembarked on 24 April. Six days later,
they marched on the Vatican, but assorted Italian democrats – with
up to nine thousand men commanded by, among others, Garibaldi –
beat them back, causing considerable carnage: the French lost five
hundred dead and wounded.

Although Oudinot brazenly claimed that this disastrous opera-
tion had merely been a 'reconnaissance' and a 'gloriously executed'
one at that,[32] the defeat was deeply embarrassing to Louis-
Napoleon, whose fundamental resonance with the French electorate
was associated with the military glories of his uncle. He was now
under political pressure, facing a National Assembly that was overtly

hostile to Oudinot's 'new' mission. On 7 May, in a republican charge led by the lawyer Jules Favre, the government's policy was rejected by the Assembly. Yet fresh elections gave Bonaparte the conservative majority he desired. Moreover, it was becoming clear that, unless he moved quickly, he would be denied his victory because the Austrians, Spanish and Neapolitans were on the move. The Austrians threw themselves against Bologna on 8 May and, after eight days of fighting, broke the city's resistance under the weight of a bombardment. They then marched down to Ancona, laying siege to the port. The French were anxious that the hated Austrians would soon grab the jewel of Rome: Thiers later remarked that 'to know that the Austrian flag was flying on the Castle of Saint Angelo is a humiliation under which no Frenchman could bear to exist'. Among those who agreed was the new French foreign minister, none other than Alexis de Tocqueville, who had taken office on 2 June and for whom it was essential to assert France's presence as a great power.[33] Action appeared to be all the more urgent because the Spanish had embarked some five thousand men bound for Fiumicino. The Neapolitans had also struck, occupying the countryside around Palestrina, but they were routed by Garibaldi at Velletri on 19 May. As Ferdinand's broken troops tumbled back across the frontier, those who had seen Garibaldi in his distinctive shirt described him as a bullet-proof 'red devil'. It was time for the French to make their move, so their peace envoy, de Lesseps, was recalled. Oudinot was furnished with new and ominous hardware: heavy siege guns were seen being hauled ashore at Civita Vecchia.

The coming fight would be hopelessly unequal: Oudinot now had thirty thousand men ranged against Rome's determined but motley force of sixteen thousand loyal regulars, *carabinieri*, civic guards, citizen volunteers and, of course, Garibaldi's men, some of whom had been with him since South America. Having been badly burned in April, Oudinot changed the focus of his assault to the Janiculum Hill, a long ridge along which ran the city's western defences. From there, he could mount artillery and rain shells on to Rome with impunity, which was precisely why Garibaldi's defence of this position was so determined and desperate. In the early hours of 3 June French troops swooped on the Italian outposts, the Pamfili and Corsini villas. The former was taken easily, but the Corsini, whose position on a knoll gave it a commanding view of the San Pancrazio city gate, was shattered by cannon fire and musketry after some sixteen hours of relentless combat. By the end of the fighting on 4 June the Italians had lost at least 550 killed and wounded, many in the narrow hornets' nest of the road between the Porta San Pancrazio and the Corsini, which had fallen to the French. Only the Vascello, a building on that same road, held out, supported by the Italian guns mounted on the city walls.

'The third of June', wrote Garibaldi dramatically, 'sealed the fate of Rome.'[34] Yet the French had sustained at least 264 casualties themselves and had lost the opportunity to storm the city by surprise. Mazzini also proved to be an inspiring leader (though Garibaldi, whom the troublesome Sterbini wanted to make dictator, was loath to admit it). Ordinary citizens, men and women, rallied to the city's defence. The French shells that were fired – particularly those falling on to the narrow streets and houses of the Trastevere, huddling immediately below the Janiculum – failed to break popular morale. Some six thousand women offered to help, and Princess Belgiojoso led a team of volunteer nurses. Meanwhile, the French were suffering from malaria. Rome might just have held out for long enough to provoke British diplomatic intervention, and for the French to be sufficiently weary to accept it. Eventually it was the Romans who were worn down. By sheer weight of numbers, in the night of 21–2 June, Oudinot's siege works finally came to within rushing distance of the bastions to the south of the Porta San Pancrazio. When they were breached, the French were at last on the city walls. Remarkably, the Vascello held on for another eight days until, blasted relentlessly by cannon, the building was nothing more than a smouldering heap of rubble. Garibaldi's men fell back to a second line of defence, pivoting at the Villa Spada (nowadays the Irish Embassy to the Vatican), which was blasted apart by gunfire over several days. (It was at this point that Garibaldi's indomitable and pregnant wife, Anita, chose to rejoin her husband.) The Italians held out desperately until the night of 29–30 June, when, fighting tooth and nail, the French took the shattered ruins of the Spada. The defenders wore the famous red shirts, which had been issued to Garibaldi's rank-and-file legionaries for the first time the previous day. On 30 June, after hearing Garibaldi's assessment of the military situation, and overriding Mazzini, the Constituent Assembly voted to capitulate. As one last monument of defiance, however, the deputies ratified the constitution of the Roman republic, which, though it was being framed while French shells burst around the parliament, stated that 'the Republic declares all nations as sisters: it respects every nationality: it supports the Italian'.[35]

Garibaldi – who, like Mazzini, wanted to continue the fight – gathered those among the remnants of his forces who were willing to follow him on Saint Peter's Square. He left Rome with some three thousand people – among them Cicerruacchio, Ugo Bassi (who since the spring had been chaplain to Garibaldi's force) and Anita, who cut her hair short and wore a green military uniform until her pregnancy was more advanced.[36] During the arduous march across the Apennines, pursued by the French and shunned by the fearful peasantry, Garibaldi's force gradually melted away through exhaustion, illness and desertion until, by the time he reached the Adriatic, he was left with no more than two hundred loyal followers. They commandeered boats to sail for Venice but were caught at sea by the Austrians. Making land, Garibaldi and his now tiny party hid in the Comacchio Forest, with Garibaldi carrying the now seriously ill Anita in his arms (she had caught a fever, probably malaria, on the long march). When she – and her unborn child – died, Garibaldi wept bitterly and had to be coaxed away from her lifeless body.[37] The Austrians captured Bassi and, with barbaric vengeance, tore the skin off his hands and forehead (where he had been anointed as a friar) before shooting him. Garibaldi recrossed the mountains, reaching the Tuscan coast, from where he sailed for Genoa, where the Piedmontese authorities threw him into prison before sending him into exile. He travelled the world doing various jobs for ten years before returning to Italy, this time triumphantly.

Mazzini remained in Rome for a week after the French troops marched in. The French, having accomplished their mission, were now keen to ensure that there were no reprisals. He eventually boarded a French ship bound for Marseille from where he made his way back to Switzerland and exile.

Back in Rome, Oudinot declared papal rule restored in mid-July and handed over power to the 'Red Triumvirate', so called because it consisted of three cardinals who dressed in scarlet cassocks. French soldiers, with bayonets fixed, prevented the republican Constituent Assembly from reassembling and censorship was restored, but Louis-Napoleon did try to cajole Pius into retaining some of the reforms of 1848: 'the French Republic', he told the Pope in true Bonapartist style, 'has not sent an army to Rome to crush Italian liberty, but to regulate it, and save it from its own excesses'.[38] Pius responded by refusing to return to Rome and withdrawing in high dudgeon to King Ferdinand's palace at Portici. There, he issued a declaration on 12 September which, while offering some mild concessions, effectively restored absolute rule. He offered amnesty only to a small group of people, but because this left such a large number liable to prosecution, it significantly blunted the effectiveness of the repression: witnesses refused to give evidence and in the end only thirty-eight of those targeted were punished. Meanwhile, the Red Triumvirate reintroduced the Inquisition; furthermore, capital punishment (by the guillotine) was restored, as were public floggings. Even moderate liberals were exiled and the Jews, who had been given full rights under the republic, were forced back into the ghetto. When the Pope eventually returned to Rome in April 1850, it was to a noticeably sullen reception.

Only Venice remained as the last pocket of Italian resistance. Despite his republicanism, Manin was pragmatic enough to realise that, as 1849 opened, the city's fate lay in a Piedmontese victory, since Franco-British mediation seemed to be getting nowhere. He also tried – as far as he could without angering the Piedmontese government – to enter into diplomatic relations with Tuscany and Rome. For recognising the Roman republic, however, he was bitterly

denounced by Tommaseo, who as a devout Catholic resented the
revolution against the Pope. Yet Manin's popularity did not suffer
with the voters in the January elections for the new Venetian assembly. There was some opposition – from the Mazzinians trying to
regain the initiative after the government crackdown in October,
and from conservatives who wanted to end the war by coming to
terms with Austria. These left- and right-wing opponents formed an
unlikely alliance in the assembly, but Manin retained the support of
most working people in Venice – including the gondoliers (the elite
of the working class), whose leader had given the triumvirs a ringing
endorsement. On 5 March, an overzealous crowd of Venetians, abet-
ted by the benign neutrality of the civic guard, stormed the assembly
in the Doge's Palace to demand that Manin be made dictator. Only
the diminutive man himself, sword drawn, stood in their way and
persuaded them to disperse. Two days later, however, the assembly
voted to give Manin full powers anyway, including the right to dissolve the assembly itself for fifteen days and, in its absence, to issue
emergency decrees. Hopes were revived when Piedmont once again
went to war with Austria, and Charles Albert's ships reappeared in
the lagoon,[39] but on 2 April came the devastating news of Novara.

The assembly rose to the challenge. Manin told the delegates of
the city's now dire situation, finishing with a call to fight to the bitter
end: 'Does the assembly wish to resist the enemy?' 'Yes,' the delegates
shouted back. 'At every cost?' To a man the delegates rose and roared,
'Yes!' It would not be long before the Austrians would bring up
crushing numbers against Venice. The siege trenches dug by the
Austrian sappers threaded their way ever closer to the walls of Fort
Marghera, the focal point for their assault.[40] From 4 May that fortress
was blasted by an estimated sixty thousand shells and rockets – a
quarter of them on 25 May alone, the climax of this rain of fire. The
Venetians had 130 cannon and mortars with which they replied, but
they ran low on munitions, and by the time the fort (now in heaps
of rubble) fell, one in three gunners had been killed. In addition to
the utter carnage, the defenders were racked by cholera and malaria.
On 26 May, seeing the Austrians cramming their trenches with
men – the ominous sign of an impending assault – the survivors beat

a retreat across the railway bridge, back into the city, or were rowed across the lagoon in boats. Five arches of the bridge were blown up to cut off the obvious route for an Austrian assault. The occasional railway platforms on the bridge were fortified with artillery; to be assigned to the front battery was to receive an order of almost certain death. Raked by Austrian gunnery every day, the Venetian dead and wounded in the front positions were carried back into the city at night while the shattered defences were shored up.

As the Austrian siege intensified, there were calls to replace Pepe, who was accused of being too old and phlegmatic to continue as Venetian commander. The Italian Club invited all soldiers to attend their meetings and to voice their opinions. Recognising the threat to discipline and the challenge to his authority, Manin closed down the club on 3 June, but he did make a major concession to the pressure for change: a new three-member military commission, which included General Ulloa, hero of the stubborn resistance of Fort Marghera, would take control of the armed forces. Pepe resigned, but Ulloa tactfully made him the president of the commission. This body was one of the reforms for which the Italian Club had been campaigning – and Manin bowed to the vote of the assembly when it accepted the change.[41] Meanwhile, Venice had acquired a new ally: Hungary. In May Kossuth had sent an envoy to negotiate with Manin at a time when he believed that the Magyars might successfully send an army through Croatia and occupy Trieste, the home of the imperial fleet. The alliance between Venice and Hungary was sealed on 20 May, with the Hungarians promising the Venetians financial support in return for a diversionary sortie from Venice when the Magyars reached the sea.[42]

This alliance gave false hope to the Venetians. The Austrian noose was slowly but surely tightening around them. Radetzky called for the city's surrender, but when Manin demanded autonomy within the empire as a condition, the field marshal offered nothing more than an amnesty for soldiers and free passage for anyone who wished to go into exile. True to its promise to resist, the assembly overwhelmingly rejected these uncompromising terms at the end of June. It was a display of defiance that cost the brave city dear. While soldiers killed each other on the lagoon, the Venetian civilians were subjected to a prolonged artillery bombardment. The guns, with their barrels removed from their carriages and slipped into specially constructed wooden slides propped up at a forty-five-degree angle, aimed into the night sky and sent twenty-four-pound shells high over the lagoon and tumbling on to the city, travelling a distance of three and a half miles.[43] The shelling began in the night of 29–30 July and lasted for three weeks. The loss of life from the bombardment and the fires that it caused was far lower than one might have expected, though, partly because of the fire-fighting efforts of the Venetians, but also because the cannonballs, while red hot, had covered such a distance that their force was often spent. They made gaping holes in roofs, but they did not always explode on impact and frequently did not even penetrate down to the lower floors. The Venetian festivals and processions continued and the theatres still put on performances. The Austrians fired a thousand projectiles a day at the city, but the Venetians defiantly dubbed the burning shells 'Viennese oranges'.[44]

But there were two enemies that Venice could not resist: disease and hunger. Some four thousand Venetians succumbed over the summer to typhus and cholera, and all the citizens were hungry, living off thin servings of vegetables and polenta, since meat and fish were becoming scarce: a chicken cost a week's wages for the average worker. Medical supplies had run out and there was no more wine (which is especially devastating in a time of cholera, since alcohol kills the bacteria). Furthermore, the troops were running low on gunpowder. By mid-July, the situation was becoming desperate and the Venetians, who had remained steadfast throughout the siege, were growing restive. A priest warned the military commission: 'The women who had gathered to buy bread were swearing and praying, and tearing the earrings from their ears and the wedding rings from their fingers . . . We must not wait until the People take matters into their own hands.'[45] With the threat of widespread rioting, on 16 July Tommaseo's proposal to introduce a system of rationing was adopted. With people moving out of the western districts of the city, which were the most exposed to the shelling, the rest of Venice was crammed with human life, much of it living in dank ground-floor rooms, sometimes sharing a bed with the dead and the cholera-ridden dying. Manin knew that the city's food supply would run out by the end of August so – over Tommaseo's fierce opposition, but supported by Pepe – a wafer-thin majority in the assembly authorised him to negotiate with the Austrians on 6 August. It was a bitter moment for Manin, who addressed the Venetian crowd for the last time on the Piazza San Marco on 13 August. Overwhelmed with emotion, he could not finish his speech. As he stepped back from the balcony, he declared: 'Such a people! To be forced to surrender with such a people!'[46] Venice could not even hope for Hungarian assistance, since news arrived of the Magyar surrender to the Russians on 18 August. Five days later, the Venetian volunteers defending the railway bridge saw a gondola emerge from the landward side of the lagoon: in it was Manin's fellow triumvir, Cavedalis, who, in the late hours of 22 August, had signed the surrender. He told the crestfallen soldiers to return to the city and hoist the white flag.

The terms were, in the circumstances, generous: all those involved in the Venetian revolution were amnestied, except for forty leaders who were allowed to go into exile: a steamer provided by the sympathetic French consul carried away Manin and his family, Pepe, Ulloa, Tommaseo and the others.[47] Manin finished up in Paris. When the imperial troops (who had sustained eight thousand deaths through disease or combat during the siege) entered the city on 27 August, leading the way were the Magyar battalions that Kossuth, back in the summer of 1848, had refused to recall to Hungary in the hope of securing permanent Austrian recognition of the April Laws. This bitter irony is perhaps the most poignant illustration of the painful contradictions of the 1848 revolutions.

III

The year 1849 dawned bleakly for Hungary. The Austrians were in control of Budapest. The National Assembly had gathered in remote Debrecen, where only 145 deputies out of 415 turned up to its first reconvening on 9 January. Eventually, that number would rise to three hundred, but for now the small rump was dominated by those who wanted to negotiate with the Austrians. Yet liberal Hungary clung on. It was able to do so because of the vigorous efforts of the government to mobilise national resources and to encourage a counter-attack. Resolution and determination became the qualities that decided promotion for junior officers and, while most of them were still of noble background, non-nobles were raised from the ranks. The army that would determinedly drive out the Austrians in the spring of 1849 was for the large part the cit-izens' force of Honvéd battalions. Their number had expanded dramatically from 16 in September 1848 to 140 by June 1849; in the same period, including regulars, the army had expanded from 100,000 to 170,000. Much of this was thanks to the introduction of conscription, which had been brought in at the outbreak of the war, so while a tenth of the ranks were filled with students, intellectuals and landowners, most of the recruits (about two-thirds) were drawn from the poorer peasantry. A fifth comprised artisans and journey-men. These figures probably reflect the fact that those who drew a short straw in the conscription ballot and who were sufficiently wealthy could pay someone else (usually poorer) to take their place. Yet none of this absolutely precludes patriotic fervour as a motiva-tion among the rank and file – for instance, the 9th Battalion, the 'red caps', became famous for its commitment and determination. And the hard patriotic core in the ranks was strengthened by the quality of the leadership. Officers from the old imperial army who joined the Honvéd battalions were almost automatically given a higher rank in the new units, while non-commissioned officers were made officers. These experienced soldiers and the educated rank-and-file volunteers who were made NCOs formed a solid group of instructors who could train the rest. Efforts to recruit from among the rebellious Romanian and southern Slav popula-tions were virtually futile, so the brunt of the enlistment was borne by the Magyars, although among the officers there were plenty of Poles and Germans. The latter made up some 15 per cent of the officer corps at the start of 1849, so Leiningen was by no means unique.[48]

The National Defence Committee, led by Kossuth, purchased – and smuggled – arms from abroad, paying with Hungary's gold reserves. Meanwhile, Hungarian workshops hammered out close to five hundred muskets a day. Others had already been purchased from abroad, particularly Belgium, by the Batthyány government in the summer of 1848. Equipping the army, however, proved to be a greater challenge than recruiting it. By the time the war had broken out, many of the volunteers were still without cloaks, just as the cold weather was closing in, and boots were not being cobbled together with sufficient speed. To try to ease the crisis, the government sent raw materials into the provinces, placing orders with local craft workers, allowing the battalions raised locally to be directly supplied.[49] The committee offered large loans to manufacturers to switch to wartime production; it weeded out skilled workers from the Honvéd battalions, sending them into the workshops; it bought up grain surpluses for the military; and it created a military academy and new field hospitals. The printing presses for Hungarian banknotes had been hauled from Budapest to Debrecen. Some eighty government commissioners, with wide-ranging and in some cases absolute powers, were sent across the country to mobilise the population and its resources for the war effort, to supervise the military and to report back to the committee. They were sorely needed as a counterweight against the local county officials, who were showing an alarming tendency to turn with the political tide – which in the New Year was flowing Austria's way.

Unfortunately, the Hungarian counter-attack was not achieved without internal bloodshed. The crisis gave renewed vigour to the radicals, who at Debrecen pressed for universal male suffrage, the proclamation of a republic, the abolition of the nobility and a law that defined as treason the demands of the national minorities. Parliament responded by establishing revolutionary tribunals to try traitors. Radicals and moderates alike were angry at the rebelliousness of the ethnic minorities and, in the end, these tribunals handed down 122 death sentences – mostly against non-Magyars.[50]

The government also faced a challenge from one of its own commanders – Görgey. The general's political convictions rested on the defence of the April Laws, and now he was worried that Hungary was being steered towards a republic. His army was riven with discontented officers who believed that they would have legality on their side for as long as they were fighting for the constitution, but nothing more radical than that. The officer corps of whole units were deserting to the imperial forces. With his army looking likely to disintegrate before his eyes, Görgey made a resounding proclamation on 5 January at Vác, where his Corps of the Upper Danube was defending the approaches to Budapest: this army 'faithful to its oath for the maintenance of the Constitution of Hungary . . . intends to defend that Constitution against all foreign enemies'. It would obey the legitimate minister of war – in other words, the one approved by the King and responsible to the Hungarian parliament – but not the committee. This was a rejection of the radical liberalism – and the suspected republicanism – of the political leadership of the Hungarian revolution.[51] The bold proclamation stemmed the flow of desertions – at last, declared Charles Leiningen, he had met a leader who was a determined enemy of the 'republican party' and who wanted 'nothing more than the constitution of 1848'.[52] Kossuth, faced with this mutiny against the committee, privately accused Görgey of being a traitor. The general was no turncoat, however: when Windischgrätz called on him to surrender and to bring his entire army with him, Görgey simply demanded negotiations with the Austrians on the basis of the April Laws. In any case he had little political backing: the moderate 'peace party' at Debrecen ought to have seen him as an ally, but they feared that he aspired to military dictatorship. The soldier heartily reciprocated their distrust, feeling that all politicians were shady characters. Yet he soon proved to be the temporary saviour of the liberal regime. After the Austrians took Budapest, he kept his army intact by withdrawing into the Slovakian hills. Forging on through bitter winter weather and over mountainous terrain, his troops fell on the Austrian units that were feeling their way towards Debrecen, forcing them to retreat and seek the safety of Windischgrätz's main army in the west. Görgey then marched southwards towards the River Tisza, where the main body of Hungarian forces held the line against the Austrians.

Owing to Görgey's obvious capabilities, Kossuth was eventually left with little choice but to appoint him to lead the counter-offensive in the spring, though he refused to make him commander-in-chief. In early April the Hungarians fought a series of bloody battles and pressed forward towards Budapest. Görgey tried to persuade Kossuth that the bulk of his forces should avoid getting bogged down in recapturing the capital, but rather should circumvent it and relieve the fortress of Komárom, which was of greater strategic importance. It was as the Hungarians were driving the Austrians before them that a momentous event occurred: on 14 April Kossuth proclaimed Hungarian independence before the excited parliament and a packed crowd of spectators: 'an act of the last necessity', the opening paragraph protested, 'adopted to preserve from utter destruction a nation persecuted to the limits of the most enduring patience'.[53] The declaration was formally published five days later.

The catalyst had been the new imperial constitution imposed by the Emperor on 5 March. It stripped Hungary of its April constitution and reduced its territory and status within the monarchy. There could, in other words, be no compromise between the liberal regime in Hungary and the monarchy in Vienna. Moreover, besides discrediting the Hungarian peace party and making war and independence the only option for the Magyar liberals, the imperial constitution sent out a very dispiriting message to the other nationalities of the kingdom. The Voivodina Serbs, who had been sustaining the full horrors of ethnic conflict in southern Hungary since the summer of 1848, were put on notice that, contrary to their hopes and expectations, the Emperor would not reward their loyalty by recognising their national aspirations. Weary of the brutalities of the conflict, Serb resistance to the Hungarians now began to disintegrate. In Transylvania General Bem had used a combination of force and diplomacy to subdue resistance. He had provoked Kossuth's anger by offering an amnesty to all Romanian fighters who surrendered their arms. He had tried to pacify the population by offering them some degree of self-government and the local use of their language. For Kossuth – as for other Hungarian nationalists – Transylvania was an integral part of the lands of Saint Stephen and should have been incorporated without such concessions. Now, though, with the declaration of independence, Kossuth at last reached out to the Romanians, sending a Romanian member of parliament into the Transylvanian mountains to meet with the remaining guerrilla fighters, who gave their unambiguous answer by killing him.[54]

Kossuth left the precise form of the new Hungary – whether it would be a republic or a monarchy – to a constituent assembly to be elected after the war. On 23 April the Austrians in Budapest, aware of Görgey's advance on Komárom (which fell shortly afterwards), abandoned the city to avoid being encircled. They did, though, leave a garrison in Buda Castle. Hungarian troops marched into the city hours later to an ecstatic welcome. Görgey, who had now been made minister of war by Kossuth, believed that the army needed a rest – and he knew that many of his officers would have been shaken by the implications of the declaration of independence. Kossuth, however, believed that the complete liberation of Budapest would bring international diplomatic recognition for independent Hungary. Time was pressing, for the Austrians would soon be reinforced by troops redeployed from Italy after Novara. Görgey bowed to the political pressure and transferred the bulk of his Honvéd forces from Komárom to the siege of Buda Castle.[55] It was a fatal mistake: had the Hungarians pressed on towards Vienna, they might at least have secured a negotiated peace.

So it was that, on 4 May, the castle hill was encircled by forty thousand Hungarian troops. The brutal fighting lasted two and a half weeks. In these critical days the Austrian guns shelled the city from the castle and even tried, albeit unsuccessfully, to zero in on Széchenyi's chain bridge. Finally, the Hungarian siege guns that had been hauled down from Komárom blasted a breach in the citadel's walls and, in a night assault on 20–1 May, the Honvéd forces surged up the slope and through the gap under murderous

Austrian fire. Görgey had ordered that no quarter be given, while the Austrians had pledged to fight to the very end, so the combat at close quarters, in a darkness lit by the bursting of shells and the flashes of musketry, was desperate, brutal and bloody: in this one night, one thousand Austrians lost their lives.[56] Though an important symbolic victory, the Hungarian forces had lost precious weeks that could have been used in pushing the Austrians further west. As Görgey had feared, his men were now too exhausted to press on into Austria, and the imperial forces remained camped on the western fringes of the country. Moreover, with victory and independence apparently in sight, the Hungarian revolutionaries now manoeuvred for domestic political advantage.

The National Assembly had elected Kossuth governor-president of Hungary, but he was no dictator, since on 2 May he had appointed a cabinet led by his close colleague Bertalan Szemere, with Görgey as minister of war. Parliament still sat and the government commanded the support of the majority. While Kossuth accepted the right to determine the general direction of policy, he willingly agreed that the ministers had to countersign his decrees and that he was bound to obey the laws passed by the National Assembly – and so ran the oath of office which he took on 14 May.[57] Thus Kossuth's presidential powers and the legislative authority of parliament sat together awkwardly. At the end of May, Szemere asked the Assembly to dissolve itself and to reconvene in Budapest on 2 July.

By that point, a great noose was being prepared for liberal Hungary. Tsar Nicholas I had agreed to the Emperor Franz Joseph's plea for Russian military intervention in the name of 'the holy struggle against anarchy'.[58] Görgey, who as minister of war now had overall supervision of all the Hungarian army corps, was among the first to read the writing on the wall. Never happy with the idea of resistance to the bitter end, he and many of his officers wanted to negotiate rather than see Hungary put to the sword. Their desire for a rapid, negotiated peace was no doubt sharpened when two Hungarian officers were captured by the Austrians, summarily tried as rebels and shot on 5 June under the orders of the new Austrian commander, the infamously ruthless General Ludwig Haynau (who had been transferred from Italy, where he had brutally suppressed an insurrection at Brescia, which had finished with the flogging of civilians, including women). Such a negotiated peace was impossible for as long as Kossuth was in charge. Görgey considered the possibility of a military coup, but he failed to secure any support from the civilian politicians. He angrily returned to the army.

On hearing the first news of the Emperor's appeal to the Tsar, Kossuth called on the Hungarian people to rise up against the Russian hordes. The government also made vain efforts to obtain international support for Hungarian independence, pointing out the dangers of a surge of Russian military might into Central Europe. Unfortunately, though, Prussia was downright hostile to Hungary: the conservative government certainly feared the consequences of Russian military intervention, but rather than help the Magyars, it offered to send its own troops to take part in the invasion, so that Prussia would have some control over the situation. The Western powers were less overtly hostile, but still offered no help. Louis-Napoleon's France was in no mood to challenge the Russians and was in any case on the cusp of crushing the Roman republic. The Hungarians found sympathy primarily on the French radical left, but it could do little more than make the right noises through its newspapers. The Paris government itself received Hungarian pleas with stony silence. Meanwhile, the British insisted that, legally, Hungary was still part of the Austrian Empire. Hungary's only ally was therefore Manin's Venetian republic. The United States was sympathetic but offered only diplomatic recognition – and the distances to be covered by the Hungarian envoys meant that by the time they arrived in Washington the revolution at home had already been extinguished.[59]

The Hungarian government also made belated efforts to secure its eastern frontiers by negotiating with Romanian nationalists, who in mid-July agreed to support the Magyars in return for official recognition of Romanian as the local language of government, law and education, as well as the abolition of compulsory peasant labour services. The 'nationality law' of 28 July extended these concessions to all the kingdom's ethnic groups. It guaranteed to each the freedom to develop their national identity. While Hungarian would be the language of central government, the counties could use whatever tongue was deemed appropriate to local circumstances. The same day, Jews were given equal rights to those of other citizens. The government also tried to prod the peasantry into rising up against the Austrians. On 19 April, a decree protecting peasant property rights had been passed. Whenever land ownership was in dispute between nobles and peasants, the law would give the benefit of the doubt to the latter. This would end one of the sources of tension since the emancipating decrees of a year previously. However, both the peasant and the nationality laws were too little, too late, to save Hungary from the final onslaught. There was to be no far-reaching programme of social reform that might stir the enthusiasm of the mass of the population for the great struggle. Moreover, the laws on nationality offered *less* to the minorities than the Emperor's centralising constitution of March 1849.

Tsar Nicholas I of Russia had his reasons to help the young Franz Joseph in destroying the Hungarian revolution. He suspected the Hungarians of trying to foment revolution in the Danubian principalities and he feared that an independent Hungary would weaken Austria, allowing Prussia to dominate Germany; he was also anxious about the effect that the Hungarian example would have on his perennially rebellious Polish subjects. These fears combined when the Polish commander of the Hungarian forces in Transylvania, József Bem, allowed his troops to surge into Bukovina in January 1849, which caused some alarm among Russian officials in neighbouring Poland. In response Nicholas gave Field Marshal Ivan Paskevich, his viceroy in Poland, 'full powers to cross the frontier and to enter into battle with the insurgents in case Austrian officials request it'. This was before the new Austrian foreign minister, Schwarzenberg, had even made a formal request for Russian help – and for now, with the Hungarians on the ropes, he was reluctant to invite the great bear into Central Europe. He wanted to prove that Austria 'is strong enough to quiet its own domestic tremors'.[60] In fact, the Russians made a brief foray into Transylvania, responding not to a formal request from Vienna but to a local plea from General Puchner for help against the Magyars. The small, six-thousand-strong Russian army was among the imperial and Romanian forces that were driven back by Bem in the spring, and it caused some embarrassment to Vienna, though not to the Russians, who remained unrepentant about acting in the name of 'humanity' against the depredations of Hungarian revolutionaries.

Nevertheless, it was a humiliating reverse for the Russians, and the Tsar was still smarting from it when Görgey drove Windischgrätz almost entirely out of Hungary in April. So Nicholas was receptive when Schwarzenberg swallowed his Austrian pride and allowed the Austrian ambassador in Saint Petersburg to make a formal plea for Russian assistance. Nicholas readily assented: while he privately admitted to Paskevich that he had 'no burning desire' to get entangled in Hungary, he also saw 'in Bem and in the other rascals in Hungary not only the enemies of Austria but also the enemies of order and tranquillity in the entire world, the personification of villains, scoundrels and destroyers, whom we must destroy for the sake of our own tranquillity'.[61] So when Franz Joseph made his appeal to Nicholas in person on 21 May to join the Habsburgs in saving 'modern society from certain ruin' and to share in the glory of maintaining 'the holy struggle of the social order against anarchy', he was pushing on an open door.[62] The young Habsburg Emperor had travelled to Warsaw to meet the Tsar, who was gratified to have the Austrian fall on his knees and kiss his hand.

The Hungarians could field at most 170,000 men, supported by 500 guns. Against them the Austrians and the Russians mustered a crushing numerical superiority, with a combined total of 375,000 men, divided between, in the west, Haynau's force of 83,000, backed by 330 artillery pieces; in the south, the 44,000 men under Jelačić, with 190 cannon; and some 48,000 Romanian guerrillas and imperial troops holding out in Transylvania. The rest of the allied numbers comprised the Russians under Paskevich. The latter was a veteran of the wars of expansion in the Caucasus and a hero (if one can really call him that) in the suppression of the Polish uprising in 1831. He fielded an overwhelming force of 200,000, with an awe-inspiring 600 guns, poised in the Romanian principalities and in Poland, but he was not prepared to be bounced by Austrian impatience into a premature assault. Although the Russians had promised to invade by 17 June, Paskevich waited until he was satisfied that his troops were ready and that he had stockpiled enough supplies and equipment to sustain his army. So it was that the belligerent Haynau struck first, driving into western Hungary towards Budapest, wisely bypassing Komárom. Meanwhile, the war in the south remained a horribly squalid affair revolving around ethnic strife.

When the Russians finally attacked in the east, they met with little resistance because the Hungarians were already engaged against the Austrians. Paskevich advanced ponderously into Transylvania, where the sheer weight of Russian numbers tipped the balance in favour of the Romanian and imperial forces. Contrary to what many people expected, the Russians behaved with restraint: Hungarian prisoners were well treated, and there was little or no looting or violence against the local population. Apparently, both the Russian invaders and the Magyars agreed that the real villains were 'the cowardly and rapacious Austrians'.[63] While the Russians seeped slowly through eastern Hungary, suffering from ghastly bouts of cholera, the Austrians in the west advanced energetically, taking Budapest on 13 July. Görgey withdrew his forces intact to the Tisza – his men exhausted and many of them barefoot – but even his skill and determination could only delay Hungary's final collapse. On 8 July the Hungarian parliament and government once again fled Budapest and reconvened – the National Assembly now numbering two hundred – at Szeged, far to the south, where it was expected that the Hungarian revolution would make its last great stand. Szeged – like Debrecen a town with muddy streets and primitive housing – was the backdrop to the last meeting of the revolutionary Hungarian parliament, for a mere week between 21 and 28 July. It was here that the Magyars made their belated concessions to the Jews and the national minorities. Meanwhile,

Görgey, marching southwards with his corps towards Szeged, was negotiating the terms of his own surrender to the Russians, trying to secure the highly unlikely prize of tsarist support for peace on the basis of the April Laws. Kossuth, whom Görgey had the brass neck to keep informed about his freelancing diplomacy, was especially infuriated. In any case Paskevich would accept no terms other than unconditional surrender. The Hungarian government and parliament fled again on 30 July, this time to Arad. The day before, the radical poet Sándor Petőfi, serving as General Bem's adjutant, was killed in action by Cossacks during the fighting in Transylvania; his body was never found. Haynau's army had by now penetrated so far into Hungary that it had reached Temesvár, where on 9 August a murderous exchange of artillery fire terrified the soldiers of the Honvéd units, many of whom were then crushed under the hooves of the Austrian heavy cavalry as they fled.

When Kossuth heard of this final disaster on 11 August, he resigned and unceremoniously handed over full civil and military powers to Görgey. Shaving off his distinctive moustache, beard and leonine sideburns, he took two false passports and fled into exile, travelling first to Constantinople. He was followed by Szemere, who spirited off the crown of Saint Stephen, which he buried at Orsova, on the frontier with the Ottoman Empire. Also on 11 August, a mere twelve members of the National Assembly met at Arad and dissolved the parliament, while Görgey made arrangements for the surrender of his forces to the Russians, in order to keep his officers from the vengeful clutches of the Austrians. The capitulation was carried out in a ceremony at the village of Világos, near Arad, two days later, but the last Hungarian resistance, in the fortress of Komárom, was not snuffed out until 2 October. In all both sides had lost fifty thousand dead. On the Austro-Russian side, most of the casualties were sustained by the Austrians. The Russians, meanwhile, suffered much more from disease than on the battlefield: they lost 550 killed in action but over 11,000 to cholera.[64]

The Russians (and Nicholas himself) admired the courage of their Hungarian adversaries and pressed for a full amnesty, but the

Vienna government on 20 August granted this only to the rank and file, the junior officers – who were conscripted into the imperial army – and Görgey. The rest faced the summary judgement of a military tribunal. Up to the end of 1850, over 4,600 Hungarians were tried and some 500 were sentenced to death, with 120 of these judgements being carried out. Some 1,500 people were imprisoned for long periods – usually the sentence ranged between ten and twenty years – many weighed down by chains. Kossuth, Szemere and other exiles were tried *in absentia*, found guilty and symbolically 'hanged' by having their names nailed to the gallows in the military prison in Budapest. The most notorious executions were those of fourteen Hungarian commanders at Arad early in the morning of 6 October, and that of Batthyány in Budapest on the same day. Among those shot or hanged at Arad was Leiningen, who managed to write one last moving letter to his beloved wife, Lizzie, before he faced the hangman. When he reached the gibbet, he joked with a guard, 'They ought at least to have treated us to a breakfast.' The sentences were carried out individually, so the whole ceremony of death lasted three agonising hours, until the bodies dangled lifelessly from a line of gibbets or slumped from their poles.[65] Batthyány had been hauled before a court martial at Olmütz in August and, by Schwarzenberg's personal command, was to be hanged. Transferred to Budapest, though, he had slit his own throat with a dagger smuggled into the prison by his wife. Although he survived, the wound ensured that he could not be killed by the noose. Instead, he was shot by firing squad at sunset on 6 October, having refused a blindfold and insisting on giving the order to fire himself.[66]

Why the 'War of Independence' (as it is remembered in Hungary) should have failed is a subject of some controversy. For Istvan Deak, ethnic strife was the key, particularly the Magyar–Romanian conflict in Transylvania, since that, he argues, was an entirely avoidable war: with timely concessions by the Hungarians, the Romanians might have been quiescent at precisely the time when the government was confronting Jelačić's invasion from the south and then the Austrian assault from the west. Yet, as Alan Sked points out, the Hungarians saw off the Croatian challenge and, after the initial shock in Transylvania, they soon mastered the situation there, too. Sked and Deak appear to agree when they dismiss the importance of Russian intervention. Paskevich's gargantuan army moved slowly across eastern Hungary, undertaking no great decisive battles against the Hungarians. Had the war dragged on for longer than it did, then Russian numbers certainly would have told; but as it was, the Hungarians were defeated repeatedly and decisively by the Austrians in the summer of 1849. Ultimately, therefore, the Hungarians lost because the Austrians themselves mustered military superiority, particularly in the unglamorous but vital sphere of logistics. The Austrians were better supplied, better equipped and better trained than the hastily assembled Hungarian Honvéd battalions. The improvised Hungarian armaments industry may have turned out an impressive number of firearms each day, but they were not reliable: in battle, muskets misfired every fourth shot and a shortage of weaponry meant that attacks could not always be followed up rigorously. Austria, meanwhile, had an overwhelming superiority in manufacturing capacity – including the all-important works in iron and steel. The Hungarians desperately sought to make up for their shortage of munitions (Görgey himself had been put to work on this task), but they never succeeded in closing the gap. Moreover, since the great Hungarian arms works was in Budapest, a city that was twice captured by the Austrians in 1848–9, production was disrupted as the manufacturing was relocated in Nagyvárad. Furthermore, for much of 1849, it was impossible for Hungary to make up the deficit in arms and munitions through imports because the country was cut off from the outside world.[67]

While not denying the importance of inherent Austrian military strength (and relative Hungarian weakness), it is difficult to escape the conclusion that the key lies either in the ethnic conflict or in the Russian intervention. There is strong evidence that it was the convergence of these two factors that was decisive in the Habsburg victory. It is true that in 1848 Jelačić was disposed of with relative ease and that General Bem managed to drive back the Romanians, but the very persistence of the southern Slav and Romanian opposition to Magyar nationalism meant that, when the Austrian counter-attack came, the Hungarian forces could not focus fully on the west to see it off. As it was, Görgey faced the 83,000-strong Austrian force with just 63,000 men at a time when the Hungarian armed forces in total numbered 170,000. The rest had to remain in the interior, deployed against Croats, Serbs, or Romanians. They were also preparing to meet the Russians. Consequently, even though the Russian blow did not fall like the skull-crushing hammer one might have expected, the *potential* dangers prevented the Hungarians from concentrating their forces until the liberal regime's last stand. Görgey's numerical inferiority against the Austrians may not have been enormous, but if different circumstances had allowed a commander of his mettle to field equal or greater numbers, then the balance might have been tipped in Hungary's favour.

The persistence of the Hungarian revolution had serious consequences for the rest of the Habsburg Empire. It provided the perfect excuse for the Austrian government not to convene the parliament promised in the March 1849 constitution. The people running the empire were the bureaucrats, the army and the police, using German as their language. Moreover, once the revolution had been stamped out in Hungary and Italy, the government was strong enough to retract the promised constitution altogether. On 19 October 1850 Franz Joseph asked Baron Karl von Kübeck, a conservative, to define the role of the Reichsrat, or imperial council, which was meant to be the upper house of parliament nominated by the Emperor. Together, the Emperor and Kübeck outmanoeuvred the more reform-minded Schwarzenberg. It was announced that the Reichsrat was going to be the only part of the constitution to be implemented. The Emperor, in other words, had no intention of sharing any power with an elected lower house. The Reichsrat first met in April 1851, and in August it was ordered to investigate whether the constitution of March 1849 was viable. Unsurprisingly, it reported that it was unworkable, and the constitution was abolished on 31 December 1851 by the 'Sylvester Patent', which restored absolutism in the Habsburg Empire.

By then, centralisation was more complete than it had been before 1848. The Hungarian constitution had been torn up and, as the Russian and Austrian troops had advanced, pro-Austrian officials had taken up the running of government in Hungary. Austrian law was introduced, and the Supreme Court in Budapest was abolished: henceforth, all appeals were to be heard in Vienna. The Hungarian police, the Pandurs, were replaced by the Austrian gendarmerie. Henceforth, the empire was not meant to be a multinational but an a-national state, in which everyone was bound together by their equal submission to the Emperor. In reality, of course, this meant that the political advantage now fell to the Germans, since their language would be the tongue of the state bureaucracy. In Hungary the German-speaking officials who had descended on the country wore a special uniform based on that of the famous Magyar cavalry, earning them the sobriquet 'Bach's hussars', after the minister who drove through this policy of forcible assimilation. Romanian hopes of being rewarded for their loyalty were rapidly dashed: with the Hungarian revolution crushed, Austrian officials, supported by the army, descended on to Transylvania, Bukovina and the Banat as surely as they did on to Hungary itself, seeking the same, uniform obedience to the Emperor.[68] Even the faithful Serbs and Croats received no reward for their dogged opposition to the Hungarians. Jelačić was removed from office in 1853, after which the Croatian governor was an Austrian general. Voivodina was given notional recognition as a separate province, but its governor was another Austrian army commander. As one Croat sighed to a Hungarian friend, 'we received as a reward what you were given as a punishment'. He was right: Hungary may well have remained under martial law until 1854, but Croatia, frontier country that it was, continued to be controlled, in effect, by the imperial army.[69]

IV

Writing half a century after the revolutions, Bolton King, who had known Mazzini and sympathised strongly with the Italian cause, crushingly remarked that the French intervention in Rome was 'one of the meanest deeds that ever disgraced a great nation'. Indeed, witnesses noticed that, as Oudinot's men occupied the city, some of them seemed ashamed.[70] And the act of crushing the life out of a sister republic provoked the French radicals, who rose up in Paris on 13 July 1849. The *démoc-socs* had been gaining in strength since the triumph of Louis-Napoleon in the presidential election the previous December. Many Parisian politicians still believed that Bonaparte was merely the creature of monarchists such as Thiers, who were using him to erode the gains of February 1848 and to decay the republic from within. This impression was reinforced when Louis-Napoleon asked the Orléanist Odilon Barrot to form a government. Barrot's cabinet included just one republican. The other ministers were monarchists who set about purging all levels of the administration of those appointed since the February revolution. The moderate republican majority in the National Assembly shared the government's obsession with 'order', but it was clear that the ministry was going beyond a reaction against social revolution to a campaign against republicanism as a whole. The government pressure therefore had the remarkable effect of radicalising the Assembly, where the moderate republicans – who had supported Cavaignac in June – were suddenly bolstered by their erstwhile critics on the left.[71] It was, in essence, a fragile coalition of republican defence against a monarchist and authoritarian resurgence.

The National Assembly flexed its muscles by insisting that it would not separate until it had voted ten 'organic laws' (concerned with harmonising existing institutions with the new constitution). Moreover, it thrust a stick into the government's spokes when, in the last days before the New Year, Barrot resorted to traditional fiscal policies to weather the continuing financial crisis: he reimposed the unpopular taxes on salt and wine that had been abolished earlier in the year. As indirect impositions, they fell with disproportionate weight on the poor. Bonaparte appears to have let his populist mask slip, revealing a president who was looking to support the interests of the old elites more than those of the peasant masses. As Karl Marx put it (in a terrible pun), 'with the salt tax, Bonaparte lost his revolutionary salt'.[72] The republicans mutilated the bill as it passed through parliament, slashing the two taxes – the salt tax to a third of its original value. On 26 January, it also rejected a government motion to ban all political clubs, with the deputies of the left going so far as to introduce a bill of impeachment against Léon Faucher, the minister of the interior responsible for the suggestion. Although the conservative government was clearly struggling to command a majority in what was still primarily a republican assembly, Bonaparte insisted that the cabinet retained his confidence. In other words he was suggesting that ministers were accountable to him, not to the legislature – an alarming claim for anyone who believed in parliamentary government.[72] It was also becoming obvious that the president and his ministers supported the idea of dissolving the difficult Assembly as soon as was possible to allow for new elections.

The radical Parisian movement began to stir once again in response to the conservative challenge. Ledru-Rollin urged calm, but he also suggested in an article in *La Réforme* on 28 January that violations of the people's fundamental liberties 'have always sounded the hour of revolution'.[74] This thinly veiled threat of insurrection illustrated how polarised the government and the republican movement had now become. However, as Karl Marx perceptively saw, an uprising at that moment would have played directly into the hands of Barrot and Bonaparte, since it would have allowed them, 'under the pretext of public safety . . . to violate the constitution in the interests of the constitution itself'.[75] The day after Ledru-Rollin's article appeared, the government put forward its motion for an early dissolution of the Assembly. It was supported by the intimidating appearance of troops led by the royalist General Changarnier, who surrounded the Assembly under the pretext of defending it against a popular insurrection. To be fair, the prospect of an uprising was not merely the figment of overheated conservative imaginations: the radical left mobilised the armed sections of the old insurrectionary society, the Rights of Man, while the Sixth Legion of the National Guard offered the deputies an alternative meeting-place in the Conservatoire des Arts et Métiers (which in itself was a revolutionary gesture, since it meant that the Assembly would continue to meet in defiance of the government and the military). None the less, the very threat of a new insurrection was enough to fracture the delicate unity of moderate and radical republicans, and the parliament agreed to a quick dissolution. Elections were to be held on 13 May. In one of its last significant acts, on 7 May the Assembly forbade the government from pursuing its campaign against the Roman republic.

The elections were held in the same atmosphere of political polarisation and social fear that had prevailed since the June days of 1848. The middle way charted by the moderate republicans would end in 'shipwreck'.[76] Conservative notables used their finances and their local influence to ensure that candidates whom they favoured led the electoral lists. Although few published openly monarchist views, it was clear that the republican experiment since February 1848 was being derided in these circles, and these attitudes were printed in election literature aimed at a wider, peasant readership. 'Socialism is Famine', warned one leaflet intended for the rural electorate. The provisional government in particular was demonised, blamed especially for the 'forty-five centimes' tax. Republicans associated with social reform – democratic humanitarians like Ledru-Rollin and reforming socialists like Blanc, along with firebrand revolutionary 'communists' like Raspail and Blanqui – were indiscriminately lumped together as 'reds'. The conservatives were helped by government officials, who obstructed the publication and distribution of left-wing literature and 'advised' voters to choose candidates opposed to 'doctrines destructive of society'. Some moderate republicans, while also emphasising the need for 'order', condemned excessive government power and repression. Their voices were drowned out as the middle ground crumbled beneath their feet.

The radicals expected to do well in these elections. They had woken up to the fact that they could not expect to win anything more than a small rump in the new National Assembly unless they won the peasant vote. 'Thanks to universal suffrage,' wrote the

socialist journalist Pierre Joigneaux (who edited *La Réforme* for a
year while a deputy in the old Assembly), 'we must, whether we like
it or not, take into account the populations of our countryside.
That is where the big battalions now lie.'[77] He wrote those words in
January 1850, but he was merely re-emphasising a strategy that the
radicals had already begun to apply in 1849: the elections of April
1848 and their aftermath had shown that it was not enough to rely
on the support of the urban workers and artisans. *La Réforme*
admitted: 'No one had given a thought to the countryside since the
First Republic. From now on we shall have to.'[78] They were helped
in this by the ongoing economic crisis, which bit deep in the countryside, since those agricultural regions that depended heavily on
selling their produce to the market were suffering from a collapse of
prices in wine, silk, grain and hemp. Economic distress was almost
certainly not enough, in itself, to radicalise the peasantry and to
make them support the *démoc-socs* (who by this stage were coming
to be known simply as 'socialists'). The countryside had been rav-
aged with poverty and famine in the past, yet this had not turned
the peasants into revolutionaries. Indeed, some historians have
argued that the evidence of peasant politicisation under the Second
Republic has been misread: the peasantry, argues Eugen Weber,
were merely reacting to their own local economic concerns, or to
village feuds, and followed the lead of the rural notables, some of
whom were certainly 'reds'. The point Weber makes is that the sincerity and depth of peasant radicalisation were rather superficial,
merely dressing up traditional loyalties, conflicts and concerns in
modern political clothing.[79] But in a sense, as Weber himself argues
in a later article, this does not matter: the politics of universal male
suffrage empowered the peasants at least to choose sides between
rival local politicians, and this was expressed in political terms,
marking a start in bringing the rural community into national
politics.[80]

This was achieved in no small part by radical propagandists who
not only followed the obvious tactic of exploiting peasant economic
distress and disillusionment with President Bonaparte but did so in
ways that slotted easily into rural life. Rural almanacs interspersed

advice on farming, climate and remedies with political articles, sometimes taking the form of a dialogue between a knowledgeable (for which read *démoc-soc*) peasant successfully convincing one of his less enlightened associates of the wisdom of the radical, republican way. Though subscribers to the radical press tended to be those literate villagers who had some cultural ties with the wider world – teachers, café-owners, the village mayor, postal workers, doctors and veterinarians – they acted as 'culture brokers' who disseminated the ideas to a wider audience. Café-owners, in particular, had a strong sense of grievance because business was hit by the wine tax, so they had good reason to marshal their customers against the government.[81] In the electoral campaign of 1849 the *démoc-socs* did not merely harp on about some golden, utopian future, but rather offered practical solutions to the immediate rural crisis. They promised reductions in taxation and cheap credit, both of which would appeal to despairing peasant smallholders. In some areas 'red' candidates lent their weight to peasant resistance against the 'forty-five centimes' tax. In Paris a *démoc-soc* committee was elected from workers, shopkeepers and intellectuals from the surviving political clubs and workers' associations, representing a broad spectrum of left-wing opinion. In April this committee tried, for the first time, to forge what had been lacking in the previous year: a truly nationwide electoral organisation, corresponding with other provincial committees and coordinating policies with the left-wing members of the outgoing National Assembly. It also issued a single electoral programme for all *démoc-soc* candidates standing in Paris and its environs, declaring that deputies would resist all violations of the constitution and that 'the right to work is the most important of all human rights; it is the right to life'.[82] Perhaps the notoriously fractious French left managed to keep its unity until the elections because much of the extremist leadership had been in prison since the previous summer, so there was less pressure from them.

When the elections came, 500 of the 750 seats were taken by conservatives, most of them monarchists with 200 of them ultraroyalist Legitimists. The centre, as expected, collapsed, with only seventy seats falling to the moderate republicans. The radicals and

the *démoc-socs* took an impressive 180 seats. Moreover, this success –
which was remarkable, given the official hostility and obstruction
that left-wing candidates faced – was not restricted to the traditionally militant districts of Paris and Lyon (in the latter city, the
démoc-socs secured almost 70 per cent of the vote). They did well in
certain rural regions, capturing more than 40 per cent of the vote in
the Massif Central, the Rhône and Saône valleys and Alsace, and
performed impressively in the Midi and the far north. Thus, 'a "red
France" was revealed'.[83] The diffusion of *démoc-soc* propaganda
proved to be most effective in those areas where there was a high
proportion of small plots of land, where the peasants were vulnerable to the desperate economic conditions of the later 1840s and
where the influence of large landowners was weak. This was especially true of the vine- and olive-growing regions of the south, where
the smallholders did not live on isolated farmsteads but together in
the village, where they socialised, allowing for both the exchange of
ideas and cooperation. Such a social environment often had a small
middle class of 'culture brokers' who were eager to challenge the
local notables. The *démoc-socs* made a particular impact in villages
that enjoyed regular interaction and interdependence with towns. In
south-eastern France the small towns and *bourgs* (rural towns with
markets) provided regular meeting- and trading-places for the
inhabitants of the outlying hamlets and villages. They therefore
proved to be important conduits for the dissemination of radical
republican ideas into the countryside, through low-level political
organisations that quietly flourished without attracting unwelcome
attention from the authorities. In some of these areas the left sowed
seeds that bore political fruit for over a hundred years.[84] In the
nearer future the *démoc-socs* hoped to build on their success of 1849
and win the next national elections, when both the three-year term
of the new legislature and Bonaparte's presidency expired. The left
dared to believe that 1852 was going to be 'their year'.

As left-wing ambitions flourished, so conservative fears grew.
'Terror', wrote Tocqueville, 'was universal.' The monarchists understood that the continuing republican vigour did not allow the
new National Assembly to abandon the republic altogether. As

Tocqueville put it, the conservatives 'rediscovered tolerance and modesty, virtues which they had practised after February [1848], but which they had largely forgotten in the last six months'.[85] That, though, did not stop them from looking for ways to defeat the radicals once and for all. Short-term repression coupled with harassment was one answer, but so too was a more permanent, authoritarian solution. As early as 16 May, Charles, Duc de Morny – and Louis-Napoleon's half-brother – wrote to a friend that 'the Empire is the only thing that can save the situation. Some of the leading politicians have been nibbling at the idea.'[86] The conflict between conservatives and the republican left could only become more intense.

The first clash came when Oudinot's troops attacked the Roman republic in June. This action was illegal, as it ignored the parliamentary decree forbidding the use of force against Rome. It also broke the constitution, which loftily declared that the Second Republic 'respects foreign nationalities, as she intends to have her own respected; she will not undertake any war of conquest or employ her forces against the liberty of any other people'.[87] Tocqueville, who had recently taken office as foreign minister, was horrified by the predictable domestic consequences of such a barefaced breach of the law:

> The first thing I learned when I joined the cabinet [on 2 June] was 'that the order to attack Rome had been sent three days previously to our army. This flagrant disobedience against the injunctions of a sovereign Assembly, this war begun against a people in revolution, because of its own revolution, and despite the very terms of the constitution . . . made inevitable and very close the conflict which everyone feared . . . All the letters from the prefects which we saw, all the police reports which came to us, were of a kind which threw us into a deep sense of alarm.[88]

Writing here with hindsight, Tocqueville was being a little disingenuous, since he agreed that the war on Rome was essential for French prestige. But he did not exaggerate when he wrote that the intervention set the battle lines for the next domestic political clash. Paris in the summer of 1849 was feverish, both politically and literally, for an outbreak of cholera was sweeping murderously through the city. The *démoc-soc* committee's April programme, with precisely the Roman expedition in mind, had proclaimed that 'Nations like men have mutual obligations – the use of French troops against the liberty of another people is a crime – a violation of the constitution.'[89] Shortly after the May elections, the same group sent a delegation to the parliament to warn that if the government insisted on using force against Rome, it would be overthrown. While the orders to Oudinot were kept secret, news of the first attack reached Paris on 10 June. The 'Mountain', or the left of the Assembly, exploded in anger in the next day's session. Ledru-Rollin – who had emerged as leader of the left-wing opposition – rose in the National Assembly to denounce the war, declaring that he and his colleagues would defend the constitution by all means, even by taking up arms. He called for the impeachment of President Bonaparte and the cabinet. A furious debate followed,[90] but, facing an overwhelming conservative majority, there was little the parliamentary left could do but hurl its best rhetoric against the government. The impeachment motion, inevitably, was easily defeated.

The attack on Rome, however, became a cause around which Parisian radicalism could mobilise its supporters. Prior to the parliamentary debate, on the morning of 11 June, delegates from the *démoc-soc* committee had discussed tactics with the editors of the republican press. They agreed on a mass demonstration, knowing full well – as one of their number, Victor Considérant, pointed out – that it would be met with violence. Only Émile Girardin of *La Presse* stood against it, arguing that the cholera outbreak had weakened the popular movement. The plan was for a peaceful, unarmed protest to march on the National Assembly, where the deputies of the Mountain would declare the government and existing parliament incompetent and proclaim themselves as a new 'National Convention'. That same morning the Montagnards – the nickname for the *démoc-socs*, recalling the days of the 1789 revolution – met in caucus in the chamber. They agreed to this plan, so by the time Ledru-Rollin issued his call for impeachment, he and his colleagues had already committed themselves to support what was, in effect, a revolutionary (albeit hopefully bloodless) *coup d'état*. This was no sudden impulse, but it flowed from a sincere belief that they were defending democracy in France and abroad. It was also, frankly, a bid for power where electoral politics had failed, justified by the left to themselves on the basis of the April programme's rather ambiguous claim that 'the Republic is superior to the right of majorities'.[91]

On the morning of 13 June, the people of Paris awoke to read three proclamations pasted on street walls and published in the republican press. The Mountain declared that the Assembly and the government, by violating the constitution and siding 'with the kings against the people', had abdicated power; the second, issued by the *démoc-soc* committee, called on the National Guard and the army to support the popular protest; the third summoned all the people to a 'calm demonstration' in defence of the constitution.

Led by Étienne Arago, a crowd of 25,000, including some 5,000 National Guards, gathered on the boulevards in the morning. Marx, summoned from his lodgings on the rue de Lille by a fellow German exile, may have been among the demonstrators. Herzen, who certainly was there, left a graphic eyewitness account. The crowd marched down the boulevards, singing 'The Marseillaise' and chanting, '*Vive la constitution! Vive la république!*' 'One who has not heard the Marseillaise,' wrote Herzen, 'sung by thousands of voices in that state of nervous excitement and irresolution which is inevitable before certain conflict, can hardly realise the overwhelming effect of the revolutionary hymn.'[92] Marx, though, was unimpressed: sceptical about the Montagnard leadership, which he saw as 'petty bourgeois', and certain that 'the memory of June 1848 surged through the ranks of the Parisian proletariat more vigorously than ever', he thought that the slogans were 'uttered mechanically, icily, and with a bad conscience'.[93] As the column reached the rue de la Paix, they were confronted by infantry and cavalry led by Changarnier, who succeeded in separating the demonstrators into two sections and driving some of them northwards, away from the boulevards. Some of the protesters bared their chests to the bayonets, daring the troops to impale their brothers; others called on the soldiers to defend the republic and pleaded the cause of Rome. Herzen found himself 'nose to nose with a horse which was almost snorting in my face, and a dragoon swearing likewise in my face and threatening to give me one with the flat [of his sabre] if I did not move aside'. He ran into Arago, whose hip was dislocated as he tried to escape the cavalry.[94]

Changarnier's intervention had been swift and decisive: the Mountain, according to the original plan, was to wait for the arrival of the protesters at the National Assembly, but they had been stopped short and dispersed. Ledru-Rollin and his colleagues were therefore isolated until a unit of left-wing National Guards arrived to protect them. They made their way to the Conservatoire des Arts et Métiers, arriving at 2.15 p.m., and began their deliberations behind a protective cordon of barricades. The left-wing caucus – initially numbering 119 – called the people to arms. Yet Paris did not explode as it had the previous June, not least because Changarnier had moved quickly to secure all the main intersections and strategic points. Some of the demonstrators who had been dispersed by Changarnier certainly ran home, gathered up their weapons and built barricades, but these hastily constructed defences – one of them merely a flimsy pile of wicker chairs plundered from a nearby café – were easily stormed by the government troops. As the forces closed in on the Conservatoire, the Mountain started to appoint a provisional government, but its futile work was interrupted when Changarnier's men broke into the courtyard. Some of the deputies, mistaking the soldiers for reinforcements, rushed out to greet them, but found themselves literally forced up against a wall. It seemed that they were about to be summarily shot when, for reasons that are not clear, the troops suddenly withdrew, allowing all but six of the deputies to flee through back doors and windows and from there into exile. Ledru-Rollin made good his escape to London, but first (it is said) he had to squeeze his corpulent body through one of the Conservatoire's windows. Herzen escaped arrest by picking up his passports and leaving France for Geneva.

The insurrection seems to have failed because its original plan – to be effectively a parliamentary coup backed by the threat of force – had been shattered by Changarnier's ruthless and decisive response. There was no contingency plan, so by the time the Mountain tried to set itself up as a revolutionary government in the Conservatoire, the forces of order had already taken the initiative and prevented the uprising from escalating. By contrast, the Mountain had to direct a full-blown insurrection of a type for which it had not planned. In this respect the absence of the battle-hardened Blanqui and other revolutionary leaders of the extreme left was a tactical weakness. It deprived the insurrection of the fierce leadership, seasoned in barricade fighting, which might have brought out a hard core of determined, working-class revolutionaries.[95] As Tocqueville bluntly put it, 'in June 1848, the leaders lacked an army; in June 1849 the army lacked leaders'.[96] Herzen agreed: when the provisional government was being established, he saw workers wandering aimlessly about the streets, 'with inquiring faces and finding neither advice nor leadership, [they] went home, convinced once more of the bankruptcy of the *Montagnard* fathers of the country'. He came across one man who, fighting back tears, sobbed, 'All is lost!'[97] The Parisian uprising had echoes in the provinces – in the Allier and the Rhône, an indication of the success of *démoc-soc* propaganda, but especially in Lyon, where barricades were thrown up by silk-weavers, only to be blown apart by artillery. In the fighting twenty-five people were killed on each side and afterwards twelve hundred insurgents were arrested. Some soldiers faced the firing squad for joining the uprising.[98]

Repressive legislation followed, in which the government was given the power to ban any political club or public meeting; a press law defined new offences, including insulting the president and inciting disobedience among soldiers, and ordered that hawkers of political literature (*colporteurs* – a traditional means by which the printed word reached the countryside) would henceforth require a permit from the local prefect. Some thirty-four Montagnard deputies were later condemned by a court meeting in Versailles, removing at a stroke some of the most experienced and recognisable leaders of the left. Yet the uprisings had been essentially urban phenomena, with the most serious outbreaks being in Paris and Lyon. With universal suffrage and with the constitution violated but still intact, the surviving left-wing militants, though temporarily demoralised by the defeats of June 1849, could still work with some confidence amongst the rural electorate.[99]

On 10 March 1850 by-elections were held for the seats left vacant by the expulsions and arrests of deputies after 13 June. Only eleven were retained by *démoc-socs*, indicating that the left may have passed its electoral high-water mark. Yet the conservatives were still alarmed that three of those seats were in Paris, suggesting that all the blows delivered against the radicals had not sapped their vitality in the capital. They interpreted the results not as a sign that the left was weakening, but that it was stubbornly persistent. Still, the right asserted its strength in the legislature by voting through a law on education on 15 March. Produced by the education committee, which included Thiers, and sponsored by the royalist Comte de Falloux, it reduced the curriculum in primary schools to religious education and basic reading, writing and arithmetic. While expanding the role of the Catholic Church in the state education system, it also permitted the establishment of privately run schools, which meant, primarily, Catholic institutions. The parish clergy were to keep watch on the state schoolteachers and to report on them to the prefect. This law was a product of conservative anxieties: republican schoolteachers were seen as notorious disseminators of subversion. Falloux himself wrote that the law, by reinforcing the role of the Church and of religious instruction, was an urgent remedy to the 'existence of social peril'.[100] It aimed to inculcate conservative values in the young, and the government had already begun its assault by dismissing twelve hundred teachers whom it considered unreliable. On 28 April, however, a further by-election in Paris returned an outspoken opponent of the Falloux law, Eugène Sue.

This clear protest vote further suggested that the left was still a danger, so the Assembly passed the electoral law of 31 May. This disenfranchised all men with criminal records, all those who had lived less than three years in their constituency and all who could not prove their residence from the tax registers. These provisions again reflected the social fears of the conservatives: this time of a rootless, criminal underclass whom they had held responsible for all the political instability since the June days. Approximately 2.8 million men lost their right to vote, accounting for 30 per cent of the electorate, although that figure was higher in some areas, including Paris (62 per cent) and the industrial department of the Nord (51 per cent), since workers tended to move about in search of affordable housing. Many on the left saw this law as a deliberate provocation, an attempt by the right to force the *démoc-socs* into insurrection in defence of universal male suffrage, the more easily to crush and outlaw the opposition. The left and moderate republicans alike urged their supporters to act with restraint. The *démoc-socs* organised a petitioning campaign, gathering fifty thousand signatures, most of which were those of rural inhabitants, a further sign that radical republicans were making inroads into the French countryside. None the less, it is hardly surprising that the republicans at the grass roots returned to their old habits and went underground. A network of secret republican societies, centred on Lyon and extending across south-eastern France, was discovered by the police in August 1850, but they found no evidence of plans for an insurrection. Still, the trial of three of the leaders in the spring of 1851 caused a sensation because of the harshness of the sentences – deportation to the distant Marquesas.

The conservatives, however, were still alarmed by the buoyant mood of the *démoc-socs* as 'their year' of 1852 approached. Louis-Napoleon Bonaparte's term of office was coming to an end and, according to the constitution, he could not be re-elected. Yet he was the only right-wing candidate who could gather enough of the vote to be certain to deny the *démoc-socs* victory in the presidential election. Victor Hugo listened to a friend who told him that she had a nightmare in which bolting horses dragged a flaming coach over a precipice, to which the great writer remarked: 'You have dreamt of 1852.'[101] For conservatives, Bonaparte was the only figure who stood between order and catastrophe. Many of them therefore supported his campaign to have the constitution amended to allow him a second term of office. Tocqueville, who as an intelligent conservative feared Louis-Napoleon as much as he feared the 'reds', remarked caustically that the very people who were angry at 'the people' for violating the constitution (a reference to 13 June) were now trying to do the same themselves.[102]

Bonaparte himself, meanwhile, had been working tirelessly to garner popular support and, above all, to distance himself from the reactionary policies of the right. On 7 September 1849 he had leaked a telegram that he had sent to the French commander in Rome. In it he denounced the cardinals' repressive regime and lamented that French foreign policy had taken a reactionary turn. When Odilon Barrot, facing a hostile reaction among the majority in the Assembly, had failed to defend the president, Bonaparte dismissed his ministry on 31 October 1849. Explaining his actions to the National Assembly, he presented himself as being above party politics, as the man who represented the will of the people and who could provide the firm leadership that the country needed:

> A whole system triumphed on 10 December [1848], for the name of Napoleon is in itself a programme. At home it means order, authority, religion and the welfare of the people; and abroad it means national self-respect. This policy, which began with my election, I shall, with the support of the National Assembly and of the people, lead to its final triumph.[103]

The conservatives were learning that Bonaparte was not their passive tool, but had ideas of his own. Some of them, such as Falloux, were beginning to wake up to the dangers of 'Caesarism'. Tocqueville noted that Louis-Napoleon constantly met with the leaders of the monarchist parliamentary majority, but that 'he none the less bore their yoke impatiently, that he was humiliated to appear to submit to their tutelage and that he secretly burned to escape from it'.[104] Nevertheless, most of the right was still more afraid of the 'reds' than they were of Louis-Napoleon's authoritarian populism. Conservative resistance to him, as he appointed a new government of his own and insisted that ministers were responsible to him, not to the National Assembly, was therefore feeble. Moreover, the conservatives could not agree on an alternative to Bonaparte, as the Orléanists wanted to support the heirs of Louis-Philippe, while the Legitimists insisted on the Bourbon Comte de Chambord. Meanwhile, Bonaparte travelled around the country as if on campaign, making no fewer than fourteen tours in 1849–51. He distributed generous quantities of wine and sausages to soldiers, whom he inspected in their barracks. Some were heard shouting, '*Vive l'Empereur!*' He stopped to talk to peasants working in the fields and he addressed public meetings, shamelessly telling audiences precisely what they wanted to hear. To republicans he offered his support of the constitution of 1848 (an implicit condemnation of the May 1850 electoral law), while to conservatives he hinted that he might support a restoration of the monarchy. He used his presidential patronage to appoint his supporters as prefects, army commanders and government officials. Within the National Assembly the right was fragmenting between Legitimists, Orléanists and those who had opted to support Bonaparte as the best man to maintain order.

This last group began to press for constitutional revision in the spring of 1851, buoyed by a petition bearing 1.5 million signatures. At the end of July the amendment was defeated in parliament by an alliance of republicans and Orléanists, for whom the Bonapartes were now dangerous competitors as claimants to the throne. The Legitimists supported Bonaparte because they wanted to revise the constitution anyway, but their backing was not enough to obtain the three-quarters of the votes needed to carry the amendment. Louis-Napoleon therefore turned away from legal means and started to think in terms of a *coup d'état*. He prepared the ground when, on 4 November, he proposed the restoration of universal male suffrage to the National Assembly. His bill was rejected, which simply undermined the democratic legitimacy of parliament while allowing Bonaparte to pose as the champion of popular sovereignty.

The date chosen for the coup was 2 December, the anniversary of Napoleon I's greatest military victory at Austerlitz. That night police arrested leading opposition leaders, including Orléanists like Thiers, *démoc-soc* deputies, republican army officers (including Cavaignac) and eighty popular militants identified as possible leaders of a counter-insurrection. The coup succeeded partly because it was not aimed at seizing power – Louis-Napoleon already had it, and he had made sure that the key ministries of police, war and interior were in loyal, if unscrupulous, hands – but simply at consolidating it. The National Printers had already been quietly taken over the previous night, and it was from there that Bonaparte's proclamation was produced and then posted up by police patrols. It justified dictatorship through a direct appeal to the 'people', over the heads of their allegedly corrupt and fractious representatives. The National Assembly, Bonaparte declared, was 'making a bid for power which I wield directly by virtue of the people's will. It fosters every wicked passion. It is jeopardising the stability of France. I have dissolved the National Assembly and I invite the whole people to adjudicate between it and me'.[105] To pre-empt parliamentary resistance, the chamber was occupied by troops. This did not stop some 220 deputies – including Tocqueville, Barrot, Falloux and Rémusat – from holding an improvised session in the *mairie* of the 10th Arrondissement (roughly corresponding with today's Sixth), from where they denounced the coup. They were expelled by soldiers and briefly arrested. Some republican deputies tried to organise resistance in the artisanal districts and some barricades went up on 3 December, but Bonaparte's shrewd proclamation restoring universal male suffrage made even the republican movement hesitate. By 4 December what Parisian resistance existed had been overwhelmed.

In the provinces, however, the coup was challenged by the 'largest provincial uprising in nineteenth-century France'.[106] Nearly seventy thousand people – including women, who stood guard in the villages when the men marched off – recruited from at least 775 communes took up arms against the government. Of those, some 27,000 were involved in violent clashes with troops or the gendarmerie. The focus of the armed resistance was in the rural districts of south-eastern and central France. The uprising usually began in the small market towns, but the surrounding villages were rapidly drawn in too. By comparison the inhabitants of the larger towns tended to protest peacefully. In over a hundred villages and market towns the insurgents expelled the local officials and put their own candidates in their place. These seizures of power were frequently a direct response to orders from *démoc-soc* leaders, suggesting that their organisations had succeeded in forming a radical republican network extending into the countryside. In the end, however, the uprising was too distant from the centres of power – Paris in particular – to pose a threat. The insurgents seized power only in the small *bourgs*, where the only armed forces were the tiny brigades of gendarmes. Only in the Basses-Alpes did the rebels succeed in capturing a departmental *chef-lieu* (capital), and they did not hold on to it for long. Once the authorities managed to marshal their forces and bring their troops to bear on the insurrection, it was easily crushed.[107]

In the short term the uprising justified Bonaparte's coup retrospectively, allowing his supporters to discredit the *démoc-socs* as dangerous enemies of order and stability. Charlemagne de Maupas, the prefect of police in Paris, proclaimed: 'Robbery, pillage, assassination, rape, arson, nothing was wanting to this mournful exhibition of the programme of 1852.'[108] The repression was efficient and sweeping: almost 27,000 people were arrested. Of these, 239 were sent to the living hell of Devil's Island in French Guiana, known as the 'dry guillotine' because of its fatal, disease-ridden conditions. A further 9,500 were exiled to Algeria, 3,000 were jailed and another 5,000 were kept under police surveillance. Ever the populist, Bonaparte, who had no stomach for such widespread recrimination, commuted the sentences of several thousand others. Although he had committed the coup in the name of universal male suffrage, the unexpected violence that it unleashed shrouded his new regime with the sulphurous odour of repression, ensuring that many republicans would never be reconciled to the new order.[109] None the less, the violence of the 'red threat' had been graphically displayed, and when Bonaparte put his actions to the people in a plebiscite on 20 December, conservatives rallied to his support. Comte Charles de Montalembert wrote in the Orléanist newspaper *Constitutionnel* that 'to vote against Louis-Napoleon is simply to give in to the socialist revolution . . . It is calling in the dictatorship of the reds to replace the dictatorship of a prince who over the last three years has done incomparable good in the causes of law and order and of Catholicism.'[110] The referendum approved the coup by an overwhelming 7.5 million votes against 640,000, although there were 1.5 million abstentions and martial law imposed in some thirty-two departments undoubtedly discouraged a much wider expression of opposition.

None the less, the Second Republic had been resoundingly rejected. Louis-Napoleon was now officially addressed as 'Your Imperial Highness'. In November 1852, with the blessing of a further plebiscite, he was made 'Emperor of the French' and was crowned Napoleon III on the first anniversary of his *coup d'état*. Victor Hugo caustically labelled him 'Napoleon le Petit' to distinguish him derisively from the 'great' Napoleon. For such impudence he was obliged to flee Paris and seek exile in the Channel Islands. His was a witty, bitter cry of protest: the revolutions of the mid-nineteenth century were well and truly over.

CONCLUSION

This book began with Alexander Herzen's hopeful journey into Europe in 1847. It ends with his disillusionment. The middle years of the century had been a time of personal as well as political tragedy for the Russian socialist. After their exile from France, Herzen and his wife Natalie lived first in Geneva and then in Nice with Georg and, eventually, Emma Herwegh, the German republicans. At the opening of 1851, however, Natalie confessed to having had an affair with Georg, and there followed months of recriminations and depression. Then tragedy struck an even heavier blow: in November, Herzen's mother and his seven-year-old son, Kolia, returning to Nice after a visit to Paris, were killed when their vessel was shipwrecked. Natalie, heartbroken, died in May the next year. The traumatised Herzen travelled around Europe over the summer until, in the autumn of 1852, he settled in London with his thirteen-year-old son, Sasha.[1] It was to him that he addressed his thoughtful reflections on the revolutions of 1848. It was a dispirited man who wrote *From the Other Shore*, dedicating it to his son on New Year's Day 1855. The old social and political order would be torn down in its entirety by a revolution; that, for Herzen, was a historical inevitability. But clearly it had not occurred in 1848. It was up to the current generation to destroy and root out the old regime, but it would be the people of the future who would reap the rewards: 'Modern man', he told Sasha, 'only builds a bridge – it will be for the unknown man of the future to pass over it. You may be there to see him . . . But do not, I beg, remain on *this shore* . . . Better to perish with the revolution than to seek refuge in the almshouse of reaction.'[2]

The revolutions were seen subsequently as failures, but one should not be too pessimistic. The events of 1848 gave millions of Europeans their first taste of politics: workers and peasants voted in elections and even stood for and entered parliament. The civil liberties that flourished all too briefly in that year also provided Europeans with the free space in which they – including women – were politicised, through participation in political clubs and workers' organisations. That some of these were conservative rather than liberal or radical does not weaken the argument, for conservatism was in itself a political stance that many members of the masses *consciously* took. Perhaps the most important achievement was the abolition of serfdom, of the compulsory labour services and dues enforced against the peasantry. Quite besides the social and economic implications of this reform, it had an important long-term political impact: it enhanced the power of the state at the expense of the landed nobility. For, along with ending peasant servitude, the emancipation entailed the destruction of the nobles' judicial rights over their peasants, who would henceforth live under the immediate jurisdiction of the state. In other words, the nobles would no longer act as intermediaries between the peasants and the government, but rather the peasantry now shared the same legal and civil rights as other subjects. In the long run this paved the way for them to become fully integrated citizens of the modern state.[3] Moreover, the problems that came boiling to the surface in 1848 – constitutionalism, civil rights, the social question, nationalism – did not disappear simply because the counter-revolution stifled discussion and protest about them. Instead, conservatives were forced to reckon with them more than ever, not least because of the accelerating pace of economic and social change in the second half of the nineteenth century. Some conservatives were realistic enough to recognise this shortly after the collapse of the liberal regimes: the historian Leopold von Ranke told one of Frederick William IV's advisers that 'the storms of today must be met with the institutions of today'.[4] Many of the solutions that were eventually adopted – social reform, national unification – may have been imposed in an authoritarian rather than a constitutional manner, and they may have been carried out for the sake of conservative interests, but they were often adapted from those originally proposed by the 'forty-eighters'. Occasionally they were even implemented with the help of some of those repentant revolutionaries who had made their peace with the conservative order. To cite but one example, in 1867, Franz Joseph's absolute monarchy in Austria finally yielded to renewed pressure and – at the expense, it is true, of the other nationalities – negotiated a compromise with the Magyars. This converted the Austrian Empire into Austria-Hungary, with both parts theoretically on equal terms and with representative institutions for Hungary, Austria and the empire as a whole. Significantly, its leading architects on the Hungarian side were both former 'forty-eighters', Gyula Andrássy and Ferenc Deák. The dogged Lajos Kossuth, however, remained in exile for the rest of his life (he died in Turin in 1894, aged ninety-two), steadfastly refusing to have any dealings with the Habsburgs.

Yet, in the context of longer-term national histories, 1848 has generally been regarded as a missed opportunity to set most of Europe permanently on a liberal, constitutional path. The implication, of course, is that if the revolutions had succeeded, the horrors of twentieth-century totalitarianism would have been avoided. A. J. P. Taylor famously remarked that 1848 was the moment when history reached a turning point, but 'Germany failed to turn'.[5] The German revolution of that year has been seen by historians as the moment when unification could have been achieved by liberal, parliamentary means, 'from below', rather than imposed 'from above' by Bismarck armed with Prussian military might (a process that was completed by 1871). Although there was a parliamentary system in

Bismarck's Reich, the imperial state was authoritarian and militarist. The argument continues that the middle classes – who in France were the backbone of the democratic, revolutionary movement – in Germany submitted to the dominance of the Prussian Junkers. Pushing still further this notion of Germany's 'special path' – *Sonderweg* – in its historical development, some historians have seen in the authoritarian German Empire of the later nineteenth century the seeds of the much darker, murderous Third Reich of the twentieth.[6] In this interpretation the failure of 1848 was a tragedy of catastrophic proportions. The great lesson drawn from the revolution was that German unity could be achieved only with power – and Prussian power in particular. Unification failed in 1848 because the revolutionaries themselves had no military strength at their disposal – and in the end they were unceremoniously overthrown by the armies of the conservative German states. Bismarck outraged his liberal Prussian audience in 1862 when he told them, 'the great questions of the age are not decided by speeches and majority decisions – that was the big mistake of 1848 and 1849 – but by blood and iron'.[7] Yet the German 'forty-eighters' were not merely idealists: they, too, were interested in power, and especially German power, as their debates on the future course of Germany revealed all too well. When forced to choose between national unity and political freedom, the liberals – with some exceptions, such as Johann Jacoby – opted for the former. That, perhaps, was the deeper tragedy of 1848: even the liberals were all too ready to sacrifice freedom to power.

A similar process can be seen at work in Italy. In the 1930s the Italian Marxist Antonio Gramsci, imprisoned by Mussolini, sought to explain how Italy, which was finally united in 1860, should have slid under the heel of the Fascist dictatorship. He found the answer in the weakness of the liberal Italian middle classes, the very people who led the struggle for national unity and freedom in 1848–9. The lesson learned from the failures of the revolutions in Italy, as in Germany, was that liberation and unification could be achieved only with the help of the armed forces of monarchist Piedmont and the cooperation of the landed elites. Consequently, unification was a 'passive revolution', imposed from above by conservative forces rather than made by the people (as Mazzini and other republicans would have liked). The Italian kingdom that emerged therefore had a weak parliamentary system which struggled to develop into a viable democracy. And that is what made the state vulnerable to the Fascist counter-revolution.[8] Once again, the process by which the revolutionaries were willing to shelve or surrender their democratic or liberal ideas to achieve power and so further the cause of national unity could already be seen at work during 1848. The Italian revolutionaries of 1848–9 also planted some cultural seeds that would bear a great deal of illiberal fruit. The revolution itself was a war, after which the hero willing to sacrifice himself for the national cause was lionised. The epitome of such selfless heroism was Garibaldi, whose memoirs of course did little to dispel the myth. Besides introducing a militarist germ into the movement for national freedom, the contrast between the heroic myth and the reality of defeat also injected the ideas of decadence and betrayal into the story of the Risorgimento, or the Italian national 'resurgence'.[9] The tension between heroism, military glory and self-sacrifice on one hand and the corruption within Italian politics and society on the other was a theme that would have a deep appeal among those who would later seek authoritarian solutions to Italy's problems.

The French experience was rather different. While no one would argue that the short-lived Second Republic was a runaway success, it has been seen (by Maurice Agulhon, among others) as a republican 'apprenticeship',[10] a preparation for the permanent establishment of parliamentary democracy in France. After many storm-tossed decades, the emergence of the Third Republic after 1870 is seen as the long-awaited triumph of the principles of the revolution of 1789: it was the 'French Revolution coming into port', as François Furet puts it.[11] Yet this does not account for the persistence of the deep-rooted political divisions within French society, which erupted during the Dreyfus Affair of the 1890s and, most bitterly, during the Nazi occupation and Vichy regime, and its aftermath, in the 1940s. Historians are still faced with the challenge of explaining why France eventually arrived, after 1945, at a permanent parliamentary democracy by such a fiery and traumatic route, having passed since 1789 through three monarchies, two Bonapartist empires, five republics and no fewer than fifteen constitutions. Lying among the corpses of the other regimes that litter this circuitous and bloody journey, 1848 begins to look less like a democratic apprenticeship and more like yet another failure to create a viable political settlement. A French political system would survive only if it could bridge the great schism between the liberal, democratic France that accepted the inheritance from 1789 and the conservative France that rejected it – or to end, as some historians have put it, the 'Franco-French War'.[12]

Central to the gloomy assessments of 1848 was the realisation that democracy was not always progressive. The elections in France in April 1848 returned a strongly conservative parliament, prompting Proudhon to remark bitterly that 'universal suffrage is counter-revolution'.[13] This opinion was reinforced by the plebiscites in favour of Louis-Napoleon Bonaparte and, later, by Bismarck, who listened intently to the German socialist Ferdinand Lassalle who promised him: 'Give me suffrage and I will give you a million votes.'[14] European popular conservatism and nationalism were a means by which authoritarian governments could outflank and enfeeble the liberal opposition, whose support frequently rested on the numerically smaller middle classes or landed elites. Yet, while ideas of French exceptionalism, of the German *Sonderweg* and of Italy's 'passive revolution' all have explanatory power, it is important not to be too downbeat. These interpretations can lead to a one-track view of historical developments: for example, at its most extreme, the idea of the *Sonderweg* can give rise to the impression that all German roads led inexorably to the Nazis and the Holocaust. It was still a long way from 1848 to 1933, but one disillusioned German 'forty-eighter' who was a harbinger of that dark future was the composer Richard Wagner, who wrote bitterly that the German people of 1848 had misunderstood the real nature of 'French–Jewish–German democracy' and so the 'authentic German suddenly found himself and his name represented by a kind of human being utterly foreign to him'.[15] However, while

Wagner certainly expressed an anti-Semitism that was latent in German society, it did not become a marked feature of the political landscape until later in the nineteenth century, when populist, ultra-nationalist currents seeped into the debates in the wake of German unification and with the rise of mass politics. Until then Jewish liberals had been happy to strive for German unity: for them that process marked further progress along the path of their own emancipation.

One could argue (as the present author has) that, while the twentieth century certainly inherited its authoritarian tendencies from concepts, movements and problems rooted in the nineteenth, it was the catastrophe of the First World War and the immense strain that it placed on European politics and society which ensured that they were able to predominate in the decades after that conflict.[16] One can, however, discern these tendencies in 1848, not as the overgrown jungle that they were to become in the twentieth century, but as germinating bulbs: in this sense 1848 was, as Lewis Namier suggests, the 'seed-plot of history'.[17] The revolutions were a 'seed-plot' in another important way, too: the 'social question', which had caused a great deal of anxiety in the years before 1848, erupted violently on to the political agenda in that year.

When, in 1848, the German democrat Ludwig Bamberger first heard the news of the June days in Paris, he immediately focused on one of the great problems that throbbed relentlessly through the entire industrial age: how to reconcile social justice with individual liberty? This was a great moral and political issue, which would produce many different 'answers', from communism to liberal capitalism. 'The social question', Bamberger saw, 'had thrown its sword into the turmoil of the political struggle, never again to disappear from the battle and to make more difficult if not impossible for all time the victory of . . . political freedom.'[18] In 1848 the social question ulcerated the liberal regimes because there was no revolutionary consensus. There was, first, no agreement over the form that the new political order would take: republic or monarchy, democratic or liberal, unitary or federal. Second, liberals and radicals did not see eye to eye over the extent to which the revolutions should overhaul social relations – how far the state should intervene to alleviate poverty, to mediate in labour disputes, and to regulate economic activity. In other words, to what extent should the new regime go beyond political reform and head into social revolution? These two sources of dissension were related, because the failure to resolve the first meant that there was no legal framework in which all sides had confidence and within which the second issue could be peacefully resolved through the political process. The failure of the 1848 revolutions to address the social question was therefore inextricably linked to the political failure of the revolutionaries to forge constitutions that could integrate those at the sharp end of the economic crisis.

This was one of the great tragedies of 1848: that the social and political unity that had secured the victory of the opposition in the initial revolutionary outbursts proved to be so fragile. Some historians have been damning of the radicals, in particular, for irreversibly damaging the liberal order while it was still in its vulnerable, early life. Frank Eyck, for example, says that in the long term, the radicals may have been right, 'but in the short term they for a time destroyed constitutionalism and the tender beginnings of representative government by using force when they could not gain their ends by persuasion. It was they who made the task of moderate liberal governments impossible.'[19] One may have sympathy for this view, as the present writer certainly does. However, while it is true that the radicals were rarely the true representatives of the impoverished masses for whom they claimed to speak, they did voice some of the widespread frustration over the social question and, in some cases, offered constructive (if sometimes unrealistic) solutions to the problems of poverty. In the long term it is true that capitalism dramatically improved the overall standards of living in Europe. With the benefit of hindsight, therefore, Eyck's chastisement of radical impatience with the limitations of the emerging liberal order in 1848 seems entirely justified. With more forbearance in 1848, it could be argued, the liberal order would have survived, and within a generation or more Europeans would have enjoyed both constitutional government and the wealth created by maturing industrial economies. Yet in 1848 it was far from clear to contemporaries that capitalism would bring the benefits of sustained economic growth and prosperity. Herzen expressed the problem rhetorically while in Paris in 1848: 'How will you persuade a workman to endure hunger and want while the social order changes by insensible degrees?'[20]

Namier's term, a 'seed-plot of history', can be applied to this aspect of 1848 because the revolutions of that year witnessed the fatal consequences of the perennial tension between, on the one hand, the liberal emphasis on political freedom and civil liberty and, on the other, the socialist stress on social justice, or the friction between the individual and society. Since 1848 this tension has provoked a wide range of responses, ranging from liberal capitalism to totalitarianism and all points between. Most modern democracies cope with the social question because it is debated within a constitutional framework on which all parties are (more or less) agreed and which protects democratic freedoms. In 1848, no such political consensus existed in most European countries. The 'social question' could therefore not be resolved within a peaceful, legal framework. So the revolutions faced the great challenge that confronts all modern states: how to integrate the masses into the state and to resolve the social question without provoking instability? Some states, such as the French Third Republic and Britain, managed to forge a political consensus by appealing to traditions (in the French case, to the democratic inheritance of 1789), which enabled them to offer some social reform through liberal, parliamentary systems. Others imposed reform from above through more authoritarian regimes, as in Bismarck's Germany during the 1880s. A third solution was revolutionary, where integration of the masses failed, or was not even seriously attempted, and where alienation led to a violent challenge to the old order, as in Russia, where the result was a totalitarian answer to the social question, in which the needs of society and, above all, the state took precedence over the liberty of the individual.

The revolutions of 1848 were also a 'seed-plot' in the sense that they comprised a truly European phenomenon, throwing up similarities in aims and ideals that bound together liberals and radicals of different nationalities, while also creating the circumstances that would soon drive them apart. This was Europe's great year of revolutions, rivalled only by the fall of communism in Central and Eastern Europe in 1989. Yet the question of whether or not 1848–9 really was a 'European' revolution – and if so, in what way? – has exercised historians.[21] It is an important problem, since underlying the historical question is (implicitly) the wider, more contemporary issue of whether Europe's political and social development rests on a broadly shared historical experience or, conversely, whether the differences between the countries are so deep that 'European' history amounts to little more than the sum of its constituent parts. Certainly, some historians have argued that 1848 was so complex that the revolutions did not sit on any common European ground, but were simply 'the sum of local events'.[22] There is no doubt, of course, that there were important national differences in the experiences of 1848. Rudolph Stadelmann, for example, stresses that the aims of the liberal majority of the German revolutionaries indicate the 'independence of German liberalism from the French example', concentrating as they did on state-building under a constitutional monarchy rather than acting on a republican–socialist impulse for radical political innovation.[23] The implications can be read in two conflicting ways: that the German revolutionaries were more moderate and concerned for legality, stability and continuity with the past; or that the German concern for state-building and monarchy gave both nationalism and conservatism priority over liberal freedom. Also, of course, not all European countries underwent a revolution: Britain, Sweden–Norway, the Low Countries, Spain, Portugal, Russia and Ottoman Europe (with the exception of the Romanian principalities) were all scarcely troubled.

But if 1848 does not stand out as a genuinely 'European' phenomenon in the sense that every country had a revolution, it is equally true that no country was wholly unaffected by the upheavals, even if they did not directly experience an uprising. Britain, Belgium, the Netherlands, Sweden and Norway all felt tremors, if not actual revolts. And in the broader framework of international politics, all the European powers were affected. Britain and Russia, at various stages, felt obliged to intervene in the revolutions. Both brought diplomatic pressure to bear over the Schleswig-Holstein crisis, and Russia intervened militarily against the revolutions in Romania and in Hungary. That 1848 did not degenerate into a major European conflict on the scale of the Napoleonic or First World wars was largely due to the fact that the five great European powers – Britain, France, Prussia, Austria and Russia – all wanted to avoid such a war at all costs. All governments – even the French Second Republic – understood that a general European conflagration would simply radicalise an already dangerous political situation and could lead to the complete disintegration of the multinational empires of Central and Eastern Europe. The task of maintaining a lasting peace in the aftermath of such turmoil would be much harder than it already was. Moreover, except in France, foreign policy and the armed forces remained under the control of the very monarchies who had the greatest interest in keeping the existing European order intact. Consequently, the Prussian government refused to bend to liberal enthusiasm for a nationalist war against Russia and yielded to combined British and Russian protests over its invasion of Schleswig-Holstein. When Russia invaded Romania and Hungary, Britain and France remained neutral; and, of course, in the case of Hungary, the Russian attack came in response to Austrian pleas for help. The French intervention against Rome in 1849 was set against a backdrop of wider international concern for the Pope, so while French forces took the city itself, Spanish, Neapolitan and Austrian forces were all involved in the wider conflict. As these examples show, the European international system based on the hegemony of five great powers remained intact, and in the end this benefited the counter-revolution.[24] It is significant that once the great European states put other interests over the maintenance of the international status quo – and this would happen soon enough, in the Crimean War of 1854–6 – one of the fundamental aims of the 'forty-eighters' – Italian, German and Romanian unification – all took place within less than two decades.

The 1848 revolutions were also European in the sense that they were genuinely spontaneous across the continent. By comparison, the assault on the old European regime after the French revolution of 1789 might have had the assistance of some local Jacobins in various countries, but the central impulse undeniably came from France. The overhaul of the Napoleonic era would not have been possible without the military might unleashed by that nation. While it is true that in 1848 perhaps the single greatest shock to jolt Europe was, once again, a revolution in France, it was the fall of Metternich in March which really drove forward the revolutionary impulse. Where tensions had been stored up in northern Italy, Hungary, Transylvania, Bohemia and Prussia, it was not the events in Paris that unleashed the fresh revolutionary charge, but the insurrection in Vienna. The outbreak of the 1848 revolutions, in other words, was a genuinely European phenomenon, precisely because they did not all burst from a single fountainhead. The European revolution of 1848 was essentially polycentric, expressed in localised varieties of liberalism that were bound together by broad and important similarities in aims, by the patterns in which the revolutions themselves progressed, and in the problems that the newly formed liberal regimes faced.

The broad similarities in the revolutionary experience were all the more remarkable in a Europe where political, social and economic structures varied widely from one country to the next. The obvious explanation as to why so many very different countries should experience revolution in 1848 is that their peoples were all suffering in the dire agrarian and industrial crisis. That underlying cause gave the revolutions a strong pan-European dimension, even though different people experienced the hardship in different ways. However, without downplaying the centrality of these economic pressures, the revolutions also followed strikingly similar patterns across Europe. Their success was invariably due, first, to a crisis of confidence both in and within the existing governments in their ability to deal with the challenges of social distress and political opposition. Second, they owed their victory to political unity between liberals and radicals and to a momentary social unity among the middle class, workers, peasants (and sometimes even the nobility) against the old order. The problems began when this unity proved to be short lived and fractured, as liberals and radicals vied with each other for control of the direction of the new regime, as property-owners sought to protect their wealth from a second, more radical revolution, and as peasants, having gained what they could from the initial upheaval, fell back in line with the conservatives. As the all-too-brief revolutionary consensus fell apart (sometimes with bloody consequences), so politics became more polarised, cutting away the middle ground as moderates turned towards increasingly authoritarian solutions to counter the threat of a second, 'social' revolution. In this sense, therefore, the revolutions self-destructed by internecine fighting. By the end of the year the conservatives had recovered their nerve, marshalled their redoubtable advantages (control of the army, the loyalty of the peasantry) and regained the initiative.

The European liberals did not only undergo similar revolutionary experiences but shared comparable (in John Breuilly's sense of 'essentially similar') aims.[25] While there were certainly important local variants in aims and ideology, liberals across Europe were all bound by a common desire to see political reform, particularly in the shape of constitutions with a limited suffrage, and everywhere except in France under the benign hand of a constitutional monarch. Radicals, on the other hand, shared the common goal of universal, or near-universal, male suffrage, and in a great many cases under a republic. The liberals and radicals of one nationality were themselves acutely conscious that they shared similar goals with their European neighbours: Hartmut Pogge von Strandmann cites the illuminating example of a German republican poster which called for a mass meeting in Berlin on 3 April 1848, in honour of the 'great European revolution', promised speeches in German, English and French, and hailed the republic in those three languages.[26]

The revolutionaries with the most 'European' outlook tended to be those whose national aspirations would benefit most from a political reshaping of the continent. Carlo Cattaneo, in an address to the Hungarian Diet shortly after the March revolutions, reminded the Magyars that for centuries Poland, Hungary and Venice had stood together as left, centre and right flanks against the Turks. Now the same nations (for 'Venice', read 'the Italians') should stand shoulder to shoulder against the new common enemy: Russia.[27] It is perhaps no coincidence that Cattaneo should – rhetorically at least – have named as allies the three nationalities who would have had the most to gain from a reordering of the European states system. Above all, the Poles, whose homeland had been torn apart by the three great 'eastern' powers, had everything to gain from such an upheaval. This was reflected in the truly internationalist language adopted by the Polish Democratic Society when it appealed to the French for arms on 28 March 1848:

> Frenchmen! Your revolution has not achieved its legitimate results! The day when your Republic was proclaimed, Europe believed itself to be free . . . it is not . . . For want of being sheltered by an independent Poland, the edifice of European freedom lacks a rooftop and remains exposed to the storms of the absolutist reaction. The fraternity of peoples is still an empty phrase . . . Frenchmen! Is that what you want? . . . Is it the egotistical 'every man for himself' style of monarchist nationalism? No, no, a thousand times no! Your Government itself proclaimed this, when, in tearing up the liberticide protocols of Vienna, it laid the will of peoples – and not that of the cabinets usurping their rights – as the basis for international relations in the future.[28]

The Polish democrats (not for the last time) were claiming for Poland the role of European buttress against the forces of repression and reaction.

Although such appeals were based on broadly European rhetoric, they were not pacifist, for everyone understood that the restoration of Poland, in particular, would require a war, and most likely a general European war at that. For ultimately, too, all European nationalists of 1848 wanted to realise, first and foremost, their own dreams of freedom, independence and greatness. Consequently, the cosmopolitan language was largely empty rhetoric. Since the

national aspirations of the liberals of one country invariably over-
lapped with those of their neighbours, the talk of Europe and of
international fraternity was all too much hot air. There was no
overarching European liberal movement to secure the revolutionary
gains of 1848; rather, the liberals acted within their own national
frameworks and, ultimately, for their own national interests. The
fact that so many of these interests worked against each other is one
of the primary explanations for the failure of the revolution.[29] As
Axel Körner argues, 'despite its idealism, Europe was not one of the
revolution's priorities'.[30] Arguably, Europeans paid a terrible price
for ignoring this bitter lesson of 1848: only after two murderous
world wars and, more recently, several bitter ethnic conflicts are
truly European political and economic structures being forged. It
can only be hoped that these will act as a conduit for the peaceful
resolution of future conflicting national interests. The extremes of
European nationalisms and the conflicts that they have engendered
in the century and a half since 1848 are, Reinhart Koselleck argues,
reason enough not to forget the common experience of the mid-
nineteenth-century revolutions.[31]

   In some parts of Europe they have never been forgotten. Despite
their intensely problematic legacy of failure, the revolutions of
1848 remained an inspiration for later generations. Socialists saw
the bloody repression in the summer of that year as the martyrdom
of the working classes, which confirmed that their interests – and
democracy itself – would always be betrayed by the property-
owning bourgeoisie. In East Germany the communist regime
appropriated the legacy of 1848 'as an indisputable element in the
revolutionary tradition of the German Democratic Republic'. It
claimed that the 'achievements of the socialist German state also
have their roots in the battles and endeavours of the revolutionary
masses of 1848'.[32] Yet, for others, 1848 was a confirmation of democratic principles. After the creation of the Weimar Republic in
1918 the Social Democratic chancellor, Friedrich Ebert, worked
hard to reconnect with the liberal heritage of 1848. At a ceremony
at Saint Paul's Church in Frankfurt in 1923, commemorating the
seventy-fifth anniversary of the opening of the first German

parliament, he told his huge audience that 18 May 1848 had been the day when the German people slipped from the grasp of reactionary governments and took its destiny in its own hands. After the same church was bombed during the Second World War, it was rebuilt after the conflict in time for the revolution's centenary, as a 'credo of German democracy'.[33] The memories of 1848 were also held dear in Hungary, where in 1941 left-wing demonstrators protested against the authoritarian regime's entry into the Second World War on the side of Nazi Germany by laying wreaths at the statues of Kossuth and Petőfi on the symbolic date of 15 March. While the post-war communist regime appropriated these revolutionary figures as its own heroes, they also became symbols of protest against totalitarianism. During the anti-communist uprising of 1956 the Hungarian insurgents sang Petőfi's patriotic hymns. After seizing control of the state radio station, they called it Radio Kossuth.[34]

Finally, the revolutions of 1989 in Central and Eastern Europe had profound echoes of 1848. The parallel is by no means exact, not least because many of the intellectuals and dissidents who led the resistance to communism were adamant that they wanted to break with Europe's heritage of revolution, not reignite it. Above all, they wanted their revolution to be an 'anti-revolution', a rejection of what the novelist and sociologist György Konrád (explicitly linking 1789 with 1917) dubbed the 'Jacobin–Leninist' tradition, which was foisted on Eastern Europe after 1945. In 1984 the Czech playwright Václav Havel had declared himself in favour of 'antipolitical politics',[35] by which he meant that the opposition to communism was not about a violent seizure of power, but rather involved elevating the cultural opposition in civil society to greater importance than the repressive state. For Konrád, the revolutionary tradition would be rejected by occupying the polar opposite of centralised political authority: 'decentralized spiritual authority'.[36]

Nevertheless, the revolutions of 1989 brought about the collapse of communism – and Havel himself, of course, did take power, as Czechoslovakia's first post-communist president. It was one thing to speak of 'antipolitics' while a dissident, but the old regime was replaced by a new democratic order that required the engagement of those who had done so much to create it. Ultimately, therefore, the 1989 revolutions were not just the process by which the peoples of Eastern and Central Europe rejected the legacy of 1917. They were also (perhaps despite themselves) the means by which those peoples became reacquainted with traditions of the French revolution of 1789 – the principles of 'liberty, democracy, civil society, nation-hood'.[37] But these ideals were not merely imported from the West; they tapped into the history of Eastern and Central Europe itself. On the eve of the collapse of communism, Timothy Garton Ash remarked that 'Czechs, Hungarians, and Poles are rediscovering their own history; and they are making it again'.[38] The uprisings of 1989 may have rejected the communist revolutionary tradition, but in so doing they reconnected their peoples to the liberal revolutions of 1848.

ACKNOWLEDGEMENTS

In writing this book I have received a lot of help and support, so I have many people to thank. My former doctoral supervisor and friend Bill Doyle first brought me to the attention of Tim Whiting at Little, Brown, so 'Salut et Fraternité!' I am grateful to Tim for his enthusiasm in the early stages of this book, and to his successor, Steve Guise, who has been a patient, kind and generous editor. I should also like to thank Iain Hunt, Kerry Chapple, Philip Parr (a superb copy editor: all blunders and errors – of judgement and of fact – are of course my own) and Jenny Fry at Little, Brown for their great work in the editing process and the publicity. Among colleagues, I salute Jim Smyth, who has been a good friend and a fine head of department; and Bob McKean, whom we were sorry to lose to retirement, for his generosity and his irrepressible enthusiasm – he has always taken a great interest in my work, such as it is. Looking beyond the history department, I should thank the University of Stirling for granting me a semester's sabbatical leave to allow me to start work on this project in the autumn of 2005. Kevin Adamson set me right on some important details, while Daniela Luigia Caglioti gave me a copy of her interesting article on foreign Protestants in southern Italy during 1848. My friend and colleague, the excellent Dave Andress, read a full copy of the typescript: if this book is ever thought to be any good, it will be largely thanks to his perceptive comments. The library staff at the University of Stirling have, as always, been cheerfully helpful. In particular, this book could not have been written without the assistance of the nice people at the Document Delivery Service. I should also add that the staff at Glasgow University Library are excellent and the collections there superb. Furthermore, I acknowledge the help of the National Library of Scotland, the Bibliothèque Nationale de France and the Archives Nationales in Paris. Thanks also go to my mother and Mike for putting up with me during the research trips to Paris, while my father and Jane provided me with urgently needed computer technology at an important stage of this project. My mother-in-law, Elizabeth Comerford, and Brenda Swan, Maureen and Robert Burns, Michael Bell and Sophie Rickard, also helped ease the pressure at a crucial stage in the editing.

During the writing of this book, our little daughter, Lily Jessica Anita, arrived: she is a firecracker with all her mother's strength of will. She has made the late evenings of tapping at the laptop worth it – and, besides all the joy she has brought us, I thank her for sleeping through the night! Finally, the last year has been one of the busiest, but perhaps one of the happiest, of my life: this is thanks to Helen, who has done so much to make this book possible. I have no doubt that, given her feisty nature, she would have been among the women standing on the barricades in 1848. This book is dedicated to her with gratitude and love.

It is also a tribute to the memory of my grandfather, a great, expansive, generous and good man, and to that of my brother-in-law, John, a kind, gentle, decent and dependable friend who passed away suddenly during the last day of editing. Both are sorely missed. Eternal and blessed memory.

Mike Rapport
Stirling, April 2008

NOTES

PREFACE

1 Most notably (among many others) by Priscilla Robertson, *Revolutions of 1848: A Social History* (Princeton: Princeton University Press, 1952); Jonathan Sperber, *The European Revolutions, 1848–1851* (Cambridge: Cambridge University Press, 1994); Roger Price, *The Revolutions of 1848* (Basingstoke: Macmillan, 1998); David Ward, *1848: The Fall of Metternich and the Year of Revolution* (London: Hamish Hamilton, 1970).
2 J. A. Hawgood, '1848 in Central Europe: An Essay in Historical Synchronisation', *Slavonic and East European Review*, vol. 26 (1947–8), pp. 314–28.
3 J. Keates, *The Siege of Venice* (London: Chatto and Windus, 2005), p. 2.

CHAPTER 1

1 A. Herzen, *My Past and Thoughts: The Memoirs of Alexander Herzen* (Berkeley, Los Angeles, London: University of California Press, 1982), pp. 313–14.
2 On Herzen, see E. H. Carr, *The Romantic Exiles* (London: Serif, 1998); I. Berlin, 'Introduction', in A. Herzen, *From the Other Shore* (Oxford: Oxford University Press, 1979), pp. vii–xxv; J. E. Zimmerman, *Midpassage: Alexander Herzen and European Revolution, 1847–1852* (Pittsburgh: University of Pittsburgh Press, 1989); E. Acton, *Alexander Herzen and The Role of the Intellectual Revolutionary* (Cambridge: Cambridge University Press, 1979).
3 R. Tombs, *France 1814–1914* (London: Longman, 1996), p. 357.
4 Quoted in A. Palmer, *Metternich, Councillor of Europe* (London: Phoenix, 1997), p. 132.
5 Quoted in ibid., p. 35.

6 Prince Richard de Metternich (ed.), *Mémoires, documents, et écrits divers laissés par le Prince de Metternich*, vol. 3 (Paris, 1881), pp. 440–1.

7 Ibid., vol. 3, p. 444.

8 I. Deak, *The Lawful Revolution: Louis Kossuth and the Hungarians 1848–1849* (New York: Columbia University Press, 1979), pp. 3–4, 15–16.

9 P. Robertson, *Revolutions of 1848: A Social History* (Princeton: Princeton University Press, 1952), pp. 335–6.

10 A. Sked, *The Decline and Fall of the Habsburg Empire 1815–1918* (London: Longman, 1989), pp. 46–50.

11 R. Okey, *The Habsburg Monarchy c. 1765–1918: From Enlightenment to Eclipse* (Basingstoke: Macmillan, 2001), p. 78.

12 R. Tempest, 'Madman or Criminal: Government Attitude to Petr Chaadaev in 1836', *Slavic Review*, vol. 43 (1984), pp. 281–7.

13 Quoted in H. A. Winkler, *Germany: The Long Road West, 1789–1933* (Oxford: Oxford University Press, 2006), p. 78.

14 Ibid., pp. 64–5.

15 Quoted in S. J. Woolf, *A History of Italy 1700-1860: The Social Constraints of Political Change* (London: Routledge, 1991), p. 227.

16 Quoted in Sked, *Decline and Fall*, p. 10.

17 Quoted in ibid., p. 10.

18 Quoted in Palmer, *Metternich*, p. 246.

19 Metternich, *Mémoires*, vol. 3, p. 629.

20 R. Gildea, *The Past in French History* (New Haven and London: Yale University Press, 1994), p. 35.

21 D. Mack Smith, *Mazzini* (New Haven and London: Yale University Press, 1994), pp. 33–4.

22 Quoted in ibid., pp. 35–6.

23 Quoted in L. Riall, *Garibaldi: Invention of a Hero* (New Haven and London: Yale University Press, 2007), p. 10.

24 Quoted in Mack Smith, *Mazzini*, p. 13.

25 Herzen, *My Past and Thoughts*, p. 366.

26 Quoted in Mack Smith, *Mazzini*, p. 12.

27 Ibid., p. 50.

28 Ibid., p. 31–2; Carr, *Romantic Exiles*, p. 29; J. Ridley, *Garibaldi* (London: Phoenix, 2001), pp. 105–6.

29 M. Rapport, *Nineteenth Century Europe, 1789–1914* (Basingstoke: Palgrave, 2005), p. 66.

30 Quoted in D. Blackbourn, *The Fontana History of Germany 1780–1918: The Long Nineteenth Century* (London: Fontana, 1997), p. 128.

31 Herzen, *My Past and Thoughts*, p. 321.

32 J. Keates, *The Siege of Venice* (London: Chatto and Windus, 2005), pp. 61–2.

33 M. Price, *The Perilous Crown: France between Revolutions 1814–1848* (London: Pan Macmillan, 2007), pp. 165–71.

34 F. Crouzet, 'French Economic Growth in the Nineteenth Century Reconsidered', *History*, vol. 59 (1974), pp. 167–79.

35 J. Harsin, *Barricades: The War of the Streets in Revolutionary Paris, 1830–1848* (New York: Palgrave, 2002), pp. 101–2.

36 Quoted in T. E. B. Howarth, *Citizen-King: The Life of Louis-Philippe, King of the French* (London: Eyre and Spottiswoode, 1961), p. 229.

37 Tombs, *France*, p. 363.

38 Quoted in R. J. Goldstein, *Political Repression in Nineteenth-Century Europe* (London: Croom Helm, 1983), p. 148.

39 Harsin, *Barricades*, pp. 114–15.

40 Extracts in D. Beales and E. F. Biagini, *The Risorgimento and the Unification of Italy*, 2nd edn (Harlow: Pearson Education, 2002), pp. 229–33.

41 H. Kohn, *Absolutism and Democracy 1814–1852* (Princeton: Van Nostrand, 1965), pp. 156–7.

42 Quoted in Winkler, *Germany*, p. 75.

43 C. A. Macartney, *The Habsburg Empire 1790–1918* (London: Weidenfeld and Nicolson, 1968), p. 218.

44 J. Droz, *Les Révolutions Allemandes de 1848* (Paris: Presses Universitaires de France, 1957), pp. 106–7.

45 J. Polišenský, *Aristocrats and the Crowd in the Revolutionary Year 1848: A Contribution to the History of the Revolution and Counter-Revolution in Austria* (Albany, N.Y.: State University of New York Press, 1980), p. 39.

46 Quoted in L. O'Boyle, 'The Problem of an Excess of Educated Men in Western Europe, 1800–1850', *Journal of Modern History*, vol. 42 (1970), p. 488.

47 Droz, *Révolutions Allemandes*, p. 81.

48 S. Z. Pech, 'Czech Peasantry in 1848', in M. Rechcigl, Jr., *Czechoslovakia Past and Present* (The Hague and Paris: Mouton, 1968), pp. 1277–9.

49 J.-P. Himka, *Galician Villagers and the Ukrainian National Movement in the Nineteenth Century* (Basingstoke: Macmillan, 1988), pp. 2–3, 11, 13–14.

50 Droz, *Révolutions Allemandes*, p. 78.

51 Polišenský, *Aristocrats and the Crowd*, p. 39.

52 Ibid., p. 39.

53 Quoted in W. H. Sewell, *Work and Revolution in France: The Language of Labour from the Old Regime to 1848* (Cambridge: Cambridge University Press, 1980), p. 224.

54 Quoted in L. Chevalier, *Labouring Classes and Dangerous Classes: Paris during the First Half of the Nineteenth Century* (London: Routledge and Kegan Paul, 1973), p. 206.

55 Droz, *Révolutions Allemande*, pp. 79–80; Polišenský, *Aristocrats and the Crowd*, p. 54.

56 Quoted in R. J. W. Evans, *Death in Hamburg: Society and Politics in the Cholera Years, 1830–1910* (Oxford: Oxford University Press, 1987), p. 119.

57 M. Gailus, 'Food Riots in Germany in the late 1840s', *Past and Present*, no. 145 (1994).

58 Price, *Perilous Crown*, pp. 326–7.

59 Sked, *Decline and Fall*, p. 76.

60 Quoted in L. Namier, *1848: The Revolution of the Intellectuals* (London: Oxford University Press, 1946), p. 5.

61 E. Hobsbawm, *The Age of Revolution, 1789–1848* (London: Abacus, 1977), p. 370.

62 Quoted in Robertson, *Revolutions of 1848*, p. 11.

63 S. Kieniewicz, *The Emancipation of the Polish Peasantry* (Chicago: Chicago University Press, 1969), pp. 113–26.

64 Quoted in Namier, *1848*, p. 3.

65 Herzen, *My Past and Thoughts*, p. 332.

CHAPTER 2

1 A. de Tocqueville, *Souvenirs* (Paris: Gallimard, 1999), pp. 23–6.

2 D. Beales and E. F. Biagini, *The Risorgimento and the Unification of Italy*, 2nd edn (Harlow: Longman, 2002), pp. 87–8; Ward, *1848*, p. 118.

3 Quoted in Sked, *Decline and Fall*, pp. 62–3.

4 P. Ginsborg, *Daniele Manin and the Venetian Revolution of 1848–49* (Cambridge: Cambridge University Press, 1979), pp. 67–80.

5 D. Mack Smith, *A History of Sicily: Modern Sicily after 1713* (London: Chatto and Windus, 1968), pp. 415–18; S. J. Woolf, *A History of Italy 1700–1860: The Social Constraints of Political Change* (London: Routledge, 1991), pp. 373–5; D. Mack Smith (ed), *The Making of Italy 1796–1870* (London: Macmillan, 1968), pp. 126–35.

6 A. Herzen, *Letters from France and Italy 1847–1851*, trans. J. E. Zimmerman (Pittsburgh: University of Pittsburgh Press, 1995), pp. 98, 100.

7 G. Pepe, *Histoire des révolutions et des guerres d'Italie en 1847, 1848 et 1849*, 3 vols (Paris, 1850), i, pp. 14–15.

8 Settembrini in Beales and Biagini, *Risorgimento*, p. 249.

9 Herzen, *Letters from France and Italy*, p. 87; Count de Liedekerke de Beaufort in Beales and Biagini, *Risorgimento*, pp. 239–40.

10 Robertson, *Revolutions of 1848*, p. 329.

11 Archives Nationales, Paris [hereafter AN], BB/30/296 (Jacques Richard's testimony).

12 D. Stern, *Histoire de la Révolution de 1848* [1850–2] (Paris: Balland, 1985), p. 98.

13 Ibid., p. 100.

14 Ibid., p. 101.

15 Lamartine, *History of the French Revolution of 1848*, 2 vols (Boston, 1852), i, p. 35.

16 J. Harsin, *Barricades: The War of the Streets in Revolutionary Paris, 1830–1848* (New York: Palgrave, 2002), pp. 255–6.

17 Stern, *Histoire*, p. 103.

18 AN, BB/30/298 (dossier 9843).

19 Stern, *Histoire*, p. 110.

20 Ibid., p. 111; Tocqueville, *Souvenirs*, pp. 43–5; D. Johnson, *Guizot: Aspects of French History 1787–1874* (London: Routledge and Kegan Paul, 1973), pp. 258–9.

21 AN, BB/30/298 (dossier 'Dispositions des citoyens ayant combattu contre les troupes'); G. Duveau, *1848: The Making of a Revolution* (London: Routledge and Kegan Paul, 1967), p. 30, Stern, *Histoire*, p. 122.

22 Ibid., pp. 124–5.

23 Tocqueville, *Souvenirs*, pp. 54–5.

24 Ibid., pp. 60–1.

25 Harsin, *Barricades*, p. 258.

26 Tocqueville, *Souvenirs*, pp. 78–9.

27 A. de Circourt, *Souvenirs d'une Mission à Berlin en 1848*, 2 vols (Paris: Picard, 1908), i, pp. 37–8.

28 G. Flaubert, *L'Education sentimentale* [1869] (Paris: Gallimard, 1965), pp. 314–16. A very useful English version is the recent Penguin edition of *Sentimental Education*, translated by Robert Baldick and annotated by Geoffrey Wall (London, 2004).

29 Stern, *Histoire*, pp. 150–4, 157–8.

30 AN, BB/30/298 (dossier 'Dispositions des citoyens ayant combattu contre les troupes').

31 T. E. B. Howarth, *Citizen-King: The Life of Louis-Philippe, King of the French* (London: Eyre and Spottiswoode, 1961), pp. 324–34.

32 Flaubert, *L'Education sentimentale*, pp. 316–18; Stern, *Histoire*, p. 169.

33 Tocqueville, *Souvenirs*, pp. 66, 68, 77–8.

34 Lamartine, *History*, i, p. 89.

35 Quoted in Duveau, *1848*, p. 50.

36 W. H. Stiles, *Austria in 1848–49: Being a History of the Late Political Movements in Vienna, Milan, Venice, and Prague*, 2 vols (New York, 1852), i, p. 96.

37 C. Schurz, *The Reminiscences of Carl Schurz*, 3 vols (London: John Murray, 1909), i, pp. 111, 116.

38 'Declaration of the Heidelberg Assembly', in F. Eyck, *The Revolutions of 1848–49* (Edinburgh: Oliver and Boyd, 1972), pp. 48–50.

39 Stiles, *Austria in 1848–49*, i, p. 102.

40 C. A. Macartney, *The Habsburg Empire, 1790–1918* (London: Weidenfeld and Nicolson, 1968), p. 323.

41 Quoted variously in ibid., p. 323; L. Deme, *The Radical Left in the Hungarian Revolution of 1848* (Boulder and New York: East European

Quarterly and Columbia University Press, 1976), p. 15; I. Deak, *The Lawful Revolution: Louis Kossuth and the Hungarians, 1848–1849* [1979] (New York: Columbia University Press, 1979), p. 67.

42 R. J. Rath, *The Viennese Revolution of 1848* [1957] (New York: Greenwood Press, 1969), p. 43–4.

43 Robertson, *Revolutions of 1848*, p. 207; Palmer, *Metternich*, p. 307.

44 August Silberstein, quoted in Rath, *Viennese Revolution*, p. 49.

45 Quoted in Palmer, *Metternich*, p. 309.

46 Fischhof's speech is quoted in full in Rath, *Viennese Revolution*, pp. 59–60.

47 Stiles, *Austria in 1848–49*, i, p. 105.

48 C. von Hügel, 'The Story of the Escape of Prince von Metternich', *National Review*, vol. 1 (1883), p. 590.

49 Ibid., p. 589.

50 W. Siemann, *The German Revolution of 1848–49* (Basingstoke: Macmillan, 1998), pp. 61–2.

51 Rath, *Viennese Revolution*, p. 66.

52 Stiles, *Austria in 1848–49*, i, p. 106.

53 Hügel, 'The Story', pp. 594–601; Palmer, *Metternich*, p. 310.

54 Quoted in Macartney, *Habsburg Empire*, p. 332.

55 Stiles, *Austria in 1848–49*, i, p. 112.

56 Quoted in Rath, *Viennese Revolution*, p. 85.

57 Quoted in G. Spira, *A Hungarian Count in the Revolution of 1848* (Budapest: Akadèmai Kiadó, 1974), p. 67.

58 L. Deme, 'The First Soldiers of the Hungarian Revolution: The National Guard in Pest in March–April, 1848', in B. K. Király and G. E. Rothenberg (eds), *War and Society in East Central Europe*, vol. 1, *Special Topics and Generalizations on the 18th and 19th Centuries* (New York: Brooklyn College Press, 1979), p. 82.

59 Quoted in C.-L. Chassin, *Alexandre Petoefi: poète de la révolution hongroise* (Brussels and Paris, 1860), p. 201.

60 Quoted in Deme, *Radical Left*, p. 18; Deak, *Lawful Revolution*, p. 71.

61 Eyewitness Ákos Birányi, quoted in Deme, *Radical Left*, p. 19.

62 Deme, 'First Soldiers', p. 83.

63 Quoted in Deme, *Radical Left*, p. 20.

64 Quoted in Deak, *Lawful Revolution*, p. 73.

65 S. Z. Pech, *The Czech Revolution of 1848* (Chapel Hill: University of North Carolina Press, 1969), pp. 3–4.

66 Ibid., p. 58.

67 Ibid., pp. 66, 68.

68 Stiles, *Austria in 1848–49*, i, p. 377.

69 Quoted in ibid.

70 Pech, *Czech Revolution*, p. 62.

71 Circourt, *Souvenirs*, i, p. 150.

72 Quoted in ibid., p. 125 n.
73 R. Stadelmann, *Social and Political History of the German Revolution* (Athens, Ohio: Ohio University Press, 1975), p. 56.
74 Quoted in ibid.
75 Eyck, *Revolutions of 1848–49*, pp. 51–3.
76 Circourt, *Souvenirs*, i, p. 148.
77 Quoted in Eyck, *Revolutions of 1848–49*, p. 53.
78 Anonymous account in ibid., p. 62.
79 Anonymous account in ibid., pp. 63–4.
80 Quoted in G. A. Craig, *The Politics of the Prussian Army 1640–1945* (Oxford: Clarendon Press, 1955), p. 99.
81 Gerlach and anonymous account in Eyck, *Revolutions of 1848–49*, pp. 64–5.
82 Gerlach in ibid., p. 56.
83 Quoted in Stadelmann, *Social and Political History*, p. 61.
84 Gerlach in Eyck, *Revolutions of 1848–49*, p. 57.
85 Quoted in full in Circourt, *Souvenirs*, i, pp. 172–4.
86 Gerlachin in Eyck, *Revolutions of 1848–49*, p. 58.
87 V. Valentin, *1848: Chapter of German History* (London: Allen and Unwin, 1940), pp. 210–11.
88 Quoted in Robertson, *Revolutions of 1848*, p. 122.
89 Proclamation of 21 March in Eyck, *Revolutions of 1848–49*, pp. 68–9.
90 Quoted in Robertson, *Revolutions of 1848*, p. 122.
91 Siemann, *The German Revolution*, p. 66.
92 O. von Bismarck, *Reflections and Reminiscences*, 2 vols (London, 1898), i, p. 27.
93 Excerpts in Beales and Biagini, *Risorgimento*, pp. 254–5.
94 Ginsborg, *Daniele Manin*, p. 132.
95 J. de Hübner, *Une Année de ma vie, 1848–1849* (Paris, 1891), pp. 22–3.
96 C. Cattaneo, 'L'Insurrection de Milan en 1848', in *Tutti le opere di Carlo Cattaneo*, ed. L. Ambrosoli, 7 vols (Verona: Arnoldo Mondadori, 1967), iv, pp. 199, 205.
97 Hübner, *Une Année*, p. 54.
98 Ginsborg, *Daniele Manin*, p. 132 n.
99 C. Osio, 'Alcuni fatti delle Cinque Gloriose Giornate', in F. Della Peruta (ed.), *Milan nel Risorgimento dall'età napoleonica all' Cinque Giornate* (Milan: Edizione Comune dil Milano, 1998), pp. 215–16.
100 Quoted in Ginsborg, *Daniele Manin*, p. 133.
101 Hübner, *Une Année*, p. 60.
102 Cattaneo, 'L'Insurrection', p. 212.
103 Osio, 'Alcuni fatti', p. 216.
104 Cattaneo, 'L'Insurrection', pp. 215, 227.
105 Hübner, *Une Année*, pp. 60–3, 66–78, 80.
106 Cattaneo, 'L'Insurrection', p. 247.

107 Ibid., p. 219; Robertson, *Revolutions of 1848*, p. 344.

108 Cattaneo, 'L'Insurrection', p. 228.

109 Hübner, *Une Année*, pp. 78–9, 81–3.

110 Cattaneo, 'L'Insurrection', pp. 223–5.

111 Ibid., pp. 229–31.

112 Ginsborg, *Daniele Manin*, pp. 135–6.

113 Cattaneo, 'L'Insurrection', p. 238.

114 Ibid., p. 245.

115 Ibid., p. 245.

116 Ginsborg, *Daniele Manin*, pp. 133, 138–41.

117 Osio, 'Alcuni fatti', pp. 222–7.

118 Hübner, *Une Année*, pp. 104, 107.

119 Quoted in F. Walker, *The Man Verdi* (London: Dent and Sons, 1962), p. 188.

120 J. Keates, *The Siege of Venice* (London: Chatto and Windus, 2005), pp. 97–104.

121 J. Quero Morales, 'Spain in 1848', in F. Fejtö (ed.), *The Opening of an Era: 1848, an Historical Symposium* (London: Allan Wingate, 1948), pp. 148, 155–6.

122 R. Carr, *Spain, 1808–1975* (Oxford: Clarendon Press, 1982), p. 242; Rapport, *Nineteenth Century Europe*, pp. 124–5.

123 E. J. Evans, *The Forging of the Modern State: Early Industrial Britain, 1783–1870* (London: Longman, 1983), pp. 261–2.

124 Quoted in J. Saville, *1848: The British State and the Chartist Movement* (Cambridge: Cambridge University Press, 1987), p. 89.

125 Quoted in L. Mitchell, 'Britain's Reaction to the Revolutions', in R. J. W. Evans and H. Pogge von Strandmann, *The Revolutions in Europe, 1848–49: From Reform to Reaction* (Oxford: Oxford University Press, 2000), p. 93.

126 Quoted in Saville, *1848*, p. 105.

127 Quoted in Mitchell, 'Britain's Reaction', p. 92.

128 Saville, *1848*, p. 112.

129 O'Connor and Jones quoted in Saville, *1848*, p. 119.

130 Quoted in J. P. T. Bury, 'Great Britain and the Revolution of 1848', in Fejtö, *Opening of an Era*, p. 186.

131 R. Davis, *Revolutionary Imperialist: William Smith O'Brien* (Dublin: Lilliput Press, 1998), p. 224.

132 Ibid., pp. 266–76.

133 This section on Ireland draws heavily on the trenchant pages by J. S. Donnelly, Jr., 'A Famine in Irish Politics', in W. E. Vaughan (ed.), *A New History of Ireland*, vol. 5, *Ireland under the Union (Part One), 1801–70* (Oxford: Clarendon Press, 1989), pp. 366–71. See also R. F. Foster, *Modern Ireland, 1600–1972* (Harmondsworth: Penguin, 1989), p. 314.

134 Quoted in G. D. Homan, 'Constitutional Reform in the Netherlands in 1848', *Historian*, vol. 28, no. 3 (May 1966), p. 413.

135 Quoted in ibid., p. 425. See also E. H. Kossmann, *The Low Countries 1780–1940* (Oxford: Clarendon Press, 1978), pp. 192–5.

136 Ibid., p. 195.

137 J. Bartier, 'Belgium in 1848', in Fejtö, *The Opening of an Era*, pp. 160–6.

138 T. K. Derry, *A History of Scandinavia: Norway, Sweden, Denmark, Finland and Iceland* (London and Minneapolis: University of Minnesota Press, 1979), p. 223.

139 Ibid., pp. 224–5; L. Tissot, 'The Events of 1848 in Scandinavia', in Fejtö, *Opening of an Era*, p. 170.

140 Quoted in D. Saunders, *Russia in the Age of Reaction and Reform 1801–1881* (London: Longman, 1992), p. 190.

141 Quoted in ibid., p. 170 ('to meet') and in B. Goriely, 'The Russia of Nicholas I in 1848', in Fejtö, *Opening of an Era*, p. 394 ('unless').

142 Quoted in Saunders, *Russia*, p. 171.

143 I. Berlin, 'Russia and 1848', *Slavonic and East European Review*, vol. 26 (1947–8), p. 348.

144 J. H. Seddon, *The Petrashevtsy: A Study of the Russian Revolutionaries of 1848* (Manchester: Manchester University Press, 1985), pp. 194–5, 208–27; Saunders, *Russia*, p. 194.

145 Quoted in Goriely, 'Russia of Nicolas I', p. 395.

146 D. Saunders, 'A Pyrrhic Victory: The Russian Empire in 1848', in Evans and Pogge von Strandmann, *Revolutions in Europe*, pp. 135–55.

147 N. V. Riasonovsky, *A Parting of Ways: Government and the Educated Public in Russia, 1801–1855* (Oxford: Clarendon Press, 1976), pp. 248–90.

148 Berlin, 'Russia and 1848', p. 358.

149 J. Breuilly, '1848: Connected or Comparable Revolutions?', in A. Körner (ed.), *1848: A European Revolution/International Ideas and National Memories of 1848* (Basingstoke: Palgrave, 2000), pp. 32–3.

150 Gerlach in Eyck, *Revolutions of 1848–49*, p. 56.

151 Circourt, *Souvenirs*, i, p. 169.

152 Rémusat in R. Price, *Documents on the French Revolution of 1848* (Basingstoke: Macmillan, 1996), p. 43.

153 Hübner, *Une Année*, pp. 8, 10.

154 Cattaneo, 'L'Insurrection', p. 252.

155 Hübner, *Une Année*, pp. 95–6.

156 C. Osio, 'Alcuni fatti', p. 215.

157 Anonymous account in Eyck, *Revolutions of 1848 49*, p. 63.

158 Tocqueville, *Souvenirs*, pp. 56–7.

159 Duveau, *1848*, pp. 53–104.

Chapter 3

1 F. Lewald, *A Year of Revolutions: Fanny Lewald's 'Recollections of 1848'*, trans. H. B. Lewis (Oxford: Berghahn, 1997), p. 24.

2 Heidelberg declaration in Eyck, *Revolutions of 1848–49*, p. 49.

3 For the immediate diplomatic and military reaction to the February revolution, see L. C. Jennings, *France and Europe in 1848: A Study of French Foreign Affairs in Time of Crisis* (Oxford: Clarendon Press, 1973), pp. 1–5.

4 R. C. Canevali, 'The "False French Alarm": Revolutionary Panic in Baden, 1848', *Central European History*, vol. 18 (1985), pp. 119–42.

5 Jennings, *France and Europe*, pp. 22–3.

6 L. M. Caussidière, *Mémoires de Caussidière: ex-préfet de police et représentant du peuple*, 2 vols, 3rd edn (Paris, 1849), i, pp. 199–200.

7 E. J. Kisluk, *Brothers from the North: The Polish Democratic Society and the European Revolutions of 1848–1849* (Boulder, Co.: East European Monographs, 2005), p. 33.

8 Quoted in J. D. Randers-Pehrson, *Germans and the Revolution of 1848–1849* (New York: Lang, 1999), p. 323.

9 Kisluk, *Brothers from the North*, p. 38.

10 This is a reference to the massacre on the Champ de Mars on 17 July 1791, when republican petitioners were fired on by the National Guard, who killed some fifty protesters. Prior to this, the Paris authorities, as the law demanded, had raised the red flag to show that martial law had been proclaimed – which is the early origin of the symbolism of that banner.

11 Quoted in Duveau, *1848*, p. 61.

12 Quoted in Saville, *1848*, p. 82.

13 Lamartine, *History*, ii, p. 12. An English translation of the text can be found on pp. 19–24.

14 M. L. Stewart-McDougall, *The Artisan Republic: Revolution, Reaction, and Resistance in Lyon 1848–1851* (Kingston, Montreal, and Gloucester: McGill-Queen's University Press and Alan Sutton, 1984), pp. 50–4.

15 Jennings, *France and Europe*, pp. 54–6; Caussidière, *Mémoires*, i, pp. 201–7.

16 Stewart-McDougall, *Artisan Republic*, pp. 50–4; Jennings, *France and Europe*, pp. 51–3.

17 Ibid., pp. 57–9.

18 Quoted in Siemann, *The German Revolution*, p. 58.

19 Schurz, *Reminiscences*, i, pp. 124–5.

20 Valentin, *1848*, pp. 218–20; Randers-Pehrson, *Germans and the Revolution*, pp. 305–6.

21 Lewald, *Year of Revolutions*, p. 124.

22 Quoted in J. J. Sheehan, *German Liberalism in the Nineteenth Century* (London: Methuen, 1982), p. 54.

23 Valentin, *1848*, pp. 118–20; Robertson, *Revolutions of 1848*, pp. 150–1.

24 Schurz, *Reminiscences*, i, p. 137.

25 Siemann, *German Revolution*, p. 68.

26 Valentin, *1848*, pp. 224–7; Randers-Pehrson, *Germans and the Revolution*, pp. 321–2 (von Arnim is quoted on p. 322).

27 Ibid., pp. 328–9.

28 Jennings, *France and Europe*, pp. 68–9; Valentin, *1848*, pp. 228–9.

29 Randers-Pehrson, *Germans and the Revolution*, pp. 335–6; Valentin, *1848*, p. 231.

30 Randers-Pehrson, *Germans and the Revolution*, pp. 339–41.

31 Quoted in ibid., p. 341.

32 Siemann, *German Revolution*, pp. 69–71.

33 L. Tissot, 'The Events of 1848 in Scandinavia', in Fejtö, *Opening of an Era*, p. 171.

34 Derry, *History of Scandinavia*, p. 223.

35 Tissot, 'Events of 1848 in Scandinavia', pp. 168–9, 171–4; Derry, *History of Scandinavia*, p. 224.

36 Proclamation in Eyck, *Revolutions of 1848–49*, p. 70.

37 Schurz, *Reminiscences*, i, pp. 129–31.

38 Robertson, *Revolutions of 1848*, p. 158.

39 N. Davies, *God's Playground: A History of Poland*, 2 vols (Oxford: Clarendon Press, 1981), ii, pp. 340–6.

40 See M. K. Dziewanowski, '1848 and the Hotel Lambert', *Slavonic and East European Review*, vol. 26 (1947–8), pp. 361–73.

41 Kisluk, *Brothers from the North*, pp. 1–15.

42 Namier, *1848*, p. 58.

43 Quoted in P. S. Wandycz *The Lands of Partitioned Poland, 1795–1918* (Seattle: University of Washington Press, 1975), p. 139; pre-parliament's resolution in Eyck, *Revolutions of 1848–49*, pp. 83–4.

44 Quoted in Namier, *1848*, p. 55.

45 Circourt, *Souvenirs*, i, pp. 303, 315.

46 K. Popiołk and F. Popiołek, '1848 in Silesia', *Slavonic and East European Review*, vol. 26 (1947–8), pp. 374–81.

47 Quoted in Namier, *1848*, pp. 71, 73. Other details in A. Zamoyski, *Holy Madness: Romantics, Patriots and Revolutionaries 1776–1871* (London: Phoenix, 2001), pp. 330–1; Kisluk, *Brothers from the North*, pp. 49–52.

48 Ibid., pp. 66–7; Zamoyski, *Holy Madness*, p. 346; Wandycz, *Lands of Partitioned Poland*, pp. 140–1; Namier, *1848*, pp. 76–7.

49 Namier, *1848*, pp. 88–9.

50 Quoted in ibid., p. 87.

51 Stiles, *Austria in 1848–49*, i, p. 119.

52 K. A. Graf von Leiningen-Westerburg, *Letters and Journal (1848–49) of Count Charles Leiningen-Westerburg: General in the Hungarian Army* (London: Duckworth, 1911), p. 86.

53 Pech, *Czech Revolution*, pp. 74–80.

54 The letter is translated by W. Beardmore in 'Letter sent by František Palacký to Frankfurt', *Slavonic and East European Review*, vol. 26 (1947–8), pp. 303–8. See also J. Polišenský, *Aristocrats and the Crowd in the*

Revolutionary Year 1848: A Contribution to the History of Revolution and Counter-Revolution in Austria (Albany: State University of New York Press, 1980), pp. 129–30, and Pech, *Czech Revolution*, pp. 80–5.

55 Polišenský, *Aristocrats and the Crowd*, pp. 61–70.
56 On this issue, see A. G. Whiteside, 'The Germans as an Integrative Force in Imperial Austria: The Dilemma of Dominance', *Austrian History Yearbook*, vol. 3 (1967), pp. 157–200.
57 Pech, *Czech Revolution*, pp. 89–90; Polišenský, *Aristocrats and the Crowd*, p. 131.
58 Quoted in Pech, *Czech Revolution*, p. 93.
59 Deak, *Lawful Revolution*, p. 109.
60 Stiles, *Austria in 1848–49*, i, pp. 127–8.
61 Ibid., p. 129.
62 Ibid., pp. 131–2.
63 Quoted in Rath, *Viennese Revolution*, p. 196.
64 Quoted in ibid., p. 178.
65 For the revolution in Galicia, see Kisluk, *Brothers from the North*, pp. 52–64; Wandycz, *Lands of Partitioned Poland*, pp. 141–5.
66 Quoted in J.-P. Himka, *Galician Villagers and the Ukrainian National Movement in the Nineteenth Century* (Basingstoke: Macmillan, 1988), pp. 32–3.
67 S. Kieniewicz, 'The Social Visage of Poland in 1848', *Slavonic and East European Review*, vol. 27 (1948–9), pp. 101–3.
68 Deme, *Radical Left*, pp. 39, 40.
69 Deak, *Lawful Revolution*, pp. 95–9.
70 Deme, *Radical Left*, p. 25.
71 Quoted in ibid., p. 43.
72 Quoted in Deak, *Lawful Revolution*, p. 122.
73 Quoted in I. Deak, 'István Széchenyi, Miklós Wesselényi, Lajos Kossuth and the Problem of Romanian Nationalism', *Austrian History Yearbook*, vols 12–13 (1976–7), p. 75.
74 'Carpathinus', '1848 and Roumanian Unification', *Slavonic Review*, vol. 26 (1947–8), p. 392.
75 K. Hitchins, *The Romanians 1774–1866* (Oxford: Clarendon Press, 1996), pp. 251–2.
76 Quoted in Deme, *Radical Left*, pp. 72–3.
77 Hitchins, *The Romanians*, pp. 253–5.
78 Quoted in 'Carpathinus', '1848 and Roumanian Unification', p. 400.
79 Hitchins, *The Romanians*, p. 257.
80 M. Glenny, *The Balkans 1804–1999: Nationalism, War and the Great Powers* (London: Granta, 1999), pp. 39–40.
81 G. E. Rothenberg, 'Jelačić, the Croatian Military Border, and the Intervention against Hungary in 1848', *Austrian History Yearbook*, vol. 1 (1965), pp. 50–2.

82 Hitchins, *The Romanians*, pp. 261–2.

83 Quoted in Glenny, *The Balkans*, p. 40.

84 Sked, *Decline and Fall*, pp. 126–8.

85 Rothenberg, 'Jelačić', pp. 53–6.

86 Quoted in G. F. H. Berkeley and J. Berkeley, *Italy in the Making*, 3 vols (Cambridge: Cambridge University Press, 1940), iii, p. 173.

87 Herzen, *Letters from France and Italy*, p. 113.

88 D. Mack Smith, 'The Revolutions of 1848–1849 in Italy', in Evans and Pogge von Strandmann, *Revolutions in Europe*, p. 67.

89 Herzen, *Letters from France and Italy*, pp. 115–17.

90 Berkeley and Berkeley, *Italy in the Making*, iii, pp. 154–5.

91 Ibid., pp. 130, 139.

92 Mack Smith, *History of Sicily*, p. 418.

93 Princess C. T. de Belgiojoso, 'Les Journées révolutionnaires à Milan', in J. Godechot, *Les Révolutions de 1848* (Paris: Albin Michel, 1971), pp. 375–6.

94 G. M. Trevelyan, *Manin and the Venetian Revolution of 1848* (London: Longman, Green and Co., 1923), p. 184.

95 House of Commons Parliamentary Papers, *Correspondence Respecting the Affairs of Italy*, Part II (January–30 June 1848) (London, 1849), p. 522.

96 Ibid., p. 498.

97 Pepe, *Histoire*, i, pp. 67–72, 76, 79–80.

98 'Carlo Alberto's proclamation of 23 March 1848', in Mack Smith, *Making of Italy*, p. 148.

99 Quoted variously in H. Hearder, *Cavour* (London: Longman, 1994), p. 35; and Woolf, *History of Italy*, p. 380.

100 G. Mazzini, *Mazzini's Letters to an English Family 1844–1854*, ed. E. F. Richards (London, 1920), p. 79.

101 'Indirizzo dell'Associazione italiana in Parigi ai Lombardi', in G. Mazzini, *Scritti editi e inediti di Giuseppe Mazzini*, 12 vols (Milan, 1863), vi, pp. 165–7.

102 Ginsborg, *Daniele Manin*, pp. 141–2.

103 Mazzini, *Letters to an English Family*, p. 85.

104 D. Mack Smith, *Mazzini* (New Haven, Conn., and London: Yale University Press, 1994), p. 60; Mack Smith, 'The Revolutions of 1848–1849 in Italy', p. 66.

105 Mack Smith, *Making of Italy*, pp. 149–50.

106 Mazzini, *Scritti*, vi, p. 172.

107 Quoted in Ginsborg, *Daniele Manin*, p. 206.

108 Mazzini, *Scritti*, vi, p. 214.

109 B. King, *A History of Italian Unity, Being a Political History of Italy from 1814 to 1871*, 2 vols (London, 1899), i, p. 244; Berkeley and Berkeley, *Italy in the Making*, iii, p. 327.

110 Quoted in Keates, *Siege of Venice*, p. 176.

111 Quoted in Ginsborg, *Daniele Manin*, p. 185.

112 Ibid., pp. 207–8.

113 Mack Smith, 'Revolutions of 1848–1849 in Italy', pp. 66–7.

114 Quoted in Berkeley and Berkeley, *Italy in the Making*, iii, p. 164.

115 Text in Mack Smith, *The Making of Italy*, pp. 151–2.

116 Quoted in Berkeley and Berkeley, *Italy in the Making*, iii, pp. 183–4.

117 B. King, *History of Italian Unity*, pp. 236–9; Woolf, *History of Italy*, p. 384.

118 House of Commons Parliamentary Papers, *Correspondence Respecting the Affairs of Italy*, Part II, pp. 482–4, 495–7, 511–13; B. King, *History of Italian Unity*, p. 240.

119 Pepe, *Histoire*, i, pp. 89–107.

120 Details of the military campaign in northern Italy during the spring can be read in Berkeley and Berkeley, *Italy in the Making*, iii, pp. 111–27, 195–270, 287–319.

121 G. Garibaldi, *My Life*, trans. S. Parkin (London: Hesperus Classics, 2004), pp. 6–7.

122 Quoted in A. Sked, *The Survival of the Habsburg Empire: Radetzky, the Imperial Army and the Class War, 1848* (London: Longman, 1979), p. 142.

123 F. Eyck, *The Frankfurt Parliament 1848–49* (London: Macmillan, 1968), pp. 99–100.

124 Ibid., pp. 241–5.

125 Siemann, *German Revolution*, p. 186.

126 Eyck, *Frankfurt Parliament*, p. 241.

127 Pech, *Czech Revolution*, pp. 139–40, 293–4.

128 Quoted in Macartney, *Habsburg Empire*, p. 356 n.

129 Deak, *Lawful Revolution*, pp. 85–6,

130 Deme, *Radical Left*, pp. 29–30, 48–9.

131 Deak, *Lawful Revolution*, pp. 102, 113–16.

132 Siemann, *German Revolution*, p. 186.

133 R. Price, *The French Second Republic: A Social History* (London: Batsford, 1972), p. 119.

134 AN, BB/18/1461 (dossier 5282A).

135 M. Agulhon, *1848 ou l'apprentissage de la République 1848–1852* (Paris: Seuil, 1973), pp. 150–2.

136 Quoted in S. Zucker, 'German Women and the Revolution of 1848: Kathinka Zitz-Halein and the Humania Association', *Central European History*, vol. 13, no. 3 (1980), p. 240.

137 Quoted in J. Sperber, *Rhineland Radicals: The Democratic Movement and the Revolution of 1848–1849* (Princeton: Princeton University Press, 1991), p. 252.

138 T. M. Roberts and D. W. Howe, 'The United States and the Revolutions of 1848', in Evans and Pogge von Strandmann, *Revolutions in Europe*, p. 175.

139 Quoted in Pech, *Czech Revolution*, p. 327.

140 W. Walton, 'Writing the 1848 Revolution: Politics, Gender, and Feminism in

the Works of French Women of Letters', *French Historical Studies*, vol. 18, no. 4 (1994), p. 1013.

141 Sheehan, *German Liberalism*, p. 49.

142 F. Engels, *Germany: Revolution and Counter-Revolution* (London: Lawrence and Wishart, 1969), p. 57.

143 Quoted in Namier, *1848*, p. 51.

144 Quoted, most recently, in T. Baycroft and M. Hewitson, 'Introduction: What Was a Nation in Nineteenth-Century Europe?', in T. Baycroft and M. Hewitson (eds), *What is a Nation? Europe 1789–1914* (Oxford: Oxford University Press, 2006), p. 1.

145 A. D. Smith, *National Identity* (Harmondsworth: Penguin, 1991), pp. 8–13; A.-M. Thiesse, *La Création des identités nationales: Europe XVIIIe–XXe siècle* (Paris: Seuil, 1999), p. 14.

CHAPTER 4

1 Tocqueville, *Souvenirs*, p. 156.

2 Ibid., p. 160.

3 Quoted in M. Dommanget, *Auguste Blanqui et la révolution de 1848* (Paris: Mouton, 1972), p. 34.

4 Quoted in ibid., p. 86.

5 Quoted in Harsin, *Barricades*, p. 289.

6 Accounts of 15 May in ibid., pp. 288–93; Tocqueville, *Souvenirs*, pp. 154–69.

7 Ibid., pp. 117–18.

8 P. H. Amman, *Revolution and Mass Democracy: The Paris Club Movement in 1848* (Princeton: Princeton University Press, 1975), p. 196.

9 Quoted in Price, *French Second Republic*, p. 99.

10 Quoted in ibid., p. 109.

11 Tocqueville, *Souvenirs*, pp. 129–30.

12 Quoted in Price, *French Second Republic*, p. 145.

13 AN, BB/30/333 (dossier 1).

14 Amman, *Revolution and Mass Democracy*, pp. 192, 194.

15 Dommanget, *Auguste Blanqui*, p. 159.

16 From Sobrier's letter-book, pp. 192–3, in AN, W//574 ('Pièces concernant Sobrier').

17 Quoted in Harsin, *Barricades*, p. 295.

18 Document in M. Agulhon (ed.), *Les Quarante-huitards* (Paris: Gallimard-Julliard, 1975), p. 152.

19 Document in Price, *Documents*, pp. 79–80.

20 Document in ibid., pp. 83–4.

21 M. du Camp, *Souvenirs de l'année 1848* (Paris, 1876), pp. 238–9.

22 Ibid., p. 241.

23 Caussidière, *Mémoires*, ii, p. 222.

24 K. Marx, *Class Struggles in France 1848–1850* (New York: International Publishers, 1964), p. 56.

25 Extract in Price, *Documents*, p. 83.

26 F. A. de Luna, *The French Republic under Cavaignac* (Princeton: Princeton University Press, 1969), pp. 135–6.

27 A. Herzen, *From the Other Shore* (Oxford: Oxford University Press, 1979), p. 46.

28 Document in Agulhon, *Quarante-huitards*, pp. 155–6.

29 Herzen, *From the Other Shore*, p. 46.

30 Price, *French Second Republic*, p. 171.

31 Du Camp, *Souvenirs*, p. 242.

32 Quoted in de Luna, *French Republic*, p. 140.

33 Robertson, *Revolutions of 1848*, p. 90. Robertson quotes the women as screaming, 'Cowards, do you dare fire on the belly of a woman?', but one suspects that 'belly' was not the exact word used. The story originates, I think, with Victor Hugo.

34 Quoted in de Luna, *French Republic*, p. 142.

35 Tocqueville, *Souvenirs*, p. 196.

36 Du Camp, *Souvenirs*, pp. 253, 256–7.

37 Ibid., pp. 270–2.

38 Document in Price, *Documents*, p. 94.

39 Ibid., pp. 94–5.

40 Price, *French Second Republic*, pp. 176–7.

41 AN, BB/18/1465A (dossier 59: Insurrection du 23 juin à Paris).

42 Caussidière, *Mémoires*, ii, p. 224.

43 Price, *French Second Republic*, pp. 159, 168, 171.

44 L. Blanc, *Histoire de la Révolution de 1848*, 5th edn (Paris, 1880), ii, pp. 153–4.

45 Ibid., pp. 153–4.

46 R. L. Hoffman, *Revolutionary Justice: The Social and Political Theory of P.-J. Proudhon* (Urbana, Chicago and London: University of Illinois Press, 1972), pp. 137–8.

47 Blanc, *Histoire*, ii, p. 147.

48 Quoted in de Luna, *French Republic*, p. 147.

49 Extract in Agulhon, *Quarante-huitards*, p. 168.

50 Extract in Price, *Documents*, pp. 101–2.

51 Ibid., p. 98.

52 De Luna, *French Republic*, p. 150; Price, *French Second Republic*, p. 187; Marx, *Class Struggles*, pp. 56–7.

53 Flaubert, *Sentimental Education*, Part 3, Chapter 1.

54 Caussidière, *Mémoires*, ii, pp. 232–3.

55 Herzen, *From the Other Shore*, p. 47.

56 Tocqueville, *Souvenirs*, pp. 190–1.

57 Ibid., p. 182.

58 Marx, *Class Struggles*, p. 56.

59 Price, *French Second Republic*, pp. 162–6.

60 Quoted in S. Zucker, *Ludwig Bamberger: German Liberal Politician and Social Critic, 1823–1899* (Pittsburgh: University of Pittsburgh Press, 1975), p. 26.

61 Engels, *Germany: Revolution and Counter-Revolution*, p. 63.

62 Quoted in Siemann, *German Revolution*, p. 92.

63 Quoted in Stadelmann, *Social and Political History*, p. 163.

64 'Demands of the Communist Party in Germany', in Engels, *Germany: Revolution and Counter-Revolution*, pp. 132–4.

65 Sperber, *Rhineland Radicals*, p. 228.

66 Quoted in ibid., p. 227.

67 Zucker, *Ludwig Bamberger*, p. 25.

68 Stadelmann, *Social and Political History*, p. 170; Siemann, *German Revolution*, p. 90.

69 Quoted in ibid., p. 90.

70 Stadelmann, *Social and Political History*, pp. 168–9.

71 Ibid., pp. 170–3.

72 Siemann, *German Revolution*, p. 91.

73 Lewald, *Year of Revolutions*, pp. 102–3.

74 Sheehan, *German Liberalism*, p. 53.

75 Lewald, *Year of Revolutions*, pp. 97, 100.

76 Siemann, *German Revolution*, pp. 137–8.

77 Lewald, *Year of Revolutions*, pp. 113–14.

78 Quoted in Robertson, *Revolutions of 1848*, p. 135.

79 Quoted in Valentin, *1848*, pp. 293–4.

80 Bismarck, *Reflections and Reminiscences*, i, p. 52.

81 Quoted in Valentin, *1848*, p. 294.

82 Bismarck, *Reflections and Reminiscences*, i, p. 50.

83 Siemann, *German Revolution*, p. 166.

84 H. W. Koch, *A Constitutional History of Germany in the Nineteenth and Twentieth Centuries* (London: Longman, 1984), pp. 55–6.

85 Siemann, *German Revolution*, pp. 80–1.

86 Quoted in Winkler, *Germany: The Long Road West*, vol 1, p. 98.

87 Letter of Theodor Paur, 19 September 1848, quoted in Eyck, *Revolutions of 1848–49*, p. 112.

88 Schurz, *Reminiscences*, i, pp. 142–3.

89 Ibid., vol. i, p. 143.

90 Lewald, *Year of Revolutions*, pp. 121, 129, 133.

91 Letter of C. Koch-Gontard, in Eyck, *Revolutions of 1848–49*, p. 112.

92 Stiles, *Austria in 1848–49*, i, p. 136.

93 Ibid., vol. 1, p. 142.

94 Rath, *Viennese Revolution*, p. 253.

95 Hübner, *Une Année*, pp. 267–9.

96 Stiles, *Austria in 1848–49*, i, p. 153; Engels, *Germany: Revolution and Counter-Revolution*, p. 68.

97 Hübner, *Une Année*, pp. 278–9; Stiles, *Austria in 1848–49*, i, p. 156.

98 Quoted in Rath, *Viennese Revolution*, p. 296.

99 Engels, *Germany: Revolution and Counter-Revolution*, p. 68.

100 Rath, *Viennese Revolution*, pp. 292–6.

101 Pech, *Czech Revolution*, p. 291.

102 Polišenský, *Aristocrats and the Crowd*, pp. 127–8; Pech, *Czech Revolution*, p. 140.

103 Polišenský, *Aristocrats and the Crowd*, pp. 138–9.

104 Ibid., pp. 153–62; Pech, *Czech Revolution*, pp. 145–7.

105 L. D. Orton, *The Prague Slav Congress of 1848* (Boulder, Col.: East European Quarterly, 1978), pp. 33–6.

106 Namier, *1848*, p. 111.

107 Orton, *Prague Slav Congress*, p. 94.

108 Namier, *1848*, p. 103.

109 Orton, *Prague Slav Congress*, pp. 107–15.

110 Quoted in Rath, *Viennese Revolution*, pp. 262–3.

111 Deme, *Radical Left*, pp. 49–51.

112 Ibid., pp. 60–5, 75; Deak, *Lawful Revolution*, pp. 142–4.

113 Spira, *Hungarian Count*, p. 229.

114 Deak, *Lawful Revolution*, p. 146.

115 Hitchins, *The Romanians*, pp. 262–3.

116 Quoted in 'Carpathinus', '1848 and Roumanian Unification', pp. 393–4.

117 Quoted in Hitchins, *The Romanians*, p. 233.

118 Glenny, *The Balkans*, pp. 61–3; Hitchins, *The Romanians*, pp. 233–6.

119 Ibid., pp. 237–8; D. V. Pleshoyano, *Colonel Nicolae Pleşoianu and the National Regeneration Movement in Walachia* (Boulder, Col.: East European Monographs, 1991), pp. 18–19.

120 Quoted in Pleshoyano, *Colonel Nicolae Pleşoianu*, p. 26.

121 Hitchins, *The Romanians*, pp. 238–45; Glenny, *The Balkans*, p. 63.

122 'Carpathinus', '1848 and Roumanian Unification', p. 403.

123 Pleshoyano, *Colonel Nicolae Pleşoianu*, pp. 80–2.

124 Hitchins, *The Romanians*, pp. 240, 245–9; Pleshoyano, *Colonel Nicolae Pleşoianu*, pp. 70–1, 86–96.

125 Quoted in Glenny, *The Balkans*, pp. 40–1.

126 Quoted in Deak, *Lawful Revolution*, p. 139.

127 Quoted in Rothenberg, 'Jelačić', p. 55.

128 Quoted in Sked, *Decline and Fall*, p. 97.

129 Quoted in ibid., p. 98.

130 Glenny, *The Balkans*, pp. 54–55.

131 Quoted in Deme, *Radical Left*, p. 99.
132 A. Urbán, 'The Hungarian Army of 1848–49', Kiraty and Rothenberg, *War and Society in East Central Europe*, vol. 1, pp. 97–100.
133 Quoted in Deme, *Radical Left*, p. 91.
134 Quoted in Spira, *Hungarian Count*, p. 247.
135 Sked, *Survival of the Habsburg Empire*, pp. 145–6.
136 Berkeley and Berkeley, *Italy in the Making*, iii, pp. 352–73.
137 B. King, *History of Italian Unity*, i, pp. 259–60.
138 Quoted in Sked, *Survival of the Habsburg Empire*, p. 149.
139 Quoted in B. King, *History of Italian Unity*, i, p. 263.
140 L. Ambrosoli, notes to Cattaneo, 'L'Insurrection', pp. 957–8.
141 C. Hibbert, *Garibaldi and his Enemies: The Clash of Arms and Personalities in the Making of Italy* (Harmondsworth: Penguin, 1987), p. 32.
142 Garibaldi, *My Life*, p. 8.
143 Quoted in Woolf, *History of Italy*, p. 393.
144 Garibaldi, *My Life*, p. 8.
145 Ibid., pp. 10–11.
146 Mack Smith, *Mazzini*, p. 63; Garibaldi, *My Life*, pp. 12–14.
147 E. Flagg, *Venice: The City of the Sea from Napoleon to Radetzky*, 2 vols (New York: Scribners, 1853), ii, p. 92.
148 Quoted in Ginsborg, *Daniele Manin*, p. 254.
149 Pepe, *Histoire*, pp. 124–30.
150 Ginsborg, *Daniele Manin*, pp. 254–66; Keates, *Siege of Venice*, pp. 233–49.
151 Ginsborg, *Daniele Manin*, pp. 266–9; Keates, *Siege of Venice*, pp. 250–1.
152 Woolf, *History of Italy*, pp. 393–4; Ginsborg, *Daniele Manin*, pp. 269–74.
153 B. King, *History of Italian Unity*, i, pp. 269–72; Berkeley and Berkeley, *Italy in the Making*, iii pp. 389–90.
154 Ibid., pp. 333–51, 388–9; Bolton King, *History of Italian Unity*, i, pp. 273–7.
155 Quoted in Mack Smith, *History of Sicily*, p. 418.
156 Ibid., pp. 416–22; B. King, *History of Italian Unity*, i, pp. 308–10, 316.
157 Quoted in Hobsbawm, *Age of Revolution*, p. 359.

CHAPTER 5

1 Bismarck, *Reflections and Reminiscences*, i, p. 50.
2 Quoted in L. Gall, *Bismarck: The White Revolutionary*, 2 vols (London: Allen and Unwin, 1986), i, p. 45.
3 Sperber, *European Revolutions*, p. 131.
4 Agulhon, *1848*, pp. 62–3.
5 Sperber, *European Revolutions*, p. 140.
6 Bismarck, *Reflections and Reminiscences*, i, p. 50.
7 Quoted in Rath, *Viennese Revolution*, p. 304.

8 Hübner, *Une Année*, p. 302.

9 Tocqueville, *Souvenirs*, p. 228.

10 Sperber, *European Revolutions*, pp. 184–5.

11 AN, BB/30/333 (dossier 1: Avocat-général of Rennes to the Minister of Justice, 6 June 1848).

12 Siemann, *German Revolution*, pp. 103–4; Sperber, *European Revolutions*, p. 162.

13 Deme, *Radical Left*, pp. 53–4.

14 Pech, *Czech Revolution*, pp. 67–8.

15 S. Z. Pech, 'Czech Peasantry in 1848', M. Rechcigl, Jr, *Czechoslovakia Past and Present*, 2 vols (The Hague and Paris: Mouton, 1968), ii, pp. 1280–3.

16 Quoted in Blum, *End of the Old Order*, p. 382.

17 Quoted in Pech, 'Czech Peasantry', p. 1285.

18 Quoted in Blum, *End of the Old Order*, p. 402.

19 Rath, *Viennese Revolution*, p. 127.

20 Blum, *End of the Old Order*, pp. 389–90.

21 Quoted in Pech, 'Czech Peasantry', p. 1289.

22 Deme, *Radical Left*, pp. 51–2.

23 Leiningen-Westerburg, *Letters and Journal*, pp. 73, 74–5.

24 Quoted in Himka, *Galician Villagers*, p. 27 n.

25 Price, *French Second Republic*, p. 118.

26 AN, BB/30/333, dossier 1.

27 Blum, *End of the Old Order*, p. 371.

28 W. J. Orr, Jr., 'East Prussia and the Revolution of 1848', *Central European History*, vol. 13 (1980), pp. 303–31, p. 316.

29 Bismarck, *Reflections and Reminiscences*, i, p. 49.

30 P. Ginsborg, 'Peasants and Revolutionaries in Venice and the Veneto', *Historical Journal*, vol. 17 (1974), pp. 503–50, p. 537.

31 Stiles, *Austria in 1848–49*, i, p. 172.

32 Ibid., ii, pp. 92-6; Rath, *Viennese Revolution*, pp. 324–6.

33 Stiles, *Austria in 1848–49*, ii, pp. 97–101; Rath, *Viennese Revolution*, pp. 326–9.

34 Stiles, *Austria in 1848–49*, ii, p. 110.

35 Hübner, *Une Année*, p. 342.

36 Rath, *Viennese Revolution*, pp. 331–4.

37 Ibid., p. 343.

38 Ibid., p. 345.

39 Hübner, *Une Année*, pp. 359–60.

40 Rath, *Viennese Revolution*, pp. 346–8.

41 Quoted in Deak, *Lawful Revolution*, p. 180.

42 Stiles, *Austria in 1848–49*, ii, p. 129.

43 Hübner, *Une Année*, p. 396.

44 Stiles, *Austria in 1848–49*, ii, p. 132.

45 A. Görgey, *My Life and Acts in Hungary in the Years 1848 and 1849*, 2 vols (London, 1852), i, p. 70.

46 Deak, *Lawful Revolution*, pp. 180–2. See also Görgey's account in *My Life and Acts*, i, pp. 78–92.

47 Hübner, *Une Année*, p. 396.

48 Ibid., p. 393.

49 Fröbel's testimony in Eyck, *Revolutions of 1848–49*, pp. 127–33.

50 Hübner, *Une Année*, pp. 434–5.

51 Sked, *Decline and Fall*, pp. 137–9.

52 Quoted in ibid., p. 133.

53 Hübner, *Une Année*, p. 451–2.

54 Rath, *Viennese Revolution*, p. 364.

55 Quoted in Siemann, *German Revolution*, p. 166.

56 Valentin, *1848*, pp. 340–1.

57 Gall, *Bismarck*, i, p. 50.

58 Siemann, *German Revolution*, pp. 105–7; Sperber, *European Revolutions*, p. 161.

59 Gall, *Bismarck*, i, pp. 46–51.

60 Quoted in Craig, *Politics of the Prussian Army*, p. 117.

61 Randers-Pehrson, *Germans and the Revolution*, pp. 424–9.

62 Quoted in Craig, *Politics of the Prussian Army*, p. 119.

63 Lewald, *Year of Revolutions*, p. 141; Stadelmann, *German Revolution*, p. 154.

64 Lewald, *Year of Revolutions*, pp. 145–6.

65 Craig, *Politics of the Prussian Army*, p. 120.

66 Lewald, *Year of Revolutions*, pp. 148–9.

67 Randers-Pehrson, *Germans and the Revolution*, pp. 431–6; Siemann, *German Revolution*, pp. 168–9; Stadelmann, *Social and Political History*, p. 155; Koch, *Constitutional History*, p. 71.

68 Quoted in Winkler, *Germany: The Long Road West*, i, p. 104.

69 Allen and Hughes, *German Parliamentary Debates*, p. 33.

70 Ibid., p. 92.

71 Ibid., p. 53.

72 Ibid., p. 57.

73 Ibid., p. 50.

74 Ibid., pp. 97–8; Winkler, *Germany: The Long Road West*, i, pp. 104–7.

75 German constitution in Eyck, *Revolutions of 1848–49*, pp. 149–60.

76 Quoted in Stiles, *Austria in 1848–49*, ii, p. 142.

77 Quoted in Hübner, *Une Année*, pp. 426–7.

78 Quoted in Eyck, *Revolutions of 1848–49*, p. 122.

79 Quoted in Sked, *Decline and Fall*, p. 125.

80 Spira, *Hungarian Count*, p. 275.

81 Quoted in Deme, *Radical Left*, p. 101.

82 Ibid., p. 105.

83 Quoted in Spira, *Hungarian Count*, pp. 284 ('I am to be blamed'), 289 ('Kossuth's name').
84 Spira, *Hungarian Count*, pp. 295–301.
85 Quoted in Deme, *Radical Left*, p. 109.
86 Deak, *Lawful Revolution*, pp. 171–2.
87 Ibid., p. 172.
88 Deme, *Radical Left*, pp. 112–13.
89 Deak, *Lawful Revolution*, *passim*, but especially p. 174.
90 Leiningen-Westerburg, *Letters and Journal*, pp. 92–5.
91 Ibid., pp. 99, 103.
92 Deak, *Lawful Revolution*, pp. 208–10; Hitchins, *The Romanians*, p. 259.
93 R. R. Florescu, 'Debunking a Myth: The Magyar–Romanian National Struggle of 1848–1849', *Austrian History Yearbook*, vols 12–13 (1976), p. 82.
94 Leiningen-Westerburg, *Letters and Journal*, p. 112.
95 Hitchins, *The Romanians*, pp. 259–60.
96 Leiningen-Westerburg, *Letters and Journal*, pp. 94–5.
97 Ibid., p. 105.
98 Ibid., pp. 144, 154.
99 Stiles, *Austria in 1848–49*, ii, pp. 155–7.
100 Leiningen-Westerburg, *Letters and Journal*, pp. 207–8.
101 Görgey, *Life and Acts*, i, p. 2.
102 Deak, *Lawful Revolution*, p. 186; for Görgey's account of the court martial and his judgement, see *Life and Acts*, i, pp. 8–31.
103 Ibid., p. 54.
104 Deak, *Lawful Revolution*, pp. 182–7.
105 Görgey, *Life and Acts*, i, p. 109.
106 Ibid., p. 120.
107 Deak, *Lawful Revolution*, pp. 211–15
108 Quoted in Ginsborg, *Daniele Manin*, p. 296.
109 See Pepe's account in *Histoire*, pp. 185–8; Keates, *Siege of Venice*, pp. 270–2, 278–9, 284–6; Ginsborg, *Daniele Manin*, pp. 296–301; Trevelyan, *Manin*, p. 215; Bolton King, *History of Italian Unity*, i, pp. 342–3.
110 Quoted in Ginsborg, *Daniele Manin*, p. 278; see also Keates, *Siege of Venice*, pp. 256–7.
111 Ginsborg, *Daniele Manin*, pp. 279–89.
112 Quoted in ibid., p. 276.
113 Ibid., pp. 274–7.
114 Quoted in Berkeley and Berkeley, *Italy in the Making*, iii, p. 411.
115 Woolf, *History of Italy*, p. 392.
116 Quoted in Berkeley and Berkeley, *Italy in the Making*, iii, p. 401.
117 Bolton King, *History of Italian Unity*, i, p. 288.
118 Quoted in Berkeley and Berkeley, *Italy in the Making*, iii, p. 425.
119 Quoted in Beales and Biagini, *Risorgimento*, p. 245.

120 Quoted in Berkeley and Berkeley, *Italy in the Making*, iii, p. 434.

121 Quoted in G. M. Trevelyan, *Garibaldi's Defence of the Roman Republic 1848–9* (London: Longman, 1988), p. 88.

122 Berkeley and Berkeley, *Italy in the Making*, iii, pp. 440–1.

123 Details on Rossi's ministry, his murder and the November revolution in Rome in ibid., pp. 395–463; Bolton King, *History of Italian Unity*, i, pp. 280–5.

124 Quoted in Trevelyan, *Garibaldi's Defence*, p. 78.

125 Quoted in Woolf, *History of Italy*, p. 396.

126 Quoted in Hibbert, *Garibaldi and his Enemies*, p. 33.

127 Garibaldi, *My Life*, p. 16.

128 Ibid., p. 17.

129 Quoted in Trevelyan, *Garibaldi's Defence*, p. 85.

130 Garibaldi, *My Life*, p. 19.

131 Ibid., p. 21.

132 Ibid., p. 20.

133 Woolf, *History of Italy*, pp. 397–9.

134 Quoted in J. F. Macmillan, *Napoleon III* (Harlow: Longman, 1991), p. 13.

135 Quoted in Tombs, *France*, p. 398.

136 Details on Louis-Napoleon's early life in Macmillan, *Napoleon III*, pp. 7–17; Stern, *Histoire*, pp. 556–65.

137 Macmillan, *Napoleon III*, p. 28.

138 Quoted in Stern, *Histoire*, p. 568.

139 AN, W/574, pc. 17 (minutes of the Club de la Révolution de 1793–1848, 17 June)

140 Lamartine, *History*, ii, p. 259.

141 Stern, *Histoire*, p. 567.

142 Quoted in ibid., p. 582.

143 Ibid., p. 583.

144 AN, BB/18/1465A (letter to the Minister of Justice, 2 July 1848).

145 Stern, *Histoire*, p. 578.

146 Tocqueville, *Souvenirs*, pp. 236–7.

147 De Luna, *French Republic*, pp. 366–7.

148 Quoted in ibid., p. 369.

149 Stern, *Histoire*, p. 572.

150 Agulhon, *1848*, pp. 97, 100–101.

CHAPTER 6

1 Eyck, *Revolutions of 1848–49*, pp. 156–9; Koch, *Constitutional History*, p. 65; 'every state and every community', quoted in Randers-Pehrson, *Germans and the Revolution*, p. 446.

2 Eyck, *Revolutions of 1848–49*, pp. 159–60; Koch, *Constitutional History*, pp. 65–6.

3 Bismarck, *Reflections and Reminiscences*, i, p. 63.

4 Valentin, *1848*, p. 373.

5 Quoted in Siemann, *German Revolution*, p. 200.

6 Quoted in Randers-Pehrson, *Germans and the Revolution*, p. 463.

7 Quoted in Valentin, *1848*, p. 407.

8 Quoted in Sperber, *Rhineland Radicals*, p. 360.

9 Schurz, *Reminscences*, i, p. 170.

10 Quoted in Sperber, *Rhineland Radicals*, p. 364.

11 For a detailed account and analysis on the revolution in the Rhineland, see Sperber, *Rhineland Radicals*, pp. 349–465.

12 This was the ill-fated 'May Conspiracy' in Prague, described by Stanley Pech, *Czech Revolution*, pp. 237–60.

13 E. Newman, *The Life of Richard Wagner*, 4 vols (New York: Knopf, 1968), ii, p. 80.

14 Siemann, *German Revolution*, p. 205.

15 Schurz, *Reminiscences*, i, pp. 195–6.

16 Stadelmann, *Social and Political History*, p. 188.

17 Schurz, *Reminiscences*, i, pp. 195–6.

18 Ibid., pp. 211–32.

19 Quoted in Valentin, *1848*, p. 420.

20 Quoted in Mack Smith, *History of Sicily*, ii, p. 424.

21 Quoted in Mack Smith, *Making of Italy*, p. 162.

22 Mack Smith, *Mazzini*, p. 65.

23 Quoted in B. King, *History of Italian Unity*, vol. 1, p. 294.

24 Mack Smith, *Mazzini*, p. 65.

25 Ibid., p. 66.

26 Quoted in B. King, *History of Italian Unity*, i, pp. 356 (Victor Emmanuel) and 361 (D'Azeglio).

27 The following paragraphs are based on Trevelyan, *Garibaldi's Defence*, pp. 99–228; B. King, *History of Italian Unity*, i, pp. 326–40; Mack Smith, *Mazzini*, pp. 67–76.

28 Quoted in Trevelyan, *Garibaldi's Defence*, p. 98.

29 Quoted in ibid., p. 99.

30 Quoted in ibid., p. 107.

31 Quoted in Mack Smith, *Mazzini*, p. 68.

32 Quoted in B. King, *History of Italian Unity*, i, p. 335.

33 H. Brogan, *Alexis de Tocqueville: A Biography* (London: Profile, 2006), pp. 481–2 (Thiers quotation on p. 481).

34 Garibaldi, *My Life*, p. 34.

35 Extracts of the constitution in Beales and Biagini, *Risorgimento*, pp. 245–7.

36 J. Ridley, *Garibaldi* (London: Phoenix, 2001), pp. 306, 311, 317.

37 Garibaldi, *My Life*, p. 42.
38 Quoted in B. King, *History of Italian Unity*, i, p. 364.
39 Trevelyan, *Manin*, pp. 217–19.
40 Ibid., pp. 221, 223.
41 Ginsborg, *Daniele Manin*, pp. 340–1.
42 Ibid., p. 345.
43 Flagg, *Venice*, ii, pp. 418–19.
44 Ginsborg, *Daniele Manin*, p. 352.
45 Quoted in ibid., p. 349.
46 Quoted in ibid., p. 333.
47 Trevelyan, *Manin*, pp. 237–40; Ginsborg, *Daniele Manin*, pp. 362–3.
48 Urbán, 'Hungarian Army', pp. 100–5, 109.
49 Ibid., p. 102.
50 Deak, *Lawful Revolution*, p. 220.
51 Stiles, *Austria in 1848–49*, ii, pp. 406–8.
52 Leiningen-Westerburg, *Letters and Journal*, p. 235.
53 Stiles, *Austria in 1848–49*, vol. 2, p. 409.
54 Deak, *Lawful Revolution*, pp. 270–3.
55 Ibid., pp. 267–70.
56 Ibid., p. 273.
57 Ibid., p. 279.
58 Quoted in ibid., p. 289.
59 Ibid., pp. 291–300.
60 Quoted in K. W. Rock, 'Schwarzenberg versus Nicholas I, Round One: The Negotiation of the Habsburg–Romanov Alliance against Hungary in 1849', *Austrian History Yearbook*, vol. 6 (1970), p. 119.
61 Quoted in ibid., p. 135.
62 Quoted in ibid., p. 136.
63 Quoted in Deak, *Lawful Revolution*, p. 306.
64 Ibid., p. 329.
65 Stiles, *Austria in 1848–49*, ii, p. 443.
66 Deak, *Lawful Revolution*, pp. 321–37.
67 Ibid., pp. 127, 305–6; Sked, *Decline and Fall*, pp. 94–5, 101–2, 107–8.
68 Hitchins, *The Romanians*, pp. 264–6.
69 Sked, *Decline and Fall*, p. 147.
70 B. King, *History of Italian Unity*, i, p. 340.
71 Agulhon, *1848*, p. 102.
72 Marx, *Class Struggles*, p. 69.
73 Price, *French Second Republic*, p. 227.
74 Quoted in B. H. Moss, 'June 13, 1849: The Abortive Uprising of French Radicalism', *French Historical Studies*, vol. 13 (1984), p. 397.
75 Marx, *Class Struggles*, p. 75.
76 Price, *French Second Republic*, p. 227.

77　Quoted in R. W. Magraw, 'Pierre Joigneaux and Socialist Propaganda in the French Countryside, 1849–1851', *French Historical Studies*, vol. 10 (1978), p. 602.

78　Quoted in Tombs, *France*, p. 389.

79　E. Weber, 'The Second Republic, Politics, and the Peasant', *French Historical Studies*, vol. 11 (1980), pp. 521–50.

80　E. Weber, 'Comment la Politique Vint aux Paysans: A Second Look at Peasant Politicization', *American Historical Review*, vol. 87 (1982), p. 365.

81　Price, *French Second Republic*, p. 241.

82　Quoted in Moss, 'June 13, 1849', p. 399.

83　Price, *French Second Republic*, p. 238.

84　T. W. Margadant, *French Peasants in Revolt: The Insurrection of 1851* (Princeton: Princeton University Press, 1979), pp. 338–41.

85　Tocqueville, *Souvenirs*, p. 252.

86　In Price, *Documents*, p. 123.

87　Agulhon, *Quarante-huitards*, p. 229.

88　Tocqueville, *Souvenirs*, pp. 271–2.

89　Quoted in Moss, 'June 13, 1849', p. 399.

90　Tocqueville, *Souvenirs*, pp. 275–6.

91　Moss, 'June 13, 1849', pp. 402–3 (April programme quoted on p. 399).

92　Herzen, *My Past and Thoughts*, p. 355.

93　Marx, *Class Struggles*, pp. 90, 92.

94　Herzen, *My Past and Thoughts*, p. 355.

95　Moss, 'June 13, 1849', pp. 411–14.

96　Tocqueville, *Souvenirs*, p. 280.

97　Herzen, *My Past and Thoughts*, pp. 356–7.

98　Moss, 'June 13, 1849', pp. 405–11.

99　Agulhon, *1848*, p. 108.

100　Quoted in Price, *French Second Republic*, p. 255.

101　Tombs, *France*, p. 390.

102　Tocqueville, *Souvenirs*, p. 294.

103　Louis-Napoleon's message to the National Assembly in Price, *Documents*, p. 128.

104　Tocqueville, *Souvenirs*, p. 295.

105　Price, *Documents*, p. 142.

106　Margadant, *French Peasants*, p. 8.

107　Ibid., pp. 3–39.

108　Ibid., p. xix.

109　Macmillan, *Napoleon III*, p. 48.

110　Price, *Documents*, p. 167.

CONCLUSION

1 Zimmerman, *Midpassage*, pp. 175–7.
2 Herzen, *From the Other Shore*, p. 3.
3 Blum, *End of the Old Order*, pp. 364, 373–4.
4 Quoted in J. J. Sheehan, *German History 1770–1866* (Oxford: Oxford University Press, 1989), p. 727.
5 A. J. P. Taylor, *The Course of German History* (London: Routledge, 1978), p. 69.
6 For the best introduction in English on the idea of a *Sonderweg*, see D. Blackbourn and G. Eley, *The Peculiarities of German History: Bourgeois Society and Politics in Nineteenth-Century Germany* (Oxford: Oxford University Press, 1984), pp. 1–35.
7 Quoted in G. Mann, *The History of Germany since 1789* (Harmondsworth: Penguin, 1974), p. 204.
8 J. A. Davis, 'Introduction: Italy's Difficult Modernization', in *Italy in the Nineteenth Century* (Oxford: Oxford University Press, 2000), pp. 15–16.
9 L. Riall, *Garibaldi: Invention of a Hero* (New Haven, Conn., and London: Yale University Press, 2007), pp. 93–7.
10 Agulhon, *1848*, which is subtitled *L'Apprentissage de la République.*
11 F. Furet, *Revolutionary France 1770–1880* (Oxford: Blackwell, 1992), p. 537.
12 Tombs, *France*, pp. 2–3.
13 Quoted in A. J. P. Taylor, *Europe: Grandeur and Decline* (Harmondsworth: Penguin, 1967), p. 30.
14 Quoted in A. J. P. Taylor, *Bismarck: The Man and the Statesman* (London, 1965), p. 47.
15 Quoted in Winkler, *Germany: The Long Road West*, p. 205.
16 Rapport, *Nineteenth Century Europe*, p. 363.
17 L. Namier, '1848: Seed-Plot of History', *Vanished Supremacies: Essays on European History, 1812–1918* (Harmondsworth: Penguin, 1962), pp. 31–45.
18 Quoted in S. Zucker, *Ludwig Bamberger*, p. 26.
19 Eyck, *Revolutions of 1848–49*, p. 180.
20 Herzen, *From the Other Shore*, p. 68.
21 See, for example, the essays by Axel Körner, John Breuilly and Reinhart Koselleck in A. Körner (ed.), *1848: A European Revolution? International Ideas and National Memories of 1848* (Basingstoke: Palgrave, 2000), pp. 3–28, 31–49, 209–21 and H. Pogge von Strandmann, '1848–1849: A European Revolution?', in Evans and Pogge von Strandmann, *Revolutions in Europe*, pp. 1–8.
22 Charles Pouthas cited in ibid., p. 6.
23 Stadelmann, *German Revolution*, p. 50.
24 Reinhart Koselleck, 'How European was the Revolution of 1848/49?', in Körner, *1848*, p. 213.

25 John Breuilly, '1848: Connected or Comparable Revolutions?', in Körner, *1848*, p. 31.

26 Pogge von Strandmann, '1848–1849', pp. 3–4.

27 C. Cattaneo, 'Indirizzo alla Dieta Ungarica', *Tutti le Opere*, vol. 4 (1967), p. 118.

28 AN, W//574, pièce 25 ('Au nom du Peuple de Pologne').

29 Koselleck, 'How European was the Revolution of 1848/49?', p. 212

30 A. Körner, 'The European Dimension in the Ideas of 1848 and the Nationalization of its Memories', in Körner, *1848*, p. 17.

31 Koselleck, 'How European was the Revolution of 1848/49?', p. 221.

32 Quoted in Siemann, *German Revolution*, p. 6.

33 R. Gildea, '1848 in European Collective Memory', in Evans and Pogge von Strandmann, *Revolutions in Europe*, pp. 207–8, 213.

34 Ibid., pp. 229–30.

35 Quoted in T. Garton Ash, *The Uses of Adversity: Essays on the Fate of Central Europe* (London: Penguin, 1999), p. 170.

36 Quoted in R. Sakwa, 'The Age of Paradox: The Anti-Revolutionary Revolutions of 1989–91', in M. Donald and T. Rees (eds), *Reinterpreting Revolution in Twentieth-Century Europe* (Basingstoke: Macmillan, 2001), p. 165.

37 K. Kumar, 'The Revolutionary Idea in the Twentieth-Century World', in Donald and Rees, *Reinterpreting Revolution*, p. 193.

38 Garton Ash, *Uses of Adversity*, p. 258.

INDEX

MIKE RAPPORT

is a Lecturer in History at the University of Stirling,
where he is also Director of the Masters Program in
Revolution and Counter-Revolution. A graduate of
the Universities of Edinburgh and Bristol, he is the
author of *Nationality and Citizenship in Revolutionary
France* and *Nineteenth-Century Europe*. He was Secretary
of the UK Society for the Study of French History
between 2000 and 2005 and was until 2007 the
Reviews Editor of the journal *French History*. He lives
in Scotland.